Artificial Intelligence: Emerging Technologies

Artificial Intelligence: Emerging Technologies

Edited by Mick Benson

CLANRYE
INTERNATIONAL
www.clanryeinternational.com

Clanrye International,
750 Third Avenue, 9th Floor,
New York, NY 10017, USA

ISBN: 978-1-63240-972-0

Cataloging-in-Publication Data

Artificial intelligence : emerging technologies / edited by Mick Benson.
    p. cm.
Includes bibliographical references and index.
ISBN 978-1-63240-972-0
1. Artificial intelligence. 2. Artificial intelligence--Engineering applications. 3. Neural computers.
4. Digital computer simulation. I. Benson, Mick.
Q335 .A78 2020
006.3--dc23

For information on all Clanrye International publications
visit our website at www.clanryeinternational.com

Contents

Preface

This book has been a concerted effort by a group of academicians, researchers and scientists, who have contributed their research works for the realization of the book. This book has materialized in the wake of emerging advancements and innovations in this field. Therefore, the need of the hour was to compile all the required researches and disseminate the knowledge to a broad spectrum of people comprising of students, researchers and specialists of the field.

The intelligence demonstrated by machines is known as artificial intelligence, or AI. Several capabilities of modern machines such as understanding human speech effectively and operating cars autonomously are classified as artificial intelligence. There are 3 types of systems into which artificial intelligence can be categorized- analytical, human inspired and humanized. Analytical artificial intelligence only possesses characteristics from cognitive intelligence. Human inspired artificial intelligence combines elements from both cognitive and emotional intelligence. Humanized artificial intelligence is self-aware and is able to show attributes of cognitive, social and emotional intelligence. There are several tools used in AI such as artificial neural networks, search and mathematical optimization and methods based on probability, economics, statistics etc. This book unfolds the innovative aspects of artificial intelligence which will be crucial for the progress of this field in the future. The topics included herein are of utmost significance and bound to provide incredible insights to readers. This book will serve as a valuable source of reference for graduate and post graduate students.

At the end of the preface, I would like to thank the authors for their brilliant chapters and the publisher for guiding us all-through the making of the book till its final stage. Also, I would like to thank my family for providing the support and encouragement throughout my academic career and research projects.

Editor

Density-Based Histogram Partitioning and Local Equalization for Contrast Enhancement of Images

M. Shakeri, M.-H. Dezfoulian, H. Khotanlou[*]

Department of Computer Engineering, Bu-Ali Sina University, Hamedan, Iran.

*Corresponding author: khotanlou@basu.ac.ir (H. Khotanlou).

Abstract

Histogram Equalization technique is one of the basic methods available in image contrast enhancement. The use of this method in the case of images with uniform gray levels (with a narrow histogram) causes the loss of image details and the natural look of the image. In order to overcome this problem and to have a better image contrast enhancement, a new two-step method is proposed. In the first step, the image histogram is partitioned into some sub-histograms according to the mean value and standard deviation, which is controlled with the PSNR measure. In the second step, each sub-histogram is improved separately and locally with the traditional histogram equalization. Finally, all sub-histograms are combined to obtain the enhanced image. The experimental results show that this method would not only keep the visual details of the histogram but also enhance the image contrast.

Keywords: *Contrast Enhancement, Histogram Modification, Image Quality Evaluation, Image Quality Enhancement.*

1. Introduction

Image enhancement methods have been widely used in many applications of image processing. Contrast is a main factor in any subjective evaluation of image quality. Contrast enhancement is one of the most important areas in the image processing for human and machine vision, and many techniques have been proposed for contrast enhancement and applied to problems in image processing. This area has great applications in medical image processing, remote sensing [1-4], digital photography [5], video surveillance systems [6], recovery of underwater visibility [7], and face recognition [8-31].

The histogram modification technique is the most common method available in image contrast enhancement, which expands the histogram using a transfer function [9]. The transfer function can be used in the global or local mode. In the global mode, the transfer function is calculated based on all gray levels in the histogram, while in the local mode, the transfer function is obtained from a special interval of histogram [10-13]. Histogram Equalization is a well-known method in the global contrast enhancement. Histogram equalization uses a transfer function based on cumulative distribution of all intensities in the image. Histogram equalization is not suitable for keeping the mean brightness of the image, and causes intensity saturation problems [14]. In [14], Kim has proposed a method called BBHE, which is based upon histogram equalization on each one of the two sub-histograms that are separated by the mean value. In the output images of the BBHE method, the over-enhanced regions can be seen due to the application of only one separation on the histogram. In [15], Wang has presented a method called DSIHE. In this method, in the first step, the histogram is divided into two equal sub-histograms based on the middle value of gray levels. Then the histogram equalization is applied to each sub-histogram. Since DSIHE divides the histogram into just two sub-histograms, this method has the same problem of BBHE. In order to overcome this problem, Sim presented the RSIHE method in [16] based on DSIHE. The RSIHE method, in a recursive operation, divides the histogram of the image into two equal sub-histograms. This operation is repeated for r times.

The histogram is divided into 2r sections, and then the histogram equalization is applied for each sub-histogram. A large r is suitable for preserving mean brightness but there is no special enhancement. With a small r, this method operates similar to DSIHE.

In [25], the bi-histogram equalization plateau limit (BHEPL) has been proposed to control the BBHE enhancement rate. BBHE applies a higher stretching process to the contrast of the high-histogram regions and compresses the contrast of the low histogram regions, possibly causing intensity saturation in the low histogram regions. A clipping process is applied to each sub-histogram of BBHE to deal with the intensity saturation problem and to control the enhancement rate through setting the plateau limit as the average number of intensity occurrence. If the bins for any intensity exceed the plateau limit, they are replaced by the plateau limit level; otherwise, they remain the same as the original bins of the input histogram. Finally, HE is implemented to the clipped sub-histograms.

In [17], Draa has proposed a method based on finding the best transfer function using the Artificial Bee Colony (ABC) algorithm with a fitness function based on entropy and Sobel operator. In [21], Pourya Hoseini has proposed a hybrid algorithm including Genetic Algorithm (GA), Ant Colony Optimisation (ACO), and Simulated Annealing (SA) metaheuristics for increasing the contrast of images. Ant colony optimization is used to generate the transfer functions, which map the input intensities to the output one. Simulated annealing, as a local search method, is utilized to modify the transfer functions generated by ant colony optimization. Genetic algorithm has the responsibility of evolutionary process of ants' characteristics.

In [18], Khan has proposed a method based on the local histogram equalization. In this method, the image histogram is divided into several parts according to the middle and mean values. The narrow areas of the histogram are then discovered and are expanded to a full brightness area, like in the HE method.

After equalization of every part with the HE method, the image is normalized in order to prevent the brightness saturation issues. In [19], Huang has proposed a method in which, according to the mean value of image, the histogram is divided into several parts, and the histogram equalization is then applied for each part. In this method, after histogram equalization, the image details would be lost due to some large divisions and lots of changes in brightness.

In [24], Huang has proposed a combinatorial method, which contains the gamma correction and the traditional histogram equalization. This method has created a balance between a high level of visual quality and a low computational cost.

Gu [26] has used saliency preserving to increase the image contrast without dealing with the artifact problem. The proposed framework includes the histogram equalization and its relevant visual pleasing conducted by the sigmoid function. Finally, this method exploits a quality determination measure based upon saliency preserving to automatically select parameters.

In [27], a method has been proposed to avoid over-enhancement and noise addition, while improving the contrast of an image. The method is a combination of Contrast Limit Adaptive Histogram Equalization (CLAHE) and Discreet Wavelet Transform (DWT). High frequencies of the image and its low counterparts are first decomposed by DWT. The image frequency coefficients are equalized by CLAHE, while leaving image high frequency with no alteration. Eventually, the reverse DWT is employed to reconstruct the image. In the last step, a weighted factor is obtained from the original and the enhanced image to control the possible over-enhancement.

Estimating and compressing the illumination component is a good method to enhance the degraded images by an uneven light. In [28], Liang has proposed a novel method to estimate the illumination by an iterative solution of non-linear diffusion equation.

In [29], Celik has proposed a new algorithm to enhance images using special information of pixels. This algorithm computes the spatial entropy of pixels by considering the distribution of spatial locations of gray levels.

In the proposed method, which is based on [19], the histogram is divided into several optimal parts according to density, mean, and standard deviation of image intensities. Then the large sections are identified and again divided into several parts. Finally, the enhanced image is constructed with local histogram equalization. The results obtained show that this method not only keeps the pixel mean and features but also enhances the image contrast.

2. Proposed method
One of the common methods used for enhancing image contrast is an approach based on histogram modification. These methods map image pixels aiming at expanding image histogram using a transfer function. The transfer function used for

enhancing image contrast can be in two modes; global and local. In the global mode, the transfer function is calculated in proportion to the entire histogram. In the local mode, this transferring function is applied for a special interval of histogram. The proposed method is divided into two parts.

The first part is histogram division, and the histogram is divided into parts to calculate the transfer function locally. The second part is the local equalization of histogram. One of the famous methods used for contrast enhancement is the histogram equalization method. Histogram equalization produces an image whose density levels of brightness are uniform, resulting in an increase in the pixel intervals, which has a considerable effect on the image quality. In this part, the actions of histogram equalization in local mode are discussed.

2.1. Histogram division

In this part, the image histogram is divided according to diffusion of the existing brightness levels in the image. If the brightness values for the image are in the [a,b] interval, H(i), i = a, a + 1, a + 2, …, b, indicates the number of image pixels with an i brightness level. In fact, H is the histogram function of the image brightness level. Based on this, the mean and standard deviation of the image brightness value are calculated using (1) and (2).

$$\mu = \frac{\sum_{i=a}^{b} H(i) * i}{\sum_{i=a}^{b} H(i)} \tag{1}$$

$$\sigma = \left(\frac{1}{\left(\sum_{i=a}^{b} H(i)\right) - 1} \sum_{i=a}^{b} H(i)(i - \mu)^2 \right)^{1/2} \tag{2}$$

The algorithm of histogram division is:

Algorithm 1: Suppose that the brightness level value of image is in [0,255].
- In the first step, initialize a = 0 and b = 255.
- Mean and standard deviation of image are calculated in [a,b].
- Two threshold values to separate and divide the histogram are calculated by (3) and (4).

$$T_1 = \mu - \sigma \tag{3}$$

$$T_2 = \mu - \sigma \tag{4}$$

- Now, [a,T_1] and [T_2,b] are two parts of the histogram that are stored.
- In this step, to divide [T_1,T_2] into smaller parts, we replace the pixels values of the image that were in [a,T_1] with mean pixel value of [a,T_1]. Also we replace the pixel values of the image in

[T_2,b] with the mean pixels value of [T_2,b] ((5) and (6)).

$$\frac{\sum_{i=a}^{T_1} i * H(i)}{T_1 - a} \tag{5}$$

$$\frac{\sum_{i=T_2}^{b} i * H(i)}{b - T_2} \tag{6}$$

- Put the "a" value equal to $T_1 + 1$ and "b" equal to $T_2 - 1$, and repeat the algorithm from step 2. The stopping criterion of this loop is that the difference between the image PSNR criteria for two successive steps would be more than 0.1. Otherwise, this image can be still divided into smaller intervals. 0.1 is obtained experimentally.

PSNR is most commonly used to measure the quality of reconstruction of lossy compression codecs. Since histogram division is a kind of compression, and has less complexity, we use the PSNR measure to compute the similarity of two images. PSNR is a criterion that shows the ratio between the peak possible power of signal and the noise failure power and its effects on displaying signal. In fact, it calculates the similarity of two images, and its value is calculated as follows ((7) and (8)).

$$PSNR = 20 * \log_{10} \frac{255}{RMSE} \tag{7}$$

$$RMSE = \left(\frac{1}{MN} \sum_{x=0}^{M-1} \sum_{y=0}^{N-1} [I'_{xy} - I_{xy}]^2 \right)^{1/2} \tag{8}$$

I and I' show the mean level of the original and enhanced image with M*N pixels. RMSE is the root of mean square error, and is calculated from the difference between the estimated values by the model and real observed values. The output of this step is shown in figure 1. In the i'th step of applying algorithm 1, where i = 1, 2, …, t, the two $[a^{(i)}, T_1^{(i)}]$ and $[T_2^{(i)}, b^{(i)}]$ intervals are stored in S matrix. t is a step, in which the difference value of PSNR between t and t-1 is greater than 0.1, and S matrix indicates dividing intervals of the histogram in algorithm 1. Different steps of algorithm 1 are shown in a diagram in figure 8a. Figure 4 shows the divided histogram and obtained intervals with algorithm 1 for figure 9a. In this figure, t or steps of algorithm would be equal to 3.

As it can be seen in figure 4, based on density, mean, and standard deviation, algorithm 1 divides the histogram into intervals but some of the selected intervals, which are shown in figure 4 with arrows, have covered a vast scope of the histogram. This causes an increasing brightness value change in these intervals in the local histogram equalization step, failure to maintain image mean, and loss of some image features (Figure 5). As specified in figure 5, in great intervals (two intervals have been shown), the brightness changes are too much and the image details would disappear (shown in the results section).

$$\begin{bmatrix} a^{(1)} & T_1^{(1)} \\ a^{(2)} & T_1^{(2)} \\ \vdots \\ a^{(t)} & T_1^{(t)} \end{bmatrix}, \begin{bmatrix} T_2^{(1)} & b^{(1)} \\ \vdots \\ T_2^{(2)} & b^{(2)} \\ T_2^{(t)} & b^{(t)} \end{bmatrix} \rightarrow S = \begin{bmatrix} a^{(1)} & T_1^{(1)} \\ a^{(2)} & T_1^{(2)} \\ \vdots \\ a^{(t)} & T_1^{(t)} \\ T_1^{(t)}+1 & T_2^{(t)}-1 \\ T_2^{(t)} & b^{(t)} \\ \vdots \\ T_2^{(2)} & b^{(2)} \\ T_2^{(1)} & b^{(1)} \end{bmatrix}$$

Figure 1. intervals obtained from implementation of algorithm 1.

In order to overcome this problem, it is necessary to prevent the creation of great intervals. Considering a constant value of p as a threshold value for each pair of consecutive intervals in S that has a difference greater than p is a solution. Algorithm1 can again be applied for the original (input) image. However, the stopping condition, PSNR criterion, should be greater than 0.1 in the two consecutive algorithm steps and the difference between a and b should be greater than the threshold value for p in each step. Thus:

- If the difference between $T_1^{(i)}$ and $a^{(i)}$, i = 1,2,...,t, is greater than p, algorithm 1 in step 2 starts with the values $a = a^{(i)}$ and $b = T_1^{(i)}$, and the intervals obtained, like the structure in figure 1, would be added to the new T set. Otherwise, $[a^{(i)}, T_1^{(i)}]$ would be added to the T set.
- The $[T_1^{(t)}+1 , T_2^{(t)}-1]$ interval is added to the T set.
- Accordingly, for the second section of S, if the difference between $b^{(i)}$ and $T_2^{(i)}$, i = 1,2,...,t, is greater than p, algorithm 1 of step 2 is carried out with starting values of $a = T_2^{(i)}$ and $b = b^{(i)}$, and the intervals obtained with structures like that in figure 1 would be added to the T set; otherwise, $[T_2^{(i)}, b^{(i)}]$ would be added to the T set.

After this procedure with p parameter greater than 50, the histogram intervals of figure 9a would be as in figure 6. As observed, with re-implementation of algorithm 1, the intervals greater than 50 in figure 4 are divided into smaller intervals, based on mean and variance (Figure 6).

This procedure causes the mean brightness pixels to be more preserved after the histogram local equalization, which is applied for each interval.

Figure 7 shows that selecting smaller intervals causes histogram uniformity, and the mean brightness of pixels is completely preserved (enhanced image is shown in the results section). In figure 8b, the diagram of steps of re-division of histogram by algorithm 1 and the place of histogram equalization are shown. In order to determine the optimum value for the PSNR threshold and "p", four images were analyzed. Figure 2 shows the PSNR threshold to number of sub-histograms ratio. For values greater than 0.1, the number of sub-histograms does not change too much.

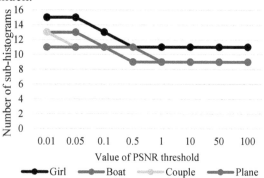

Figure 2. PSNR threshold to number of sub-histograms ratio.

Figure 3 shows the "p" value to number of sub-histograms greater than "p" ratio. For values bigger than 50, the number of sub-histograms greater than "p" reaches zero, which makes the proposed method ineffective.

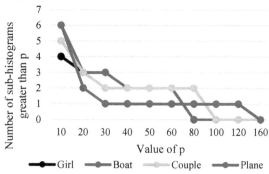

Figure 3. Value of "p" to number of sub-histogram greater than "p" ratio.

2.2. Local Equalization of Histogram

Up to this point, image histogram is partitioned into parts, and the existing intervals are obtained in set T. We will save the number of produced intervals via the previous step algorithm, in e parameter.

The method of histogram local equalization is as follows:

First, for each e interval of the histogram, in the original (input) image, the probability density function is calculated based on (9).

$$\text{pdf}^{k}(i) = \frac{n_i}{\sum_i n_i} \qquad (9)$$

$k = 1, 2, \ldots, e,$

$i = T(k,1), T(k,1)+1, T(k,1)+2, \ldots, T(k,2)$

i is the brightness level in the k'th interval; the first index of the T set shows row, and the second index shows column. n_i also shows the number of i brightness levels in the original image. Also the cumulative distribution function (CDF) is calculated for each part of the histogram in the original image by (10).

$$\text{cdf}^{k}(i) = \sum_{h=T(k,1)}^{i} \text{pdf}^{k}(h) \qquad (10)$$

$k = 1, 2, \ldots, e,$

$i = T(k,1), T(k,1)+1, T(k,1)+2, \ldots, T(k,2)$

i is the brightness level in the k'th interval; the first index of the T set shows row, and the second index shows column. Using a mapping function, and applying k'th cdf on the k'th interval of the original image (sub-image), we will reach the enhanced image with (11).

$$P^{k}(i) = T(k,1) + (T(k,2) - T(k,1)) * \text{cdf}^{k}(i) \qquad (11)$$

$k = 1, 2, \ldots, e,$

$i = T(k,1), T(k,1)+1, T(k,1)+2, \ldots, T(k,2)$

$P^{k}(i)$, in fact, is the histogram value in the k'th interval of brightness level of i in the original image.

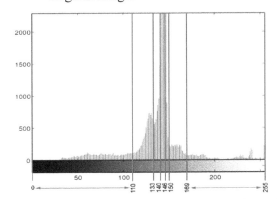

Figure 4. Histogram divisions and the obtained intervals by initial implantation of algorithm1.

3. Results

In this part, the proposed methods will be compared with the other methods. The results of test with parameter p = 50 were evaluated in two cases.

3.1. Qualitative evaluation

Different contrast enhancement algorithms are evaluated for four famous image visually. Figure

9a shows the image that the histogram equalization algorithm is applied to, where there are lots of inconsistencies among background, hair, body, and face in the two original and enhanced images. Results of the BBHE, DSIHE, and RSIHE algorithms are shown in figure 9c, figure 9f, and figure 9b, respectively. These methods use the local sub-histograms for decreasing the histogram equalization effect but many result aspects still exis as a result of applying the histogram equalization in these methods. For example, hair and clothes are rather dark, face is too bright, there are lots of changes in the pixel brightness values, and therefore, lots of image details have been lost.

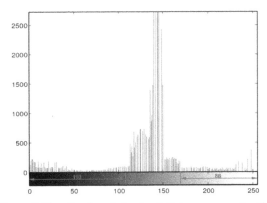

Figure 5. Results of applying local histogram equalization on initial intervals by algorithm 1 on Figure 9a.

$$T = \begin{bmatrix} 0 & 54 \\ 55 & 96 \\ 97 & 110 \\ 111 & 133 \\ 134 & 140 \\ \mathbf{141} & \mathbf{145} \\ 146 & 149 \\ 150 & 168 \\ 169 & 183 \\ 184 & 194 \\ 195 & 236 \\ 237 & 241 \\ 242 & 255 \end{bmatrix} \begin{bmatrix} T_1^{(t)}+1 & T_2^{(t)}-1 \end{bmatrix}$$

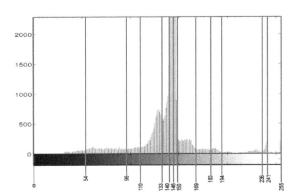

Figure 6. Histogram divisions and intervals obtained on Figure 9a after re-implantation of algorithm 1 for intervals larger than p.

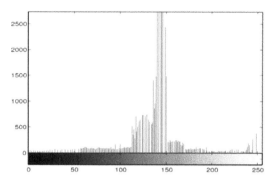

Figure 7. Result of local histogram equalization on secondary intervals formed by re-implantation of algorithm 1 on Figure 9a.

In figure 9g, the results of applying algorithm [19] can be seen where somehow the mean of image brightness is preserved and great enhancement is applied. However, due to the long length of some intervals, some image details have been lost; for example, hair area is completely dark.

In figure 9i, the result of SDDMHE method is shown, which is not enhanced enough. In figure 9h, the enhanced image from the proposed algorithm has been shown. Because of using the local sub-histograms with optimum intervals, in addition to enhanced contrast, the mean value of pixels is preserved, and therefore, none of the image details have been lost; for example, hair area seems more natural. Also figure 9d shows the result of the ABC method that presents the same enhanced results with the proposed method, except the bow tie and face area. Also in figures 10 and 11, the proposed ABC and RSIHE methods; and in figure 12, the proposed method generate the best output image.

If you choose not to use this document as a template, prepare your technical work in single-spaced, double-column format. Set bottom margins to 25 millimeters (0.98 inch) and top, left and right margins to about 20 millimeters (0.79 inch). Margin of First page is different from other pages. For first page set top margin to 30 millimeters (1.18 inch), and bottom, left and right margins are similar to other pages. Do not violate margins (i.e., text, tables, figures, and equations may not extend into the margins). The column width is 78 millimeters (3.07 inches). The space between the two columns is 13 millimeters (0.51 inch).

3.2. Quantitative evaluation

In addition to the qualitative evaluation, measuring the accuracy is one of the requirements to compare the proposed method and the other existing methods.

There are five measuring criteria used in this paper: PSNR, AMBE [20], FSIM [22], KL[30] distance, and DE [23].

AMBE is the absolute difference between the mean values of input image X and output image Y to define the normalized absolute mean brightness error (12) (AMBE $\in$ [0,1]).

$$\text{AMBE}(X, Y) = \frac{1}{1 + |\text{MB}(X) - \text{MB}(Y)|} \tag{12}$$

where, MB(X) and MB(Y) are the average values of X and Y, respectively. In table 1, the AMBE values for the contrast enhancement methods are shown on 10 images. The proposed ABC and SDDMHE methods can completely preserve the mean values of image pixels because they use the local histogram equalization with optimum intervals instead of the global histogram equalization. Therefore, they can effectively decrease AMBE. Table 2 shows the PSNR values obtained by applying a different algorithm on the previous images. We can see that the PSNR values obtained by the proposed method have maximum values. A greater PSNR value indicates that there is more similarity between the original and enhanced images. Histogram equalization refers to processing the input image to utilize the dynamic range efficiently by mapping an input into output image such that there is an equal number of pixels at each grey-level in the output. Thus it is expected that the equalized output image has flattened the grey-level distribution. However, it should be noted that the process should not change the overall shape of the input histogram to protect the image content. In order to quantitatively measure how flattened the output grey-level distribution is, the Kullback–Leibler (KL) distance between the distribution of the processed output image $p(y_k)$ and the uniform distribution $q(y_k)$ was used. The KL-distance (13) is a natural distance function from a "true" probability distribution, $p(y_k)$, to a "target" probability distribution, $q(y_k)$.

$$\text{KL}(p, q) = \sum_{\forall k} p(y_k) \log_2 \left(\frac{p(y_k)}{q(y_k)} \right) \tag{13}$$

The lower the value of KL, the better the histogram equalization is. Table 3 shows that the proposed method output generates the lowest KL-distance between other methods.

Another quantitative evaluation is the discrete entropy (DE). The discrete entropy of the input image X with K distinct grey-levels is in (14).

$$\text{DE}(X) = -\sum_{k=1}^{K} p(x_k) \log p(x_k) \tag{14}$$

where, $p(x_k)$ is the probability of pixel intensity x_k, which is estimated from the normalized histogram. Similarly, the discrete entropy of the output image Y_w with L distinct grey-levels is defined as (15).

$$DE(Y_w) = -\sum_{l=1}^{L} p(y_l) \log p(y_l) \qquad (15)$$

where, $p(y_l)$ is the probability of pixel intensity y_l. A higher value of DE indicates that the image has richer details. Using the metrics $DE(X)$ and $DE(Y_w)$, the normalized discrete entropy ($DE_N(X,Y_w) \in [0,1]$) between the input image X and the output image Y_w is defined as (16).

$$DE_N(X,Y_w) = \frac{1}{1 + \dfrac{(\log(256) - DE(Y_w))}{(\log(256) - DE(X))}} \qquad (16)$$

where, log(256) is the maximum value of entropy that can be achieved using the 8-bits data representation. The higher the value of normalized discrete entropy, the better the enhancement is in terms of utilizing the dynamic range and providing better image details. Table 4 shows the DE value for different algorithms.

The visual information in an image is often very redundant, while HVS understands an image mainly based on its low-level features.

Table 1. Comparing various methods with AMBE.

Test Images	HE	BBHE	DSIHE	[21]	[19]	Proposed	RSIHE	SDD MHE	ABC
baboon	0.0673	0.0796	0.0652	0.3382	0.0813	0.1816	0.1383	**0.4077**	0.1296
boat	0.0447	0.3169	0.0213	0.3637	0.0708	**0.4878**	0.2756	0.1442	0.3584
City	0.0145	0.0503	0.0137	0.0347	0.1267	**0.5220**	0.1599	0.3816	0.2209
Couple	0.1884	0.1051	0.1092	0.3665	0.2765	**0.9831**	0.3293	0.6331	0.6260
Girl	0.0565	0.0474	0.0390	0.1007	0.2899	**0.6501**	0.2898	0.4218	0.3858
Jet	0.0194	0.3142	0.1232	0.0473	0.1490	**0.4975**	0.1566	0.2983	0.2002
Lenna	0.2249	0.1146	0.3467	0.1416	0.1313	**0.9657**	0.2057	0.6089	0.4375
Man	0.0252	0.0400	0.0220	0.0445	0.1204	0.2735	0.1325	1.3892	**0.9874**
Peppers	0.0599	0.1392	0.1615	0.2256	0.1665	0.3582	0.1467	**0.4971**	0.2245
Plan	0.0205	0.3762	0.1197	0.0315	0.3680	**0.4284**	0.2349	0.2148	0.1977
Average	0.0721	0.1584	0.1022	0.1694	0.1780	**0.5348**	0.2069	0.4997	0.3768

Table 2. Comparing various methods with PSNR.

Test Images	HE	BBHE	DSIHE	[21]	[19]	Proposed	RSIHE	SDD MHE	ABC
baboon	18.23	18.56	13.97	22.20	26.24	**30.80**	23.64	27.64	18.91
boat	17.97	18.14	13.08	18.56	24.13	**32.83**	32.82	31.13	18.47
City	11.03	16.38	10.50	15.58	20.64	**32.92**	22.66	29.85	20.90
Couple	17.22	17.26	14.20	17.69	22.59	**30.58**	28.10	28.10	17.55
Girl	13.85	14.60	17.77	16.68	20.15	**35.16**	30.12	30.28	23.96
Jet	12.84	21.91	16.87	18.82	27.32	**34.28**	26.04	28.43	21.89
Lenna	20.13	20.15	21.95	24.01	28.98	27.33	25.23	**31.23**	24.63
Man	16.53	19.09	14.38	19.84	23.28	**34.03**	25.38	28.14	18.03
Peppers	20.35	21.75	21.13	26.85	**31.36**	26.18	26.21	30.55	21.20
Plan	10.23	14.29	19.02	13.20	18.80	**36.09**	33.66	31.28	27.90
Average	15.84	18.21	16.29	19.34	24.35	**32.02**	27.39	29.66	21.34

Table 3. Comparing various methods with KL.

Test Images	HE	BBHE	DSIHE	[21]	[19]	Proposed	RSIHE	SDD MHE	ABC
baboon	2.0242	1.6299	0.7356	0.7242	0.7142	**0.3449**	0.7736	0.9156	0.7613
boat	2.0464	2.1224	1.0737	1.0394	0.9349	**0.4332**	1.004	1.1302	0.5865
City	2.0721	1.7622	1.2515	1.2133	1.1363	0.9895	1.1606	1.4986	**0.5757**
Couple	2.0408	1.5532	1.0101	0.9909	0.9307	**0.5226**	0.9379	1.1099	0.7561
Girl	3.1498	3.8185	2.8002	2.5443	2.4394	**1.7853**	2.5175	2.7288	2.1528
Jet	2.2886	2.0348	1.4453	1.4004	1.4258	**0.7586**	1.4959	1.7674	4.4943
Lenna	2.0307	1.2927	0.73	0.659	0.6627	0.4748	0.6915	0.8386	**0.2135**
Man	2.0486	1.065	0.709	0.7335	0.638	**0.3984**	0.6771	0.6962	0.6952
Peppers	2.0267	0.6835	0.6313	0.6029	0.595	0.6256	0.6197	0.7135	**0.4291**
Plan	4.2533	4.2304	4.32	4.0942	4.0119	**3.0112**	4.0353	3.9958	3.0218
Average	2.3981	2.0193	1.4707	1.4002	1.3489	**0.9344**	1.3913	1.5395	1.3686

In other words, the salient low-level features convey crucial information for HVS to interpret the scene. Accordingly, perceptible image

degradations will lead to perceptible changes in image low-level features, and hence, a good IQA metric could be devised by comparing the low-level feature sets between the reference image and the distorted image. Based on the physiological and psychophysical evidence, the visually discernable features coincide with the points where the Fourier waves at different frequencies have congruent phases, i.e. at points of high phase congruency (PC), we can extract highly informative features. Therefore, PC is used as the primary feature in computing FSIM. Meanwhile, considering that PC is contrast invariant but image local contrast does affect HVS' perception on the image quality, the image gradient magnitude (GM) is computed as the secondary feature to encode contrast information. PC and GM are complementary, and they reflect different aspects of HVS in assessing the local quality of the input image. After computing the local similarity map, PC is utilized again as a weighting function to derive a single similarity score. Suppose that we are going to calculate the similarity between images f_1 and f_2. Denote by PC_1 and PC_2 the PC maps extracted from f_1 and f_2, and G_1 and G_2, the GM maps extracted from them. It should be noted that for color images, the PC and GM features are extracted from their luminance channels. FSIM is defined and computed based on PC_1, PC_2, G_1, and G_2. Computation of the FSIM index consists of two stages. In the first stage, the local similarity map is computed, and then in the second stage, we pool the similarity map into a single similarity score. We separate the feature similarity measurement between $f_1(x)$ and $f_2(x)$ into two components, each for PC or GM. First, the similarity measure for $PC_1(x)$ and $PC_2(x)$ is defined as (17).

$$S_{PC}(X) = \frac{2PC_1(x).PC_2(x) + T_1}{PC_1^2(x) + PC_2^2(x) + T_1} \quad (17)$$

where, T_1 is a positive constant to increase the stability of S_{PC}. Similarly, the GM values $G_1(x)$ and $G_2(x)$ are compared, and the similarity measure is defined as (18).

$$S_G(x) = \frac{2G_1(x).G_2(x) + T_2}{G_1^2(x) + G_2^2(x) + T_2} \quad (18)$$

where, T_2 is a positive constant depending on the dynamic range of the GM values. In our experiments, both T_1 and fixed to all databases so that the proposed FSIM can be conveniently used. Then $S_{PC}(x)$ and $S_G(x)$ are combined to get the similarity $S_L(x)$ of $f_1(x)$ and $f_2(x)$. We define $S_L(x)$ as (19).

$$S_L(x) = S_{PC}(x).S_G(x) \quad (19)$$

Having obtained the similarity $S_L(x)$ at each location x, the overall similarity between f_1 and f_2 can be calculated.

However, different locations have different contributions to the HVS perception of the image. For example, the edge locations convey more crucial visual information than the locations within a smooth area. Since the human visual cortex is sensitive to the phase congruent structures, the PC value at a location can reflect how likely it is a perceptibly significant structure point. Intuitively, for a given location x, if anyone of $f_1(x)$ and $f_2(x)$ has a significant PC value, it implies that this position x will have a high impact on HVS in evaluating the similarity between f_1 and f_2. Therefore, we use $PC_m(x)$ to weight the importance of $S_L(x)$ in the overall similarity between f_1 and f_2, and accordingly, the FSIM index between f_1 and f_2 is defined as (20) and (21).

$$PC_m(x) = \max\left(PC_1(x), PC_{2(x)}\right) \quad (20)$$

$$FSIM = \frac{\sum_{x \in \Omega} S_L(x).PC_m(x)}{\sum_{x \in \Omega} PC_m(x)} \quad (21)$$

As specified in table 5, the proposed RSIHE and the ABC method generate the best FSIM values, respectively.

Table 4. Comparing various methods with DE.

Test Images	HE	BBHE	DSIHE	[21]	[19]	Proposed	RSIHE	SDD MHE	ABC
baboon	0.2341	0.2751	0.4568	0.4607	0.4641	**0.6102**	0.4443	0.4032	0.5483
boat	0.2832	0.2759	0.4296	0.4376	0.4505	**0.6512**	0.4461	0.4171	0.4638
City	0.3259	0.3624	0.4446	0.4522	0.4572	0.4685	0.4633	0.4006	**0.535**
Couple	0.1968	0.2685	0.4261	0.4391	0.4544	**0.6937**	0.4377	0.3846	0.4616
Girl	0.4208	0.3747	0.4497	0.4735	0.4827	**0.5617**	0.4762	0.4561	0.484
Jet	0.3599	0.3873	0.4709	0.4788	0.4626	**0.5997**	0.4624	0.4213	0.4743
Lenna	0.2146	0.3003	0.4319	0.4571	0.4513	**0.6221**	0.4452	0.3982	0.4558
Man	0.1886	0.309	0.4018	0.3937	0.4066	0.4066	**0.4429**	0.4062	0.4274
Peppers	0.1806	0.3952	0.4143	0.4256	0.4165	**0.5757**	0.4188	0.385	0.4288
Plan	0.4844	0.4857	0.4805	0.4939	0.499	0.499	0.4975	0.5	**0.6432**
Average	0.2889	0.3434	0.4406	0.4512	0.4545	**0.5688**	0.4534	0.4172	0.4922

Table 5. Compare various method with FSIM.

Test Images	HE	BBHE	DSIHE	[21]	[19]	Proposed	RSIHE	SDD MHE	ABC
baboon	0.8395	0.9365	0.8936	0.9571	0.9449	**0.9929**	0.9194	0.8947	0.9194
boat	0.6859	0.8236	0.8077	0.9208	0.8889	**0.9933**	0.9829	0.8728	0.983
City	0.7566	0.8328	0.7893	0.9173	0.8858	0.9863	**0.9907**	0.8407	0.9382
Couple	0.8938	0.8205	0.8137	0.9044	0.8838	**0.9895**	0.9577	0.8192	0.9577
Girl	0.5737	0.6302	0.5986	0.7161	0.8377	**0.9732**	0.962	0.6521	0.9692
Jet	0.8464	0.8744	0.7514	0.9595	0.9196	0.9795	**0.9965**	0.9185	0.9648
Lenna	0.9112	0.9576	0.9284	0.9729	0.9328	**0.99**	0.9561	0.9321	0.9561
Man	0.9165	0.9377	0.9486	0.947	0.9521	0.9874	**0.9889**	0.9366	0.9599
Peppers	0.9476	0.967	0.9479	0.9798	0.9709	**0.99**	0.9595	0.9454	0.9603
Plan	0.5057	0.6026	0.5681	0.7403	0.9066	0.9708	**0.9777**	0.6207	0.9773
Average	0.7877	0.8383	0.8047	0.9015	0.9123	**0.9853**	0.9691	0.8433	0.9586

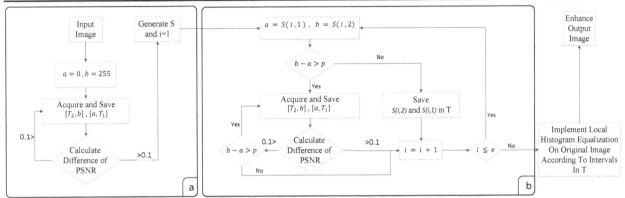

Figure 8. (a) Algorithm 1 steps (b) steps of re-implantation of algorithm 1 for intervals. larger than p.

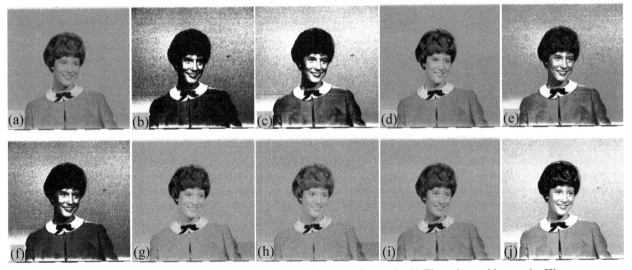

Figure 9. Girl (a) The original Image, The experimental image under study (b) The enhanced image by Histogram Equalization (c) The enhanced image by BBHE (d) The enhanced image by ABC (e) the enhanced image by RSIHE (f) The enhanced image by DSIHE (g) The enhanced image by [19] (h) The enhanced image by the proposed method (i) The enhanced image by SDDMHE (j) The enhanced image by [21].

4. Conclusion

In this paper, a new method was proposed for image contrast enhancement without losing image details. Intensity saturation and over-enhancement is one of the main issues in the other proposed contract enhancement methods. In order to overcome this problem and also to obtain a desired contrast enhancement, the image histogram is first divided into some sub-histograms according to the mean value and standard deviation. Then every single sub-histogram is enhanced separately using the traditional histogram equalization. Finally, these enhanced sub-histograms are combined to make the enhanced image. The qualitative and quantitative results of comparing different contrast enhancement methods with the proposed method show that the proposed method not only keeps the details and image brightness level mean but also enhances the image contrast effectively, and leads to an increased image quality. Selecting the parameters related to the number of sub-histograms was one of the problems faced with in this work. A solution is using a method to obtain

the value of "p" and PSNR threshold according to the input image.

Figure 10. Boat (a) Original Image (b) Enhanced image by Histogram Equalization (c) Enhanced image by BBHE (d) Enhanced image by ABC (e) Enhanced image by RSIHE (f) Enhanced image by DSIHE (g) Enhanced image by [19] (h) Enhanced image by proposed method (i) Enhanced image by SDDMHE (j) Enhanced image by [21].

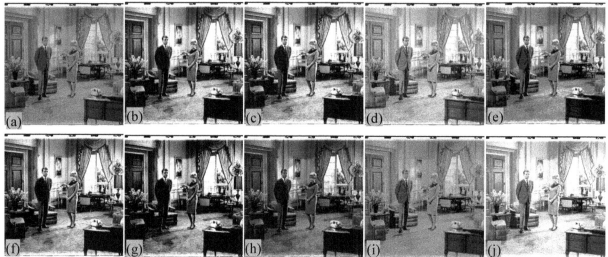

Figure 11. Couple (a) Original Image (b) Enhanced image by Histogram Equalization (c) Enhanced image by BBHE (d) Enhanced image by ABC (e) Enhanced image by RSIHE (f) Enhanced image by DSIHE (g) Enhanced image by [19] (h) Enhanced image by proposed method (i) Enhanced image by SDDMHE (j) Enhanced image by [21].

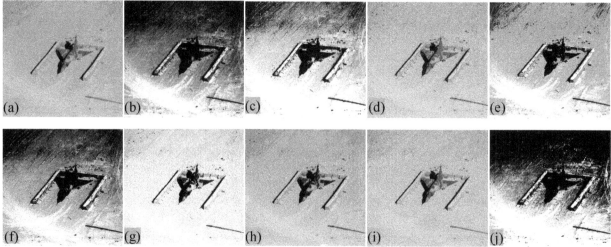

Figure 12. Plan (a) Original Image (b) Enhanced image by Histogram Equalization (c) Enhanced image by BBHE (d) Enhanced image by ABC (e) Enhanced image by RSIHE (f) Enhanced image by DSIHE (g) Enhanced image by [19] (h) Enhanced image by proposed method (i) Enhanced image by SDDMHE (j) Enhanced image by [21].

References

[1] Chen, C. Y., Lin, T. M., & Wolf, W. H. (2008). A visible/infrared fusion algorithm for distributed smart cameras. IEEE Journal of Selected Topics in Signal Processing, vol. 2, no. 4, pp. 514-525.

[2] Lai, C. C., & Tsai, C. C. (2008). Backlight power reduction and image contrast enhancement using adaptive dimming for global backlight applications. IEEE Transactions on Consumer Electronics, vol. 54, no. 2, pp. 669-674.

[3] Kim, Y. T. (1997). Contrast enhancement using brightness preserving bi-histogram equalization. IEEE transactions on Consumer Electronics, vol. 43, no. 1, pp. 1-8.

[4] Kim, J. Y., Kim, L. S., & Hwang, S. H. (2001). An advanced contrast enhancement using partially overlapped sub-block histogram equalization. IEEE transactions on circuits and systems for video technology, vol. 11, no. 4, pp. 475-484.

[5] Wang, Y., Chen, Q., & Zhang, B. (1999). Image enhancement based on equal area dualistic sub-image histogram equalization method. IEEE Transactions on Consumer Electronics, vol. 45, no. 1, pp. 68-75.

[6] Sim, K. S., Tso, C. P., & Tan, Y. Y. (2007). Recursive sub-image histogram equalization applied to gray scale images. Pattern Recognition Letters, vol. 28, no. 10, pp. 1209-1221.

[7] Xie, X., & Lam, K. M. (2005). Face recognition under varying illumination based on a 2D face shape model. Pattern Recognition, vol. 38, no. 2, pp. 221-230.

[8] van Bemmel, C. M., Wink, O., Verdonck, B., Viergever, M. A., & Niessen, W. J. (2003). Blood pool contrast-enhanced MRA: improved arterial visualization in the steady state. IEEE transactions on medical imaging, vol. 22, no. 5, pp. 645-652.

[9] Arici, T., Dikbas, S., & Altunbasak, Y. (2009). A histogram modification framework and its application for image contrast enhancement. IEEE Transactions on image processing, vol. 18, no. 9, pp. 1921-1935.

[10] Abdullah-Al-Wadud, M., Kabir, M. H., Dewan, M. A. A., & Chae, O. (2007). A dynamic histogram equalization for image contrast enhancement. IEEE Transactions on Consumer Electronics, vol. 53, no. 2, pp. 593-600.

[11] Lamberti, F., Montrucchio, B., & San, A. (2006). CMBFHE: A novel contrast enhancement technique based on cascaded multistep binomial filtering histogram equalization. IEEE Transactions on Consumer Electronics, vol. 52, no. 3, pp. 966-974.

[12] Chen, Z., Abidi, B. R., Page, D. L., & Abidi, M. A. (2006). Gray-level grouping (GLG): an automatic method for optimized image contrast Enhancement-part I: the basic method. IEEE transactions on image processing, vol. 15, no. 8, pp. 2290-2302.

[13] Chen, S. D., & Ramli, A. R. (2003). Contrast enhancement using recursive mean-separate histogram equalization for scalable brightness preservation. IEEE Transactions on Consumer Electronics, vol. 49, no. 4, pp. 1301-1309.

[14] Kim, Y. T. (1997). Contrast enhancement using brightness preserving bi-histogram equalization. IEEE transactions on Consumer Electronics, vol. 43, no. 1, pp. 1-8.

[15] Wang, Y., Chen, Q., & Zhang, B. (1999). Image enhancement based on equal area dualistic sub-image histogram equalization method. IEEE Transactions on Consumer Electronics, vol. 45, no. 1, pp. 68-75.

[16] Sim, K. S., Tso, C. P., & Tan, Y. Y. (2007). Recursive sub-image histogram equalization applied to gray scale images. Pattern Recognition Letters, vol. 28, no. 10, pp. 1209-1221.

[17] Draa, A., & Bouaziz, A. (2014). An artificial bee colony algorithm for image contrast enhancement. Swarm and Evolutionary computation, vol. 16, pp. 69-84.

[18] Khan, M. F., Khan, E., & Abbasi, Z. A. (2014). Segment dependent dynamic multi-histogram equalization for image contrast enhancement. Digital Signal Processing, vol. 25, pp. 198-223.

[19] Huang, S. C., & Yeh, C. H. (2013). Image contrast enhancement for preserving mean brightness without losing image features. Engineering Applications of Artificial Intelligence, vol. 26, no. 5, pp. 1487-1492.

[20] Kim, M., & Chung, M. G. (2008). Recursively separated and weighted histogram equalization for brightness preservation and contrast enhancement. IEEE Transactions on Consumer Electronics, vol. 54, no. 3, pp. 1389-1397.

[21] Hoseini, P., & Shayesteh, M. G. (2013). Efficient contrast enhancement of images using hybrid ant colony optimisation, genetic algorithm, and simulated annealing. Digital Signal Processing, vol. 23, no. 3, pp. 879-893.

[22] Zhang, L., Zhang, L., Mou, X., & Zhang, D. (2011). FSIM: a feature similarity index for image quality assessment. IEEE transactions on Image Processing, vol. 20, no. 8, pp. 2378-2386.

[23] Shannon, C. E. (2001). A mathematical theory of communication. ACM SIGMOBILE Mobile Computing and Communications Review, vol. 5, no. 1, pp. 3-55.

[24] Huang, S. C., Cheng, F. C., & Chiu, Y. S. (2013). Efficient contrast enhancement using adaptive gamma correction with weighting distribution. Image Processing, IEEE Transactions on, vol. 22, no. 3, pp. 1032-1041.

[25] Ooi, C. H., Kong, N. S. P., & Ibrahim, H. (2009). Bi-histogram equalization with a plateau limit for

digital image enhancement. IEEE Transactions on Consumer Electronics, vol. 55, no. 4, pp. 2072-2080.

[26] Gu, K., Zhai, G., Yang, X., Zhang, W., & Chen, C. W. (2015). Automatic contrast enhancement technology with saliency preservation. IEEE Transactions on Circuits and Systems for Video Technology, vol. 25, no. 9, pp. 1480-1494.

[27] Lidong, H., Wei, Z., Jun, W., & Zebin, S. (2015). Combination of contrast limited adaptive histogram equalisation and discrete wavelet transform for image enhancement. IET Image Processing, vol. 9, no. 10, pp. 908-915.

[28] Liang, Z., Liu, W., & Yao, R. (2016). Contrast Enhancement by Nonlinear Diffusion Filtering. IEEE Transactions on Image Processing, vol. 25, no. 2, pp. 673-686.

[29] Celik, T. (2014). Spatial entropy-based global and local image contrast enhancement. IEEE Transactions on Image Processing, vol. 23, no. 12, pp. 5298-5308.

[30] Kullback, S., & Leibler, R. A. (1951). On information and sufficiency. The annals of mathematical statistics, vol. 22, no. 1, pp. 79-86.

[31] Shafeipour Yourdeshahi, S., Seyedarabi, H., & Aghagolzadeh, A. (2016). Video-based face recognition in color space by graph-based discriminant analysis. Journal of AI and Data Mining, vol. 4, no. 2, pp. 193-201.

2

Tuning Shape Parameter of Radial Basis Functions in Zooming Images using Genetic Algorithm

A. M. Esmaili Zaini[1], A. Mohammad Latif[2,*] and Gh. Barid Loghmani[1]

Department of Applied Mathematics, Yazd University, Yazd, Iran.

Department of Computer Engineering, Yazd University, Yazd, Iran.

Corresponding author: alatif@yazd.ac.ir(A. Latif).

Abstract

Image zooming is one of the current issues of image processing that maintains the quality and structure of an image. In order to zoom an image, it is necessary to place the extra pixels in the image data. Adding the data to the image must be consistent with the texture in the image in order to prevent artificial blocks. In this work, the required pixels are estimated using the radial basis functions and calculating the shape parameter c with the genetic algorithm. Then all the estimated pixels are revised on the basis of the sub-algorithm of edge correction. The proposed method is a non-linear one that preserves the edges and minimizes the blur and block artifacts on the zoomed image. This method is evaluated on several images for calculating the suitable shape parameter of the radial basis functions. The numerical results obtained are presented using the PSNR and SSIM fidelity measures on different images as compared to some other methods. The average PSNR of the original image and image zooming was found to be 33.16, which shows that image zooming by factor of 2 is similar to the original image, which emphasizes that the proposed method has an efficient performance.

Keywords: *Image Zooming, Radial Basis Function, Genetic Algorithm, Interpolation.*

1. Introduction

Image zooming is used to enhance the resolution of an image in order to achieve a high-quality image. It plays an important role in image processing and machine vision, and has a variety of applications in the printing industry, electronic publishing, digital cameras, medical imaging and sampling, images on web pages, license plate recognition, and face recognition systems [1].

Recent studies have shown that in many applications the main task regards the visual quality of images. Resolution of the edges and lack of blurred and additional artifacts are two important factors involved in the quality of zoomed images.

In most algorithms of image zooming, the interpolation method is used. This is to find a set of unknown pixel values from a set of known pixel values in the image.

In image zooming, several basic parameters affect the image quality, as follow [2]:

1. The zooming method should maintain the edges and borders of the image.

2. The method should not produce constant undesirable pieces or blocks of other areas.

3. The method should involve efficient computations, and it should not depend on the inner parameters too much.

Traditional technologies use linear interpolation methods to create high resolution samples in zooming images. Pixel replication, bi-linear interpolation, quadratic interpolation, bi-cubic interpolation, and spline interpolation are among the linear interpolation methods [3-5]. These methods serve to smooth out image edges, and, in some cases, to produce stair edges. Also the outputs of these methods are blurred images.

In the bi-linear interpolation method, artificial blocks and undesirable visual effects appear at a high zooming rate, and the edges are preserved to an acceptable degree.

In the bi-cubic interpolation method, at a suitable zooming rate, the artificial blocks and the undesirable visual effects are fewer than in the bi-linear interpolation method, and the edges are preserved as well. Determining the image quality in these methods is difficult but in terms of high quality, one may refer to the spline interpolation, bi-cubic interpolation, quadratic interpolation, and bi-linear interpolation methods in a descending order [6].

To modify the linear methods in terms of improving the image quality and solving the problem of image blur, the non-linear interpolation technique has been used. The changes in the non-linear methods depend on their interpolation. This means that the performance of these methods with sharp edges is different from their performance with soft edges. Indeed, it is in contrast with the linear methods that treat all pixels equally [7-9].

In non-linear methods, a subset of edge pixels is estimated [8], and resampling, parameter optimization, contextual interpolation, and edge direct interpolation are conducted to preserve the image quality and edges [10-13].

In reference [10], statistical methods have been used to set the structure of the edges and the correction technique of bi-linear interpolation, and the interpolation error theorem [11] have been used in the edge-adaptive method.

In reference [14], as a part of the edge-directed non-linear interpolation method, the technique of filtering direction and data fusion has been used, and a missed pixel has been interpolated in different directions. Then the results of edge-directed interpolation have been combined with the linear least squares estimation, and thus the desirable outcome has been achieved.

In reference [15], the LAZ method has been introduced as a local adaptive zooming algorithm in order to find the edges in different directions using the information of discontinuity or sharp brightness changes. Also two threshold values have been considered, and the missed pixels have been estimated regarding the direction of the edge.

In the recent years, some methods based on the partial differential equations (PDEs) have been proposed and have shown better performance than the previous methods. In references [16 and 17], the edge-directed interpolation methods have been discussed based on the diverse issues with PDEs.

In reference [18], the non-linear curvature interpolation method and PDEs for image-zooming have been provided.

In reference [19], the non-linear fourth-order PDEs method is a combination of the locally adaptive zooming algorithm for image zooming.

In reference [20], an image zooming algorithm has been presented using non-linear PDE combined with edge-directed bi-cubic algorithm.

Most PDE-based methods provide clear images with sharp edges. The effects resulting from blurring and the artificial blocks are minimized in these methods.

In reference [21], a non-linear image-zooming method has been provided based on the radial basis functions and the contextual edge correction techniques. Given that the radial basis functions have the shape parameter c in this method, an interval has been proposed for c by performing numerical experiments.

In reference [22], the artificial neural network methods have been used for zooming operations on digital images.

In reference [23], a non-linear image interpolation algorithm based on the moving least squares technique has been presented. In this method, ability for image zooming and preserving edge features is demonstrated.

In reference [24], image magnification by least squares surfaces has been presented in such a way that extra pixels are estimated using the surface of least squares.

In the present work, using the Genetic Algorithm (GA) and the measure of similarity of two images, the required pixels were calculated regarding the radial basis functions, and the shape parameter c was desirably obtained. Then all the estimated pixels were revised based on the proposed edge correction sub-algorithm.

The structure of this paper is as what follows. In Section 2, the radial basis functions and their properties are discussed. In Section 3, GA and image zooming are briefly reviewed. In Section 4, the proposed method is provided. In Section 5, the evaluation criteria and the results of running and calculating the shape parameter c are discussed using GA in radial basis functions and compared with other methods. In the final part, the conclusion and the future research works in this field are given.

2. Radial basis functions

Radial basis functions play a key role in various fields of engineering and applied mathematics including functions in the discussion of interpolation and solving partial differential equations. Solving a high-dimensional interpolation problem is not as easy as solving univariate functions because the amount of calculations and the complexity of the algorithm are high. According to Hardy [25], a multivariate interpolating function is not unique.

Due to these obstacles, Hardy [26] provided new-basis functions in 1971. Later, on the basis of this provision, radial basis functions emerged as a standard method of approximation. These functions and their importance and applied properties are defined as follow:

Definition 1-2: function $\phi : R^n \to R$ is called 'radial function' if $\|x\| = \|y\|$, then $\phi(x) = \phi(y)$, where $\|.\|$ is the Euclidean norms. in fact, suppose that $\bar{X} = (x_1, x_2, ..., x_d) \in \Omega \subseteq R^d$ and $\phi : R^d \to R$. Then $\bar{X} = (x_1, ..., x_d) \to \phi(\|x_1, .., x_d\|_2)$, where

$$\|\bar{X}\|_2 = \sqrt{\sum_{i=1}^{d} X_i} \ .$$

$\|\bar{X}\|_2$ is the distance of $\bar{X}$ from the origin. Thus the above functions are called 'radial functions' because the discussion is on the distances of the points from a particular center that is the origin.

If the constant points $\bar{x}_1, \bar{x}_2, ..., \bar{x}_n \in R^d$ are given and the following linear composition is displayed from the functions g to the center of the points $\bar{x}_i$:

$$f : R^d \to R$$

$$\bar{x} \to \sum_{i=1}^{n} \alpha_i g(\bar{x} - \bar{x}_i) = \sum_{i=1}^{n} \alpha_i \phi(\|\bar{x} - \bar{x}_i\|) \qquad (1)$$

where, $\|\bar{x} - \bar{x}_i\|$ is an Euclidean norm between the points $\bar{x}, \bar{x}_i$, ϕ, is the radial basis function, and α_i is the real coefficient. Then function f can be displayed as (2). Also the obtained function f is placed in a space composed of the radial basis functions with a finite dimension.

$$f(\bar{x}) = \sum_{i=1}^{n} \alpha_i \phi(\|\bar{x} - \bar{x}_i\|) \qquad (2)$$

Definition 2-2: we suppose a set of n distinct points $\{x_i\}_{i=1}^{n}$ with the corresponding distinct values $\{f_i\}_{i=1}^{n}$ given. In this case, the interpolating function is defined as (3) using the radial basis function.

$$s(x) = \sum_{i=1}^{n} \lambda_i \phi(\|x - x_i\|) \qquad (3)$$

where, the interpolation condition is:
$S(x_i) = f(x_i), \ i = 1, 2, ..., n$.
Equation (3) is equivalent with the linear equations system (4), where the coefficient λ_i can be calculated.

$$A\lambda = F \qquad (4)$$

where

$$A = \begin{pmatrix} \phi(\|x_1 - x_1\|) & \phi(\|x_1 - x_2\|) & \cdots & \phi(\|x_1 - x_n\|) \\ \phi(\|x_2 - x_1\|) & \phi(\|x_2 - x_2\|) & \cdots & \phi(\|x_n - x_2\|) \\ \vdots & \vdots & \ddots & \vdots \\ \phi(\|x_n - x_1\|) & \phi(\|x_n - x_2\|) & \cdots & \phi(\|x_n - x_n\|) \end{pmatrix}$$

A is an interpolating matrix of $n \times n$ with the element $A_{ij} = \phi(\|x_i - x_j\|), \ i, j = 1, ..., n$.

In addition,

$$\lambda = \begin{pmatrix} \lambda_1 \\ \lambda_2 \\ \cdot \\ \cdot \\ \cdot \\ \lambda_n \end{pmatrix}, \ F = \begin{pmatrix} f_1 \\ f_2 \\ \cdot \\ \cdot \\ \cdot \\ f_n \end{pmatrix}$$

In matrix A, ϕs are radial basis functions, and it is clear that matrix A is a symmetric matrix regarding the radial basis function.

Shoenberg [27] has proved that any non-constant function $\phi : [0, \infty) \to R$ is strictly positive definite if and only if the function $\psi : r \to \phi(\sqrt{r})$ on $[0, \infty)$ is completely monotonic. In his article, Michely [28] has shown that if $\phi \in C^{\infty}[0, \infty)$ and ϕ' are completely monotonic and non-constant, and $\phi(0) \ge 0$, then matrix A is non-singular for each $\psi(r) = \phi(\sqrt{r})$.

If the positive definite radial basis functions are used to form matrix A, then A is positive definite and the system always has a solution. However, if the conditional positive definite radial basis functions are used to form matrix A, the interpolating system will be in a specific form; according to (3), if ϕs are the positive definite functions with the order Q where $q = \begin{pmatrix} Q - 1 + d \\ d \end{pmatrix}$,

then with the condition in which:

$$s(x) = \sum_{i=1}^{n} \lambda_i \phi(\|x - x_i\|) + \sum_{k=1}^{q} B_k P_k(x) \qquad (5)$$

$$\sum_{i=1}^{n} \lambda_i P_k(x_i) = 0, \ 1 \le k \le q \qquad (6)$$

Equations (5) and (6) are converted to matrix (7):

$$\begin{pmatrix} A & P \\ P^T & 0 \end{pmatrix} \begin{pmatrix} \lambda \\ B \end{pmatrix} = \begin{pmatrix} F \\ 0 \end{pmatrix} \qquad (7)$$

where, $A_{ij} = \phi(\|x_i - x_j\|)$ for $i, j = 1, ..., n$ and $P_{ij} = P_j(x_i)$ are the assumptions of the interpolating matrix A, for a given ϕ.

Using this trick, the new matrix is non-singular, and the system will have a solution without any damage to the generality of the problem of interpolation.

In general, the radial basis functions are classified into two groups: extremely smooth functions and piecewise smooth functions. Table 1 shows some extremely smooth and piecewise functions.

In extremely smooth radial basis functions, c > 0 is a shape parameter that plays a key role in the accuracy of the methods based upon these functions. Finding the optimal parameters has been considered for many years and they are often calculated through trial and error. Selecting an appropriate c often depends on the problem, and c cannot be selected with certainty.

3. Genetic algorithm and image zooming

Genetic algorithm (GA) is used as a method for finding suitable solutions to most engineering and optimization problems. This algorithm, which uses the evolutionary computation to find suitable solutions, has been inspired by the Darwinian evolutionary theory. This algorithm has been developed by Holand [29], starting with a completely random population and going on through generations. In each generation, the entire population is evaluated, based on the principal of the survival of the fittest, and the better results are selected based on the targeted function (fitness) and transmitted to a new generation. This process is repeated until the termination condition of the algorithm is established. Choosing a fitness function in GA is very important. Therefore, it must be proportionate to the problem. This algorithm leads to suitable solutions by using the operators of selection, cross-over, and mutation.

Table 1. Radial basis function.

Name of function	Type of function	$\phi(r)$
Gaussian function	Extremely smooth	e^{-cr^2}
Multiple quadratic	Extremely smooth	$\sqrt{c^2 + r^2}$
Reverse quadratic	Extremely smooth	$\dfrac{1}{c^2 + r^2}$
Reverse multiple quadratic	Extremely smooth	$\dfrac{1}{\sqrt{c^2 + r^2}}$
Linear spline	Piecewise smooth	r
Cubic spline	Piecewise smooth	r^3
Thin plate spline	Piecewise smooth	$r^2 \ln r$

In image zooming, a number of new pixels are placed among the original pixels of the image. In zooming, the aim is to estimate the amount of new pixels, which is determined on the basis of their neighboring pixels. There are two kinds of neighborhoods in 2D images, namely 4-cell and 8-cell neighborhoods. These neighborhoods are shown in figure 1. In most of the proposed methods, attempt is made to keep the zooming rate at a power of two but it should be noted that this algorithm is usable for every zooming rate.

Suppose that the dimensions of the original image, n × n, spread regularly to 2n × 2n.

More precisely, if S(i ,j) represents the pixel of the original image in the ith row, and the jth column and Z(l, k) represent the pixel of the zoomed image in the lth row and the kth column, then function f defined by (8) places the values for the original image pixels in the interlaced places of the new image.

$$f : S \rightarrow Z$$
$$f(S(i,j)) = Z(2i-1, 2j-1) \qquad (8)$$
$$i, j = 1, 2, ..., n$$

The result is shown in figure 2. The original image pixels are shown with ●, and the other pixels that must be estimated in three steps are shown with ○. These steps estimate the pixels with even columns and even rows, odd rows and even columns, and even rows and odd columns. In order to estimate the values for these pixels, the radial basis functions and the related linear system are used, and then all the pixels are revised with the edge-modified sub-algorithm.

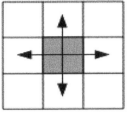 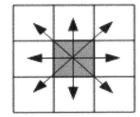

4-cell neighborhood   8-cell neighborhood

Figure 1. Types of neighborhoods.

For the image zooming by factor of 4, the original image expands to the image according to figure 2. Then all the required pixels are estimated. This process is repeated once more.

4. Proposed method

In this method, the points are referred to the pixel coordinate of the image whose brightness and number of columns and rows are considered as a point in a 3D space. In order to estimate the required pixels based on the 4-cell neighborhood, the intended point is selected, and then the intended pixels are estimated by selecting the radial basis function and solving the related linear system by (4).

Thus the shape parameter c is determined in the radial basis function with GA.

The flow chart of the proposed method is shown in figure 3. It should be noted that to approximate the pixels of the last column and row, the penultimate row and column are repeated.

The steps of the proposed algorithm are as follow:

Step 1. The radial basis function is selected.

Step 2. GA is called to determine the random shape parameter c.

Step 3. The linear equation system with regard to the selected radial basis function is formed.

Step 4. The linear equation system and the coefficient are solved.

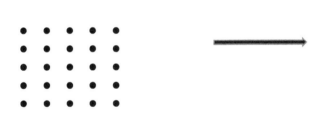

Figure 2. Image zooming.

Step 5. The intended pixels are estimated by replacing the number of columns and rows in the radial basis function.

Step 6. Steps 3 to 5 in three stages are repeated according to the zooming algorithm and estimating the required pixel.

Step 7. The measure PSNR or SSIM of the original image with the zoomed image is calculated.

Step 8. If the stop condition is satisfied, go to step 9; otherwise, go to step 2.

Step 9. The suitable parameter c of the radial basis function in zooming the images with regard to the termination condition in GA is determined.

Step 10. All the estimated pixels, again based on the directed edge sub-algorithm, are revised (explained in the next part).

4.1. Modified sub-algorithm of image edges

After estimating all the required pixels, they are revised to improve the edges, as shown in figure

4. Based upon the following conditions, they are modified if required [15]. A, B, C, and D are the original pixels, and X, Y1, Y2, Z1, and Z2 are the estimated pixels. The advantage of this sub-algorithm is that there is no threshold for the image edges. The steps of the proposed sub-algorithm are as follow:

Step 1. If $|A - D| > |B - C|$, then $X \leftarrow \dfrac{B + C}{2}$. In fact, the edge is in the NE-SW direction.

Step 2. If $|A - D| < |B - C|$, then $X \leftarrow \dfrac{A + D}{2}$. In fact, the edge is in the NW-SE direction.

Step 3. If $(A - D)(B - C) > 0$ then $Y1 \leftarrow \dfrac{A + B}{2}$ and $Y2 \leftarrow \dfrac{C + D}{2}$. In fact, the edge is in the NS direction.

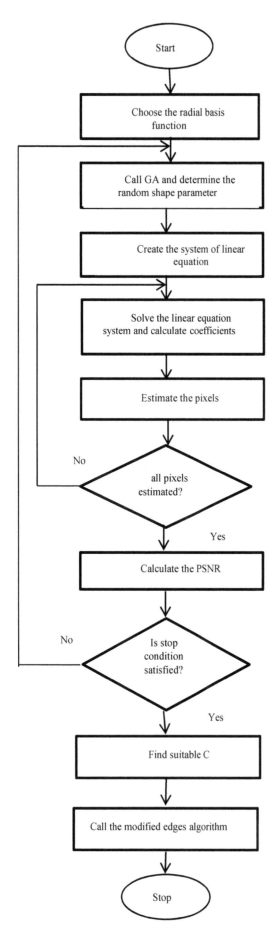

Figure 3. A flow chart of proposed algorithm.

Step 4. If $(A-D)(B-C)<0$ then $Z1 \leftarrow \dfrac{A+C}{2}$ and $Z2 \leftarrow \dfrac{B+D}{2}$. In fact, the edge is in the EW direction.

$\bullet$ A	$\circ$ $Y1$	$\bullet$ B
$\circ$ $Z1$	$\circ$ X	$\circ$ $Z2$
$\bullet$ C	$\circ$ $Y2$	$\bullet$ D

Figure 4. A design for correcting edges.

5. Experimental results

In order to evaluate the proposed method, for image zooming by factor of 2, a digital image was first considered as an original image, and then reduced to half its size by removing its rows and columns alternately. Next, it was enlarged to double its size using the proposed method and the other existing methods. As it was expected, the more similar the original and the zoomed images, the better the performance of the algorithm.

In the next section, evaluation of quality metrics is presented.

5.1. Assessment criteria

The PSNR and SSIM criteria are used to compare two images in terms of their similarity. The greater the amount of PSNR and the closer the amount of SSIM is to one, the more is the conformity of the two images [30]. The measure PSNR is calculated on the basis of (9) and (10):

$$PSNR=10*Log_{10}\left(\frac{MAXI^2}{MSE}\right) \quad (dB) \qquad (9)$$

$$MSE=\frac{1}{m\,n}\sum_{i=0}^{m-1}\sum_{j=0}^{n-1}[I(i,j)-K(i,j)]^2 \qquad (10)$$

where, $I(i,j)$ and $K(i,j)$ are the pixels of the original image and the estimated image, respectively, and $MAXI$ is the maximum amount of the image pixels.

The measure SSIM, which includes the structural elements of the picture, measures the quality of the structural content and the similarity between the two images, that is a number between zero and one, and is calculated by (11). The closer the measure is to one, the more similar the two images are. However, the closer the measure is to zero, the less similar the two images are.

SSIM(x,y)=

$$\frac{(2\mu_x\mu_y+c_1)(2\sigma_x\sigma_y+c_2)(\sigma_{xy}+c_3)}{(\mu_x^2+\mu_y^2+c_1)(\sigma_x^2+\sigma_y^2+c_2)(\sigma_x\sigma_y+c_3)} \qquad (11)$$

where, μ, σ^2 and σ_{xy} are the mean, variance, and co-variance of the pixels, respectively, and c_1, c_2, and c_3 are three constants to prevent the denominator from being zero.

5.2. Numerical experiments of proposed method

The shape parameter c of radial basis function is determined using GA. Important parameters in GA are shown in table 2.

Table 2. GA setting.

Scaling function	Rank
Cross-over rate	0.8
Mutation rate	0.2
Mutation function	Adaptive feasible
Cross-over function	Constraint dependent
Selection function	Uniform

The results of running the proposed algorithm in the MATLAB software were tabulated in tables 3 and 4. In table 3, the measures PSNR and SSIM were used to zoom the image. Also 10 different standard images are shown in figure 5, in which their size is 512×512 [31].

Lifting body Elaine Disk Fire

Dog Balloons House Airplane

Fruit   Swan

Figure 5. Different standard images for image zooming.

The results of the proposed method were obtained using the extremely smoothly Gaussian radial basis function e^{-Cr^2} (GRBF). In GA, the used range was [-10, 10], and the initial population was considered to be 10. However, a better number of population was considered to be 5 so that the next

generation would be continued regarding the values for PSNR and SSIM.

For the proposed images, on average, the termination condition was achieved after 70 repetitions. After running the algorithm, a suitable value for c was found to be 2.4335. Figure 6 shows the process of reaching a suitable solution in zooming the image with GA.

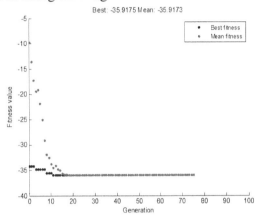

Figure 6. Process of reaching a suitable solution using GA and GRBF in image of lifting body.

It should be noted that PSNR was used in the algorithm because in a GA, the minimum value for the targeted function is calculated. After running the algorithm and calculating a suitable value for the shape parameter c, the sub-algorithm of edge correction was run on the image.

The results obtained were tabulated in table 3. The minimum difference of PSNR by the GRBF method with edge correction and without edge correction was 0.08 and the maximum was 0.47, whilst the average was 0.21. Also it could be seen that the quality of the images was preserved at a desirable level.

Table 4 shows the results of implementing the proposed method using the extremely smoothly reverse quadratic radial basis function $\frac{1}{c^2+r^2}$ (RQRBF). In GA, the applied range was [0,100], and the initial population was considered to be 20; however, a better number of population was considered to be 10 so as to the next generation to continue with regard to the values for PSNR and SSIM.

For the proposed images, on average, the termination condition was achieved after 51 repetitions. A suitable value for c, obtained after running the algorithm, is shown in table 3. Figure 7 shows the process of reaching a suitable solution in zooming the image with GA. After running the algorithm and calculating the optimal value for the shape parameter c, the directed edge sub-algorithm was run on the image.

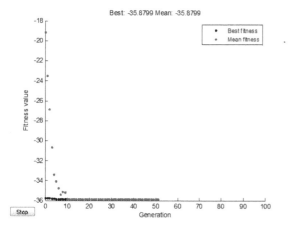

Figure 7. Process of reaching a suitable solution using GA
and RQRBF in image of lifting body

The results obtained were tabulated in table 4. The least difference of PSNR between with and without edge correction by the RQRBF method was 0.07, the most was 0.51, and its average was 0.21. As it can be seen, the quality of the images is preserved at a desirable level.

According to the results obtained, it can be concluded that a suitable value for the shape parameter c in the Gaussian radial basis function is independent from the image but the reverse quadratic radial basis function depends on it.

Table 3. Results of running GRBF with suitable c on different images using SSIM and PSNR, with and without edge correction by factor of 2 in zooming.

Methods	Without edge correction		With edge correction	
images	SSIM	PSNR	SSIM	PSNR
Lifting body	0.9766	35.92	0.9769	36.39
Elaine	0.9601	34.58	0.9589	34.66
Disk	0.9952	33.00	0.9956	33.08
Fire	0.9850	32.09	0.9857	32.21
Swan	0.9835	33.09	0.9842	33.22
Dog	0.9806	33.78	0.9814	33.94
Balloons	0.9889	32.31	0.9894	32.55
House	0.9860	33.83	0.9867	33.99
Airplane	0.9792	29.65	0.9812	29.95
Fruits	0.9616	31.24	0.9608	31.59

Table 4. Results of running RQRBF with suitable c on different images using SSIM and PSNR, with and without edge correction by factor of 2 in zooming.

Methods	Without edge correction		With edge correction		suitable values of the shape
images	SSIM	PSNR	SSIM	PSNR	parameter c
Lifting body	0.9766	35.88	0.9769	36.39	12.781
Elaine	0.9601	34.59	0.9589	34.66	17.875
Disk	0.9952	33.00	0.9956	33.08	0.607
Fire	0.9850	32.10	0.9857	32.21	18.625
Swan	0.9835	33.08	0.9842	33.22	20.026
Dog	0.9806	33.78	0.9814	33.94	17.688
Balloons	0.9890	32.34	0.9893	32.57	10.188
House	0.9860	33.86	0.9867	34.00	13.75
Airplane	0.9792	29.67	0.9812	29.97	12.938
Fruits	0.9617	31.24	0.9608	31.59	14.871

5.3. Comparison of results of proposed method with other methods

In order to evaluate the proposed algorithm, the results were obtained using the extremely smoothly GRBF e^{-Cr^2}. This was compared with non-linear PDE with edge directed bi-cubic (PDEWBC) [20] and least square ellipsoid (LSE) methods [24], bi-linear interpolation (BIL) method, bi-cubic interpolation (BIC) method, and curvature interpolation method (CIM) [18].

The results obtained are presented in table 5. As one can see in this table, the average difference of PSNR between the GRBF and LSE methods is 0.24, between GRBF method and PDEWBC is 1.33, and between the GRBF method and CIM is 1.75. Also the average difference of PSNR between the GRBF and BIC methods is 2.26, and between the GRBF and BIL method is 2.16.

With regard to comparison of the results, it can be concluded that the proposed GRBF method has a better performance than the other methods on the selected image.

It is to emphasize that the results are also obtained by zooming factor of 4 with GRBF with suitable c, as shown in table 6.

Table 5. Comparison of GRBF and other methods by PSNR criterion by factor of 2 in zooming.

Methods images	BIL	BIC	CIM	PDEWBC	LSE	GRBF
Lifting body	33.34	33.30	33.87	34.41	36.17	**36.39**
Elaine	31.26	31.08	31.49	31.80	34.61	**34.66**
Disk	30.94	30.82	31.56	31.93	32.70	**33.08**
Fire	31.66	31.71	31.82	31.97	31.95	**32.21**
Swan	31.19	30.74	31.44	31.88	32.73	**33.22**
Dog	31.83	31.37	32.05	32.65	33.63	**33.94**
Balloons	31.29	31.73	32.28	32.77	34.07	**32.55**
House	32.64	32.60	32.97	33.24	33.83	**33.99**
Airplane	29.70	29.59	30.12	30.49	31.30	**29.95**
Fruits	26.17	26.08	26.49	27.12	28.20	**31.59**
Average	31.00	30.90	31.41	31.83	32.92	**33.16**

Table 6. Results of running GRBF using PSNR, with edge correction and compare other methods by factor of 4 in zooming.

Methods images	BIL	BIC	CIM	PDEWBC	GRBF
Lifting body	27.39	27.05	27.89	28.41	**30.43**
Elaine	26.49	26.14	28.49	29.21	**30.68**
Disk	25.77	25.56	26.68	28.74	**30.92**
Fire	25.60	25.46	25.71	26.02	**26.08**
Swan	26.90	26.75	26.93	**26.98**	26.37
Dog	27.55	27.38	27.61	27.85	**27.68**
Balloons	24.94	24.75	25.34	25.76	**26.28**
House	27.09	26.90	27.56	28.06	**28.84**
Airplane	22.49	22.12	23.85	24.34	**25.16**
Fruits	23.07	22.72	24.23	25.16	**26.99**
Average	25.73	25.48	26.43	27.06	**27.94**

These results were compared with the BIL, BIC, CIM, and PDEWCB methods. As indicated in table 6, the PSNR value, average difference of PSNR between the GRBF and BIL methods is 2.21, between the GRBF and BIC methods is 2.46, between the GRBF method and CIM is 1.51, and between the GRBF and PDEWBC methods is 0.88. The merit of the presented method is that

the objective evaluation results are better than the performance of the other methods.

From a visual perspective, figure 8 shows the sample image Elaine zoomed with the proposed method and in two modes with and without edge correction. The images obtained from the proposed method are clearer and blur less with good performance on the edges.

GRBF without edge correction

Difference with been original image and GRBF without edge correction

GRBF with edge correction

Difference with been original image and GRBF edge correction

RQRBF without edge correction

Difference with been original image and RQRBF without edge correction

RQRBF with edge correction

Difference with been original image and RQRBF with edge correction

Figure 8. Results of Elaine's image zooming by factor of 2 and using different methods.

6. Conclusion

In this research work, a suitable value for the shape parameter c was achieved by radial basis functions with the application of GA. This achieved result has been used in zooming images.

This method provided desirable results.

In addition, the edge correction technique was used to enhance the quality of images after calculating a suitable value for the shape parameter c. In the future studies, the proposed method can be developed with other edge correction techniques or non-linear methods such as the two-variable interpolation method or a combination of radial basis function isolation and edge correction techniques. It is to note that proving the independence of the shape parameter c in the Gaussian radial basis function in zooming images will be investigated in our future research project.

References

[1] Lehmann, T., Gönner, C. & Spitzer, K. (1999). Survey: Interpolation methods in medical image processing, IEEE Trans. Med. Imaging., vol. 18, no. 11, pp. 1049–1075.

[2] Lee, Y. J. & Yoon, J. (2010). Nonlinear image upsampling method based on radial basis function interpolation, IEEE Trans. Image Process., vol. 19, no. 10, pp. 2682–2692.

[3] Keys, R. G. (1981). Cubic convolution interpolation for digital image processing, IEEE Trans. Acoust., Speech, Signal Process., vol. 29, no. 6, pp. 1153–1160.

[4] Hou, H. S. & Andrews, H. C. (1978). Cubic splines for image interpolation and digital filtering, IEEE Trans. Acoust., Speech, Signal Process, vol. 26, no. 6, pp. 508–517.

[5] Thévenaz, P., Blu, T. & Unser, M. (2000). Interpolation revisited, IEEE Trans. Med. Image., vol. 19, no. 7, pp. 739–758.

[6] Padmanabhan, S. A. & Chandramathi, S. (2011). Image zooming using segmented polynomial interpolation in R^2 space, European Journal of Scientific Research, vol. 57, no. 3, pp. 447-453.

[7] Jensen, K. & Anastassion, D. (1995). Subpixel edge localization and the interpolation of still images, IEEE Trans. Image Process., vol. 4, no. 3, pp. 285–295.

[8] Allebach, J. & Wong, P. W. (1996). Edge-directed interpolation, in Proc. IEEE Int. Conf. Image. Proc., vol. 3, pp. 707–710.

[9] Carrato, S. & Tenze, L. (2000). A high quality 2X image interpolator, IEEE Signal Process., vol. 7, no. 6, pp. 132–135.

[10] Li, X. & Orchard, T. (2001). New edge directed interpolation, IEEE Trans. Image Process, vol. 10, no. 10, pp. 1521–1527.

[11] Cha, Y. & Kim, S. (2007). The error-amended sharp edge (ease) scheme for image zooming, IEEE Trans. Image Process., vol. 16, no. 6, pp. 1496–1505.

[12] Li, M. & Nguyen, T. Q. (2008). Markov random field model-based edge directed image interpolation, IEEE Trans. Image Process., vol. 17, no. 7, pp. 1121–1128.

[13] Zhang, X. & Wu, X. (2008). Image interpolation by adaptive 2-D autoregressive modeling and soft-decision estimation, IEEE Trans. Image Process., vol. 17, no. 6, pp. 887–896.

[14] Zhang, L. & Wu, X. (2006). An edge-guided image interpolation algorithm via directional filtering and data fusion, IEEE Trans. Image Process., vol. 15, no. 8, pp. 2226–2238.

[15] Battiato, S., Gallo, G. & stanco, F. (2002). A locally adaptive zooming algorithm for digital images, Image and Vision Computing, vol. 20, no. 11, pp. 805-812.

[16] Jiang, H. & Moloney, C. (2002). A new direction adaptive scheme for image interpolation, in Proc. Int. Conf. Image Processing, vol. 3, pp. 369-372.

[17] Wang, Q. & Ward, R. K. (2007). A new orientation-adaptive interpolation method, IEEE Trans. Image Process., vol. 16, no. 4, pp. 889–990.

[18] Kim, H., Cha, Y. & Kim, S. (2011). Curvature interpolation method for image zooming, IEEE Trans. Image Process., vol. 20, no. 7, pp.1895-1903.

[19] Nowrozian, N. & Hassanpour, H. (2014). Image zooming using non-linear partial differential equation, International Journal of Engineering Transactions A: Basics, vol. 27, no. 1, pp. 15-28.

[20] Warbhe, S. & Gomes, J. (2016). Interpolation technique using non-linear partial differential equation with edge directed bi-cubic, International Journal of Image Processing, vol. 10, no. 4, pp. 205-213.

[21] Lee, Y. J. & Yoon, J. (2010). Nonlinear image upsampling method based on radial basis function, IEEE Trans. Image Process., vol. 19, no. 10, pp. 2682–2692.

[22] Youssef, D., Mohammed, B., Abdelmalek, A., Tarik, H. & EL Miloud, J. (2015). Zoom and restoring of digital image artificial neural networks, Computer Science and Engineering, vol. 5, no. 1, pp. 14-24.

[23] Lee, Y.J. & Yoon, J. (2015). Image zooming method using edge-directed moving least squares interpolation based on exponential polynomials, Applied Mathematics and Computation, vol. 269, pp. 569-583.

[24] Esmaili Zaini, A. M., Barid Loghmani, G. & Latif, A. M. (2016). Image magnification by least squares surfaces, Iranian Journal of Numerical Analysis and Optimization. In press.

[25] Watson, G. A. (1980). Approximation theory and numerical methods, Wily.

[26] Hardy, R. L. (1971). Multiquadric equations of topology and other irregular surface, J. Geophys. Res., vol. 76, pp. 1905-1915.

[27] Schoenberg, I. J. (1970). Matric space and completely monotone functions, Ann. Math. Appl. vol. 23, pp. 811-841.

[28] Michelli, C. A. (1986). Interpolation of scattered data distance matrices and conditionally positive definite functions, Constr. Approx., vol. 2, pp.11-22.

[29] Holland, J. H. (1992). Adaptation in natural and artificial systems. 1975. Ann Arbor, MI: University of Michigan Press and.

[30] Wang, Z., Bovik, A. C., Sheikh, H. R. & Simoncelli, E. P. (2004). Image quality assessment: from error visibility to structural similarity, IEEE Trans. Image Process., vol. 13, no. 4, pp. 600-612.

[31] Online. Available: www.freeimages.co.uk and sipi.usc.edu/database.

3

Multi-Output Adaptive Neuro-Fuzzy Inference System for Prediction of Dissolved Metal Levels in Acid Rock Drainage

H. Fattahi [*], A. Agah and N. Soleimanpourmoghadam

Department of Mining Engineering, Arak University of Technology, Arak, Iran.

Corresponding author: H.fattahi@arakut.ac.ir (H. Fattahi).

Abstract

Pyrite oxidation, Acid Rock Drainage (ARD) generation, and associated release and transport of toxic metals are a major environmental concern for the mining industry. Estimation of the metal loading in ARD is a major task in developing an appropriate remediation strategy. In this work, an expert system, the Multi-Output Adaptive Neuro-Fuzzy Inference System (MANFIS), is used for estimation of metal concentrations in the Shur River, resulting from ARD at the Sarcheshmeh porphyry copper deposit, SE of Iran. Concentrations of Cu, Fe, Mn, and Zn are predicted using the pH, and the sulfate (SO_4) and magnesium (Mg) concentrations in the Shur River as inputs to MANFIS. Three MANFIS models are implemented, Grid Partitioning (GP), Subtractive Clustering Method (SCM), and Fuzzy C-Means Clustering Method (FCM). A comparison is made between these three models, and the results obtained show the superiority of the MANFIS-SCM model. These results indicate that the MANFIS-SCM model has a potential for estimation of the metals with a high degree of accuracy and robustness.

Keywords: *Acid Rock Drainage, MANFIS, Grid Partitioning, Subtractive Clustering Method, Fuzzy C-Means Clustering Method.*

1. Introduction

The Sarcheshmeh copper mine is located in the Central Iranian Volcanic Belt in Kerman Province, SE of Iran [1,2]. The mine and mineral processing operation produces large tonnages of low-grade wastes and tailings materials that can generate Acid Rock Drainage (ARD) [3,4]. The waste and tailings materials contain reactive sulfide minerals, in particular pyrite, and have a short lag time before generating ARD. The mine generated acidic waters have high concentrations of dissolved iron and sulfate, a low pH (2-4.5), and variable concentrations of other elements, principally Mn, Zn, Cu, Cd, and Pb [5-9]. ARD containing metals threaten the aquatic life and surrounding environment [10-14]. The prediction of metal loadings to the Shur River is required to help develop effective mitigation strategies to minimize impacts to the river.

The Sarcheshmeh copper mine provides an excellent opportunity to investigate the processes involved in sulfide mineral oxidation and ARD generation within sulfide-bearing waste and tailings, and the impact of ARD on the Shur Rivers [15,16,2]. Numerous works have been done on different aspects of ARD at Sarcheshmeh and other mines in Iran including those outlined as what follow. Ardejani et al. [17] have offered a combined mathematical-geophysical model for prediction of pyrite oxidation. Sadeghi et al. [14] have investigated an image processing method applied to model the pyrite oxidation in the wastes of the AlborzSharghi coal washing plant, NE of Iran. Shokri et al. [18] have presented a statistical model for predicting pyrite oxidation in a coal waste pile at AlborzSharghi, Iran. Khorasanipour, Eslami [19] have investigated hydro-geochemistry and contamination by trace elements in Cu-Porphyry Mine tailings.

In the past few decades, the intelligent system approaches have gained increasing popularity in different fields of engineering for modeling and simulation of environmental problems. Kemper, Sommer [20] have estimated the metal concentrations in soils using a back propagation network and multiple linear regression. Almasri, Kaluarachchi [21] have applied modular neural networks to predict the nitrate distribution in ground water using on-ground nitrogen loading and recharge data. Back-propagation neural network and multiple linear regression were used for prediction of water quality in the Gomti River in India [22]. Tahmasebi, Hezarkhani [23] have investigated the application of an Adaptive Neuro-Fuzzy Inference System (ANFIS) for grade estimation at the Sarcheshmeh Porphyry Copper Deposit. Gholami et al. [24] have used artificial intelligence methods for prediction of nickel mobilization. Rooki et al. [25] have applied neural networks for prediction of metals in acid mine drainage. Doulati Ardejanii et al. [4]have used the general regression neural network analysis for prediction of rare earth elements in neutral alkaline mine drainage from the Razi Coal Mine, Golestan Province, NE of Iran. Sadeghiamirshahidi et al. [26] have applied artificial neural networks (ANNs) for prediction of pyrite oxidation in the spoil of the AlborzSharghi coal washing refuse pile, NE of Iran. Sayadi et al. [27] have investigated the application of neural networks to predict the net present value in mining projects. Shokri et al. [28] have applied ANNs and ANFISs for prediction of pyrite oxidation in a coal washing waste pile in Iran. Maiti, Tiwari [29] have compared Bayesian neural networks and an ANFIS in groundwater level prediction.

The literature investigated has shown that many research works have been conducted related to the application of the ANN method in mining and relevant environmental problems.

In this work, the three MANFIS models MANFIS-GP, MANFIS-SCM, MANFIS-FCM were used to build the prediction models for the estimation of the ARD-derived metals in the Shur River.

The results obtained from the estimation using MANFIS were compared with the measured concentrations of the major metals in the Shur River.

2. Site descriptions
The Sarcheshmeh open pit copper mine is located 160 km SW of Kerman and 50 km to SW of Rafsanjan in the Kerman province, Iran (Figure 1); the main access road to the studied area is the Kerman–Rafsanjan–Shahr Babak road [30].

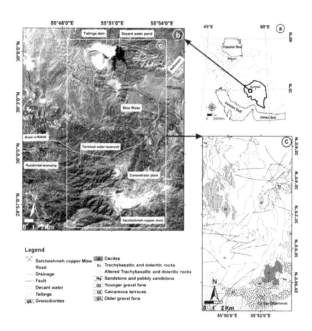

Figure 1. (a) Location of Kerman province, (b) satellite image, illustrating geographical situation of Sarcheshmeh copper complex, (c) geological map of studied area [31].

The ore body is recognized to be the fourth largest porphyry copper deposit in the world consisting of 1 billion tons of ore with copper (0.9%) and molybdenum (0.03%) [32]. The mine is situated in the rugged topography of the Band Mamazar-Pariz Mountains at an average elevation of 1,600 m. The mean annual precipitation at the site varies from 300 to 550 mm, the temperature ranges from +35 $^{\circ}$C in summer to -20 $^{\circ}$C in winter, and the area is covered with snow about 3–4 months per year [15,25]. The Sarcheshmeh ore body is oval-shaped with a width of about 1,200 m and a length of about 2,300 m. This deposit is centred on the late Tertiary Sarcheshmeh grano-diorite porphyry stock [33]. The geology of Sarcheshmeh porphyry deposit consists of a very complex series of magmatically related intrusives of Tertiary volcanic emplaced at variable distances from the edge of an older near-batholith-size granodiorite mass. The open pit mining method is used to extract the ore, the tailings impoundment is located about 20 km downstream of the open pit on the Shur River. The Shur River is the main recipient of the mine drainage including the ARD and industrial effluent of the Sarcheshmeh copper complex that discharges into the tailings impoundment [31]. The Shur River basin at the tailings dam site has a catchment area of approximately 200 km^2 and has a mean annual discharge of about 0.53 m^3/s [34].

3. Sampling and field methods
Water sampling was conducted in February

2006. In this work, 6 stations at different distances along the river between the mine and the tailings dam were selected for collecting the samples for water quality analysis.

The water samples were immediately acidified by adding HNO (10 cc acid to 1,000 cc sample) and stored under cool conditions [24]. THE Water sampling equipment included sterile sample containers, GPS, oven, autoclave, Ph-meter, and atomic adsorption and ICP analyzers. The pH values for the water samples were measured using a portable pH-meter in the field. Other quantities measured in the field included electrical conductivity (EC), total dissolved solids (TDS), and temperature. Analyses of the dissolved metals were performed using an adsorption spectrometer (AA220) in the water laboratory of the National Iranian Copper Industries Company (NICIC). The ICP (model 6000) analysis was used to analyze the concentrations of those metals, usually detected in the range of ppb [35,36].

4. Multi-Output Adaptive Neuro-Fuzzy Inference System

ANN is simple but a powerful and flexible tool for forecasting, provided that there is enough data for training, an adequate selection of the input–output samples, an appropriated number of hidden units, and enough computational resources available. Also ANN has the well-known advantages of being able to approximate any non-linear function and being able to solve problems where the input–output relationship is neither well-defined nor easily computable because ANN is data-driven. Multi-layered feed-forward ANN is specially suited for forecasting, implementing non-linearities using sigmoid functions for the hidden layer and linear functions for the output layer [37].

Just like ANN, a fuzzy logic system is a non-linear mapping of an input vector into a scalar output but it can handle numerical values and linguistic knowledge. In general, a fuzzy logic system contains four components: fuzzifier, rules, inference engine, and defuzzifier. The fuzzifier converts a crisp input variable into a fuzzy representation, where membership functions give the degree of belonging of the variable to a given attribute. Fuzzy rules are of the type ''if–then'', and can be derived from numerical data or from expert linguistic. The Mamdani and Sugeno inference engines are two of the main types of inference mechanisms. The Mamdani engine combines the fuzzy rules into a mapping from fuzzy input sets to fuzzy output sets, while the

Takagi–Sugeno type relates fuzzy inputs and crisp outputs. The defuzzifier converts a fuzzy set into a crisp number using the centroid of area, bisector of area, mean of maxima or maximum criteria [38,39].

ANN has the advantage over the fuzzy logic models that knowledge is automatically acquired during the learning process. However, this knowledge cannot be extracted from the trained network behaving as a black box. Fuzzy systems, on the other hand, can be understood through their rules but these rules are difficult to define when the system has too many variables and their relations are complex [40].

A combination of ANN and fuzzy systems has the advantages of each of them. In a neuro-fuzzy system, neural networks extract automatically fuzzy rules from numerical data and, through the learning process, the membership functions are adaptively adjusted. ANFIS is a class of adaptive multi-layer feed-forward networks, applied to non-linear forecasting where past samples are used to forecast the sample ahead. ANFIS incorporates the self-learning ability of ANN with the linguistic expression function of fuzzy inference [41].

The ANFIS network [42] is composed of five layers:

Layer 1: each node i in this layer generates a membership grades of a linguistic label. For instance, the node function of the ith node might be:

$$Q_i^1 = \mu_{A_i}(x) = \cfrac{1}{1 + \left[\left(\cfrac{x - v_i}{\sigma_i}\right)^2\right]^{b_i}} \qquad (1)$$

where, x is the input to node i, μ is the membership functions of the MANFIS system, and A_i is the linguistic label (small, large, …) associated with this node; and $\{\sigma_i, v_i, b_i\}$ is the parameter set that changes the shapes of the membership function. Parameters in this layer are referred to as the "premise parameters".

Layer 2: Each node in this layer calculates the "firing strength" of each rule via multiplication:

$$Q_i^2 = W_i = \mu_{Ai}(x).\mu_{Bi}(y) \qquad i = 1,2 \qquad (2)$$

The firing strength of a rule is given by the product of the input membership grades, and this value is passed to the membership grade of the output to the corresponding fuzzy set.

W_i is The weight of the layer 2, μ_{Ai} and μ_{Bi} are symbols for membership functions of the inputs x and y, respectively.

Layer 3: The ith node of this layer calculates the ratio of the ith rule's firing strength to the sum of all rules' firing strengths:

$$Q_i^3 = \bar{W}_i = \frac{w_i}{\sum\limits_{j=1}^{2} w_j}, \quad i = 1, 2 \tag{3}$$

$\bar{W}_i$ is normalized weights of the layer 3. For convenience, outputs of this layer will be called "normalized firing" strengths.

Layer 4: Every node i in this layer is a node function:

$$Q_i^4 = \bar{W}_i f_i = \bar{W}_i (p_i x + q_i y + r_i) \tag{4}$$

where, $\bar{W}_i$ is the output of layer 3. Parameters in this layer will be referred to as "consequent parameters".

Each node in this layer is an adaptive node. Its output is obtained by multiplying the corresponding weight of the layer 3 in a first-order polynomial that is defined as the output membership function.

Layer 5: The overall output is determined by summation of all incoming signals of the layer 4.

$$Q_i^5 = Overall\ Output = \sum \bar{W}_i f_i = \frac{\sum w_i f_i}{\sum w_i} \tag{5}$$

The MANFIS used in this paper possesses a similar architecture to a classic ANFIS system, except for a difference in the fourth layer [43,44]. The difference is the increase in the number of weights of the multi-output neuro-fuzzy system that allows improving the precision of approximation. Design of the MANFIS system for three outputs and one-input is shown in figure 2, and the system logic is described below [45].

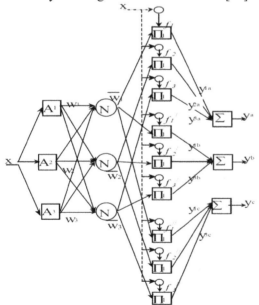

Figure 2. Architecture of MANFIS system for three outputs and one-input [45].

The following is a layer-by-layer description of a one-input one-rule first-order Sugeno system [46,43]

Layer 1: Generates the membership grades:

$$o_i^1 = g(x) \tag{6}$$

g: the membership function of the MANFIS system.

Layer 2: Generates the firing strengths:

$$o_i^2 = w_i = \prod_{j=1}^{m} g(x) \tag{7}$$

Layer 3: Normalizes the firing strengths:

$$o_i^3 = \bar{w}_i = \frac{w_i}{w_i + w_2 + w_3} \tag{8}$$

Layer 4: Calculates rule outputs based on the consequent parameters:

$$o_i^4 = y_i = \bar{w}_i.f_i = \bar{w}_i.(p_i.x + q_i.x + r_i) \tag{9}$$

$$o_i^{4'} = y_i' = \bar{w}_i.f_i' = \bar{w}_i.(p_i'.x + q_i'.x + r_i')$$

$$o_i^{4''} = y_i'' = \bar{w}_i.f_i'' = \bar{w}_i.(p_i''.x + q_i''.x + r_i'')$$

Layer 5: Sums all the inputs from layer 4:

$$o_i^5 = y_a = \sum_{i=1}^{n} y_i = \sum_{i=1}^{n} \bar{w}_i.f_i = \bar{w}_i.(p_i.x + q_i.x + r_i) \tag{10}$$

$$o_i^{5'} = y_b = \sum_{i=1}^{n} y_i' = \sum_{i=1}^{n} \bar{w}_i.f_i' = \bar{w}_i.(p_i'.x + q_i'.x + r_i')$$

$$o_i^{5''} = y_c = \sum_{i=1}^{n} y_i'' = \sum_{i=1}^{n} \bar{w}_i.f_i'' = \bar{w}_i.(p_i''.x + q_i''.x + r_i'')$$

For a given dataset, different MANFIS models can be constructed using different identification methods. Grid partitioning, subtractive clustering method, and fuzzy C-means clustering method are the three methods used in this paper to identify the antecedent membership functions. These methods are described below.

4.1. Grid Partitioning of the Antecedent Variables

This method proposes the dependent partitions of each antecedent variable [43]. The expert developing the model can define the membership functions of all antecedent variables using prior knowledge and experience. They are designed to represent the meaning of the linguistic terms in a given context. However, for many systems, no specific knowledge is available on these partitions. In that case, the domains of the antecedent variables can simply be partitioned into a number of equally spaced and equally shaped membership functions [47]. Therefore, in the grid partitioning method, the domain of each antecedent variable is partitioned into equidistant and identically shaped membership functions. Using the available input-output data, the parameters of the membership functions can be optimized.

4.2. Subtractive Clustering method

The subtractive clustering method proposed by Chiu [48] considers the data points as the candidates for the center of clusters. The algorithm is developed as follows:

At first, a collection of n data points $\{X_1, X_2, X_3, ..., X_n\}$ in an M-dimensional space is considered. Since each data point is a candidate for a cluster center, a density measure at data point X_i is defined as:

$$D_i = \sum_{j=1}^{n} \exp\left(-\frac{\|x_i - x_j\|^2}{\left(\frac{r_a}{2}\right)^2} \right) \tag{11}$$

where, r_a is a positive constant. Hence, a data point will have a high density value if it has many neighboring data points. The radius r_a defines a neighborhood; data points outside this radius contribute only slightly to the density measure. After the density measure of each data point has been calculated, the data point with the highest density measure is selected as the first cluster center. Let X_{c1} be the point selected and D_{c1} be its density measure. Next, the density measure for each data point x_i is revised as follows:

$$D_i = D_i - D_{c1} \exp\left(-\frac{\|x_i - x_{c1}\|^2}{\left(\frac{r_b}{2}\right)^2} \right) \tag{12}$$

where, r_b is a positive constant. After the density calculation for each data point is revised, the next cluster center X_{c2} is selected and all the density calculations for data points are revised again. This process is repeated until a sufficient number of cluster centers are generated.

SCM is an attractive approach to the synthesis of the MANFIS networks, which estimates the cluster number and its cluster location automatically. In the subtractive clustering algorithm, each sample point is seen as a potential cluster center. Using this method, the computation time becomes linearly proportional to data size but independent from the dimension of the problem under consideration [49-56]. Using SCM, the cluster center of all data can be found. Then the number of subtractive centers is used to generate automatic membership functions and rule

base as well as the location of the membership function within dimensions.

4.3. Fuzzy C-means Clustering method

Fuzzy C-means Clustering Method is a data clustering algorithm proposed by [Bezdek [57]], in which each data point belongs to a cluster to a degree specified by a membership grade. FCM partitions a collection of n vectors X_i, $i = 1, 2, ..., n$, into C fuzzy groups, and finds a cluster center in each group such that a cost function of dissimilarity is minimized. The stages of the FCM algorithm are described in brief in the following text. First, the cluster centers c_i, $i = 1, 2, ..., C$ are chosen randomly from the n points $\{X_1, X_2, X_3, ..., X_n\}$. After that, the membership matrix U is computed using the following equation:

$$\mu_{ij} = \frac{1}{\sum_{k=1}^{c} \left(\frac{d_{ij}}{d_{kj}}\right)^{2/m-1}} \tag{13}$$

where, $d_{ij} = \|c_i - x_j\|$ is the Euclidean distance between the ith cluster center and the jth data point, and m is the fuzziness index. Then the cost function is computed according to the following equation [58]. The process is stopped if it is below a certain threshold.

$$J(U, c_1, ..., c_2) = \sum_{i=1}^{c} J_i = \sum_{i=1}^{c} \sum_{j=1}^{n} \mu_{ij}^m d_{ij}^2 \tag{14}$$

In the final step, the new c fuzzy cluster centers c_i, $i = 1, 2, ..., C$ are computed using the following equation:

$$c_i = \frac{\sum_{j=1}^{n} \mu_{ij}^m x_j}{\sum_{j=1}^{n} \mu_{ij}^m} \tag{15}$$

5. Prediction of Metals in Acid Rock Drainage using, MANFIS model

In this work, MANFIS was used to build a prediction model for estimation of metal concentration in ARD of Sarcheshmeh porphyry copper deposit using MATLAB. Three MANFIS techniques were implemented, namely: GP, SCM and FCM. Figure 3 shows the fuzzy architecture of the MANFIS. As it can be seen in figure 3, pH, SO₄, and Mg were introduced as the input parameters into the MANFIS models, and Cu, Fe, Mn, Zn as the outputs. Part of the dataset used in this work is presented in table 1. Also descriptive statistics of the all datasets are shown in table 2.

Figure 3. Architecture of MANFIS based on GP, SCM, and FCM.

Table 1. Part of dataset used in this work (concentrations of elements are given in ppm).

	Inputs			Outputs			
	PH	SO4	Mg	Cu	Fe	Mn	Zn
Training data set	3.91	1100	78.2	69.8	0.65	49.6	15.3
	3.84	798	60.77	46.5	3.42	27.7	10.07
	4.85	770	30.48	16	2.68	20.4	8.69
	5.54	1005	51.75	3.79	7.77	12.79	4.55
	5.46	775	58.3	0.31	0.21	10.9	3.42
	5.56	698	54.29	0.899	4.065	9.52	2.8
	5.52	765	62.87	1.06	2.5	8.51	3.07
	5.8	540	40.67	0.02	8.26	7.08	7.53
	6.6	284	42	0.01	0.3	4.2	0.05
	7.2	249	34.5	0.01	0.01	0.04	0.01
Testing dataset	5.5	737	13	15	14	12	7.5
	6	650	50	13	2	15	0
	5.5	650	50	28	4	16	6
	6.2	750	50	23	2.5	16	5.6
	5.61	790	66.8	8	4	11.5	4

Table 2. Statistical description of 55 datasets used for construction of model (concentrations of elements are given in ppm).

Parameter	Min	Max	Average	Standard deviation
PH	3.3	7.2	5.34	1.01
SO4	27	1526	778.45	274.31
Mg	13	123	56.704	21.28
Cu	0	158	20.29	30.40
Fe	0.01	23	4.60	4.36
Mn	0.04	52	16.05	11.49
Zn	0	31.48	6.32	5.49

5.1. Pre-processing of data

In data-driven system modeling methods, some pre-processing steps are usually implemented prior to any calculations in order to eliminate outliers, missing values or bad data. This step ensures that the raw data retrieved from the database is suitable for modeling. In order to soften the training procedure and improve the accuracy of prediction, the data samples were normalized to the interval [0, 1] according to the following linear mapping function:

$$x_M = \frac{x - x_{min}}{x_{max} - x_{min}} \tag{16}$$

where, m x is the original value from the dataset, x_M is the mapped value, and x_{min} (x_{max}) denotes the minimum (maximum) raw input values, respectively.

The model outputs are remapped to their corresponding real values by the inverse mapping function ahead of calculating performance criterion.

5.2. Performance criteria

In order to evaluate the performance of the MANFIS models, the mean squared error (MSE) and squared correlation coefficient (R^2) tests were chosen to be the measure of accuracy. Let y_i be the actual value and $\hat{y}_i$ be the predicted value of the ith observation, and n be the number of samples. The higher the R^2, the better is the model performance. For instance, an R^2 of 100% means that the measured output has been predicted exactly (perfect model).

$R^2 = 0$ means that the model performs as poorly as a predictor using simply the mean value of the data. Also a lower MSE indicates better performance of the model. MSE and R^2 are defined, respectively, as follow:

$$MSE = \frac{1}{n}\sum_{i=1}^{n}(y_i - \hat{y}_i)^2 \tag{17}$$

$$R^2 = 1 - \frac{\sum_{i=1}^{n}(y_i - \hat{y}_i)^2}{\sum_{i=1}^{n}y_i^2 - \frac{\sum_{i=1}^{n}\hat{y}_i^2}{n}} \tag{18}$$

6. Results and discussion

The training and testing procedures of the three MANFIS models (GP, SCM, FCM) were conducted. A dataset that included 55 data points was employed in the current work, while 44 data points (80%) were utilized for constructing the model and the remainder data points (11 data points) were utilized for assessment of degree of accuracy and robustness.

The MSE and R^2 values obtained for training datasets indicate the capability of learning the structure of data samples, whereas the results of testing dataset reveal the generalization potential and the robustness of the system modeling methods. The characteristics of the MANFIS models are presented in table 3.

Table 3. Characteristics of MANFIS models.

MANFIS parameter	MANFIS (GP)	MANFIS (SCM)	MANFIS (FCM)
Membership function type	Gaussian	Gaussian	Gaussian
Output membership function	Linear	Linear	Linear
Number of nodes	286	310	166
Number of linear parameters	500	152	80
Number of nonlinear parameters	30	228	120
Total number of parameters	530	380	200
Number of training data pairs	44	44	44
Number of testing data pairs	11	11	11
Number of fuzzy rules	125	38	20

The number of fuzzy rules obtained for the GP, SCM, and FCM models are 125, 38 and 20, respectively. The membership functions of the input parameters for different models are shown in figures 4-6.

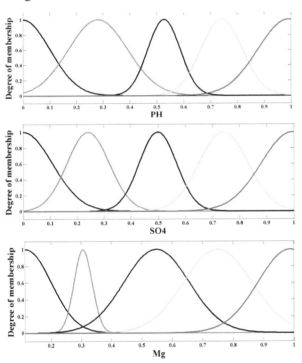

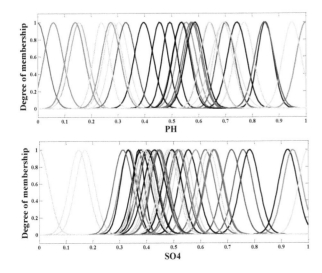

Figure 4. Membership functions obtained by MANFIS-GP model.

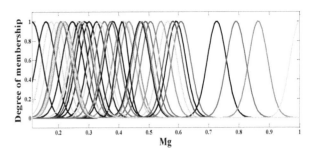

Figure 5. Membership functions obtained by MANFIS-SCM model.

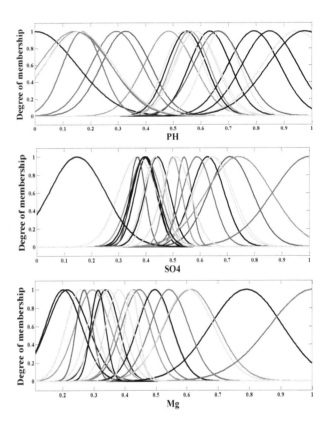

Figure 6 Membership functions obtained by MANFIS-FCM model.

In the MANFIS simulation, an expert is not required to establish the membership functions, the number of membership functions assigned to each input variable is chosen empirically by plotting the datasets and examining them visually or simply by trial and error. A comparison between the results obtained from the three models is shown in table 4. As it can be observed in this table, the MANFIS-SCM model performs better than the other two models for estimation of metals in the ARD of Sarcheshmeh porphyry copper deposit.

Correlation between the measured and predicted values of metals in ARD for testing phases is shown in figures 7-10.

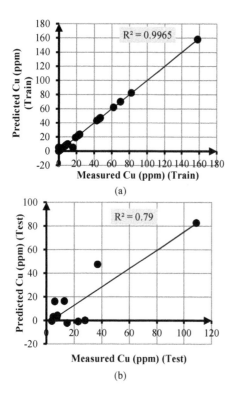

(a)

(b)

Figure 7. Correlation between measured and predicted values of Cu by MANFIS-SCM model a) training datasets, b) testing datasets.

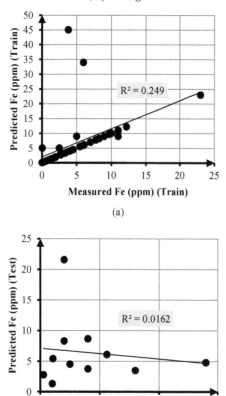

(a)

(b)

Figure 8. Correlation between measured and predicted values of Fe by MANFIS-SCM model a) training datasets, b) testing datasets.

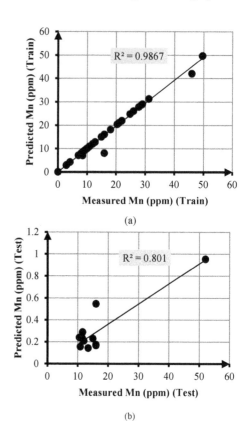

(a)

(b)

Figure 9. Correlation between measured and predicted values of Mn by MANFIS-SCM model a) training datasets, b) testing datasets.

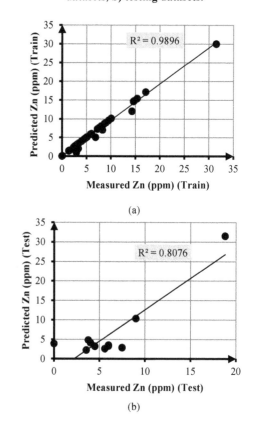

(a)

(b)

Figure 10. Correlation between measured and predicted values of Zn by MANFIS-SCM model a) training datasets, b) testing datasets

Table 4. A comparison between results of three models for testing datasets.

MANFIS model	Cu		Fe		Mn		Zn	
	MSE	R^2	MSE	R^2	MSE	R^2	MSE	R^2
MANFIS-GP	0.179	0.59	0.522	0.003	0.083	0.37	0.049	0.75
MANFIS-SCM	0.009	0.79	0.099	0.016	0.011	0.801	0.020	0.807
MANFIS-FCM	0.025	0.31	0.071	0.023	0.025	0.66	0.085	0.79

Also a comparison between the predicted values of metals in ARD by the MANFIS-SCM model and measured values is shown in figures 11-14.

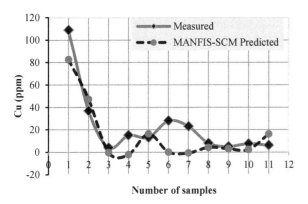

Figure 11. Comparison between measured and predicted Cu by MANFIS-SCM model for testing.

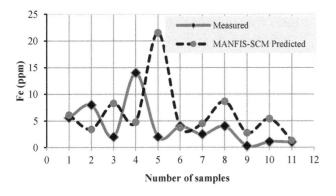

Figure 12. Comparison between measured and predicted Fe by MANFIS-SCM model for testing.

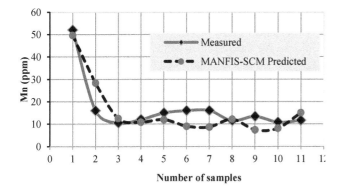

Figure 13. Comparison between measured and predicted Mn by MANFIS-SCM model for testing.

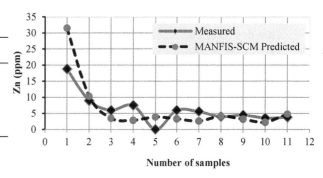

Figure 14. Comparison between measured and predicted Zn by MANFIS-SCM model for testing.

As shown in these figures, the results of the MANFIS-SCM model provided a good-fit to the measured values of Cu, Mn and Zn concentrations, and poor fit for Fe concentration. The poor-fit model for Fe ion is a result of the low correlation between Fe and the independent variables. The R^2 values for training stages of MANFIS-SCM were 0.99, 0.24, 0.98, and 0.98 for Cu, Fe, Mn and Zn, respectively. A comparison between the predicted concentrations and the measured data resulted in the correlation coefficients for testing stages of MANFIS-SCM, R^2, 0.79, 0.016, 0.80, and 0.80 for the Cu, Fe, Mn, and Zn ions respectively.

7. Conclusions

In a conventional fuzzy inference system, the number of rules is decided by an expert who is familiar with the target system to be modeled. The MANFIS method results in a better performance than the other intelligent methods due to the combination of FL and ANN. In a MANFIS simulation, however, no expert is required, and the number of membership functions (MFs) assigned to each input variable is chosen empirically, i.e. by plotting the datasets and examining them visually or simply by trial and error. For datasets with more than three inputs and two outputs, visualization techniques are not very effective and most of the time trial and error must be relied on.

Consequently, an automatic model identification method becomes a must, which is often realized by means of a training set of input-output pairs. In this paper, a new method to predict major metals (Cu, Fe, Mn and Zn) in Shur River impacted by ARD has been presented using the MANFIS method using 55 data samples and the following are concluded:

- A comparison was made between three MANFIS models, GP, SCM, and FCM and based upon the performance indices; R^2 and

MSE, MANFIS-SCM model was shown to be the best predictive model.

• Consequently, it is concluded that MANFIS-SCM is a reliable system modeling technique for estimation of metals in the AMD of Sarcheshmeh porphyry copper deposit with a highly acceptable degree of accuracy and robustness.

References

[1] Malakooti, S. J., Tonkaboni, S. Z. S., Noaparast, M., Ardejani, F. D., & Naseh, R. (2014). Characterisation of the Sarcheshmeh copper mine tailings, Kerman province, southeast of Iran. Environmental earth sciences, vol. 71, pp. 2267-2291.

[2] Shahabpour, J., & Doorandish, M. (2008). Mine drainage water from the Sar Cheshmeh porphyry copper mine, Kerman, IR Iran. Environmental monitoring and assessment, vol. 141, pp. 105-120.

[3] Ardejania, F. D., Karamib, G. H., Assadib, A. B., & Dehghan, R. A. Hydrogeochemical investigations of the Shour River and groundwater affected by acid mine drainage in Sarcheshmeh porphyry copper mine. In: 10th International mine water association congress, 2008. pp 235-238.

[4] Doulati Ardejanii, F., Rooki, R., Jodieri Shokri, B., Eslam Kish, T., Aryafar, A., & Tourani, P. (2012). Prediction of rare earth elements in neutral alkaline mine drainage from Razi Coal Mine, Golestan Province, northeast Iran, using general regression neural network. Journal of Environmental Engineering, vol. 139, pp. 896-907.

[5] Williams, R. (1975). Waste production and disposal in mining, milling, and metallurgical industries. Miller-Freeman Publishing Company, San Francisco, pp. p 485.

[6] Chen, C., & Vachtsevanos, G. (2012). Bearing condition prediction considering uncertainty: An interval type-2 fuzzy neural network approach. Robotics and Computer-Integrated Manufacturing, vol. 28, pp. 509-516.

[7] Cánovas, C., Olías, M., Nieto, J., Sarmiento, A., & Cerón, J. (2007). Hydrogeochemical characteristics of the Tinto and Odiel Rivers (SW Spain). Factors controlling metal contents. Science of the Total Environment, vol. 373, pp. 363-382.

[8] Moncur, M., Ptacek, C., Blowes, D., & Jambor, J. (2005). Release, transport and attenuation of metals from an old tailings impoundment. Applied Geochemistry, vol. 20, pp. 639-659.

[9] Lottermoser, B. (2007). Mine wastes. Springer, Berlin, pp.

[10] Kim, Y., Mallick, R., Bhowmick, S., & Chen, B.-L. (2013). Nonlinear system identification of large-scale smart pavement systems. Expert Systems with Applications, vol. 40, pp. 3551-3560.

[11] Dinelli, E., Lucchini, F., Fabbri, M., & Cortecci, G. (2001). Metal distribution and environmental problems related to sulfide oxidation in the Libiola copper mine area (Ligurian Apennines, Italy). Journal of Geochemical Exploration, vol. 74, pp. 141-152.

[12] Lee, J., & Chon, H. (2006). Hydrogeochemical characteristics of acid mine drainage in the vicinity of an abandoned mine, Daduk Creek, Korea. Journal of Geochemical Exploration, vol. 88, pp. 37-40.

[13] Sahoo, P., Tripathy, S., Panigrahi, M., & Equeenuddin, S. M. (2014). Geochemical characterization of coal and waste rocks from a high sulfur bearing coalfield, India: Implication for acid and metal generation. Journal of Geochemical Exploration, vol. 145, pp. 135-147.

[14] Sadeghi, S., Rezvanian, A., & Kamrani, E. (2012). An efficient method for impulse noise reduction from images using fuzzy cellular automata. AEU-International Journal of Electronics and Communications, vol. 66, pp. 772-779.

[15] Ardejani, F. D., Karami, G., Assadi, A., & Dehghan, R. (2008). Hydrogeochemical investigations of the Shour River and groundwater affected by acid mine drainage in Sarcheshmeh porphyry copper mine. 10th international mine water association congress, Karlovy Vary, Czech Republic, pp. pp 235–238.

[16] Marandi, R., Doulati Ardejani, F., & Marandi, A. Biotreatment of acid mine drainage using sequencing batch reactors (SBRs) in the Sarcheshmeh porphyry copper mine. In: IMWA symposium, 2007. pp 221-225

[17] Ardejani, f. D., Shokri, B. J., Moradzadeh, A., Soleimani, e., & Jafari, M. A. (2008). A combined mathematical geophysical model for prediction of pyrite oxidation and pollutant leaching associated with a coal washing waste dump. International Journal of Environmental Science & Technology, vol. 5, pp. 517-526.

[18] Shokri, B. J., Ramazi, H., Ardejani, F. D., & Moradzadeh, A. (2014). A statistical model to relate pyrite oxidation and oxygen transport within a coal waste pile: case study, Alborz Sharghi, northeast of Iran. Environmental earth sciences, vol. 71, pp. 4693.

[19] Khorasanipour, M., & Eslami, A. (2014). Hydrogeochemistry and Contamination of Trace Elements in Cu-Porphyry Mine Tailings: A Case Study from the Sarcheshmeh Mine, SE Iran. Mine Water and the Environment, pp. 1-18.

[20] Kemper, T., & Sommer, S. (2002). Estimate of heavy metal contamination in soils after a mining accident using reflectance spectroscopy. Environmental science & technology, vol. 36, pp. 2742-2747.

[21] Almasri, M. N., & Kaluarachchi, J. J. (2005). Modular neural networks to predict the nitrate distribution in ground water using the on-ground nitrogen loading and recharge data. Environmental Modelling & Software, vol. 20, pp. 851-871.

[22] Singh, K. P., Basant, A., Malik, A., & Jain, G. (2009). Artificial neural network modeling of the river water quality—a case study. Ecological Modelling, vol. 220, pp. 888-895.

[23] Tahmasebi, P., & Hezarkhani, A. (2012). A hybrid neural networks-fuzzy logic-genetic algorithm for grade estimation. Computers & Geosciences, vol. 42, pp. 18-27.

[24] Gholami, R., Kamkar-Rouhani, A., Ardejani, F. D., & Maleki, S. (2011). Prediction of toxic metals concentration using artificial intelligence techniques. Appl Water Sci, pp. 125–134.

[25] Rooki, R., Doulati Ardejani, F., Aryafar, A., & Bani Asadi, A. (2011). Prediction of heavy metals in acid mine drainage using artificial neural network from the Shur River of the Sarcheshmeh porphyry copper mine, Southeast Iran. Environmental earth sciences, vol. 64, pp. 1303-1316.

[26] Sadeghiamirshahidi, M., Eslam kish, T., & Doulati Ardejani, F. (2013). Application of artificial neural networks to predict pyrite oxidation in a coal washing refuse pile. Fuel, vol. 104, pp. 163-169.

[27] Sayadi, A. R., Tavassoli, S. M. M., Monjezi, M., & Rezaei, M. (2014). Application of neural networks to predict net present value in mining projects. Arabian Journal of Geosciences, vol. 7, pp. 1067-1072.

[28] Shokri, B. J., Ardejani, F. D., Ramazi, H., & Sadeghiamirshahidi, M. (2014). Prediction of Pyrite Oxidation in a Coal Washing Waste Pile Applying Artificial Neural Networks (ANNs) and Adaptive Neuro-fuzzy Inference Systems (ANFIS). Mine Water and the Environment, pp. 146–156.

[29] Maiti, S., & Tiwari, R. K. (2014). A comparative study of artificial neural networks, Bayesian neural networks and adaptive neuro-fuzzy inference system in groundwater level prediction. Environmental Earth Sciences, vol. 71, pp. 3147-3160.

[30] Derakhshandeh, R., & Alipour, M. (2010). Remediation of acid mine drainage by using tailings decant water as a neutralization agent in Sarcheshmeh copper mine. Res J Environ Sci 4(3):, pp. 250–260.

[31] Jannesar Malakooti, S., Shahhosseini, M., Doulati Ardejani, F., Ziaeddin Shafaei Tonkaboni, S., & Noaparast, M. (2015). Hydrochemical characterisation of water quality in the Sarcheshmeh copper complex, SE Iran. Environmental Earth Sciences, vol. 74, pp. 3171-3190.

[32] Banisi, S., & Finch, J. (2001). Testing a floatation column at the Sarcheshmeh copper mine. Miner Eng 14(7):, pp. 785–789.

[33] Waterman, G. C., & Hamilton, R. (1975). The Sar Cheshmeh porphyry copper deposit. Economic Geology, vol. 70, pp. 568-576.

[34] Monjezi, M., Shahriar, K., Dehghani, H., & Namin, F. S. (2009). Environmental impact assessment of open pit mining in Iran. Environmental Geology, vol. 58, pp. 205–216.

[35] Rooki, R., Ardejani, F. D., Aryafar, A., & Asadi, A. B. (2011). Prediction of heavy metals in acid mine drainage using artificial neural network from the Shur River of the Sarcheshmeh porphyry copper mine, Southeast Iran. Environmental earth sciences, vol. 64, pp. 1303-1316.

[36] Aryafar, A., Gholami, R., Rooki, R., & Ardejani, F. D. (2012). Heavy metal pollution assessment using support vector machine in the Shur River, Sarcheshmeh copper mine, Iran. Environmental earth sciences, vol. 67, pp. 1191-1199.

[37] Catalão, J. P. d. S., Mariano, S. J. P. S., Mendes, V., & Ferreira, L. (2007). Short-term electricity prices forecasting in a competitive market: A neural network approach. Electric Power Systems Research, vol. 77, pp. 1297-1304.

[38] Shoorehdeli, M. A., Teshnehlab, M., Sedigh, A. K., & Khanesar, M. A. (2009). Identification using ANFIS with intelligent hybrid stable learning algorithm approaches and stability analysis of training methods. Applied Soft Computing, vol. 9, pp. 833-850.

[39] Pousinho, H. M. I., Mendes, V. M. F., & Catalão, J. P. d. S. (2012). Short-term electricity prices forecasting in a competitive market by a hybrid PSO–ANFIS approach. International Journal of Electrical Power & Energy Systems, vol. 39, pp. 29-35.

[40] Rodriguez, C. P., & Anders, G. J. (2004). Energy price forecasting in the Ontario competitive power system market. IEEE transactions on power systems, vol. 19, pp. 366-374.

[41] Heidarian, M., Jalalifar, H., & Rafati, F. (2016). Prediction of rock strength parameters for an Iranian oil field using neuro-fuzzy method. Journal of AI and Data Mining, vol. 4, pp. 229-234.

[42] Zhou, Q. Q., Purvis, M., & Kasabov, N. (1997) A membership function selection method for fuzzy neural networks. In: Proc ICONIP, 1997. pp 785-788.

[43] Jang, J. S. R. (1993). ANFIS: Adaptive-network-based fuzzy inference system. IEEE Transactions on Systems, Man and Cybernetics, vol. 23, pp. 665-685.

[44] Li, H., Chen, C. P., & Huang, H.-P. (2000) Fuzzy neural intelligent systems: Mathematical foundation and the applications in engineering. CRC Press,

[45] Benmiloud, T. Multi-output adaptive neuro-fuzzy inference system. In: wseas international conference on neural networks, 2010. pp 94-98

[46] Tsoukalas, L. H., & Uhrig, R. E. (1996) Fuzzy and neural approaches in engineering. John Wiley & Sons, Inc.

[47] Fattahi, H. Indirect estimation of deformation modulus of an in situ rock mass: an ANFIS model based on grid partitioning, fuzzy c-means clustering

and subtractive clustering. Geosciences Journal, pp. 1-10.

[48] Chiu, S. L. (1994). Fuzzy model identification based on cluster estimation. Journal of intelligent and Fuzzy systems, vol. 2, pp. 267-278.

[49] Stavroulakis, P. (2004) Neuro-fuzzy and Fuzzy-neural Applications in Telecommunications (Signals and Communication Technology). Springer.

[50] Jang, J.-S. R., Sun, C.-T., & Mizutani, E. (1997). Neuro-fuzzy and soft computing-a computational approach to learning and machine intelligence [Book Review]. IEEE Transactions on Automatic Control, vol. 42, pp. 1482-1484.

[51] Chopra, S., Mitra, R., & Kumar, V. (2006). Reduction of fuzzy rules and membership functions and its application to fuzzy PI and PD type controllers. International Journal of Control, Automation and Systems, vol. 4, pp. 438.

[52] Fattahi, H., Shojaee, S., Farsangi, M. A. E., & Mansouri, H. (2013). Hybrid Monte Carlo simulation and ANFIS-subtractive clustering method for reliability analysis of the excavation damaged zone in underground spaces. Computers and Geotechnics, vol. 54, pp. 210-221.

[53] Karimpouli, S., & Fattahi, H. (2016). Estimation of P-and S-wave impedances using Bayesian inversion and adaptive neuro-fuzzy inference system from a carbonate reservoir in Iran. Neural Computing and Applications, pp. 1-14.

[54] Fattahi, H., & Karimpouli, S. (2016). Prediction of porosity and water saturation using pre-stack seismic attributes: a comparison of Bayesian inversion and computational intelligence methods. Computational Geosciences, pp. 1-20.

[55] Fattahi, H. (2017). Prediction of slope stability using adaptive neuro-fuzzy inference system based on clustering methods. Journal of Mining and Environment, vol. 8, pp. 163-177.

[56] Fattahi, H., Nazari, H., & Molaghab, A. (2016). Hybrid ANFIS with ant colony optimization algorithm for prediction of shear wave velocity from a carbonate reservoir in Iran. Int Journal of Mining & Geo-Engineering, vol. 50, pp. 231-238.

[57] Bezdek, J. C. (1973) Fuzzy mathematics in pattern classification. Cornell university, Ithaca

[58] Fattahi, H. (2016). Adaptive neuro fuzzy inference system based on fuzzy C–means clustering algorithm, a technique for estimation of TBM peneteration rate. Int J Optim Civil Eng, vol. 6, pp. 159-171.

4

Chaotic Genetic Algorithm based on Explicit Memory with a new Strategy for Updating and Retrieval of Memory in Dynamic Environments

M. Mohammadpour[1], H. Parvin[2,3]* and M. Sina[2]

1. Young Researchers and Elite Club, Yasooj Branch, Islamic Azad University, Yasooj, Iran.
2. Department of Computer Engineering, Nourabad Mamasani Branch, Islamic Azad University, Nourabad Mamasani, Iran.
3. Young Researchers and Elite Club, Nourabad Mamasani Branch, Islamic Azad University, Nourabad Mamasani, Iran.

*Corresponding author: parvin@alumni.iust.ac.ir (H. Parvin).

Abstract
Many problems considered in the optimization and learning processes assume that solutions change dynamically. Hence, the algorithms are required that dynamically adapt with the new conditions of the problem through searching new conditions. Mostly, utilization of information from the past allows to quickly adapting changes right after they occur in the environment. This is the idea underlining the use of memory in this field, what involves the key design issues concerning the memory content, update process, and retrieval process. In this work, we use the chaotic genetic algorithm (GA) with memory for solving dynamic optimization problems. A chaotic system has a much more accurate prediction of the future compared with a random system. The proposed method uses a new memory with diversity maximization. Here, we propose a new strategy for updating memory and memory retrieval. An experimental study is conducted based on the moving peaks benchmark (MPB) in order to test the performance of the developed method in comparison with several state-of-the-art algorithms from the literature. The experimental results obtained show the superiority and more effectiveness of the proposed algorithm in dynamic environments.

Keywords: *Dynamic Environments, Explicit Memory, Moving Peaks Benchmark, Offline Error, Chaos.*

1. Introduction
Nowadays in engineering problems, we are faced with what should be optimal in some of these issues with the purpose of optimization to reduce expenses (minimizing), or to increase quality (maximizing). In any of possible optimal solution, suitable quantities of all parameters are the best way to solve the problem. In optimization expression we may intend to find goal minima in dynamic or static environment. If the optima of the problem change during the evolution, we can assume the environment as a dynamic one; otherwise, we should assume the environment as a static one. Evolutionary algorithms may perform in static environments with good efficiency but these algorithms alone are not able to solve dynamic optimization with a good performance. Therefore, to solve optimization problems, dynamic optimization problems need to strong heuristics. In these environments, dynamic changes are the main reason for occurring the challenges. Some of these challenges may include

the difficulty in updating the memory after each change in the population, preserve diversity in a convergence environment to optimize the desired particle size and limited memory capacity, and identify the changes in their environment. To solve the optimization problems in the dynamic environment, the various dynamic methods are presented where each of them solves one or many of these challenges. Among the methods proposed to solve the dynamic optimization problems, methods that use a combination of strategies are of special significance. The combination memory and diversity have been used in [1-9]. Many researchers have used a composition of memory and evolutionary algorithms to solve dynamic optimization problems but our proposed method has a main difference with the other methods. We used a proper memory with a novel storage and retrieval strategy. The main goal of this work was to provide maximum diversity for the GA evolutionary algorithm. We focused on setting a memory that can be embedded with evolutionary algorithms and improved them to solve dynamic optimization problems (DOPs). The proposed method can be considered as an application or an algorithm.

2. Related work

In this section, we introduce different solutions to DOPs, each of which are able to overcome some of the DOP challenges.

a. Methods based on memory for dynamic environments

In [10], Mohammadpour and Parvin have presented a new method based on memory for the optimization problems. This paper presents a GA-based memory to deal with DOPs, and focuses on explicit placement of memory schemes.

The Memory Immigrant Genetic Algorithm (MIGA) [11], introduced by Yang et al., uses a combination of GA and memory-based immigrants. The random immigrant method aims to improve the GA performance in dynamic environments through maintaining the population diversity level with random immigrants, and the memory approach aims to move the GA directly into an old environment that is similar to the new one through reusing the better old solutions. In the memory/search method, the total population size can be divided into two populations including the "memory" and "search" populations. The first population is based upon the memory applied to memorize old and well solutions. The second one is based upon the search used to explore and introduce new peaks and their introduction to memory. The second population is randomly initialized after each change [12]. The MEGA method of memory combined with GA is used. The main populations are the randomly initialized memory and the memory used to store the previous solutions [11]. Mohammadpour and Parvin, in [13], have presented a new method for solving the optimization problems with the aid of memory and clustering in addition to the chaos theory for population creation.

b. Methods based on clustering for dynamic environments

Yang et al. have proposed the CPSOR (Clustering Particle Swarm Optimization), in which the particles to cluster are divided as the smallest particles existing in each cluster to search for the local cluster in practice. The PSO algorithm with the *gbest* model is used in the CPSOR algorithm where each particle's neighborhood is defined as the whole swarm. In order to speed up the local

search within the PSO algorithm, we introduce a learning method for the *gbest* particle used in CPSO. When a particle i in a sub-population finds a better position, we iteratively check each dimension of the *gbest* particle: replace the dimension with the corresponding dimensional value of particle i if the *gbest* particle is improved by doing so. [14]. The clustering method in CPSO will assign the particles that are close to each other into a sub-swarm, which is the same as the neighborhood defined in PSO_{lbest}. However, CPSO has several major advantages in comparison with PSO_{lbest}. First, CPSO can track multiple optimal in dynamic environments. In CPSO, if more than one sub-swarms cover a same peak, they will finally be combined with each other into one sub-swarm by the overlapping check function. Second, CPSO can control overcrowding in a single peak [15]. Yang and et al. [15] have proposed the CGAR algorithm. In this algorithm, the standard GA with simple crossover and mutation and also the k-means clustering are used.

c. Methods based on multi-Populations

Self-organizing scouts (SOS) is a state-of-the-art multi-population evolutionary algorithm approach designed to overcome this limitation of a standard memory [16]. SOS begins with some number of base subpopulations searching for good solutions. When a peak (region with good solutions) has been found, the population splits. A scout population is formed to keep track of the peak, while the base population resumes searching for other peaks [16]. In particle swarm algorithm based on quantum particles that are known in this algorithm (i.e. mQSO algorithm), the population is divided into several groups and three quantum particles called functional diversity, pluralism is anti-convergence disposal. Quantum particles are placed in random positions to maintain the diversity of groups. If you find a real function that overlaps between the two groups, the group will reinitialize worse. Anti-convergence operation will be taken when all groups are converging, i.e. the group will re-initialize worse [17]. In [18], an approach is proposed by making the number of subpopulations adaptive, and it is named "AMQSO". The method of FMSO has been used parent of a group as a group foundation for identifying promising areas and group of children for local search. Each child has its own search area. In this way there is a kind of balance between local search and global search. The method of FMSO search area to form a circle centered in the best particle group is considered.

Each particle that has a shorter distance than the radius of the circle is (closer to the center of the particle) by virtue of belonging to the group of children [19]. In the ESCA [20] and CESO [21] methods, the populations are divided into different categories, where each group uses unlike search approaches. The generalized methods based on multi-population have been presented in [32-38].

3. Dynamic environments

Most of the problems considered in optimization and learning assume that solutions exist in a static unchanging environment. If the environment does change, one may simply treat the new environment as a completely new version of the problem that can be solved as before. When a problem changes infrequently or only in small amounts, this can be a reasonable method. However, this assumption tends to break down when the environment undergoes frequent discontinuous changes. When this occurs, a search process may be slow to react; hurting performance in the time it takes to find a new solution. Instead of focusing only on finding the best solution to a dynamic problem, one must often balance the quality of solutions with the speed required to find good solutions.

a. Moment changes in environment:

When a dynamic event occurs, the fitness landscape changes. The term change is typically used to mean a change in the fitness landscape. The term environment is used to refer to the problem formulation and constraints at a given time. Typically, a change in the environment leads to a change in the fitness landscape. A dynamic environment changes cyclically over time. The cycle in which the optimization function should be changed, is considered as change frequency. The cycle at which a change occurs is referred to as *a moment of change* in the environment.

b. Response of changes the environments:

Many real world optimization problems are actually dynamic, and the optimization methods capable of continuously adapting the solution to a changing environment are required.

Most of the research works in evolutionary computation focus on optimization in dynamic environments, where changes for environments are small and algorithms must track those changes quickly. When changes to the environment are much more severe, a very different approach is necessary. After a change in the environment occurs, the location of the global optimum may change drastically. For discontinuous problems, search must be able to find areas containing good solutions in addition to refining those solutions to find the best solutions possible. Search algorithms that are able to explore widely across the search space after a change will have an advantage over those that search only locally. If search is population-based, introducing diversity into the search may help explore the search space after a change. For many problems, changes in the search space, though discontinuous, are not completely random.

3.1. Groups of dynamic environments

Dynamic environments can be taxonomy in different approaches. Branke [22] have categorized the dynamic environments into several parameters: the frequency of changes, severity of changes, predictability of changes, detectability of changes, and influence of search on the environment.

In the frequency of change, changes may be rare, while in others, changes may occur constantly. Problems are also not limited to one frequency of changes. Some problems may have small frequent changes, while others have large infrequent changes. The most important aspect of a frequency change is how long a learning or optimization algorithm has to find a solution both before it has an effect on performance and before another change occurs.

As mentioned earlier, the severity of changes also defines a dynamic problem. Some problems may have changes that are small enough to be easily tracked, while others have large discontinuous changes. Small changes may not have a large effect on the fitness landscape, while large changes may completely change the landscape.

The predictability expresses that, in some problems, changes follow a particular prototype. In others, changes are completely random. A problem with small predictable changes needs a very diverse algorithm than the ones with severe unpredictable changes.

The detectability of the change express in some problems, changes to the fitness landscape are easy to detect; one knows exactly when a change has occurred. In others, it may take some time before it is clear that the environment has changed. This can have a large effect on how an algorithm solves a problem.

Influence of search on the environment expresses that although every problem with dynamic environments suffers changes autonomous of the results of search, the search can make extra changes in the environment. For some problems, solutions have no effect on the environment. For many others, though, the particular solution changes the environment.

3.2. Benchmark Problems for Dynamic Environments

Benchmark problems are used to examine the performance of the evolutionary algorithm in dynamic environments. The benchmark problems can simulate evolutionary algorithms in dynamic environments.

3.2.1. Moving Peaks Benchmark (MPB) for simulation of Dynamic Environments

MPB is a multimodal, multidimensional dynamic problem, proposed by Branke [23]. In Moving Peaks, the landscape is composed of m peaks in an n dimensional real-valued space.

At each point, the fitness is defined as the maximum over all m peak functions. This fitness can be formulated as follows:

$$F\left(\vec{x},t\right)=max\,(B\left(\vec{x}\right),\max_{i=1...m}P(\vec{x},h_i\left(t\right),w_i\left(t\right),\vec{p}_i\left(t\right))) \tag{1}$$

where, $P(\vec{x},h_i,w_i,\vec{p}_i)$ is a function describing the fitness of a given point $(\vec{x})$ for a peak described by height (h), width (w), and peak position $(\vec{p})$.

Every Δe evaluations, the height, width, and position are changed for each peak, changing the state of the environment. The height and width of each peak are changed by the addition of *Gaussian random* variables scaled by height severity (hs) and width severity (ws) parameters. The position is shifted using a shift length s and a correlation factor λ. The shift length controls how far the peak moves, while the correlation factor determines how random a peak's motion will be. If $\lambda = 0.0$, the motion of a peak will be completely random, but if $\lambda = 1.0$, the peak will always move in the same direction until it reaches a boundary of the coordinate space where its path reflects like a ray of light. At the time of a change in the environment, the changes in a single peak can be described as

$$h_i\left(t\right)=h_i\left(t-1\right)+height_{severity}\cdot\sigma \tag{2}$$

$$w_i\left(t\right)=w_i\left(t-1\right)+width_{severity}\cdot\sigma \tag{3}$$

$$\vec{p}_i\left(t\right)=\vec{p}_i\left(t-1\right)+\vec{v}_i\left(t\right) \tag{4}$$

$$\sigma\in N\left(0,1\right) \tag{5}$$

The shift vector $\vec{v}_i(t)$ combines a random vector $\vec{r}$ with the previous shift vector $\vec{v}_i(t-1)$. The random vector is created by drawing uniformly from $[0;1]$ for each dimension, and then scaling the vector to have length s. $\vec{v}_i(t)$ is formulated by (6).

$$\vec{v}_i(t)=\frac{s}{\left|\vec{r}+\vec{v}_i\left(t-1\right)\right|}((1-\lambda)\vec{r}+\lambda\vec{v}_i\left(t-1\right)) \tag{6}$$

Peak function for h, w, and p of each peak can be calculated as follows:

$$P\left(\vec{x},h\left(t\right),w\left(t\right),\vec{p}\left(t\right)\right)=h\left(t\right)-w\left(t\right)\cdot\sqrt{\sum_{j=1...n}(x_j-p_j)^2} \tag{7}$$

Part of the radical, the distance between the point exist and the position of each peak is expressed [23]. Figure 1 shows the trend of the changes in the peaks.

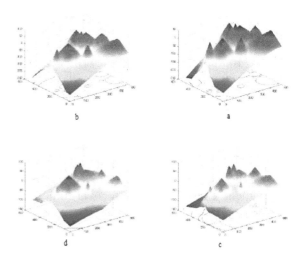

Figure 1. Trend of changes in peaks in MPB.

3.3. *Offline Error*

The performance measure used is the *Offline Error*, which is defined as follows:

$$Offline\ Error=\frac{1}{M}\sum_{t=1}^{M}\left(h\left(t\right)-f\left(t\right)\right) \tag{8}$$

where, $f(t)$ is the best solution obtained by an algorithm just before the M-th environmental change, $h(t)$ is the optimum value for the M-th environment, and M is the total number of evaluations.

4. Genetic algorithm

Genetic algorithm (GA) is based on learning method of biological evolution [24]. For a genetic algorithm to solve a particular problem, a set of candidate solutions to that problem is randomly created. This set of solutions is called population. Then, the quality of each of these potential solutions is measured and the best ones are selected as parents. The chosen individuals reproduce and undergo a variation process by means of genetic operators, e.g., recombination and mutation, defining a new offspring population. Finally, the next generation of the population is formed by combining parent and offspring populations. This process is repeated until a certain stop condition, e.g., number of generations, is attained. Figure 2 shows the pseudo code of a GA.

Algorithm 1: *Genetic Algorithm*

1. *Initialize population*
2. *Evaluate population*
3. *repeat*
4.   *Select parents*
5.   *Recombine pairs of parents*
6.   *Mutate the offspring*
7.   *Evaluate the offspring*
8. *Create new population from parents and offspring*
9. *until stop_condition is true*

Figure 2. Pseudo-Code of GA.

4.1. Population

A population is formed by a set of individuals, also called chromosomes, typically of a fixed size. Each individual represents a possible solution to the problem, and consists of a sequence of smaller components, called genes. Each gene may assume different values, or alleles.

4.2. Representation

The choice for the representation of the individuals is made according to the type of problem to solve. The representation defines how the population individuals are encoded.

4.3. Fitness function

The fitness function is used to measure the quality of the population individuals. To measure it, a decoding process is needed to obtain the individual phenotype. The fitness is a real value obtained by applying the fitness function to the phenotype.

4.4. Selection

The selection method is used to choose a pool of parents based on their fitness. The solutions with higher fitness values have more probabilities to be chosen for mating.

4.5. Genetic operators

The role of genetic operators is to create variations among the population individuals. Genetic operators can be divided in two main categories: recombination (or crossover) and mutation. Recombination is applied using two (or more) selected parents and mixing their genetic content. Mutation is applied to the individual genes by making a small change in their corresponding alleles.

5. Memory

Generally, memory is divided into two categories: explicit memory and implicit memory. The implicit memory is used to store all information (including additional information). In fact, the memory is used to store all information in one chromosome (each chromosome has two or more alleles). The convergence data, i.e. distribution of alleles can be used as the normal view of the current environment. The diploid implicit memory functions have been presented in [25]. The implicit memory is divided into two categories: a dualism memory and a diploid memory. Explicit memory is used to store useful information about the environment, and unlike implicit memory that stores additional data, it only stores useful information. Explicit memory involves the two types of direct memory and associative memory [26]. In direct memory, good solutions obtained by each individual (local information) or solutions obtained by all members of the population (general information) are directly stored in memory and reused in new environments [27]. In associative memory, environmental information are stored as well as good solutions; among the data stored in the memory, are lists of the states of problem space or the likelihood of a good solution in problem space [28] and reused in the new environment.

5.1. Memory retrieval

The information stored in memory should be used for new tracking of the optimum. Thus the best time to retrieve data from memory is the moment when the environment is changed. Several strategies can be adopted to retrieve memory. One of the memory retrieval methods is the replacing the best person in the memory instead of the worst person in the memory [29, 30].

5.2. Update strategy for memory

The previously described memory approaches used different replacing methods [29].

In general, the remaining approaches used the method called similar proposed by Branke [29]. Branke investigated and compared the following replacing schemes:

Strategy 1: This strategy analyzed the two individuals in memory with the minimum distance between them and replaced the worst with the best individual in the population. For example, suppose that individuals i and j were chosen:
- if $fit(i) < fit(j)$, replaced the individual j by the current best.
- if $fit(i) > fit(j)$, replaced the individual i by the current best.

Strategy 2:

- If $fit(j) \times \frac{d_{ij}}{d_{max}} \leq fit(new)$ replaced the individual j by the current best

- otherwise, replaced the individual i by the current best

Where d_{ij} was the distance between the individuals i and j and d_{max}
Was the maximal possible distance between the individuals i and j.

Strategy 3: In this *similarity* method, the current best individual of the population replaced the most similar individual stored in memory as long as it was a better solution. The similarity measure depended on the used representation. For binary encodings, the similarity between to individuals was measured using the Hamming distance.

6. Chaos theory

The chaos theory [27] refers to chaotic dynamical systems. Chaotic systems are non-linear dynamical systems that are very sensitive to initial conditions. The behavior of chaotic systems is apparently random, although these behaviors are not random. The random element is not necessary in creating a chaotic behavior. A famous example of such a system is the logistic map model. The features of the chaos theory can be, self-organization (adapting to environmental conditions) in dynamic environments, self-similarity (each part of the system has the features of the general form and it is similar to that form) and sensitivity to initial conditions. Figure 3 presents the sensitivity of chaotic systems to the initial conditions.

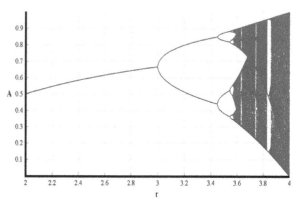

Figure 3. Sensitivity of chaotic systems to initial conditions.

In this figure, it is obvious that, in chaotic systems, not only a small initial divergence does not remain small, but also it grows exponentially. Also according to the figure, it can be clearly said that if we start moving from the end point, we will converge to the start point, which is one of the properties of a chaotic system.

In a random system, the current state of the system is independent from its previous state. In a random model, it is not possible to have an accurate prediction about the output of the model even within a short time period. A famous example is the formal logistic map as equation (9).

$$r_{n+1} = Ar_n(1-r_n) \qquad (9)$$

In this equation, r_n is a a real number in the range of [0, 1], and parameter A, which is known as the logistic factor, causes unique features in this function. In this work, the amount of parameter A was equal to 4.

7. Proposed algorithm

In this work, we proposed a chaotic genetic algorithm based on the explicit memory to maintain the appropriate solutions to increase the efficiency of the algorithm. First the population and the memory were initialized by means of the chaos theory. If the memory was updated at generation t, the next update would happen at generation $t + rand(5; 10)$. The memory size equal to $0.1 \times N$. N is the size of the population. The memory was updated as follows. Every individual in memory had a feature that specified its age. When the memory was started, all individuals had an age equal to zero. In every generation, the age of all the memory individuals was computed using a linear combination of its actual age and a contribution of its fitness. This contribution was set using a parameter called μ.

More formally, the age of an individual was calculated using (10).

$$age_i = age_i + 1 + \mu \times fit_i \qquad (10)$$

$$\forall i = 1 \ldots m, \forall \mu \grave{o} (0,1)$$

In this equation, m is the memory size. In this strategy, the individual age was not set to zero, so the older individuals were not penalized. When the memory was full and it was necessary to start replacing memory individuals, again the youngest was selected to be deleted and replaced by a new member if this individual was better. The pseudo-code for the memory update is shown in Algorithm 2 in figure 4.

Algorithm 2: *MEM Function(MEM)*
    Input: *m is memory size; $\mu \epsilon$ (0,1).*
    Output: $\emptyset$

Initialize memory based chaos theory (logistic map)
$age_i = 0$
Every Generation:
    $age_i = age_i + 1 + \mu \times fit_i$
IF *it is time to Update Memory*
    $Best_{pop}$i s the best individual of the population
    Select memory individual $Memory_{sel}$ with the lowest age
        IF *$fitness(Memory_{sel}) < fitness(Best_{pop})$*
        memory individual $Memory_{sel}$ is replaced by $Best_{pop}$
    END of IF
END of IF

Figure 4. Pseudo-code for update memory.

The memory was retrieved as follows. In order to store the most relevant information to an environment in the memory, each time an environmental change was detected, the memory was also retrieved. When the memory was retrieved, the current best individual of the memory or the elite from the previous memory was stored, replacing the worst individual of the population. After retrieval of memory individuals, the GA readapts easier to the new environment. The memory was also used to detect environmental changes: the change in the environment was analyzed in a way that if the suitability of one of the members is changed in the re-evaluate, the proposed algorithm finds that the environment is changed. At this moment, a new set of individuals was formed by merging the memory and the main population. Then these individuals were evaluated in the context of the new environment, and the best population individuals were selected to become the new search population, which evolved through the selection, crossover, and mutation. Through this process, the memory remained unchanged. The best individual from the previous population was preserved and transferred to the next population,

replacing the worst individual. The pseudo-code for the proposed algorithm is shown in figure 5.

For more explanations, we shall explain the related stages of the pseudo-code proposed method. In Step 2, the memory and population is initialized using the logistic map function. Unlike the standard GA that uses random numbers for creating initial population; in the proposed algorithm we use the chaos theory for creating initial population. A chaotic system has a precise prediction of the future compared with a random system. Thus the chaos theory can help speed convergence of the algorithm.

Algorithm3: *Proposed Algorithm*
    Input: $N, D, MCN, x_j^{min}, x_j^{max}, MemorySize$
    output: BEST Solution, BEST Fit, Error

1.   ***Begin***
2.   *Initialize POP and MEM with chaos thory*
3.   *$FitPOP_i = fitness(POP_{.i})$*
4.   *$FitMEM_i = fitness(MEM_i) \; Update\_MEM = 1$*
        $Update \; Time = rand(5,10)$
5.   *$Cycle = 1$*
Repeat:
6.   *$Chang_{flag}$:*
7.   *$Update\_MEM$:*
8.   *$Update\_MEM = 0$*
9.   *$MEM = Update\_MEM \; Function(MEM, POP)$*
10.   *$Update \; Time = rand(5,10) + Cycle$*
11.   *$POPc = Update\_POPFunction(POP)$*
    % POPc is current POP and POPFunction is genetic algorithm
12.   *$FCPOP_i = Fitness(POP_{.i})$ % Fitness for Current POP*
13.   **IF** *$FCPOP_i \neq FPOP_i$ **then** $Chang_{flag} = 1$*
    % Change Detected
14.   *$Chang_{flag}$ is active: % Reuse Memory*
    1. *$FM_i = Fitness(MEM_{.i}), FPOP_i = Fitness(POP_{.i})$*
    2. *Select $j_r \in MEM_r$ % j_r is best individual in memory*
        subject to $MEM_r \leq FM_l$
    3. *Select $d_r \in POP_r$ % d_r is worst individual in population*
        subject to $x_r \geq x_l$
    4. *$POP_r = MEM_r$ %best individual in memory replacement instead of worse individual in population*
15.   **IF** *$Update\_Time \geq Cycle$*
        then *update_mem = 1*
16.   *$Cycle = Cycle + 1$*
17.   *Until cycle = MCN*
18.   ***End***

Figure 5. Pseudo-code for proposed algorithm.

In the proposed algorithm, we used a logistic map function for the chaos theory. In this algorithm, instead of using random behaviors for individuals, we used the chaotic behaviors for each individual in the main population and memory population. For example, to create initial population, we used (11).

$$(11)$$

$$POP = LB_i + Ar_n(1 - r_n)(UB_i - LB_i)$$

$$\forall \; r_n \grave{o} [0,1], j \in (1,2,\ldots,SN), \forall i \in (1,2,\ldots,N)$$

In this equation, LB_i is the lower band, UB_i is the upper band, and *pop* is the population. In this equation, instead of a random value, we used a chaotic value.

In steps 3 and 4, as a function of efficiency, the competence for each individual memory of the main population and the memory population was calculated. If the memory update time occurs in cycle iteration then the next update for memory is in $Rand(5,10) + cycle$. The algorithm cycle begins at stage 5. Steps 6 and 7 state the function of updating for the individual and memory population. In step 8 the reassess is performed to calculate the efficiency of the individual and if the efficiency is changed even for a single individual, we understand that the environment has changed. In step 12, evaluation to calculate the fitness of individuals is done if fitness for even an individual be changed in that case alone in that environment has changed. Step 14 based on the changes in the environment, the data stored in the memory should be applied foe the new environment which is done in 4 various phases as follows:

Phase 1- Fitness is calculated for the memory population.

Phase 2- The best individual of the memory is selected; in fact, the best individual out of this memory is the individual that has the more fitness.

Phase 3- The worst individual of the population is selected; in fact, the worst individual out of this population is the individual that has the lowest fitness.

Phase 4- A replacement strategy chooses whether to replace the best individual of the memory instead of the worst individual of the main population.

Explicit memory maintains diversity for the proposed approach throughout the run. In this work, the worst individuals of the population were replaced by the new ones.

One of the approaches for increasing efficiency of the proposed algorithm is to maintain diversity throughout the run. If a population always remains diverse, then convergence may be avoided at all times, and optimization may be more adaptive to changes. The proposed approach maintains the diversity of the population by inserting chaotic initialized individuals into the population at every generation.

Step 15 explains that "if time update cycle of the algorithm is larger than a threshold, the algorithm will activate an update memory flag; otherwise, *if* finally reaches the end".

The general flowchart of this model is shown in figure 6.

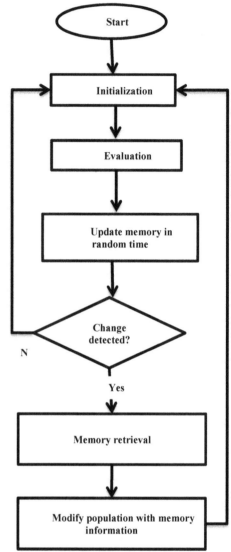

Figure 6. Flowchart of proposed algorithm.

8. Experimental settings

Branke [12] has introduced a dynamic benchmark problem called the moving peaks benchmark (MPB) problem. Numerical experiments concerning MPB, scenario 2, as proposed by Branke [12], were performed in order to test the behavior of the proposed method. The default settings and definition of the benchmark used in the experiments of this paper can be found in table 1.

The default parameter setting of MPB used in the experiments is presented in table 1 [12].

The default parameter setting of proposed method is presented in table 2. Giving different values for the parameters, different results can be obtained, through which we can reach the proper (optimal) values for the parameters used in the proposed method.

To demonstrate the dynamics of the proposed algorithm, we gave the contour-plot of the population distribution at different instances of the sample run (as shown in Figure 7). A *2D* MPB problem landscape was considered with 10 optima. Figure 7 shows that in the proposed algorithm, a very high percentage of the peaks was covered in each assessment. We implemented all algorithms using Matlab 2012, and run all algorithms on a PC with a core i5 processor and a 8 G Bytes RAM memory. The proposed algorithm was compared with AmQSO, mQSO, FMSO, cellular PSO, rPSO, and CPSO. For mQSO, we adapted the configuration 10 (5+5q), which created 10 swarms with 5 neutral (standard) particles and 5 quantum particles with $rcloud = 0.5$ and $rexcl = rconv = 31.5$, as suggested in [17].

For FMSO, there are at most 10 child swarms; each has a radius of 25.0. The size of the parent and the child swarms were set to 100 and 10 particles, respectively [19]. For FMSO, there are at most 10 child swarms each has a radius of 25.0. The size of the parent and the child swarms are set to 100 and 10 particles, respectively [16].

For cellular PSO, a 5-dimensional cellular automaton with 105 cells and Moore neighborhood with radius of two cells is embedded into the search space. The maximum velocity of particles is set to the neighborhood radius of the cellular automaton and the radius for the random local search (r) is set to 0.5 for all experiments. The cell capacity θ is set to 10 particles for every cell [31].

In CPSO, each particle learns from its own historical best position and the historical best position of its nearest neighbor other than the global best position, as in the basic PSO algorithm. Using a hierarchical clustering method, the whole swarm in CPSO can be divided into sub-swarms that cover different local regions. In order to accelerate the local search, a learning strategy for the global best particle was also introduced in CPSO [15]. Hu and Eberhart proposed re-randomization PSO (RPSO) for optimization in dynamic environments [29] in which some particles randomly are relocated after a change is detected or when the diversity is lost, to prevent losing the diversity.

Blackwell et al. [18] introduced compound particle swarm optimization (AmQSO) utilizing a new type of particles which helps explore the search space more comprehensively after a change occurred in the environment. For all algorithms, we reported the average offline error and 95% confidence interval for 100 runs.

Table 1. Standard configuration parameters for MPB problem [22].

Parameter	Value
peaks (number of peaks)	10
Frequency of change *(U)*	5000
Height severity	7.0
Width severity	1.0
Peak shape	Con
Basic function	No
Shift length *s*	1.0
Number of dimensions (D)	5
Correlation coefficient (λ)	0
Percentages of changing peaks *cPeaks*	1.0
S	[0, 100]
H	[30.0, 70.0]
W	[1, 12]
I	50.0

Table 2. Parameter values for proposed algorithm.

Parameter	Value
Lower bound	0
Upper bound	100
Total population	100
Memory Size	10
Probability of Crossover	0.6
Probability of Mutation	0.2
Logistic factor (A)	4

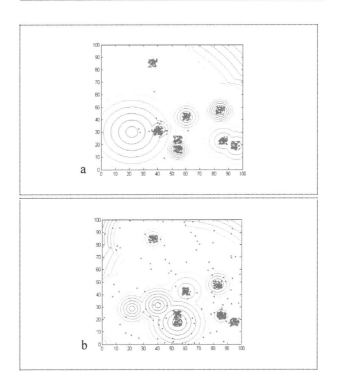

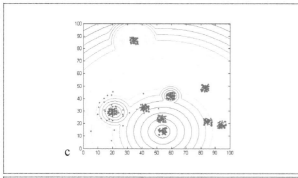

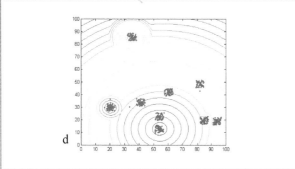

Figure 7. Trend of convergence individuals for peaks in through the run of the algorithm with population size = 100, peaks number = 10, frequency of change = 5000, and shift length = 1.

8.1. Influence of different parameter values on proposed algorithm

Table 3 shows the average offline error for the proposed method and the other methods of frequency change of 500 and different numbers of peaks.

From the results of the table 3, it can be easily seen that the proposed method outperforms all the other peer algorithms when the number of peaks is larger than one. Table 4 shows the mean offline error for the proposed method and the other methods in the frequency change of 1000 and varying the number of peaks.

Table 5 shows the mean offline error for the proposed method and the other methods in the frequency change of 5000 and varying the number

of peaks. It can be seen in table 5 that the performance of the proposed algorithm was not influenced too much when the number of peaks increased. Generally, increasing the number of peaks makes it harder for algorithms to track the optima. However, the offline error decreases when the number of peaks is larger than 50 for the proposed algorithm. Figures 8, 9, 10, and 11 show the offline error for the proposed algorithm, respectively, with frequency changes of 500 and 5000 and 10 peaks and 50 peaks. Table 6 shows the results of the proposed method with different dimensions involving peaks number 10, frequency change of 5000, and shift length of 1, in addition to those of mQSO, adaptive mQSO, rPSO, and mPSO [31]. Result of exist in table 6 shows with dimension 3, 4, 5, 10, 15, 20 of the landscape space; the performance of the proposed algorithm was better than the other algorithms. Table 7 shows the offline error for the proposed algorithm with frequency change of 500 and different dimension and different numbers of peaks. Table 8 shows offline error for the proposed algorithm with different severity of change and different number of peaks. Figure 12 shows the offline error for the proposed algorithm with shift lengths of 5 and 7. Figure 13 shows that the percentage cover of peaks for the proposed algorithm with population size is 300 and high frequency change applying as well. Increase of population size help at the speed convergence of the proposed algorithm. Figure 14 shows comparison proposed algorithm with AmQSO algorithm with different correlation coefficients, frequency of change of 500, number of peaks of 10, and shift length of 1. Figure 15 shows the average offline error for the proposed algorithm with different memory sizes and default values for MPB problem.

Table 3. Average offline error for different algorithms on MPB problem with different numbers of peaks and frequency 500.

Peak number	Proposed algorithm	mQSO	rPSO	FMSO	Cellular PSO[32]	AmQSO	CPSO
1	**2.85(0.22)**	33.67(3.4)	4.27(-)	7.58(0.9)	13.46(0.3)	3.02(0.32)	14.25(-)
5	**3.57(0.25)**	11.91(0.7)	16.19(-)	9.45(0.4)	9.63(0.49)	5.77(0.56)	36.40(-)
10	**3.96(0.21)**	9.62(0.34)	17.34(-)	18.26(0.3)	9.35(0.37)	5.37(0.42)	20.91(-)
20	**4.05(0.18)**	9.07(0.25)	17.06(-)	17.34(0.3)	8.84(0.28)	6.82(0.34)	13.11(-)
30	**4.67(0.20)**	8.80(0.21)	16.98(-)	16.39(0.4)	8.81(0.24)	7.10(0.39)	10.83(-)
40	**4.95(0.15)**	8.55(0.21)	16.64(-)	15.34(0.4)	8.94(0.24)	7.05(0.41)	10.12(-)
50	**5.23(0.17)**	8.72(0.20)	15.77(-)	5.54(0.2)	8.62(0.23)	8.97(0.32)	9.28(-)
100	**5.06(0.16)**	8.54(0.16)	14.55(-)	2.87(0.6)	8.54(0.21)	7.34(0.31)	7.77(-)
200	**4.81(0.13)**	8.19(0.17)	13.40(-)	11.52(0.6)	8.28(0.18)	7.48(0.19)	6.83(-)

Table 4. Average offline errors for different algorithms on MPB problem with different numbers of peaks and frequency 1000.

Peak number	Proposed algorithm	mQSO	rPSO	FMSO	Cellular PSO	AmQSO	CPSO
1	**1.10(0.10)**	18.60(1.3)	1.94(-)	14.42(0.9)	6.77(0.38)	2.33(0.31)	8.93(-)
5	**1.12(0.11)**	6.56(0.38)	13.77(-)	10.59(0.4)	5.30(0.32)	2.90(0.32)	8.62(-)
10	**1.28(0.13)**	5.71(0.22)	15.55(-)	10.40(0.3)	5.15(0.19)	4.56(0.40)	7.48(-)
20	**1.76(0.9)**	5.85(0.15)	15.54(-)	10.33(0.3)	5.23(0.18)	5.36(0.47)	6.10(-)
30	**2.01(0.14)**	5.81(0.15)	14.38(-)	10.06(0.4)	5.33(0.16)	5.20(0.38)	5.44(-)
40	**2.23(0.16)**	5.70(0.14)	14.11(-)	9.85(0.4)	5.61(0.16)	5.25(0.37)	5.57(-)
50	**2.56(0.10)**	5.87(0.13)	13.75(-)	9.54(0.2)	5.55(0.14)	6.06(0.14)	5.17(-)
100	**2.42(0.14)**	5.83(0.13)	12.27(-)	8.77(0.6)	5.57(0.12)	4.77(0.45)	4.26(-)
200	**2.20(0.11)**	5.54(0.11)	11.32(-)	8.06(0.6)	5.50(0.12)	5.75(0.26)	3.74(-)

Table 5. Average offline errors for different algorithms on MPB Problem with different numbers of peaks and frequency 5000.

Peak number	Proposed algorithm	mQSO	rPSO	FMSO	Cellular PSO	AmQSO	CPSO
1	0.92(0.09)	3.82(0.35)	0.56(0.04)	3.44(0.1)	2.54(0.1)	0.51(0.0)	**0.14(0.11)**
5	1.06(0.7)	1.90(0.08)	12.58(0.76)	2.94(0.0)	1.72(0.1)	1.01(0.0)	**0.72(0.72)**
10	1.15(0.10)	1.91(0.08)	12.98(0.48)	3.11(0.0)	1.76(0.1)	1.51(0.1)	**1.05(0.24)**
20	**1.18(0.06)**	2.56(0.10)	12.79(0.06)	3.36(0.0)	2.59(0.1)	2.00(0.1)	1.59(0.22)
30	**1.35(0.05)**	2.68(0.10)	12.35(0.54)	3.28(0.0)	2.95(0.1)	2.19(0.1)	1.58(0.17)
40	1.53(0.09)	2.65(0.08)	11.23(0.62)	3.26(0.0)	3.11(0.1)	2.28(0.1)	**1.51(0.12)**
50	1.65(0.07)	2.63(0.08)	11.34(0.29)	3.22(0.0)	3.22(0.1)	2.43(0.1)	**1.54(0.12)**
100	1.80(0.06)	2.52(0.06)	9.73(0.28)	3.06(0.0)	3.39(0.1)	2.68(0.1)	**1.41(0.08)**
200	1.71(0.05)	2.30(0.05)	8.90(0.19)	2.84(0.0)	3.36(0.0)	2.62(0.1)	**1.24(0.06)**

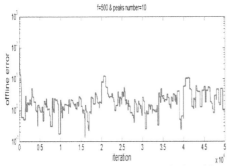

Figure 8. Offline error for proposed algorithm in frequency = 500 and peaks number = 10.

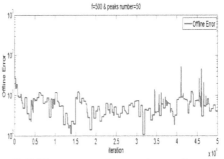

Figure 9. Offline error and current error for proposed algorithm in frequency = 500 and peak number = 50.

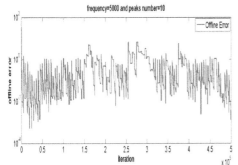

Figure 10. Offline error and current error for proposed algorithm in frequency = 5000 and peak number = 50

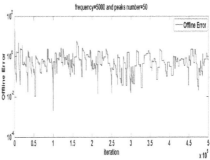

Figure 11. Offline error for proposed algorithm in frequency = 5000 and peak number = 10

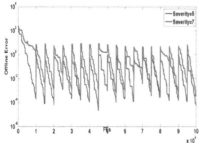

Figure 12. Offline error for proposed algorithm with shift lengths of 5 and 7 with frequency of 5000, and peaks number of 10.

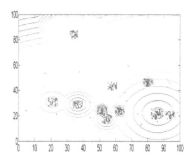

Figure 13. Cover of peaks with iteration = 500000, frequency change = 10000, peak number = 10, population size = 300, shift length = 1, and other default parameter values for MPB benchmark.

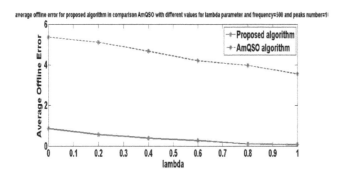

Figure 14. Comparison between proposed algorithm with AmQSO in frequency change = 500, peak number = 10, and different correlation coefficients (λ).

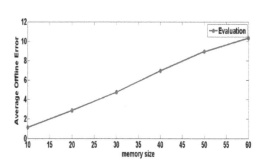

Figure 15. Average offline error for proposed algorithm with different memory sizes and default values for MPB problem.

Table 6. Result of proposed method with different dimensions involving peak number of 10, frequency change of 5000, and shift length of 1, in comparison with mQSO, AmQSO, rPSO, and mPSO.

Algorithm	Dimension						
	2	3	4	5	10	15	20
Proposed method	0.96(0.09)	**1.08(0.11)**	**1.11(0.10)**	**1.15(0.13)**	2.45(0.28)	**3.85(0.31)**	**4.25(0.35)**
Adaptive mQSO	**0.71(0.05)**	1.16(0.10)	1.33(0.08)	1.51(0.10)	**3.37(0.22)**	4.91(0.31)	5.83(0.29)
mQSO	1.01(0.04)	1.49(0.09)	1.47(0.08)	1.85(0.08)	4.22(0.20)	6.50(0.33)	8.88(0.34)
rPSO	2.62(0.08)	6.61(0.33)	10.43(0.54)	12.98(0.48)	16.87(0.83)	18.48(0.97)	18.48(0.94)
mPSO	1.24(0.07)	1.42(0.10)	1.35(0.09)	1.51(0.12)	4.32(0.26)	7.07(0.25)	10.77(0.40)

Table 7. Offline error for proposed algorithm with frequency change = 5000 and different peaks and different dimensions and shift length = 1.

peaks	Dimension				
	5	7	10	15	20
1	0.92(0.08)	1.11(0.14)	2.09(0.17)	2.80(0.20)	3.15(0.41)
5	1.06(0.09)	1.23(0.13)	2.25(0.21)	2.95(0.25)	3.26(0.40)
10	1.15(0.13)	2.09(0.16)	2.45(0.23)	3.85(0.28)	4.25(0.39)
20	1.18(0.09)	2.45(0.11)	3.56(0.25)	4.23(0.27)	6.85(0.39)
30	1.35(0.10)	2.66(0.16)	3.84(0.19)	5.25(0.29)	6.92(0.46)
40	1.53(0.12)	2.90(0.12)	3.96(0.18)	5.63(0.31)	7.12(0.48)
50	1.85(0.08)	3.56(0.10)	4.25(0.21)	5.91(0.33)	7.93(0.45)
100	1.80(0.13)	3.42(0.14)	4.15(0.21)	5.64(0.37)	7.76(0.53)
200	1.71(0.15)	3.36(0.11)	4.03(0.20)	5.45(0.30)	7.60(0.51)

Table 8. Offline error for proposed algorithm with frequency change = 5000 and different peaks and different dimensions and shift length = 1.

peaks	shift length				
	2	3	4	5	6
1	1.89(0.13)	3.02(0.19)	5.09(0.32)	6.12(0.43)	8.09(0.56)
5	2.06(0.10)	3.16(0.22)	5.23(0.30)	6.26(0.40)	8.12(0.56)
10	2.19(0.15)	3.31(0.25)	5.35(0.35)	6.45(0.45)	8.15(0.68)
20	2.36(0.17)	3.65(0.20)	5.41(0.35)	6.52(0.42)	8.53(0.70)
30	2.52(0.14)	3.74(0.22)	5.49(0.37)	6.58(0.42)	8.65(0.50)
40	2.70(0.17)	3.86(0.25)	5.62(0.33)	6.69(0.45)	8.69(0.55)
50	2.92(0.16)	3.95(0.27)	5.87(0.36)	6.87(0.47)	8.74(0.52)
100	2.80(0.14)	3.90(0.25)	5.96(0.35)	6.80(0.49)	8.79(0.60)
200	2.71(0.14)	3.86(0.26)	5.90(0.30)	6.96(0.46)	8.98(0.53)

Table 9 shows Min, Max and Std (standard divation) error for the proposed algorithm with frequency change = 5000 and different peaks and different dimension and shift length = 1.

Table 9. Min, Max, and std error for proposed algorithm with frequency change = 5000 and different peaks and different dimensions and shift length = 1.

peaks	Min error	Max error	Std error
1	0.62	0.11	0.09
5	1.00	1.21	0.7
10	1.02	1.27	0.10
20	1.07	1.29	0.06
50	1.10	1.35	0.05
100	1.12	1.41	0.09
200	1.16	1.62	0.07

9. Conclusion

In dynamic problems, storing and maintaining the memory has been one of the largest problems examined in the prior works. First, it must be decided how often to update the memory. Secondly, we should decide what should continue to be stored in the memory as one tries to add a new environment.

Memory usage information to remember environment and good storage solutions that are not too old can increase the efficiency of the algorithm. The solutions maintained from the past can be tracked for future exploration. The novel strategy designed for updating memory at the proposed algorithm maintains diversity among population through the run. The retrieval of memorized individuals, which usually occurs after a change, takes place before the re-adaptation of the proposed algorithm to the new environment.

A chaotic system has a precise prediction of the future in comparison with a random system. Using the chaos theory for initializing population helps speed up the convergence of individuals in the proposed algorithm. However, it is worth mentioning that in the dynamic environment, the diversity and convergence dilemma is foundation of local search and global search dilemma where it is gained by keeping old solutions in a memory. Therefore, the mechanism design and new algorithm change proposal to solve the issues with dynamic optimization qualities and the challenges of different options can be suitable for future works.

References

[1] Ramsey, C. L. & Grefenstette, J. J. (1993). Case-based initialization of genetic algorithms. In S. Forrest, editor, Proceedings of the Fifth International Conference on Genetic Algorithms, pp. 84-91. Morgan Kaufmann.

[2] Louis, S. J. & Xu, Z. (1996). Genetic algorithms for open shop scheduling and re- scheduling. In M. E. Cohen and D. L. Hudson, editors, Proceedings of the Eleventh International Conference on Computers and their Applications (ISCA), pp. 99-102.

[3] Mori, N., Kita, H. & Nishikawa, Y. (1996). Adaptation to a changing environment by means of the thermo dynamical genetic algorithm. In H.-M. Voigt, editor, Parallel Problem Solving from Nature (PPSN IV), volume 1141 of Lecture Notes in Computer Science, pp. 513-52.

[4] Mori, N., Kita, H. & Nishikawa, Y. (1997). Adaptation to changing environments by means of the memory-based thermo dynamical genetic algorithm. In I. Back, editor, Proceedings of the Seventh International Conference on Genetic Algorithms (ICGA 1997), pp. 299-306. Morgan Kaufmann.

[5] Mori, N., Kita, H. & Nishikawa, Y. (1998). Adaptation to a changing environment by means of the feedback thermo dynamical genetic algorithm. In Parallel Problem Solving from Nature (PPSN V), vol. 1498 of Lecture Notes in Computer Science, pp. 149-158.

[6] Uyar, A. S. & Harmanci, A. E. (2002). Preserving diversity in changing environments through diploidy with adaptive dominance. In W. B. Langdon and et al., editors, Proceedings of the Genetic and Evolutionary Computation Conference (GECCO 2002), page 679. Morgan Kaufmann.

[7] Simoes, A & Costa, E. (2003). An immune system-based genetic algorithm to deal with dynamic environments: Diversity and memory. In D. W. Pearson, N. C. Steele, and R. Albrecht, editors, Proceedings of the 6th International Conference on Artificial Neural Networks (ICANNGA 2003), pp. 168-174. Springer-Verlag.

[8] Yang, S. (2006). A comparative study of immune system based genetic algorithms in dynamic environments. In M. Keijzer and et al., editors, Proceedings of the Eighth International Genetic and Evolutionary Computation. Conference (GECCO 2006), pp. 1377-1384. ACM Press.

[9] Liu, L., Wang, D. & Yang, S. (2009). An immune system based genetic algorithm using permutation-based dualism for dynamic traveling salesman problems. In M. Giacobini and et al., editors, Evo Workshops 2009: Applications of Evolutionary Computing (EVOSTOC 2009), vol. 5484 of Lecture Notes on Computer Science, pp. 725-734. Springer.

[10] Mohammadpour, M. & Parvin, H. (2016). "Genetic Algorithm Based on Explicit Memory for Solving Dynamic Problems", In Journal of Advances in Computer Research Sari Branch Islamic Azad University. vol. 7, no. 2, pp. 53-68.

[11] Yang, S. (2005). Memory-based immigrants for genetic algorithms in dynamic environments. In H.-G. Beyer, editor, Proceedings of the Seventh International Genetic and Evolutionary Computation Conference (GECCO2005), vol. 2, pp. 1115-1122. ACM Press.

[12] Branke, J. (1999). Memory enhanced evolutionary algorithms for changing optimization problems. In Proceedings of the IEEE Congress on Evolutionary Computation (CEC 1999), pp. 1875-1882. IEEE Press.

[13] Mohammadpour, M. & Parvin, H. (2016). Chaotic genetic algorithm based on clustering and memory for solving dynamic optimization problem. Tabriz Journal of Electrical Engineering, vol. 46, no. 3 (Persian Journal).

[14] Yang, S. & Li, C. (2012). A clustering particle swarm optimizer for locating and tracking multiple optima in dynamic environments. IEEE Trans. vol. 16, no. 4. pp. 959-974.

[15] Yang, S. & Li, C. (2009). A clustering particle swarm optimizer for dynamic optimization. in Proc. Congr. Evol. Comput., pp. 439–446.

[16] Branke, J., Kauler, T. & Schmidt, C. (2000). A multi-population approach to dynamic optimization problems. In I. Parmee, editor, Proceedings of Adaptsim03ive Computing in Design and Manufacture (ACDM 2000), pp. 299-308. Spriger-Verlag.

[17] Blackwell, T. & Branke, J. (2006). Multi-Swarms, Exclusion, and Anti-Convergence in Dynamic Environments. IEEE Transactions on Evolutionary Computation 10, pp. 459–472.

[18] Blackwell, T., Branke, J. & Li, X. (2008). Particle swarms for dynamic optimization problems. Swarm Intelligence. Springer Berlin Heidelberg,. pp. 193-217.

[19] Yang, S. & Li, C. (2008). Fast Multi-Swarm Optimization for Dynamic Optimization Problems. Proc, Int'l Conf. Natural Computation, vol. 7, no. 3, pp. 624-628.

[20] Lung, R. I. & Dumitrescu, D. (2010). Evolutionary swarm cooperative optimization in dynamic environments. Natural Comput., vol. 9, no. 1, pp. 83–94.

[21] Lung, R. I. & Dumitrescu, D. (2007). A collaborative model for tracking optima in dynamic environments. In Proc. Congr. Evol. Comput, pp. 564–567.

[22] Branke, J. (2002). Evolutionary Optimization in Dynamic Environments. Kluwer Academic Publishers.

[23] Branke, J. (1999). Memory enhanced evolutionary algorithms for changing optimization problems. In Proceedings of the IEEE Congress on Evolutionary Computation (CEC 1999), pp. 1875-1882. IEEE Press.

[24] Holland, J. (1975). Adaptation in Natural and Artificial Systems. University of Michigan Press, Ann Arbor, MI.

[25] Ryan, C. (1997). Diploidy without dominance. In Nordic Workshop on Genetic Algorithms, pp. 45–52.

[26] Yang, S. (2007). Explicit memory schemes for evolutionary algorithms in dynamic environments. In S. Yang, Y.-S. Ong, and Y. Jin, editors, Evolutionary Computation in Dynamic and Uncertain Environments, volume 51 of Studies in Computational Intelligence, pp. 3-28. Springer-Verlag.

[27] Ramsey, C. & Grefenstette, J. (1993). Case-based initialization of genetic algorithms. In S. Forrest, editor, Proceedings of the Fifth International Conference on Genetic Algorithms, pp. 84-91. Morgan Kaufmann.

[28] Trojanowski, K. & Michalewicz, Z. (1999) Searching for optima in non-stationary environments. in Proc of the IEEE Congress on Evolutionary Computation (CEC 1999), pp. 1843-1850. IEEE Press.

[29] Branke, J. (1999). Memory enhanced evolutionary algorithms for changing optimization problems. In Congress on Evolutionary Computation, pp. 1875–1882.

[30] Wang, H. & Yang, S. (2012). Ip WH, Wang D, A memetic particle swarm optimization algorithm for dynamic multi modal optimization problems. Int J Syst Sci, vol. 43, no. 7, pp. 1268-1283.

[31] Hashemi, B. & Meybodi, M. R. (2009). Cellular PSO: A PSO for Dynamic Environments. In Advances in Computation and ntelligence, Lecture Notes in Computer Science, vol. 5821, pp. 422-433.

[32] Kamosi, M., Hashemi, A. B. & Meybodi, M. R. (2010). A new particle swarm optimization algorithm for dynamic environment. Swarm, Evolutionary, and Memetic Computing, SEMCO 2010, Lect. Notes in Comput. Sci. 6466, pp. 129–138.

[33] Ozsoydan, F. B. & Baykasoglu, A., (2015). A multi-population firefly algorithm for dynamic optimization problems, Evolving and Adaptive Intelligent Systems (EAIS), 2015 IEEE International Conference. pp. 1-7.

[34] Sadeghi, S., Parvin, H. & Rad, F. (2015). Particle Swarm Optimization for Dynamic Environments, Springer International Publishing, 14th Mexican International Conference on Artificial intelligence, MICAI 2015, pp. 260-269, October 2015.

[35] Nguyen, T. T., (2013). Solving dynamic optimization problems by combining Evolutionary Algorithms with KD-Tree, Soft Computing and Pttern Recogonition (SoCPaR), International Conference, pp. 247-25.

[36] Yildiz, A., Lekesiz, H. & Yi;diz A. R. (2016). "Structural design of vehicle components using gravitational search and charged system search algorithm, Material Testing, vol. 58, no, 1, pp. 79-91.

[37] Kiani, M. & Yildiz, A. R, (2015). A Comparative Study of Non-traditional Methods for Vehicle Crashworthiness and NVH Optimization, In J Crashworthiness, pp. 1-12, doi: 10.1007/s11831-015-9155-y.

[38] Motameni, H. (2016). PSO for multi-objective problems: Criteria for leader selection and uniformity distribution. Journal of Artificial Intelligence and Data Mining, vol. 4, no. 1, pp. 67-76. doi: 10.5829/idosi.JAIDM.2016.04.01.08.

5

FDiBC: A Novel Fraud Detection Method in Bank Club based on Sliding Time and Scores Window

S. M.- H. Hasheminejad[*] and Z. Salimi

Department of Computer Engineering, Alzahra University, Tehran, Iran.

*Corresponding author: SMH.Hasheminejad@Alzahra.ac.ir(S.M.-H. Hasheminejad).

Abstract

One of the recent strategies for increasing the customer's loyalty in banking industry is the use of customers' club system. In this system, customers receive scores on the basis of financial and club activities they are performing, and due to the achieved points, they get credits from the bank. In addition, by the advent of new technologies, fraud is growing in banking domain as well. Therefore, given the importance of financial activities in the customers' club system, providing an efficient and applicable method for detecting fraud is highly important in these types of systems. In this paper, we propose a novel sliding time and scores window-based method, called *FDiBC* (Fraud Detection in Bank Club), to detect fraud in bank club. In *FDiBC*, firstly, based upon each score obtained by customer members of bank club, 14 features are derived, and then based on all the scores of each customer member, five sliding time and scores window-based feature vectors are proposed. For generating training and test dataset from the obtained scores of fraudster and common customers in the customers' club system of a bank, a positive and a negative label are used, respectively. After generating the training dataset, learning is performed through two approaches: 1) clustering and binary classification with the OCSVM method for positive data, i.e. fraudster customers, and 2) multi-class classification including SVM, C4.5, KNN, and Naïve Bayes methods. The results obtained reveal that *FDiBC* has the ability to detect fraud with 78% accuracy, and thus can be used in practice.

Keywords: *Financial Fraud Detection, Club System, Banking Industry and Sliding.*

1. Introduction

Fraud is an illegal action through which a person earns a property without the permission of its owner; electronic fraud is one of the prevalent crimes growing currently and associated officials have not been so far able to uproot it. In fact, financial fraud detection means separating financial data of fraudsters from financial data related to ordinary people. With the advent of modern technologies, the techniques of committing these crimes have become more varied, consequently, trapping the culprits and proving their crimes have become more difficult. In 2013, the report of 1.44 billion fraud in European banks, and 8% growth rate compared with 2012, clarifies expediting the e-fraud growth rate, especially in the banking industry [1]. When it comes to banking business, one of the strategies for increasing the customer loyalty in banking is applying the customers' club system.

In this system, customers receive scores on the basis of financial and club activities they are performing, and due to the scores obtained, they get credits from the bank. However, by the advent of new technologies, fraud is growing in the banking domain as well. Data mining [2] has been used in different areas such as diagnosing heart diseases [3], text-mining [4], designing software architecture [5-7], selecting design pattern [8, 9], and so on. One application of data mining is to detect fraud. Fraud includes the crimes of credit card transactions, money-laundering, etc. [10]. In fact, using data mining helps abnormal scenarios identification. As a strategy, data mining can be learned as patterns using the past fraud data, and then by employing those patterns, future fraudsters can be predicted. The techniques of detecting financial fraud in banking can be divided into four categories: credit card, money-laundering, fake transactions, and false accounts. One of the primary studies in this domain can be referred to a study by [11], in which a method has been offered for detecting fraud in credit cards using the "fuzzy logic" technique. Most studies in financial domain have been related to credit card swindling that use the neural network approach [12]. Duman et al. [13] have employed a genetic algorithm (GA) for detecting credit card fraud. In [13], to each transaction a score is given, and based on this score, transactions are classified as legal or illegal. In [13], the aim is to reduce the number of transactions that are mis-classified. In another study [14], two algorithms of association rules and clustering have been used, and these two algorithms have been applied on a dataset from 114 firms. Additionally, in [15], Hidden Markov Model has been used for detecting fraud in fake transactions. West et al., in a review paper [10], have divided the fraud types into six categories including credit card fraud, securities fraud, financial statement fraud, insurance fraud, mortgage fraud, and money laundering but they did not consider the new fraud happening in bank club systems.

In this paper, a novel sliding time and scores window-based method called *FDiBC* (*Fraud Detection in Bank Club*) is proposed for detecting fraud in the customers' club system on the basis of data mining. In *FDiBC*, it is assumed that fraudsters attempt to carry out fraud using uncommon transactions and fake communications in the customers' club system. In *FDiBC*, on the basis of instance data of the scores of bank customers' club system, classifiers are learned, and then these classifiers are evaluated. In *FDiBC*, both the clustering and classifier approaches are employed and its novelties are as follow:

- Proposing a novel method based upon clustering and classification to detect fraud in the customers' club system (the proposed *FDiBC* method is described with more details in Section 3)
- Providing new sliding time and scores window-based feature vectors for summarizing the customer scores
- Identifying the best classifier in detecting fraud from the five classification methods OSCVM, SVM , C4.5, KNN, and Naïve Bayes [2]

Note that there are several techniques for classification but it cannot be said which one is better than the others. The reason is that there is no learning technique that achieves good results for all problems. In real life, some of them may achieve good results for some problems and bad results for the rest. Therefore, for a new problem

(i.e. fraud detection) to find out the best learning technique, we evaluate several learning techniques so that the best learning technique is identified. Thus one of the contributions of this paper is to identify the best learning technique compatible with the fraud detection.

In the rest of this paper, at first, the bank club system will be introduced in Section 2. Then we proceed to explain the proposed *FDiBC* method in Section 3. In Section 4, the results of evaluating the proposed *FDiBC* method will be mentioned. Finally, in Section 5, conclusions would be done and further works would be stated.

2. Bank club system

The loyalty of bank customers comes along with bank club systems. These systems, in an attempt to raise the level of customers' loyalty from its bottom and to establish effective and regular relationship with customers, provide new services appropriate with their needs to increase their satisfaction and faithfulness. Bank club systems have been usually designed for special and common customers. The customers obtain scores through activity in a bank using different ports such as Internet Bank, Mobile Bank, ATM, and POS. Then customers' loyalty cards are charged once their obtained scores reach a pre-defined limit. Furthermore, customers will be entitled to a discount for purchasing their given scores. Bank club systems usually have two panels for customers and management (both of which cover branches and administrators). Some of their most important features are mentioned below. The main features of management panel are as follow:

- Users management
- Types of deposits, their definition and management
- Types of deposit, transactional and club activity patterns, their definition and management
- Collective and individual registration of customers by bank as well as issuing and printing collective and individual password in the branches

The main features of customer panel are as follow:

- Completing the profile information
- Registration and card management
- Inviting friends
- News
- Observing the obtained scores (chart and graph)
- Sub-system of using the scores
- Issuing and managing loyalty card
- Management reports

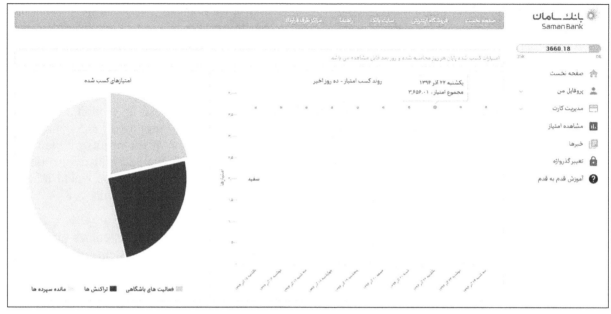

Figure 1. Customer panel of Saman Bank club system (In Persian).

In this paper, we use the archive customer scores of Saman Bank club as our case study. Saman Bank is one of the three famous private Iranian banks, and its club system has started since 2012. In figure 1, a customer panel of this club system is shown. Note that this system is displayed in Persian language. In figure 1, there is a pie chart revealing different kinds of obtained scores including deposit, transactional, and club activity.

3. Proposed *FDiBC* method

In this section, a proposed *FDiBC* method based on data mining is presented for detecting fraud, and its flowchart is illustrated in figure 2. The *FDiBC* method consists of the following eight steps: 1) Pre-processing, 2) Generating feature vectors based on sliding time and scores window, 3) Generating training and test datasets, 4) Separating the fraudster's data from common customer's data, 5) Clustering, 6) Learning several binary classifiers of OCSVM, 7) Learning multi-class classifiers for SVM, KNN, C4.5, and Naïve Bayes methods, and 8) Evaluating the learned classifiers. In the first step, some pre-processes including substitution of missed data, and noise and outliers deletion are applied on instances of scores obtained by customers from the bank club system. In the second step, according to the scores of each customer, feature vectors are built based on sliding time and score windows. In fact, the input of data mining in the proposed *FDiBC* method is a feature vector based on scores of each customer. In the third step, the entire data instances are divided into training and test sets. For this division, we used a ten-fold

cross-validation procedure [20], in which 90% of all data instances are randomly regarded as training dataset and the rest are test dataset for 10 times. In the fourth step, data instances of fraudsters in training dataset are separated from the common customers in order to identify their hidden patterns. In the fifth step, feature vector of fraudster's data is clustered. The focal point in this step is that the number of clusters in the proposed *FDiBC* method is determined automatically, so there is no need to be specified by human experts. In the fifth step, the training dataset is re-labeled, and new classifiers are identified. In the sixth step, based on new classifiers of training dataset, binary classifiers are learned with the OCSVM method. In the seventh step, on the basis of two classes of fraudsters and common customers, some classifiers with SVM, KNN, C4.5, and Naïve Bayes methods are learned. In the eighth step, the learned classifiers are evaluated by test dataset. In the following sections, each step is explained in detail.

3.1. Pre-processing

In order to conduct a desired data mining, the lost values should be replaced in the first place, outliers are identified, and inconsistencies are modified. In this step of the proposed *FDiBC* method, two major activities are performed: 1) Replacing the lost data, and 2) Removing noise and outliers. The lost values are the data that is not available to the analyst for any reason at the time of analysis. Existence of such data makes their analysis difficult to deal with. In this case, there are lost values in the data; they should be estimated properly. In *FDiBC*, to replace the lost data for each score instance, linear regression of Weka is used [16]. Existences of noise, outliers, and unwanted data always cause dire effect on the results of clustering and classification; therefore, in using the data mining method, at first, it is attempted to eliminate these instances. In the proposed *FDiBC* method, for removing the noise instances and unwanted data, the method of "RemoveMisclassified" is employed and implemented in the Weka tool [17].

3.2. Generating window-based feature vectors

Feature vector is used to display a score instance. In this paper, at the outset, based on each score given to a customer in the customers' club system, fourteen features are derived. These features are illustrated in table 1. A pivotal point is that fraud cannot be detected from one score, and it is usually detectable from some sequential scores. Therefore, in this paper, some innovative features are proposed from sequential scores, which are calculable out of the features shown in table 1.

In this paper, to detect the scores of fraudsters, two sliding windows called *SSW* (*Sliding Scores Window*) and *STW* (*Sliding Time Window*) are proposed. A sliding window is, in fact, referred to as more general features calculated according to all the scores of a member.

SSW is a window of scores having size *N*. It must be noted that the size of each sliding window is referred to the number of scores that the features of the corresponding sliding window are computed based on them. In table 2, a list of 12 overall features computable from the sequence of customer scores is provided as window-based features. As it can be implied by table 2, features of a *SSW* can be calculated on the basis of the sequence of customer scores.

STW is a window of scores having the aggregated features of customer scores given to them during the time of window, e.g. a day, a week, and a month. It should be mentioned that in the *STW* feature vectors, the window size denotes the number of scores that are obtained by the customer during the time interval of *STW*.

Moreover, it can be seen in table 2 that some features are dependent on the size of the window. These features include 1) number of purchase transactions over the size of the window, 2) number of money transfer transactions over the size of the window, 3) number of purchase mobile phone charging transactions over the size of the window, 4) number of bill payment transactions over the size of the window, 5) number of card

registrations and profile completion over the size of the window, and 6) number of friends introduced over the size of the window; in which all the activities performed are divided by the size of the window for normalization.

After deriving the features from table 2, for each feature vector, a label representing whether the sliding window-based feature vector is a fraud or a common one is provided. In figure 3, an example of a *SSW* feature vector with size 4 is given. As shown in this figure, label +1 denotes *SSW* of a fraudster customer and label -1 denotes *SSW* of a common customer.

Note that in this figure, at first, from score streams of each customer, for each score, 14 features are extracted in Step 1, and according to window size, each *SSW* feature vector is calculated in Step 2.

It should be noted that the minimum size of *SSW* equals one; however, for discovering the effective size of the *SSW* feature vectors, different values should be measured to identify the optimum size. In section 4 of this paper, evaluation of the effective *SSW* size is presented.

Due to the importance of transaction history, we proposed the *STW* feature vectors. In order to employ the historical data, we proposed four *STW* feature vectors including one-day *STW*, one-week *STW*, one-month *STW*, and hybrid *STW* with different time intervals. In figures 4 and 5, samples of these *STW* feature vectors are illustrated.

As shown in figures 4 (a-c), the 12 features of table 2 were calculated for all the scores obtained by a customer during a day, a week, and a month, respectively. Hybrid *STW* feature vector (shown in Figure 5) is generated by the three current day *STW*, week *STW*, month *STW* feature vectors. In fact, the goal of the hybrid *STW* feature vector is to consider the behaviors of a customer based on the current day and the last week and month. Note that in Section 4 of this paper, evaluation of the different *STW* feature vectors is presented.

It should be mentioned that the ABA feature shown in table 2 for the *STW* feature vectors is considered the average of balance of customer account during the *STW* time interval.

3.3. Generating training and test datasets

In the proposed *FDiBC* method, the training and test datasets are determined after conducting pre-processing and generating feature vectors. The purpose of generating the training dataset is to learn classifiers, and the aim of generating the test dataset is to evaluate the learned classifies.

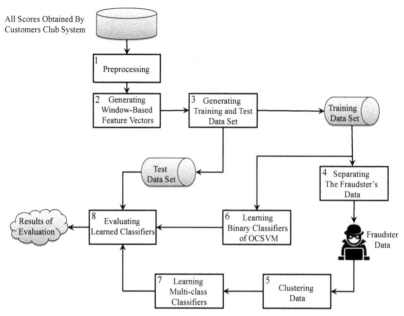

Figure 2. Process of proposed *FDiBC* method.

Table 1. Extracted features for each score obtained by customers.

No.	Feature Name	Feature Type	ACRONYM
1	Score Type	Enumeration (including 1) Account-Based, 2) Card-Based, and 3) Club Activity-Based)	SCT
2	Amount	Numerical	AMN
3	Transaction Type	Enumeration (including 1) Purchase, 2) Money Transfer, 3) Pay Bill, and 4) Purchase Mobile Phone Charging)	TRT
4	Account Type	Enumeration (including 1) Saving Account, 2) Checking Account, 3) Money Market Account, and 4) Certificates of Deposit)	ACT
5	Account Balance	Numerical	ACB
6	Port Type	Enumeration (including 1) Net Bank, 2) Branch, 3) PinPad/PoS (Point of Sale), 4) ATM (Automated Teller Machine), 5) IVR (Interactive Voice Response), and 6) Mobile Bank)	POT
7	Customer Group Type	Enumeration (including 1) Regular, 2) Special, and 3) Honorary)	CGT
8	Acquire Account Number	Numerical	AAN
9	Date	Date	DAT
10	Time	Time	TIM
11	Introduce Friend	Binary (1 denotes a new friend introduction)	FRI
12	Register Card	Binary (1 denotes a new card registration)	RCA
13	Register	Binary (1 denotes customer registration)	REG
14	Customer Profile	Binary (1 denotes customer profile completion)	CUP

Table 2. Features proposed for a sliding window-based feature vectors.

No.	Proposed Feature Name	Feature Type	Acronym
1	Average Interval Time Between Scores	Time	ATT
2	Average Amount of Transactions	Numerical	AAT
3	Average Balance of Accounts for scores belonging to *SSW* and *STW*	Numerical	ABA
4	Difference Rate of Acquire Account Numbers	Numerical	DRA
5	Customer Group Type	Enumeration	CGT
6	Difference Rate of Ports	Numerical	DRP
7	Number of Purchase Transactions over Window Size	Numerical	NPT
8	Number Money Transfer Transactions over Window Size	Numerical	NTT
9	Number of Purchase Mobile Phone Charging Transactions over Window Size	Numerical	NCT
10	Number of Bill Payment Transactions over Window Size	Numerical	NBP
11	Number of Registration Card and Complete Profile over Window Size	Numerical	NRC
12	Number of Introduced Friends over Window Size	Numerical	NIF

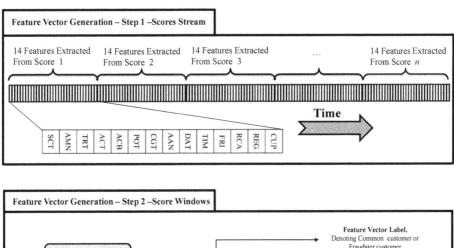

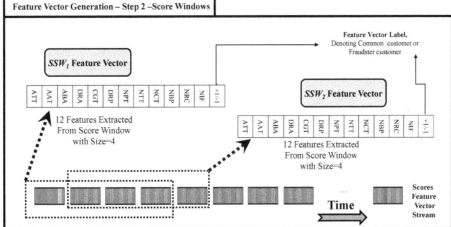

Figure 3. A Sample of SSW feature vectors with size equal to 4.

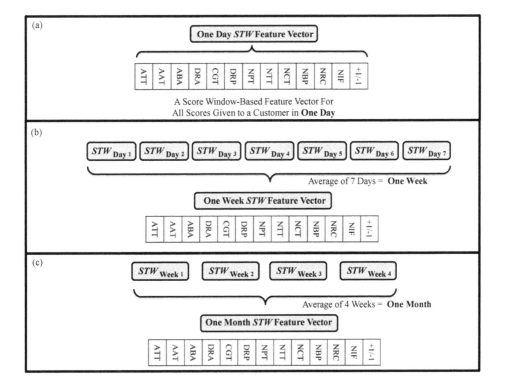

Figure 4. Samples of one-day STW (a), one-week STW (b), and one-month STW (c) feature vectors.

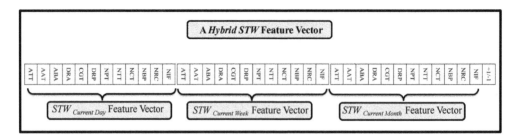

Figure 5. A Sample of a hybrid SSW feature vector.

3.4. Separating fraudster's data from common customer's data

As it can be seen in figure 2, after generating the training dataset, in order to detect the hidden patterns from fraudster's data, the data instance of fraudsters were separated from the common customer's data and sent to the clustering step (the fifth step of *FDiBC* shown in Figure 2).

3.5. Clustering

As it can be seen in figure 2, the fifth step of the proposed *FDiBC* method is to cluster the fraudster's data. The aim of this step is to re-label the labels of the fraudster's data. The reason is to find out the hidden patterns in the fraudster's data instances and to modify their labels. In order to calculate the similarity between a pair of feature vectors such as *SSW* or *STW*, we used the *Euclidean* similarity, as a popular similarity measure, which is defined in (1).

$$SIM_{Euclidean(i,j)} = \frac{1}{Dist_{Euclidean}(i,j)}$$

$$Dist_{Euclidean}(i,j) = \sqrt{\sum_{k=1}^{|FeatureVectorSize|} |x_k - y_k|^2} \quad (1)$$

where, x_k and y_k represent the values of the i and j instances for the kth feature, respectively. It is valuable to point out that to compute the similarity between a pair of feature vectors according to the *Euclidean* distance, after calculating the *Euclidean* distance between them, the inverse value of the *Euclidean* distance is considered as the similarity between them. The reason for this is that the *Euclidean* distance has an opposite relation to similarity.

In this step, the fraudster's instances are placed in several clusters, and for each fraud cluster, a separated pattern is provided, and then in the next step, for each pattern, one classifier is learned with the OCSVM classification method that is the indicator of that pattern in detecting fraud. In fact, through the clustering process, several patterns representing a group of instances can be identified, and then, in the classification step (the sixth step in the proposed *FDiBC* method shown

in Figure 2), a classifier is learned for each cluster, and the fraud detection is performed through voting among these classifiers.

So far, several methods have been offered for data clustering such as *K-means, K-mediods*, which have been studied in [18]. Among the introduced clustering methods, the evolutionary clustering methods show higher precisions than the others. For this reason, these kinds of methods are used in the proposed *FDiBC* method. Meanwhile, in *FDiBC*, we require an algorithm for clustering, in which there is no need to determine k (number of clusters) before performing clustering. Therefore, the clustering methods should be used to determine the optimal value of k automatically. One of the new methods of clustering based on the PSO (*Particle Swarm Optimization*) algorithm is called the CPSOII algorithm [19]. The cause of using the CPSOII algorithm in the proposed *FDiBC* method for clustering fraudster's data is the high precision of this algorithm, and evaluation presented in [19] revealed that the CPSOII algorithm outperforms the classical clustering methods such as *K-means* and the evolutionary clustering methods such as GA. Another reason for choosing the CPSOII algorithm in *FDiBC* is that this algorithm is able to find the optimal number of clusters automatically. The important point to be noted in this section is that clustering is only applied to the fraudster's data belonging to the training dataset and the common customer's data is not involved in the process of clustering.

3.6. Classification

In order to detect fraud from the training dataset, some classifiers are learned. A classifier is a model through which the label of new data (test dataset) can be predicted. In the proposed *FDiBC* method, the two binary and multi-class classification methods are used. The output of the fraudster's data clustering was delivered to the binary OCSVM classification method (sixth step in the proposed *FDiBC* method, according to Figure 2). The OCSVM classification does not need any data with -1 label for learning a classifier but it can learn the classifier using data with +1 label. In the multi-class classification methods (seventh step in *FDiBC*, according to Figure 2), all instances of the training dataset are used; and the instances with +1 labels are used for fraudster customers, and -1 for common customers. After learning these classifiers, in the eighth step of the proposed *FDiBC* method, according to figure 2, each instance of the test dataset is given to all classifiers and their opinions are asked, and then it is compared with its real label, and finally, the performance of each classifier is evaluated. The point to be noted is that so far, several classification methods have been provided; however, it cannot be concluded that a particular method is the best for classification. In order to find out the best classification method in any area, different methods should be evaluated. Therefore, in the current study, the SVM, KNN, C4.5, Naïve Bayes, and OCSVM classification methods were employed, and one of the innovations of this paper is to identify the best classification method for the fraud detection.

4. FDiBC evaluation

In order to evaluate the proposed *FDiBC* method, 20388 instance scores during three years registered in the customers' club system of Saman Bank as a case study. These scores belonged to 2292 customers of the customer's club, 112 of which have committed fraud with 1933 score instances. Therefore, the scores of fraudster customers have been considered as +1 label, and -1 label have been used for common customers.

Figure 6 shows the score frequencies of the club system case study including the number of customers with i scores and the total number of instance scores. As shown in figure 6, the number of scores for each customer in this case study is in the range of [1, 31].

In the first step of the proposed *FDiBC* method, some filters introduced in the pre-processing section have been applied to the collected data of the case study, and the number of instances of this data have been declined from 20388 to 19823 scores. This process in the first step of *FDiBC* has considered 565 instances as noise or outlier instances, and removed.

After removing the noise and outlier instances, in the second step of the *FDiBC*, five proposed vectors including *SSW* with default window size equaled to 4, one-day *STW*, one-week *STW*, one-month *STW*, and hybrid *STW* are generated.

In the third step of the proposed *FDiBC* method, we used the ten-fold cross-validation procedure

[20] to evaluate the performance of each classifier. In order to evaluate the clustering step of the proposed *FDiBC* method, the CPSOII algorithm with parameters of "number of particles" equaled 100, and the "maximum number of iterations" equaled 2500 have been applied on the fraudster instances belonging to the training dataset. Other parameters of the CPSOII algorithm have been supposed according to [19]. As for applying the CPSOII algorithm in the proposed *FDiBC* method, the important point is the function to be regarded from the provided functions of clustering fitness. So far, three fitness functions including 1) The sum of the squared errors (SSE), 2) Variance Rate Criterion (VRC), and 3) DBI Criterion have been used in the literature of clustering methods. Among these three methods, using the DBI criterion is suggested for automatically detecting the number of proper clusters. That is why in this paper, the CPSOII algorithm uses the DBI criterion as its fitness function. As mentioned earlier, five feature vectors including 1) *SSW* with the default window size equal to 4, 2) one-day *STW*, 3) one-week *STW*, 4) one-month *STW*, and 5) hybrid *STW* are used. Therefore, the application of the CPSOII algorithm over these five feature vectors leads to identify 5, 8, 7, 3, and 8 distinct clusters for *SSW*, one-day *STW*, one-week *STW*, one-month *STW*, and hybrid *STW*, respectively. It should be noted that the CPSOII algorithm has automatically achieved these results and converged into them; besides, the number of minimum clusters and the number of maximum clusters have been used, respectively, equal to 2 and the total number of instances. The results obtained by the CPSOII algorithm from the clustering of the fraudster instances equal to 0.58, 0.66, 0.47, 0.51, and 0.59 based on the DBI criterion for *SSW*, one-day *STW*, one-week *STW*, one-month *STW*, and one hybrid *STW*, respectively.

In the CPSOII algorithm, the *K-means* algorithm can be used in producing the primary population of particles as guided initialization. In figure 7, the convergence of the CPSOII algorithm for clustering of the fraudsters instances with a week *STW* feature vector have been illustrated for both modes including *guided & unguided* initialization (with *K-means* algorithm) and unguided initialization (without *K-means* algorithm).

In figure 7, the CPSOII algorithm has been implemented with *K-means* algorithm and without it, and the results, as it was expected, reveal that using *K-means* algorithm in the CPSOII algorithm leads to increase in the velocity of convergence; however, it has no impact on its precision.

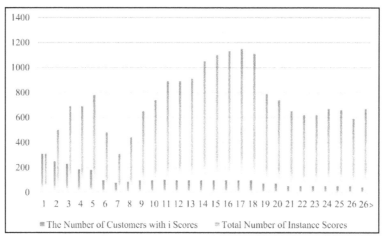

Figure 6. Score frequencies of Saman Bank club system.

Therefore, the CPSOII algorithm can identify the best or approximated to the best clusters without using the *K-means* algorithm. It should be noted that the average time of performing the CPSOII algorithm by a computer with Ci7 and main memory of 4 gigabyte is 6 minutes and 29 seconds, which can be regarded as a desirable time for pre-processing.

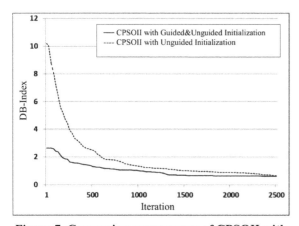

Figure 7. Comparing convergence of CPSOII with Guided & Unguided initialization toward qualified solutions (using DBI criterion) for a week STW feature vector.

In the sixth step of the proposed *FDiBC* method, a classifier is learned with the OCSVM method for each identified cluster in the fifth step. After learning, these classifiers (including 5, 8, 7, 3, and 8 distinct clusters for *SSW,* one-day *STW,* one-week *STW,* one-month *STW,* and hybrid *STW,* respectively) would be evaluated by the test dataset (including 5947 instances), which, in turn, were selected in the third step of *FDiBC* (according to Figure 2). Moreover, in the seventh step of *FDiBC,* for the training dataset, four classifiers are learned using four multi-class classifiers methods including the SVM, KNN, C4.5, and Naïve Bayes methods for five feature vectors proposed by *FDiBC* in Section 2. After

learning these four classifiers for each feature vector, the test dataset (including 5947 instances), chosen in the third step of the proposed *FDiBC* method (according to Figure 2) are evaluated. The precision, recall, and accuracy criteria [20] have been employed to examine the performance of the proposed *FDiBC* method. These criteria are calculated using the results of classifiers on the test dataset. These three criteria have been defined in (2)-(4).

$$Precision = \frac{TP}{TP + FP} \tag{2}$$

$$Recall = \frac{TP}{TP + FN} \tag{3}$$

$$Accuracy = \frac{TP + TN}{TP + FP + FN + TN} \tag{4}$$

In these equations, *TP* (True Positive) means the number of fraudster instances, which is properly predicated as the fraudster label by classifiers. *FP* (False Positive) indicated the number of fraudster instances; however, they are predicated as the common customer label erroneously. *FN* (False Negative) indicated that the number of common customer instances is wrongly predicated as fraudsters. *TN* (True Negative) includes the number of common customer instances, which is predicated correctly as the common customer label. The results of evaluation of the learned classifiers are shown in figure 8 with five classification methods and five different feature vectors. As illustrated in this figure, among the five classification methods, the OCSVM classification method with the CPSOII clustering algorithm obtains the best results based on the precision, recall, and accuracy criteria, i.e. 0.79, 0.77, and 0.78, respectively. These results revealed that the hybrid of the clustering method with the classification method was able to learn classifiers efficiently according to the precision, recall, and accuracy criteria. From this evaluation, it can be concluded that using the clustering method for detecting the hidden patterns in the fraudster's data, the degree of classification method detection can be increased. Regarding the results achieved, shown in figure 8, the one-week *STW* feature vector outperforms the other four feature vectors. After all, the hybrid *STW* feature vector has better results in comparison with the other three feature vectors. These results reveal that considering the data of only current day, the results of fraud detection are not as good as the data of current week. In addition, the results of the aggregation of scores of one month are worse than the aggregation of scores of the current week. However, the results of hybrid *STW* feature vectors are better than one-day and one-month *STW* feature vectors. From this evaluation, it can be concluded that using the data of the current week of customer scores for detecting fraudster customer outperforms other four proposed feature vectors.

As it can be noted in Section 3.2, the size of sliding scores window (*SSW*) has an effective role on the efficiency of this feature vector; therefore, for the size of windows with 1 to 30 lengths, the values of accuracy criterion for the five classification methods are illustrated in figure 9. In this figure, only the accuracy criterion is taken into consideration, and as we can see, when the size of window is equal to 11, all the five classification methods provide the most efficiency and obtain the highest value of accuracy criterion.

Note that financial fraud in bank club system is an illegal action in which a customer achieves a score without deserving it. For instance, if we assumed that scores of remaining balance of customer account are calculated at 12:00 a.m, a fraudster can deposit 1,000,000 Rial to his account at 11:00 p.m., and after his scores are calculated, he withdraws all of the remaining balance of his account at 1:00 a.m. In fact, he can repeat these actions all midnights and achieve undeserved scores.

As mentioned earlier, using CPSOII, clustering algorithm in the proposed *FDiBC* method leads to increase in accuracy. Therefore, we investigate manually the clusters of fraudsters obtained by the CPSOII algorithm. Following on from what is said earlier, for six clusters detected by CPSOII in the fifth step of *FDiBC*, six patterns of fraud are mentioned:

1. *Obtaining scores through inviting friends (Cluster 1):*
   Regarding the fact that customers can get scores through inviting friends, the evaluation results in this section reveal that it is possible for customers of a bank club system to obtain scores via sending several invitation letters to fake e-mails. After detecting this fraud by the *FDiBC* method, in order to avoid this from happening, the inviter customer should obtain scores, whenever the invited member registers his/hers first bank card in the bank club system.

2. *Obtaining scores based on bank transactions (Cluster 2):*
   Customers can achieve scores on the basis of the amount of the transactions of the registered cards in the bank club system. According to the evaluation results in this section, some customers can obtain scores on the basis of different very low amount of transactions. After detecting this fraud by the *FDiBC* method, in order to avoid this from happening, giving scores on transaction basis should prevent by applying limitation on the amount of transaction at transaction registration time and at the time of registering the pattern of giving score on the transaction basis.

3. *Obtaining scores based on purchasing through POS (Cluster 3):*
   Based upon purchasing through POS, customers can obtain scores. According to investigations, customers having POS system can perform several transactions as purchase regulating their account on POS. These transactions are transferring money from his/her account to someone else's account. For this reason, after detecting this type of fraud by the *FDiBC* method, it is required to have a bank club alarm system, in which the information about how customers obtain score is examined, and if there is any fraud possibility, it will inform.

4. *Obtaining scores based on remaining balance of customer account (Cluster 4):*
   Customers can obtain scores on the basis of the remaining amount in their accounts. According to investigations, customers can obtain scores withdrawing from their accounts during day and completing their balance at the end of day (the system calculates customer scores during night and once a day). In order to prevent this fraud, after detecting this type of fraud via the *FDiBC* method, scores will be calculated on the basis of the minimum balance of every day or using data of more than one day to fraud detection like one-week *STW* feature vector.

5. *Obtaining scores based on registering bank cards (Cluster 5):*

Customers can obtain scores on the basis of registering their cards. Based on the investigations, if customers can register gift card, they can obtain scores without creating any added value to the bank.

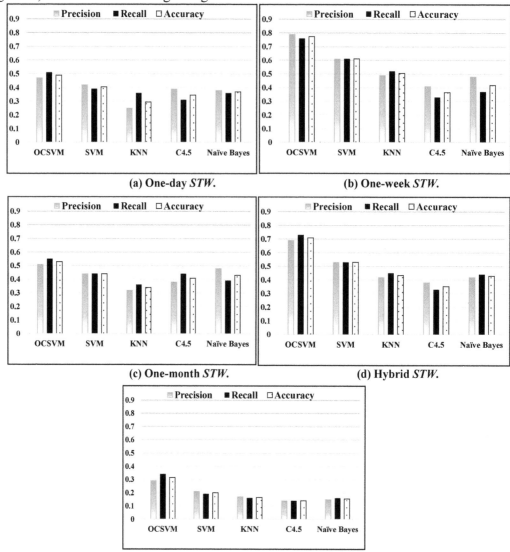

(a) One-day *STW*.

(b) One-week *STW*.

(c) One-month *STW*.

(d) Hybrid *STW*.

(e) *SSW* with its window size equaled to 4

Figure 8. Results of evaluating different classification methods with different feature vectors.

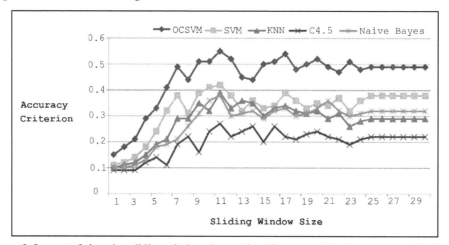

Figure 9. Impact of changing sliding window size on classifiers according to accuracy criterion.

For this purpose, after detecting this type of fraud through the *FDiBC* method, registration of this kind of cards have been prohibited in the customers' club system. In addition, each customer member can register at most 10 cards (according to the investigations) in his/her user account in order to prevent fraud based on the card registration except his/her own cards.

6. *Obtaining scores based on transactions of bill payment (Cluster 6):*
Customers can obtain scores through bank POS by paying bills. According to the investigations on the processes of bill payment of some customers, the following frauds are detected:
A- Creating different bills based on the formula of bill can identify with recognize from a major bill.
B- Paying the bills of people who are not members of the bank club. Oftentimes, corporations offering bank services adopt this technique to commit fraud.

After detecting this kind of fraud through the proposed *FDiBC* method, a number of measures have been done to restrict every individual in paying bills.

As mentioned in the Introduction Section, there is no research work in which authors considered the fraud happened in bank club systems. However, the similar approach to *FDiBC* is Duman et al. [13] work. In [13], for each transaction, a score is given, and based upon this score, transactions are classified into legal or illegal. Indeed, in [13], each score has a label, and the classification process is applied on each score. Therefore, to compare *FDiBC* with the idea presented in [13], we assigned a label to 14 features obtained by each customer's score, and the results of five used classification methods are illustrated in figure 10.

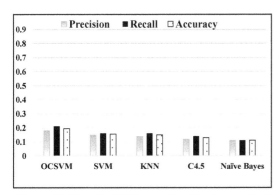

Figure 10. Results of different classification method evaluations with feature vector creating by 14 features mentioned in table 1.

As shown in this figure, as it is expected, the results of 14 features obtained by each customer's score is very poor. The reason for this case is that in bank club systems, a fraud usually happens by a

sequence of scores, and one score alone cannot show a fraud.

5. Limitation
In the course of experiments during the evaluation, a number of limitations of FDiBC are apparent. First, employing an evolutionary search algorithm, i.e. the CPSOII algorithm for clustering, leads to an increase in complexity, particularly time complexity. In addition, when FDiBC calculates the STW and SWW feature vectors, the run-time of the FDiBC algorithm is greatly increased. Of course, we can assume that such systems could be optimized without concern for real-time performance because the systems could be run offline. Therefore, it seems likely that the run-time of the FDiBC algorithm is tolerable. Finally, as the clustering is a type of NP-complete problem [20], therefore, like the other existing methods, the FDiBC algorithm cannot guarantee to achieve an optimal solution. However, instead of the use of simple heuristics like K-means, FDiBC uses a powerful search-based algorithm, i.e. the CPSOII algorithm, as a crucial alternative to solve NP complete optimization problems [20]. As shown in figure 7, CPSOII outperforms the other heuristics methods like K-means according to DBI metric.

6. Conclusion
Fraud detection in the customer club system is one of the new challenges in the banking industry. In this paper, a novel sliding time and scores window-based method, called *FDiBC (Fraud Detection in Bank Club)*, was proposed to detect fraud in bank club. In *FDiBC*, two models of feature vectors including time window-based, i.e. one-day *STW*, one-week *STW*, one-month *STW*, and hybrid *STW*, and scores window-based, i.e. *SSW*, were proposed for detecting fraud. Additionally, the dataset was divided into the training and test sets. The training dataset was learned through two approaches: 1) clustering with the CPSOII algorithm and classifying with the OCSVM binary classification method, and 2) classifying with multi-class SVM, C4.5, KNN, and Naïve Bayes classification methods. At the end, the learned classifiers were evaluated using the test dataset. The evaluation results presented in Section 4 of this paper revealed that out of the two approaches of the binary classification with clustering and multi-class classification, the binary classification with clustering provided more efficiency. Moreover, among the five proposed feature vectors, the evaluation results presented in Section 4 revealed that the one-week

STW feature vector outperformed the other four feature vectors. Meanwhile, the scores window size was more effective in the precision of the proposed *SSW* feature vector, and therefore, by changing this value and evaluating the results, the best value of the scores window size was 11.

Finally, evaluation of the proposed *FDiBC* method suggested that using the CPSOII clustering with the OCSVM classification method along with one-week *STW* feature vector detected financial fraud with an accuracy criterion equal to 0.78%. Applying *FDiBC* on the used dataset leads that six patterns of fraud are detected (see Section 4). Note that these patterns of fraud can be helpful for administration users of bank club systems to prepare solutions to deal with the problem.

For future works, we intend to use other classification methods to improve the performance of learning rate. In addition, we are going to propose a bank club alarm system like an IPS (*Intrusion Prevention System*) as a preventive measure against fraud and employ the proposed method in other banking areas [21].

References

[1] European Central Banking, (2014), Third Report on Card Fraud, https://www.ecb.europa.eu/pub/pdf/other/cardfraudreport201402en.pdf

[2] Han, J., Kamber, M., & Pei, J. (2011). Data mining: concepts and techniques: concepts and techniques. Elsevier.

[3] Homayounfar, E., Sepehri, M. M., Hasheminejad, S. M. H., & Ghobakhloo, M. (2014). Designing a chronological based framework for condition monitoring in heart disease patients-a data mining approach (DM-PTTD). Iranian Journal of Medical Informatics, vol. 3, no. 3, pp. 1-6.

[4] Sebastiani, F. (2002). Machine learning in automated text categorization. ACM computing surveys (CSUR), vol. 34, no. 1, pp. 1-47.

[5] Hasheminejad, S. M. H., & Jalili, S. (2013). SCI-GA: Software Component Identification using Genetic Algorithm. Journal of Object Technology, vol. 12, no. 2, pp. 1-35.

[6] Hasheminejad, S. M. H., & Jalili, S. (2014). An evolutionary approach to identify logical components. Journal of Systems and Software, vol. 96, pp. 24-50.

[7] Hasheminejad, S. M. H., & Jalili, S. (2015). CCIC: Clustering analysis classes to identify software components. Information and Software Technology, vol. 57, pp. 329-351.

[8] Hasheminejad, S. M. H., & Jalili, S. (2009). Selecting proper security patterns using text classification. In Computational Intelligence and Software Engineering, CiSE International Conference on IEEE, pp. 1-5.

[9] Hasheminejad, S. M. H., & Jalili, S. (2012). Design patterns selection: An automatic two-phase method. Journal of Systems and Software, vol. 85, no. 2, pp. 408-424.

[10] West, J., & Bhattacharya, M. (2016). Intelligent financial fraud detection: A comprehensive review. Computers & Security, vol. 57, pp. 47-66.

[11] Syeda, M., Zhang, Y. Q., & Pan, Y. (2002). Parallel granular neural networks for fast credit card fraud detection. In Fuzzy Systems, 2002. FUZZ-IEEE'02. Proceedings of the 2002 IEEE International Conference on IEEE (Vol. 1, pp. 572-577).

[12] Phua, C., Lee, V., Smith, K., & Gayler, R. (2010). A comprehensive survey of data mining-based fraud detection research. arXiv preprint arXiv:1009.6119.

[13] Duman, E., & Ozcelik, M. H. (2011). Detecting credit card fraud by genetic algorithm and scatter search. Expert Systems with Applications, vol. 38, no. 10, pp. 13057-13063.

[14] Gill, N. S., & Gupta, R. (2012). Analysis of Data Mining Techniques for Detection of Financial Statement Fraud. The IUP Journal of Systems Management, vol. 10, no. 1, pp. 7-15.

[15] Kumari, N., Kannan, S., & Muthukumaravel, A. (2014). Credit Card Fraud Detection Using Hidden Markov Model-A Survey. Middle-East Journal of Scientific Research, vol. 19, no. 6, pp. 821-825.

[16] Hall, M., Frank, E., Holmes, G., Pfahringer, B., Reutemann, P., & Witten, I. H. (2009). The WEKA data mining software: an update. ACM SIGKDD explorations newsletter, vol. 11, no. 1, pp. 10-18.

[17] WEKA, RemoveMisclassified, (2017), http://weka.sourceforge.net/doc.dev/weka/filters/unsupervised/instance/RemoveMisclassified.html.

[18] Hruschka, E. R., Campello, R. J., Freitas, A., & De Carvalho, A. C. (2009). A survey of evolutionary algorithms for clustering. Systems, Man, and Cybernetics, Part C: Applications and Reviews, IEEE Transactions on, vol. 39, no. 2, pp. 133-155.

[19] Masoud, H., Jalili, S., & Hasheminejad, S. M. H. (2013). Dynamic clustering using combinatorial particle swarm optimization. Applied intelligence, vol. 38, no. 3, pp. 289-314.

[20] Alpaydin, E. (2014). Introduction to machine learning. MIT press.

[21] Siami, M., & Hajimohammadi, Z. (2013). Credit scoring in banks and financial institutions via data mining techniques: A literature review. Journal of AI and Data Mining, vol. 1, no. 2, pp. 119-129.

6

Automatic Optic Disc Center and Boundary Detection in Color Fundus Images

F. Abdali-Mohammadi[1*] and A. Poorshamam[2]

1. Faculty of Engineering, Department of Computer Engineering & Information Technology, Razi University, Kermanshah, Iran.

2. Faculty of Basic Science, Department of Mathematic. Razi University, Kermanshah, Iran.

*Corresponding author: fardin.abdali@razi.ac.ir (F. Abdali-Mohammadi).

Abstract

Accurate detection of retinal landmarks like the optic disc is an important step in computer-aided diagnosis frameworks. This paper presents an efficient method for the automatic detection of the optic disc center and estimating its boundary. The center and initial diameter of the optic disc are estimated by employing an artificial neural network (ANN) classifier, which employs the visual features of vessels and their background tissue to classify the extracted main vessels of retina into two groups: vessels inside the optic disc and vessels outside optic disc. To this end, the average intensity values and standard deviation of RGB channels, the average width and orientation of the vessels, and density of the detected vessels and their junction points in a window around each central pixel of main vessels are employed. The center of the detected vessels, which belong to the inside of the optic disc region, is adopted as the optic disc center, and their average lengths in the vertical and horizontal directions are selected as the initial diameter of the optic disc circle. Then the exact boundary of the optic disc is extracted using the radial analysis of the initial circle. The performance of the proposed method is measured on the publicly available DRIONS, DRIVE, and DIARETDB1 databases, and compared with several state-of-the-art methods. The proposed method shows a much higher mean overlap (70.6%) in the same range of detection accuracy (97.7%) and center distance (12 pixels). The average sensitivity and predictive values of the proposed optic disc detection method are 80.3% and 84.6%, respectively.

Keywords: Retinal Image Segmentation, Optic Disc Center Detection, Optic Disc Border Estimation.

1. Introduction

The eye and retinal diseases such as diabetic retinopathy, occlusion, and glaucoma are the major causes of blindness in the developed and developing countries. The detection and quantitative measurement of different parts of retina such as blood vessels, optic disc, and fovea, is an important step in the computer-aided diagnosis of these diseases. Manual or semi-automatic detection of retinal landmarks is labor-intensive and time-consuming, especially in a large database of retinal images. Thus the development of automatic methods for robust detection of these landmarks is valuable. In the literature, several techniques have been reported for detecting and analyzing retinal landmarks like blood vessels [1-8], fovea [9, 10], and optic disc [11-34].

The optic disc is an important landmark for registering changes within the optic disc region due to a retinal disease. The changes in the shape, color or depth of the optic disc are used to measure abnormal features due to certain retinopathies such as glaucoma and diabetic retinopathies [4, 10-12]. It can also be used for detecting other anatomical components like fovea [14, 15]. This region has different properties, and in the literature, several methods attempt to employ one or more characterizations of it to estimate the location of the optic disc region. The optic disc is usually the brightest component on the fundus images, and therefore, a set of high-intensity pixels can be identified as the optic disc location [16-19]. The application of threshold to intensity values may work well unless there are other high-intensity components such as exudates and lesion regions.

Another feature that can be used to detect the optic disc is the intensity variation in this region because of dark blood vessels beside the bright nerve fibers [15, 16]. However, this method often fails when a large number of white lesions or light arti-facts exist in the fundus images.

Since the vessels are originated from the center of the optic disc, some methods have tried to find the strongest vessel network convergence as the primary feature for detection of the optic disc. The center of the optic disc can be estimated as the convergence point of vessels [20, 21].

The direction of vessels in the optic disc is another feature of this region that has been used to estimate the location of the optic disc [22, 23]. Since the directions of the main vessels inside the optic disc are vertical, Youssif et al. [22] have proposed the directional matched filter to highlight this feature of the optic disc region. The center of the optic disc is estimated as a point with the highest response to the directional matched filter.

Other techniques such as principal component analysis (PCA) [24], texture descriptor [25], Radon transform [26], and morphological operations [24, 27, 28] have also been used to estimate the location of the optic disc.

Some methods have tried to employ the complex feature vector obtained from the vessel network and background of the optic disc region to classify all pixels of the input image into two groups: optic disc region and non-optic disc region [29-34].

Also the optic disc boundary has been extracted by employing different techniques such as fixed circle [15], active contour models [19], genetic algorithm [18], and watershed transform [21].

In this paper, an efficient method is presented for automatic extraction of the optic disc location and boundary. To this end, the visual characteristics of the optic disc region are employed to distinguish the main vessels inside the optic disc using the artificial neural network (ANN) classifier. The center of detected vessels is adopted as the center of optic disc, and an average length of detected vessels in horizontal and vertical directions is used as the initial diameter of the optic disc circle. The precise location of the optic disc boundary is determined using the radial analysis of this circle.

The rest of this paper is organized as what follows. The proposed method for an efficient optic disc detection is presented in section 2. Experimental results are reported in section 3. Finally, conclusion is given in section 4.

2. Proposed Optic Disc Detection method

In the fundus images, as shown in figure 1, the optic disc is known as a high intensity or yellowish region. It is the entrance point of the blood vessels and optic nerves. The occurrence of the dark blood vessels beside the light optic nerves also causes a relatively rapid variation in the intensity of this region. The thickness of the blood vessels gradually reduces when distant from the optic disc center. The main blood vessels split into smaller branches, and spread out to the whole retinal surface for delivering and receiving blood supplies in the capillary system. Some of these features have been employed in the literature for localization of the optic disc. To perform robust optic disc detection, one should employ all of these features, especially in abnormal cases.

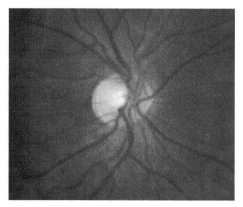

Figure 1. Color fundus image.

This paper presents a supervised method for the automatic detection of the optic disc region. To increase the reliability of detection of the optic disc center and boundary, we limited the search process to the centerline of the detected main vessels in the retinal images. By employing this limitation, not only the white lesion regions can be neglected from the list of optic disc candidates but also the speed of the search process can be increased. At first, the main vessels of retina are detected, and for each vessel point, all characteristics of the vessels and their background tissue are extracted as a feature vector. Then by employing the ANN classifier, all the detected vessel points will be classified into two classes: inside the optic disc (IOD) and outside the optic disc (OOD) vessels. Finally, the center of the IOD vessels is selected as the optic disc center and the average length of the IOD vessels in horizontal and vertical directions is used as the initial diameter of the optic disc circle. Then the precise location of the optic disc boundary is determined using the radial analysis of this circle. The flowchart of the proposed method is shown in figure. 2.

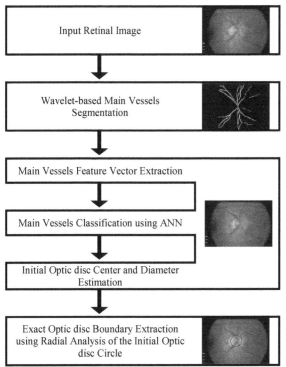

Figure 2. Flowchart of proposed method for automatic detection of center and boundary of optic disc.

2.1. Main vessels segmentation

To extract the main blood vessels, we employed a multi-resolution analyzing technique based on continuous wavelet transform [3]. In this method, complex Morlet was used as the analyzing wavelet to enhance the Gaussian-shaped line structures (vessel structures) and separate them from other non-vessel edges like edges of red lesions and bright blobs. The final vessel network is extracted by applying an adaptive thresholding process. The basic threshold value (TB) was obtained by analyzing the cumulative density function (CDF) obtained from the histogram of the vesselness values (real part of complex Morlet coefficients). Since the average ratio of all the thin and thick vessel pixels in the retinal images is less than 15% [3], and also to detect the optic disc, thick vessels are sufficient, we set the basic threshold value such that its value was equal to 90% of the existing vesselness values:

$$T_B = \arg_j \{\text{CDF(j)} = 0.90\} \qquad (1)$$

The imaginary part of the complex Morlet coefficient in each pixel is added to the basic threshold value in order to penalize the edge-shaped points. After applying an adaptive thresholding procedure, a proper length filter is also applied to the result obtained to eliminate small regions. (For more details, refer to Ref. [3].) An example of the different steps involved in the segmentation phase is shown in figure 3.

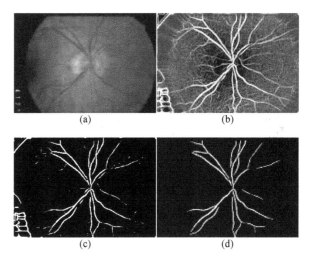

Figure 3. Results obtained in vessel segmentation phase. a) Original fundus image. b) Enhanced vessels using wavelet-based technique. c) Results of applying adaptive thresholding. d) Final detected main vessels.

2.2. Main vessels feature vector extraction

To calculate different features from vessels, we introduced a simplified variation of the local vessel pattern operator [35] and applied it to the center line of the detected main vessels. The simple local vessel pattern (SLVP) operator is defined using N equally-spaced points ($P_R(i)$ for i = 0 to $N-1$) on a circle with radius R, which is centered at the centerline pixel (x_c, y_c) of the detected vessels (I):

$$P_R(i) = I([x_c - R\sin(2\pi i / N)], [y_c + R\cos(2\pi i / N)]) \qquad (2)$$

The coordinate of each point is rounded ([.]) so that its position exactly falls into the center of a pixel. Therefore, the value of each point $P_R(i)$ is equal to "1" if it falls on the vessel points and "0" otherwise. The number of points (N) in SLVP is set to the number of pixels existing in the perimeter of the corresponding circle ($\lceil N = 2\pi R \rceil$). Also the radius of the circle is adopted such that the SLVP obtained can describe the certain features of all vessel structures. Since in the retinal images with their size of about 565 × 584 pixels (DRIVE datasets [36]) the maximum width of blood vessels (W_X) is less than 10 pixels, we set the value for radius R to 15 pixels in order to span all vessel widths. For other datasets that have a large difference to this size, this radius should be set based on its maximum width of vessels plus five ($R = W_X + 5$). Another choice is employing the resizing algorithm to resize the images to about 565 × 584 pixels (size of images in the DRIVE dataset).

By analyzing the obtained circular structure of the SLVP operator, different features of vessel points such as vessel width (V_w), vessel orientation (V_θ), and vessel junctions (J_V) can be extracted. The type of each vessel point can be determined using the number of vessel ends (V_E) that intersect with the perimeter of the corresponding circle. Each vessel end consists of one transition from 0 to 1, several 1s, and one transition from 1 to 0. Therefore, half of the number of transitions from 0 to 1 or vice versa can be used as the number of vessel ends (V_E), as below:

$$V_E = \frac{1}{2}\left(|P_R(N-1)-P_R(0)| + \sum_{i=0}^{N-2}|P_R(i)-P_R(i+1)| \right) \qquad (3)$$

Therefore, the type of current point can be determined as one of these cases based on the value of V_E:
- If $V_E \leq 2$, the current point is simple or end vessel point.
- If $V_E > 2$, the current point is a junction (bifurcation or cross-over) point.

Also the width (V_w) and orientation (V_θ) of vessel can be estimated as below:

$$V_w = 2R \times \sin(\frac{\pi N_v}{N})$$
$$V_\theta = \frac{(POFO + N_v/2) \times 2\pi}{N} \mod \pi \qquad (4)$$

where, R is the radius of the circular structure and N is the number of all points in the circular structure. Also $POFO$ is the position of the first point with value "1" from the beginning of the obtained circular structure and N_v is the average number of vessel points in the vessel ends. Therefore, the value for N_v should be calculated from the number of all vessel points existing in the circular structure divided by the number of vessel ends:

$$N_v = (\sum_{i=0}^{N-1}P_R(i))/V_E \qquad (5)$$

An example of extracting $SLVP$ for $R = 15$ and $N = 96$ (P_{15}) and the details of estimating $POFO$ and N_v are also illustrated in figure 4.

To detect the IOD vessels, all visual characteristics of the vessels and their background tissue are employed as a feature vector. To increase the reliability of the measured features, all features are calculated in a 70 × 70 window (W) centered at each point (x, y) in the centerline of the detected main vessels. Then the following set of features is measured:

1) Average intensity value in the window W for red (I_R), green (I_G), and blue (I_B) channels of the colored retinal image (Im):

$$I_C = \sum_{x,y\in W}\text{Im}(x,y,C)/|W| \quad for \ C \in \{R,G,B\} \qquad (6)$$

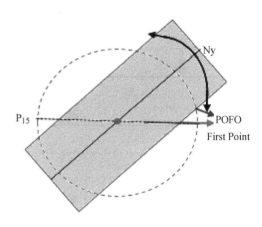

Figure 4. An example of extracting local vessel pattern for $R = 15$ and $N = 96$ and estimation of $POFO$ and N_v. Value of white circle is one (for vessel points) and black circle is zero (for non-vessel points).

where, |W| is the number of points in the window W.

2) Standard deviation of intensity value in the window W for red (S_R), green (S_G) and blue (S_B) channels of colored retinal image (Im):

$$S_C = \sqrt{(\sum_{x,y\in W}(\text{Im}(x,y,C)-I_C)^2)/|W|} \quad for \ C \in \{R,G,B\} \qquad (7)$$

3) Average width of the vessels in the window W:

$$A_w = (\sum_{x,y\in W}V_w(x,y))/|N_V^W| \qquad (8)$$

where, $|N_V^W|$ is the number of vessel centerline points in the window W.

4) Average orientation of the vessels in the window W:

$$A_\theta = (\sum_{x,y\in W}V_\theta(x,y))/|N_V^W| \qquad (9)$$

5) Density of the detected vessels (V) in the window W:

$$D_V = (\sum_{x,y\in W}V(x,y))/|W| \qquad (10)$$

6) Density of junction points (J_V) of vessels in the window W:

$$D_J = (\sum_{x,y\in W}J_V(x,y))/|N_V^W| \qquad (11)$$

2.3. Initial optic disc circle extraction

To increase the reliability of detection of the optic disc center and boundary, we limited the search process to the centerline of the main vessels in the retinal images. To separate the vessels inside the optic disc from the other main vessels, all visual characteristics of the vessels and their background tissue were extracted as a feature vector ($\vec{F}$) for each centerline point of the main vessels:

$$\vec{F} = \{I_R, I_G, I_B, S_R, S_G, S_B, A_\theta, A_w, D_V, D_J\} \qquad (12)$$

Then the extracted feature vectors for all centerline points were applied to a fully connected multi-layer perceptron ANN to be applied to a fully connected multi-layer perceptron to estimate their similarity to the IOD or OOD vessels. This ANN had 10 input neurons, 7 hidden neurons, and one output neuron. The ANN output indicated the similarity of the input feature vector to the IOD vessels (S_{IOD}) and in the range of 0 to 1. The values near 1 were related to the IOD vessels, and those near 0 were related to the OOD vessels. The structure of the proposed ANN is shown in figure 5.

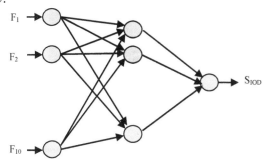

Figure 5. Structure of employed ANN to estimate similarity of main vessel to IOD vessels. Input F_k is k^{th} element of extracted feature vector corresponding to main vessel point, and S_{IOD} is similarity value of this vessel point to inside of optic disc vessels.

After estimating the similarity of all points on the centerline of main vessels to the IOD vessels by the proposed ANN, the points with S_{IOD} values greater than 0.5 were selected as the IOD vessel candidates. Then the morphological closing operator (using disk structure element with radius of 20 pixels) was applied to the IOD candidates to connect the near disjointed candidates. The biggest set of candidates was selected as the IOD vessels.

Finally, the center of detected IOD vessels was selected as the optic disc center, and the average length of IOD vessels in the horizontal and vertical directions was used as the diameter of the initial optic disc circle. The details of these steps are given in figure 6.

2.4. Exact optic disc boundary detection using radial analysis

Since the intensity of the optic disc region is very high, and it can be more visible in the red channel, this channel was selected for further processing (see Figures 7a-7c). At first, the morphological

opening operator was applied to the red channel to reduce the effect of dark vessels in the optic disc region. Then the final location of the optic disc boundary was determined using the radial analysis of initial optic disc circle on the enhanced red channel. Therefore, the position of each point on the initial optic disc circle was adjusted to a new point on the radial line whose intensity was near the optic disc boundary intensity.

To this end, for each point on the initial circle perimeter (called "Initial Position"), a radial line was defined as a line that passed through the corresponding point in the direction of the initial circle radius. The length of this line was set to the length of the radius of the initial circle, and the corresponding point fell exactly at the middle of this line (one half at inside the circle and the other half at outside of it). The position of each point on the radial line was rounded to fall on a nearest pixel. On the radial line, at first, the direction of adjustment was determined. Therefore, five points starting from Initial Position toward inside were considered, and we compared their intensities with a pre-defined threshold (the average intensity of optic disc points TOD). If the intensity of all of them was greater than the threshold TOD, the direction of adjustment was set to the outside of the initial circle, and the final position of this point was adjusted to the first point whose value was lower than the threshold TOD. Otherwise (the intensity of all of them not greater than the threshold TOD), the direction of adjustment was set to the inside of the initial circle, and the final position of this point was adjusted to the first point whose value was greater than the threshold TOD. The value for threshold TOD was set to average intensity of pixels inside the initial circle on the enhanced red channel. Finally, the morphological closing operator was applied to the adjusted border to smooth the boundary and fill the small gaps that may exist in the region of vessels. The details of the proposed method are given in figure 7.

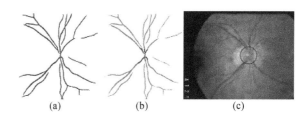

Figure 6. Results of different steps of obtaining initial optic disc circle. a) Extracted main vessel center line. b) Detected IOD vessels. c) Initial optic disc circle.

3. Experimental results

The proposed method for automatic optic disc center detection and its boundary estimation was evaluated on three publicly available databases, the DRIONS database [18], DRIVE database [36], and DIARETDB1 database [37].

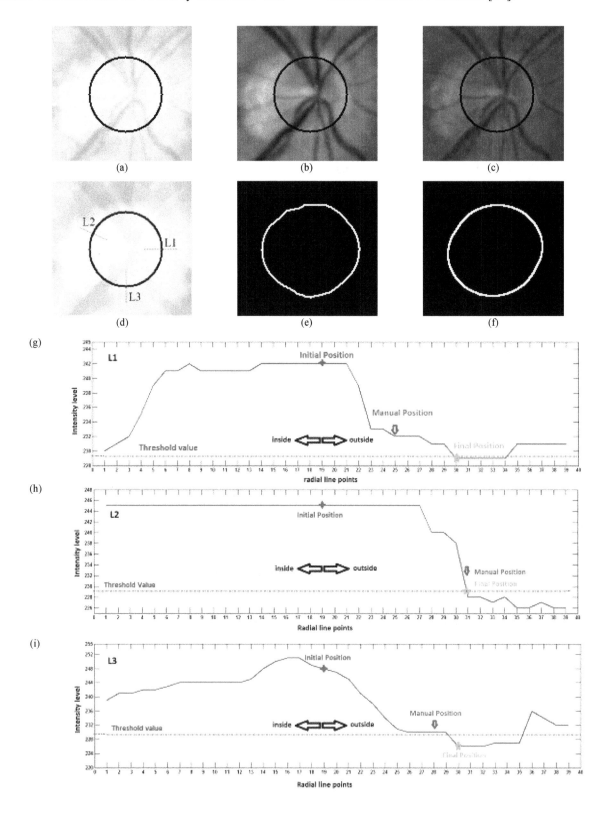

Figure 7. Details of radial analysis for adjusting border of optic disc. a) Initial optic disc circle on red channel (Initial Position). b) Initial optic disc circle on green channel. c) Initial optic disc circle on blue channel. d) Enhanced red channel for applying radial analysis method along with three radial lines L1, L2, and L3.) Finally, adjusted optic disc boundary (Final Position). f) True optic disc boundary extracted by expert (Manual Position). h-i) Details of applying radial analysis method on three radial lines L1, L2, and L3.

The DRIONS dataset consists of 110 images. This set has the same images used in Carmona et al. [18]. These images were captured in digital form using a HP-Photosmart S20 fundus camera at 45° field of view (FOV). The size of images was 600 × 400 pixels, and we used 8 bits per each color channel. Two experts manually segmented the optic disc region of all images. The union of hand-labeled images by two experts was used as ground truth.

The DRIVE database consists of 40 images along with manual segmentation of vessels. It has been divided into training and test sets, each of which containing 20 images. These images were captured in digital form using a Canon CR5 3CCD camera at 45° FOV. The size of images was 565 × 584 pixels, and 8 bits per each color channel were used. We hand-labeled the optic disc regions by one expert, and used them as ground truth.

DIARETDB1 is an image database consisting of 89 color eye fundus images along with manual detected optic disc region. The size of images is 1500 × 1152 pixels. These images were captured using a fundus camera at 50° FOV.

To evaluate the proposed method, based on the area overlap between the ground truth optic disc region and the optic disc region obtained by the proposed method, different parameters such as true positive (TP), false negative (FN), and false positive (FP) were calculated. TP is the area of the ground truth optic disc region also detected by the proposed method. FN is the area of the ground truth optic disc region that was not detected by the proposed method. FP is the area of the detected optic disc region that is outside the ground truth optic disc region, as shown in figure 8.

Using these metrics, we can obtain more meaningful performance measures like sensitivity, predictive, and overlap values, as below:

Sensitivity = TP / (TP + FN)   (13)
Predictive = TP / (TP + FP)   (14)
Overlap = TP / (TP + FP + FN)   (15)

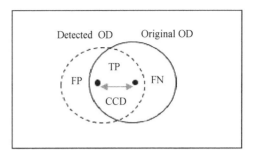

Figure 8. Areas used to estimate performance of proposed method. CDD is Euclidian distance between detected center and original center of optic disc.

Also to evaluate the performance of the optic disc detection algorithm, accuracy (ACC) and center disk distance (CDD) from the original position was used as measure. ACC is defined as the percentage of the images that the detected optic disc has overlapped with the ground truth images. CDD is also defined as the Euclidean distance between the center of the detected optic disc and the center of reference optic disc in the ground truth images.

At First, to obtain the best structure for ANN, we divided the images for the DRIONS dataset into two equal sets (each with 55 images): one set was used as the training set and the other one as the test set. We trained ANN with different numbers of nodes in the hidden layer. The training was done using the gradient decent algorithm and repeated 100 epochs for each input. This process was done when the number of hidden nodes in ANN were set to 2, 3, 4, 5, 6, 7, 8, 9, 10, 15, and 20 neurons. In each case, the performance of ANN was evaluated using the test images. The results obtained are shown in table 1. From the results obtained, the best performance was related to the case where the number of hidden nodes was set to 7 neurons. Therefore, we used this ANN in the remaining experiments.

To evaluate the proposed method on all images of the DRIONS dataset, the test and train sets were exchanged, and the performance of the proposed method was calculated again. The average of the obtained performances along with the results of Carmona et al. [18] are summarized in table 2.

Table 1. Results obtained for proposed method for different numbers of hidden neurons in ANN.

Hidden Nodes	2	3	4	5	6	7	8	9	10	15	20
ACC%	96.3	96.3	98.1	98.1	100	100	100	100	98.1	98.1	96.3
Overlap%	70.4	72.2	73.4	76.5	77.6	77.7	77.2	76.8	75.4	74.9	72.3
CDD (pixel)	14.4	13.8	12.2	11.8	10.9	8.8	10.3	11.2	12.8	13.4	13.7

From the results obtained, ACC, CDD, and overlap of the proposed method were 100%, 9 Pixels, and 76.5%, respectively. Some samples of

the results obtained for the proposed method are shown in figure 9. To compare the proposed method with some of the state-of-the-art methods, it was also applied to the DIARETDB1 database [37].

In this experiment, the previous trained ANN using DRIONS dataset was used again. Since the training and test sets are really independent, the robustness of the proposed method can also be determined.

Table 2. Obtained performance on DRIONS database.

Method	ACC%	CDD (pixel)	Overlap%
Carmona et al. [18]	96	5	-
Proposed method	100	9	76.5

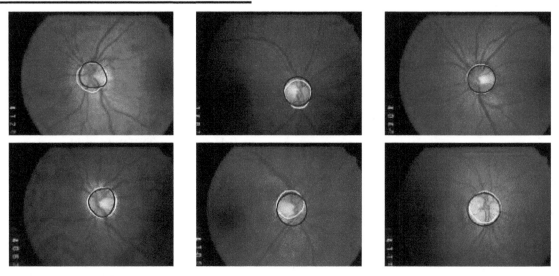

Figure 9. Results obtained for proposed method on DRIONS dataset images. Detected boundary of optic disc is shown by white curve, and ground truth is shown by black curve.

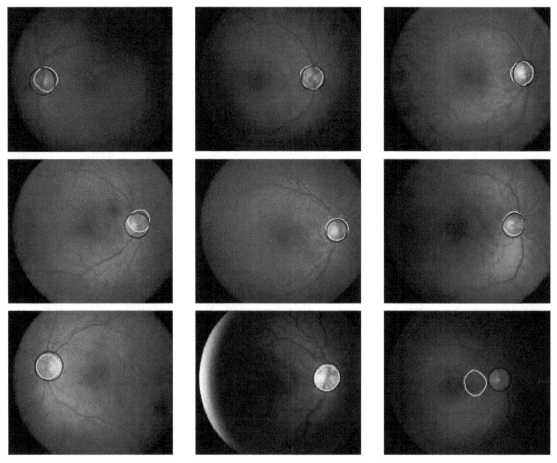

Figure 10. Results obtained for proposed method on DIARETDB1 dataset images. Detected boundary of optic disc is shown by white curve, and ground truth is shown by black curve.

Table 3. Obtained performance of all methods on DIARETDB1 database. Best values are bold.

Method	ACC%	CDD (pixel)	Overlap%	Sensitivity%	Predictive%
Walter et al. [16]	92.	15.5	37.2	65.6	93.9
Stapor et al. [17]	78.	6.0	34.1	84.9	80.3
Lupascu et al. [25]	86.	13.8	30.9	68.4	81.1
Sopharak et al. [27]	59.	16.3	29.7	46.0	95.9
Welfer et al. [28]	97.	4.9	44.5	92.5	87.6
Qureshi et al. [30]	94.	11.9	-	-	-
Proposed method	**95.**	**12.2**	**68.4**	**76.5**	**89.9**

Table 4. Obtained performance of all methods on DRIVE database. Best values are bold.

Method	ACC%	CDD (pixel)	Overlap%	Sensitivity%	Predictive%
Walter et al. [16]	77.5	12.39	30.03	49.88	86.53
Stapor et al. [17]	87.5	9.85	32.47	73.68	61.98
Youssif et al. [22]	100	17	-	-	-
Lupascu et al. [25]	95	8.05	40.35	77.68	88.14
Sopharak et al. [27]	95	20.94	17.98	21.04	93.34
Welfer et al. [28]	100	7.48	42.54	83.25	89.38
Qureshi et al. [30]	100	15.95	-	-	-
Hsiao et al. [31]	100	15	93	-	-
Ramakanth et al. [33]	100	-	-	-	-
Proposed method	**97.5**	**13.1**	**68.2**	**87.7**	**78.9**

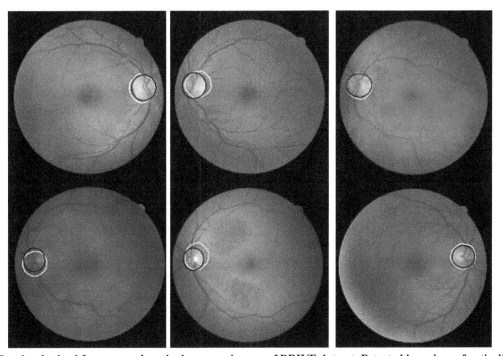

Figure 11. Results obtained for proposed method on some images of DRIVE dataset. Detected boundary of optic disc is shown by white curve, and corresponding ground truth is shown by black curve.

Table 5. Running times for different segmentation methods on DRIVE database. Best values are bold.

Method	Time	PC	Software
Walter et al. [16]	219.60s	Intel(R) Core (TM)2 Quad CPU 2.4 GHz, 4 GB RAM	MATLAB
Stapor et al. [17]	43.00s	Intel(R) Core (TM)2 Quad CPU 2.4 GHz, 4 GB RAM	MATLAB
Sopharak et al. [27]	14.92s	Intel(R) Core (TM)2 Quad CPU 2.4 GHz, 4 GB RAM	MATLAB
Welfer et al. [28]	22.66s	Intel(R) Core (TM)2 Quad CPU 2.4 GHz, 4 GB RAM	MATLAB
Proposed method	**13.24s**	Intel(R) Core (TM)2 Quad CPU 2.4 GHz, 4 GB RAM	MATLAB

For this purpose, the methods proposed by Walter et al. [16], Stapor et al. [17], Lupascu et al. [25], Sopharak et al. [27], Welfer et al. [28], and Qureshi et al. [30] were used for comparison. The results of other methods were obtained from their original papers or from Welfer et al. [28]. These results are summarized in table 3. In this table, for each evaluating parameter, the best value is bolded. The results obtained for the proposed method on some images of the DIARETDB1 database are also shown in figure 10.

From the results obtained, the overlap of the proposed method was much higher than the others (at least 22% greater), while its accuracy, sensitivity, and predictive values were high, and the mean distance between the center of detected optic disc and ground truth was about 12 pixels.

The proposed method was also compared on the DRIVE database [29] with some state-of-the-art methods. In this experiment, the methods proposed by Walter et al. [16], Stapor et al. [17], Youssif et al. [22], Lupascu et al. [25], Sopharak et al. [27] , Welfer et al. [28], Qureshi et al. [30], Hsiao et al. [31], and Ramakanth et al. [33] were used for comparison. The results of other methods were obtained from their original papers or from Welfer et al. [28]. These results are summarized in table 4. In this table, for each evaluating parameter, the best value is bolded. In this experiment, the previous trained ANN was used again. Since the training and test sets are really independent, the results obtained show the robustness of the proposed method. According to the results obtained, the sensitivity and overlap values for the proposed method were 87.7% and 68.2%, respectively, and higher than the others, while its accuracy, CDD, and predictive values were similar to the others. The results obtained for the proposed method on some images of the DRIVE database are also shown in figure 11.

Finally, the running time of the proposed method along with some state-of-the-art methods are given in table 5. The proposed method requires a low computational cost, and competes with the existing fast methods because we concentrated the feature extraction process only on the center line of the vessels. Without optimization of its MATLAB code, it will take about 13.2 seconds to process one image in the DRIVE database on a PC with a Intel(R) Core(TM)2 Quad CPU and 4.0 GB RAM. In real applications, the computation time can be significantly reduced by implementing the algorithm in C/C++ programming. In this way, our method can be seen as an interesting option to handle large image sets.

4. Conclusion

In this paper, we proposed an efficient algorithm for automatic optic disc detection and its border estimation. The proposed method is based upon estimating the similarity of the main retinal vessels into the optic disc vessels by employing the ANN along with efficient visual features of the optic discs vessels and background tissue. The center of detected inside the optic disc vessels was selected as the optic disc center, and a circle that surrounded these vessels was also selected as the initial border of the optic disc. The precise location of the optic disc boundary was adjusted by the radial analysis of the initial circle. The obtained average accuracy, overlap, sensitivity, and predictive values for optic disc segmentation on the DRIONS, DRIVE, and DIARETDB1 datasets were 97.7%, 70.6%, 80.3%, and 84.6%, respectively. The mean distance between the detected optic disc and ground truth was less than 12 pixels. The mean overlap value of the proposed method was at least 22% greater than the other state-of-the-art methods. Also the running time of the proposed method was better than the other state-of-the-art methods.

In the future works, to increase the performance of the proposed method, we can employ more reliable features, and also can employ feature learning-based techniques to this end. Also new edge detection methods [38] can be utilized to enhance results on noisy images. Finally employing other classifiers can be considered.

7. Acknowledgment

The author would like to thank Dr. Abdolhossein Fathi from Computer Engineering Department, Razi University, for his kind help and contribution in feature extraction and evaluation of results.

References

[1] Kose, C. & Ikibas, C. (2011). A personal identification system using retinal vasculature in retinal fundus images. Expert Sys. App., vol. 38, no. 11, pp. 13670-13681.

[2] Lathen, G., Jonasson, J. & Borga, M. (2010). Blood vessel segmentation using multi-scale quadrature filtering. Pattern Recognition Letters, vol. 31, pp. 762-767.

[3] Fathi, A. & Naghsh-Nilchi, A. R. (2013). Automatic Wavelet-Based Retinal Blood Vessels Segmentation and Vessel Diameter Estimation. Biomedical Signal Processing and Control, vol. 8, pp. 71– 80.

[4] Abdel-Ghafar, R. A., Morris, T., Ritchings, T., & Wood, I. (2004). Detection and characterisation of the optic disc in glaucoma and diabetic retinopathy,

presented at the Med. Image Understand. Anal. Conf., London, U.K., pp. 23-24.

[5] You, X., Peng, Q., Yuan, Y., Cheung, Y. & Lei, J. (2011). Segmentation of retinal blood vessels using the radial projection and semi-supervised approach. Pattern Recognition, vol. 44, no. 10-11, pp. 2314-2324.

[6] Manoj, S. & Muralidharan Sandeep, P. M. (2013). Neural Network Based Classifier for Retinal Blood Vessel Segmentation. International Journal of Recent Trends in Electrical & Electronics Engg, vol. 3, no. 1, pp. 44-53.

[7] Marin, D., Rábida, L., Aquino, A., Emilio, M., Arias, G. & Bravo, J.M. (2010). A New Supervised Method for Blood Vessel Segmentation in Retinal Images by Using Gray-Level and Moment Invariants-Based Features. IEEE Transactions on Medical Imaging. Vol. 30, no. 1, pp. 0278-0062.

[8] Vega, R., Guevara, E., Falcon, L. E., Sanchez, Ante, G. & Sossa, H. (2013). Blood Vessel Segmentation in Retinal Images Using Lattice Neural Networks. Advances in Artificial Intelligence and Its Applications, Vol. 8265, pp. 532-544.

[9] Chin, K. S., Trucco, E., Tan, L. & Wilson, P. J. (2013). Automatic fovea location in retinal images using anatomical priors and vessel density. Pattern Recognition Letters, vol. 34, pp. 1152-1158.

[10] Akram, M. U., Khalid, S., Tariq, A., Khan, S. A. & Azam, F. (2014). Detection and classification of retinal lesions for grading of diabetic retinopathy. Computers in Biology and Medicine, vol. 45, pp. 161-171.

[11] Abirami, P. K, Ganga, T. K., Regina, I. A. & Geetha, S. (2015). Neural Network based Classification and Detection of Glaucoma using Optic Disc and CUP Features. International Journal of Scientific Research Engineering & Technology, vol. 4, pp. 2321-0613.

[12] Vijayan, T. & Singh, A. (2015). Glaucoma Recognition and Segmentation Using Feed Forward Neural Network and Optical physics. International Journal of Advanced Research in Electrical, Electronics and Instrumentation Engineering, vol. 4, pp. 2320-3765.

[13] Wyawahare, M. V. & Patil, P. M. (2014). Performance Evaluation of Optic Disc Segmentation Algorithms in Retinal Fundus Images: an Empirical Investigation. International Journal of Advanced Science and Technology, vol. 69, pp. 19-32.

[14] Niemeijer, M., Abràmoff, M. D. & Ginneken, B.V. (2009). Fast detection of the optic disc and fovea in color fundus photographs. Med. Imag. Anal., vol. 13, pp. 859-870.

[15] Sinthanayothin, C., Boyce, D. J. F., Cook, H. L., & Williamson, T.H. (1999). Automated localization of the optic disc, fovea, and retinal blood vessels from digital colour fundus images. Ophthalmology, vol. 83, pp. 902-910.

[16] Walter, T., Klein, J. C., Massin, P. & Erginay, A. (2002). A contribution of image processing to the diagnosis of diabetic retinopathy - detection of exudates in color fundus images of the human retina. IEEE Trans. Med. Imag., vol. 21, no. 10, pp. 1236-1243.

[17] Stapor, K., Switonski, A., Chrastek, R. & Michelson, G. (2004). Segmentation of fundus eye images using methods of mathematical morphology for glaucoma diagnosis. Lecture Note. Comput. Scie., vol. 3039, pp.41-48.

[18] Carmona, E. J., Rincon, M., Garcıa-Feijoo, J. & De-la Casa, J.M.M. (2008). Identification of the optic nerve head with genetic algorithms. Artifi. Intel. Med., vol. 43, no. 3, pp. 243-259.

[19] Duanggate, C., Uyyanonvara, B., Makhanov, S. S., Barman, S. & Williamson, T. (2011). Parameter-free optic disc detection. Computerized Medical Imaging and Graphics, vol. 35, pp. 51-63.

[20] Hoover, A. & Goldbaum, M. (2003). Locating the optic nerve in a retinal image using the fuzzy convergence of the blood vessels. IEEE Trans. Med. Imag., vol. 22, no. 8, pp. 951-958.

[21] Welfer, D., Scharcanski, J., Kitamura, C. M., DalPizzol, M. M., Ludwig, L. W. B. & Marinho, D. R. (2010). Segmentation of the optic disc in color eye fundus images using an adaptive morphological approach. Comput. Bio. Med., vol. 40, pp.124-137.

[22] Youssif, A.A.H.A.R., Ghalwash, A. Z. & Ghoneim, A.A.S.A.R. (2008). Optic disc detection from normalized digital fundus images by means of a vessels' direction matched filter. IEEE Trans. Med. Imag., vol. 27, no. 1, pp. 11-18.

[23] Foracchia, M., Grisan, E. & Ruggeri, A. (2004). Detection of optic disc in retinal images by means of a geometrical model of vessel structure. IEEE Trans. Med. Imag., vol. 23, no. 10, p.p. 1189-1195.

[24] Morales, S., Naranjo, V., Angulo, J. & Alcaniz, M. (2013). Automatic Detection of Optic Disc Based on PCA and Mathematical Morphology. IEEE Transactions on Medical Imaging, vol. 32, no. 4, pp.786-796.

[25] Lupascu, C. A., Tegolo, D. & Rosa, L. D. (2008). Automated detection of optic disc location in retinal images. 21st IEEE Int. l Symp. Computer-Based Med. Sys., University of Jyvaskyla, Finland, pp.17-22.

[26] Pourreza-Shahri, R., Tavakoli, M. & Kehtarnavaz N. (2014). Computationally efficient optic nerve head detection in retinal fundus images. Biomedical Signal Processing and Control, vol. 11, pp. 63-73.

[27] Sopharak, A., Uyyanonvara, B., Barmanb, S. & Williamson, T. H. (2008). Automatic detection of diabetic retinopathy exudates from non-dilated retinal images using mathematical morphology methods. Comput. Med. Imag. Graph., vol. 32, pp. 720-727.

[28] Welfer, D., Scharcanski, J. & Marinho, D. R. (2013). A morphologic two-stage approach for automated optic disc detection in color eye fundus images. Pattern Recognition Letters, vol. 34, pp. 476-485.

[29] Tobin, K., Chaum, E., Govindasamy, V. & Karnowski, T. (2007). Detection of anatomic structures in human retinal imagery. IEEE Trans. Med. Imag., vol. 26, no. 12, pp. 1729-1739.

[30] Qureshi, R. J., Kovacs, L., Harangi, B., Nagy, B., Peto, T. & Hajdu, A. (2012). Combining algorithms for automatic detection of optic disc and macula in fundus images. Computer Vision and Image Understanding, vol. 116, pp. 138-145.

[31] Hsiao, H., Liu, C., Yu, C., Kuo, S. & Shen, S. (2012). A novel optic disc detection scheme on retinal images. Expert Systems with Applications, vol. 39, pp. 10600-10606.

[32] Mendonça, A. M., Sousa, A., Mendonça, L. & Campilho, A. (2013). Automatic localization of the optic disc by combining vascular and intensity information. Computerized Medical Imaging and Graphics, vol. 37, no. 5-6, pp. 409-417.

[33] Ramakanth, S. A. & Babu, R. V. (2014). Approximate Nearest Neighbour Field based Optic disc Detections. Computerized Medical Imaging and Graphics, vol. 38, pp. 49-56.

[34] Muramatsu, C., Nakagawa, T., Sawada, A., Hatanaka, Y., Hara, T., Yamamoto, T. & Fujita, H. (2011). Automated segmentation of optic disc region on retinal fundus photographs: Comparison of contour modeling and pixel classification methods. Computer methods and programs in biomedicine, vol. 101, pp. 23-32.

[35] Fathi, A., Naghsh-Nilchi, A. R. & Abdali-Mohammadi, F. (2013). Automatic vessel network features quantification using local vessel pattern operator. Computers in Biology and Medicine, vol. 43, pp. 587-593.

[36] DRIVE: Digital Retinal Images for Vessel Extraction. URL:http://www.isi.uu.nl/Research/ Databases /DRIVE/S.

[37] DIARETDB1: Kauppi, T., Kalesnykiene, V., Kamarainen, J.K., Lensu, L., Sorri, I., Raninen, A., Voutilainen, R., Uusitalo, H., alviainen, H. K¨ & Pietila, J., DIARETDB1 diabetic retinopathy database and evaluation protocol, Technical Report.

[38] Dorrani, Z. & Mahmoodi, M. S. (2016). Noisy images edge detection: Ant colony optimization algorithm. Journal of AI and Data Mining, Vol. 4, no. 1, pp. 77-83.

7

Target Tracking Based on Virtual Grid in Wireless Sensor Networks

F. Hoseini[1]* A. Shahbahrami[2] and A.Yaghoobi Notash[1]

1. Department of Computer Engineering, Rasht Branch, Islamic Azad University, Rasht, Iran.

2. Department of Computer Engineering, Faculty of Engineering, University of Guilan, Rasht, Iran.

*Corresponding author: farnazhoseini@iaurasht.ac.ir (F.Hoseini).

Abstract

One of the most important and typical applications of Wireless Sensor Networks (WSNs) is target tracking. Although target tracking can provide benefits for large-scale WSNs and organize them into clusters, tracking a moving target in cluster-based WSNs suffers from a boundary problem. The main goal of this paper is to introduce an efficient and novel mobility management protocol namely Target Tracking Based on Virtual Grid (TTBVG), which integrates on-demand dynamic clustering into a cluster-based WSN for target tracking. This protocol converts on-demand dynamic clusters to scalable cluster-based WSNs using boundary nodes and facilitates sensors' collaboration around clusters. In this manner, each sensor node has the probability of becoming a cluster head and apperceives the trade-off between energy consumption and local sensor collaboration in cluster-based sensor networks. The simulation results of this work demonstrate the efficiency of the proposed protocol in both the one-hop and multi-hop cluster-based sensor networks.

Keywords: *Target Tracking, Virtual Grid, Clustering, Wireless sensor networks, Dynamic Clustering.*

1. Introduction

One of the new low-cost and saving-energy network paradigms that can create applications for monitoring and controlling is Wireless Sensor Networks (WSNs). Target tracking is considered as an important element in WSNs and many practical applications including battlefield surveillance, patient monitoring devices, disaster response, and emergency rescue [1]. With target tracking, a moving target like a person or a vehicle can be tracked with sensing capability of sensors, and the information about the position and location of that moving target can be studied in each time instance [2]; it also benefits from local collaboration and routing [3, 4]. Although target tracking can provide benefits for large-scale WSNs and organize them into clusters, tracking a moving target in cluster-based WSNs suffers from a boundary problem. Recently, the cluster structure has been used to resolve the boundary problems [5,6]. Generally, the nodes that are surrounded by the target cooperate with each other to estimate the place of the target [7–9] but in a dynamic clustering approach, when the target travels in a region wake up a group of nodes used to construct a cluster of local collaborations. In other words, clusters are constituted dynamically as the target moves. It is an efficient way for local sensor collaboration since the clusters formed at each time instant change dynamically [10]. However, the dynamic clustering process has multi-problems, repeating as the target moves, is energy costly, and dynamic clustering does not consider how to efficiently transfer data to the sink [11]. While the target tracking uses the static cluster for the network scalability and energy efficiency, "static cluster" does not mean unchanging of the cluster during the network's entire lifetime; it means unchanging for a relatively long time period compared to a temporally formed dynamic cluster until the next round of clustering process starts[12–15]. In this manner, as shown in the Low-Energy Adaptive Clustering Hierarchy (LEACH) protocol [16], each sensor node has the probability of becoming a cluster head so as to balance the energy load. LEACH [17] is the first typical clustering protocol designed for WSNs. Since it is the first mature algorithm for cluster formation; LEACH becomes a baseline for successors.

A predictive real mechanism in target tracking is used to inform the cluster heads about the approaching target, and then the corresponding cluster head wakes up a number of appropriate nodes exactly before the arrival of the target. One static cluster can be saved and handed to another without costly dynamic clustering processes. Besides it can provide a scalable structure that coordinates and manages the networks. In large-scale sensor networks, static cluster-based approaches are used more suitably for target tracking. However, when the target moves across or along the boundaries of clusters, the static cluster membership prevents sensors of different clusters to collaborate and share information with each other, boundary problem.

Since the boundary problem can lead to increase the tracking uncertainty or even the scat of the target, a new protocol is necessary to solve the boundary problem and apperceive the trade-off between the energy consumption and the local sensor collaboration in cluster-based sensor networks [18]. In order to solve this problem in cluster-based WSNs, a new mobility management protocol based on virtual grid is suggested, which converts the on-demand dynamic clusters to the scalable cluster-based WSNs.

This paper is organized as what follows. Related works are given in Section 2 that includes a detailed survey of the related research works. The proposed protocol is explained in Section 3 that includes the simulation, and its results are presented in Section 4. Finally, conclusions and future works are presented in Section 5.

2. Related works

There are some important factors such as energy consumption, response time, life time, and lack of energy that are discussed throughout this paper. Energy consumption refers to the amount of energy or power by an individual or organization or to the process or system of such consumption. Response time is the time a system or functional unit takes to react to a given input. The lifetime of a network is defined as the operational time of the network during which it is able to perform the dedicated task(s). In order to clarify the specified factors, in the first part of this paper, some background information is presented.

2.1. Distributed predictive tracking

Distributed Predictive Tracking (DPT) is available in WSN [19]. There are three types of nodes in this protocol: boundary node, typical node, and cluster-head node.

There is no limit to use the clustering protocol but we should have changed some of them. In DPT, two previous locations are used to guess the next target places. After creating the clusters, DPT is executed. Cluster-head can use Target Descriptor (TD) to identify targets and to provide their location information. There is some useful information in each TD such as the target ID, the current location of the target, and the next predicted location of the target. Cluster-heads based on all sensor information are available in their database, start searching, and select the tried sensors. If the target speed or direction changes suddenly, another failure scenario can happen.

2.2. Exponential predictive tracking

Exponential Distributed Predictive Tracking (EDPT) is another tracking protocol in WSN [20]. In this protocol, in order to reduce the energy consumption and response time, an improved predictive algorithm is used that is called Exponential Smoothing Predictive Algorithm (ESPA) [21]. ESPA uses five previous points in the target path to find the next place of the target. If the target is located out of range, recovery will be at work, just like the DPT protocol.

2.3. Virtual grid

One of the most important challenges in WSNs is the lack of energy. Using the virtual grid on networks is an efficient solution to reduce energy consumption [22]. One node that is located in every cell of each type of virtual grid is in the active mode, and the others are in the passive mode, which is depicted in figure 1. As a result, life time increases and energy is stored by the network. Two types of neighborhoods have been defined for these cells. In the first type, each cell can communicate with the horizontal and vertical adjacent cells. In the second type, instead of the horizontal and vertical adjacent cells, each cell can communicate with the diagonal cells as well. Most of the protocols in the WSN context have been used as grids with square cells but there are other types of girds such as grids with triangle cells and grids with polygon cells.

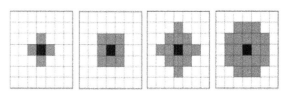

Figure 1. Virtual grid with different types of cells.

Target tracking in WSNs has received a considerable attention in the recent years from various angles, and a lot of protocols have been proposed. Zhao et al. [23] have introduced the collaboration mechanism for target tracking via information-driven dynamic sensors. Brooks et al. [24] have presented a distributed entity-tracking framework for sensor networks. Chen et al. [25] have used distributed sensor scheduling algorithms in networks with binary sensor and acoustic sensor networks, respectively. Wang et al. [26] have proposed a novel localization algorithm for target tracking. VigilNet[27, 28] has designed and implemented an energy-efficient and real-time integrated system for target tracking. Cheng et al. [29] have used distributed Time Division Multiple Access (TDMA) for target tracking. Chen et al. [30], in another research work; have handled a secure localization scheme to defend against some typical attacks.

In order to balance energy consumption and sensor collaboration, a series of dynamic clustering protocols have been applied for target tracking in WSNs [31, 32]. Yang et al. [6] have used an Adaptive Dynamic Cluster-Based Tracking (ADCT) protocol, which selects cluster heads dynamically and wakes up nodes to construct clusters with the aid of a prediction algorithm as the target moves in the network. Zhang and Cao [7] have introduced the Dynamic Convoy Tree-Based Collaboration (DCTC) method to detect and track the mobile target. Ji et al. [8] have represented a dynamic cluster-based structure for object detection and tracking since the convoy tree maybe assumed as a cluster in dynamic configuration by adding and pruning some nodes. Jinet[9] has also proposed a dynamic clustering mechanism for target tracking in WSNs and balancing the missing rate and energy consumption. Medeiros et al. [12] have presented a dynamic clustering algorithm for target tracking in wireless camera Networks. Chen et al. [5], in another work, have introduced a decentralized dynamic clustering protocol based on static sensors.

Several protocols for target tracking are based upon the static cluster structure [13–14]. Heinzelman et al. [16] have converted sensor nodes into clusters using LEACH as a suitable clustering protocol, and Younis et al. [33] have converted it using Hybrid, Energy-Efficient, and Distributed Clustering (HEED). Based on the cluster structure, a Distributed Predictive Tracking (DPT) protocol has been designed by Yang and Sikdar [13], which predicts the next place of the target and notices the cluster head regarding the approaching target. A Hierarchical Prediction Strategy (HPS) for target tracking and implementation of a real target tracking system has been proposed by Wang et al. [14], which depends on the cluster structure.

Cluster-based target tracking protocols take the advantages of underlying the cluster structure in comparison with the dynamic clustering protocols, which are especially suitable for target tracking in large-scale networks. Mobayen et al. [34] have proposed a novel recursive singularity free FTSM (Fast Terminal Sliding Mode) strategy for the finite time tracking control of non-homonymic systems. The results have been stimulated on a wheeled mobile robot and an under-actuated surface vessel, which are two benchmark examples of extended chained-form non-homonymic systems. Mobayen [35], in another work, has presented a new recursive terminal sliding mode strategy for tracking control of disturbed chained-form non-homonymic systems. The simulation results showed the efficiency of this method in the presence of external disturbances. In another work, Mobayen [36] has considered the composite non-linear feedback method for robust tracking control of uncertain linear systems with time-varying delays and disturbances. The experimental results were presented to illustrate the effectiveness of the proposed technique.

3. Proposed protocol

We used the virtual grid with rectangular cells in the proposed protocol (shown in Figure 2) because any cluster could be placed in each cell of the grid.

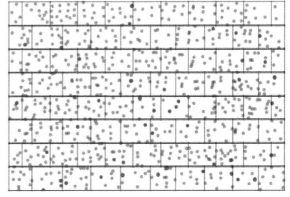

Figure 2. Virtual grid with rectangular cells in proposed protocol.

In target tracking applications in WSNs, for choosing a cluster, the nodes should be equipped with GPS or benefit from a positioning algorithm. The sensor nodes have both the short and long sensing ranges. Normally, a node is activated in short beam, and if the cluster head requests, it will switch to a high beam.

In addition, it is assumed that the nodes are distributed densely in the area of interest. Sink, which is a special node where data is collected, to be able to do its job, should know the width and length of the monitored area. There are two methods for this purpose. The first method is easier and more energy efficient but less flexible. The second one is more flexible but more complex and energy consuming. We chose the latter approach because in this way, at the starting point of grid, the nodes send a Hello message to sink. The sink node collects messages and the length and width of the grid using the flowchart in figure 3.

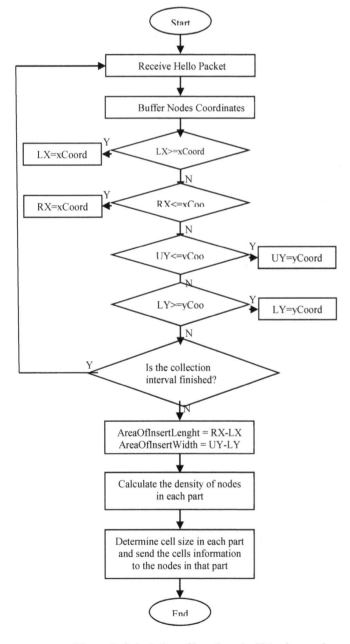

Figure 3. Calculation of length and width of area of interest and cells using sink node.

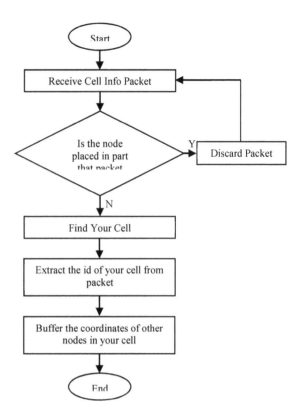

Figure 4. Finding cell and other nodes in cell.

Table 1. Simulation condition.

Parameters	Scenarios		
	Details		
Scenery Size	100×100	100×100	100×100
Antenna	Omni Directional	Omni	
	Directional	Omni Directional	
Time Simulation	1500	1500	1500
Sink Number	1	1	1
Common Node Number	200	200	200
Common Node Location	Random	Random	Random
Initial Energy of Common Node	100 Joule	100 Joule	100 Joule
Target speed	2m/s	1.5m/s	1m/s

The nodes identify their cell boundary by analysing information included in the Cell Info packet. The nodes send a Hello message, which contains their coordinates to other nodes in their cell. Then a node is elected as the cluster head based on the identity or its location with respect to the center of cell. The cluster-head node determines the border and non-border nodes. The non-border nodes are scheduled by the cluster head to sleep and wake up. The sensor unit of the non-border nodes is turned off, and it will be turned on by the cluster head demand but their communication unit is turned on if they are in the wake-up mode, otherwise it is turned off.

Tracking of the target starts when the monitored area border nodes detect its effect and report to the cluster head by the Target Entrance name. The cluster head will send a Name Request for assigning an identity number to the target by the sink node if required. Then three sensor nodes used to locate the target are elected by the cluster head. It sends a Target Detection message to them. Subsequently, it waits for the Targeted packet.

The cluster head will wait for Target Detection messages. After receiving three Target Detection messages, localizing the target is done by the cluster head. Then the cluster head sends a Target Info message to the sink and its neighbourhood cluster heads. These cluster head create a detection wall in the border of the sender cell and creates secondary clusters in that part of the border. Some border nodes will be elected as the cluster head and the others will join the nearest cluster heads. This is done by a Ready to Detection message that the cluster head sends.

4. Simulation and results

We used ns2 for evaluating our simulations in TTBVG protocol. The simulation conditions are listed in table 1. We compared TTBVG (proposed protocol) with DPT and EDPT. The difference between the scenarios is in the target speeds, then increased the target speed and evaluated its influence on the efficiency of algorithms.

4.1. Residual energy

The residual energy of the nodes was evaluated and the results obtained were shown in figures 5 and 6. These results prove the efficiency of TTBVG. As shown in figures 5 and 6, the life time is increased and energy consumptions of the nodes decreased.

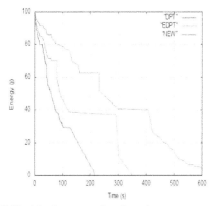

Figure 5. Residual energy of nodes when target speed is 5m/s.

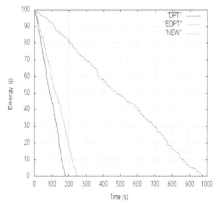

Figure 6. Residual energy of nodes when target speed is 1m/s.

4.2. Error rate

The error rate was calculated. TTBVG locates the target position more correctly. In figure 7, the error rates of DPT, EDPT, and TTBVG are shown with respect to different speeds of the target. The results obtained show the excellence of TTBVG.

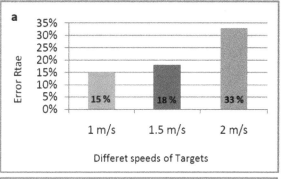

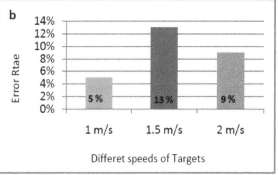

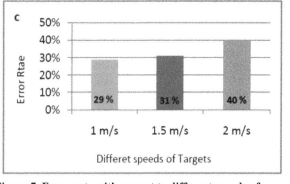

Figure 7. Error rate with respect to different speeds of target. a) DPT, b) EDPT, and c) (TTBVG) proposed protocol.

5. Conclusion and future works

Target tracking is one of the new network paradigms and important applications of WSNs. However, tracking a moving target in cluster-based WSNs suffers from the boundary problem. In this paper, in order to resolve this problem in cluster-based WSNs, a new mobility management protocol namely Target Tracking Based on Virtual Grid (TTBVG) was suggested. This protocol converts the on-demand dynamic clusters to scalable cluster-based WSNs using boundary nodes, and facilitates sensors' collaboration around clusters. In this manner, each sensor node has the probability of becoming a cluster head and apperceives the trade-off between energy consumption and local sensor collaboration in cluster-based sensor networks. The simulation results of this work demonstrated the efficiency of TTBVG in both the one-hop and multi-hop cluster-based sensor networks. TTBVG is very useful for the research groups that are interested in the development, modification or optimization of tracking algorithms for WSNs. For the future works, the proposed protocol can be of use for other applications in WSN such as emergency preparedness and habitat monitoring.

References

[1] Akyildiz, I. F., Su, W., Sankarasubramaniam, Y., & Cayirci, E. (2002). A survey on sensor networks. IEEE Communications Magazine, vol. 40, no. 8, pp. 102-114.

[2] Bandyopadhyay, S., & Coyle, E. J. (1997). Adaptive clustering for mobile wireless sensor networks. IEEE Journal on Selected Areas in Communications, vol. 15, pp. 1265-1275.

[3] Pearlman, M. R., & Haas, Z. J. (1999). Determining the optimal configuration for the zone routing protocol. IEEE Journal on Selected Areas in Communications, vol. 17, no. 8, pp. 1395-1414.

[4] Kozat, U. C., Kondylis, G., Ryu, B., & Marina, M. K. (2000). Virtual dynamic backbone for mobile ad hoc networks. In Proceedings of the International Conference on Communications (ICC '01), pp. 250-255.

[5] Chen, W. P., Hou, J. C., & Sha, L. (2004). Dynamic clustering for acoustic target tracking in wireless sensor networks. IEEE Transactions on Mobile Computing, vol. 3, no. 3, pp. 258–271.

[6] W Yang, W., Fu, Z., Kim, J., & Park, M. S. (2007). An adaptive dynamic cluster-based protocol for target tracking in wireless sensor networks. In Advances Data and Web Management, vol. 4505, pp. 156-167.

[7] Zhang, W., & Cao, G. (2004). DCTC: dynamic convoy tree-based collaboration for target tracking in sensor networks. IEEE Transactions on Wireless Communications, vol. 3, no. 5, pp.1689-1701.

[8] Zha, H., Metzner, J. J., & Kesidis, G. (2004). Dynamic cluster structure for object detection and tracking in wireless ad hoc sensor networks. In Proceedings of the IEEE International Conference on Communications, pp. 3807-3811.

[9] Jin, G. Y., Lu, X.Y. & Park, M. S. (2006). Dynamic clustering for object tracking in wireless sensor networks. In Proceedings of the 3rd Iternational Conference on Ubiquitous Computing Systems (UCS'06), pp. 200-209.

[10] Ghaffari, A., & Nobahary, S. (2015). FDMG: Fault detection method by using genetic algorithm in clustered wireless sensor networks. Journal of AI and Data Mining, vol. 3, no. 1, pp. 47–54.

[11] Hosseinirad, S. M., & Basu, S. K. (2015). Wireless sensor network design through genetic algorithm. Journal of AI and Data Mining, vol. 3, no. 1, pp. 47–54.

[12] Medeiros, H., Park, J., & Kak, A. (2008). Distributed object tracking using a cluster-based Kalman filter in wireless camera networks. IEEE Journal on Selected Topics in Signal Processing, vol. 2, no. 4, pp. 448-463.

[13] Yang, H., & Sikdar, B. (2003). A protocol for tracking mobile targets using sensor networks. In Proceedings of the 1st IEEE International Workshop on Sensor Network Protocols and Applications, pp. 71-81.

[14] Wang, Z., Li, H., Shen, X., Sun, X., & Wang, Z. (2008). Tracking and predicting moving targets in hierarchical sensor networks. In Proceedings of the IEEE International Conference on Networking Sensing and Control. pp. 1169-1174.

[15] Wang, Z., Wang, Z., Chen, H., Li, J., & Li, H. (2011). Hiertrack-energy efficient target tracking system for wireless sensor networks. In Proceedings of the 9th ACM Conference on Embedded Networked Sensor Systems, pp. 377-378.

[16] Heinzelman, W. B., Chandrakasan, A. P., & Balakrishnan, H. (2002). An application-specific protocol architecture for wireless microsensor networks. IEEE Transactions on Wireless Communications, vol. 1, no. 4, pp. 660-670.

[17] Yongtao, C. A. O., & Chen, H. E. (2006). A distributed clustering algorithm with an adaptive backoff strategy for wireless sensor networks. IEICE Transactions on Communications, vol.89, no. 2, pp.609-613.

[18] Hoseini, F., Yaghoobi, A., & Ekbatanifard, G., (2015) .Target tracking based on virtual grid. The 1st IEEE International Conference on Signal Processing and Intelligent Systems (SPIS).

[19] Toh, Y. K., Xiao, W., & Xie, L. (2007). A wireless sensor network target tracking system with

distributed competition based sensor scheduling. In 3rd International Conference on Intelligent Sensors, Sensor Networks and Information (ISSNIP), pp. 257-262. IEEE.

[20] Ramya, K., Kumar, K. P., & Rao, V. S. (2012). A survey on target tracking techniques in wireless sensor networks. International Journal of Computer Science and Engineering Survey, vol. 3, no. 4, pp. 93.

[21] Bermúdez, J. D. (2013). Exponential smoothing with covariates applied to electricity demand forecast. European Journal of Industrial Engineering, vol.7, no. 3, pp. 333-349.

[22] Akkaya, K., & Younis, M. (2005). A survey on routing protocols for wireless sensor networks. Ad hoc Networks, vol.3, no. 3, pp. 325-349.

[23] Zhao, F., Shin, J., & Reich, J. (2002). Information-driven dynamic sensor collaboration for tracking applications. IEEE Signal Processing Magazine, vol. 19, no. 2, pp. 61-72.

[24] Brooks, R. R., Griffin, C., & Friedlander, D. S. (2002). Self-organized distributed sensor network entity tracking. International Journal of High Performance Computing Applications, vol. 16, no. 3, pp. 207-219.

[25] Chen, J., Cao, K., Li, K., & Sun, Y. (2011). Distributed sensor activation algorithm for target tracking with binary sensor networks. Cluster Computing, vol. 14, no. 1, pp. 55-64.

[26] Wang, Z., Luo, J. A., & Zhang, X. P. (2012). A novel locationenalized Maximum likelihood estimator for bearing-only target localization. IEEE Transaction on Signal Processing, vol. 60, no. 12, pp. 6166-6181.

[27] He, T., et al. (2006). VigilNet: an integrated sensor network system for energy-efficient surveillance. ACM Transactions on Sensor Networks, vol. 2, no. 1, pp. 1-38.

[28] He, T., et al. (2006). Achieving real-time target tracking using wireless sensor networks. In Proceedings of the 12th IEEE Real-Time and Embedded Technology and Applications Symposium, pp. 37-48.

[29] Cheng, P., Zhang, F., Chen, J., Sun, Y., & Shen, X. (2013). A distributed TDMA scheduling algorithm for target tracking in ultrasonic sensor networks. IEEE Transactions on Industrial Electronics, no. 99.

[30] Chen, H., Lou, W., & Wang, Z. (2010). A novel secure localization approach in wireless sensor networks. Eurasia Journal on Wireless Communications and Networking, vol. 201.

[31] Fayyaz, M. (2011). Classification of object tracking techniques in wireless sensor networks. Wireless Sensor Network, vol. 3, pp.121-124.

[32] Demigha, O., Hidouci, W. K., & Ahmed, T. (2013). On energyefficiency in collaborative target tracking in wireless sensor network: a review. IEEE Communications Surveys& Tutorials, vol. 99, pp. 1-13.

[33] Younis, O., & Fahmy, S. (2004). HEED: a hybrid, energy-efficient, distributed clustering approach for ad hoc sensor networks. IEEE Transactions on Mobile Computing, vol. 3, no. 4, pp. 366-379.

[34] Mobayen, S., Yazdanpanah, M. J., & Majd, V. J. (2011). A finite-time tracker for nonholonomic systems using recursive singularity-free FTSM. In American Control Conference (ACC), pp. 1720-1725. IEEE.

[35] Mobayen, S. (2015). Finite-time tracking control of chained-form nonholonomic systems with external disturbances based on recursive terminal sliding mode method. Nonlinear Dynamics, vol. 80, no. 1-2, pp, 669-683.

[36] Mobayen, S. (2015). Design of a robust tracker and disturbance attenuator for uncertain systems with time delays. Complexity, vol. 21, no. 1, pp. 340-348.

8

A Gravitational Search Algorithm-Based Single-Center of Mass Flocking Control for Tracking Single and Multiple Dynamic Targets for Parabolic Trajectories in Mobile Sensor Networks

E. Khodayari[1], V. Sattari-Naeini[2*] and M. Mirhosseini[3]

1. Department of Computer Engineering, Payamnor University of Bardsir, Bardsir, Kerman, Iran.
2. Department of Computer Engineering, Shahid Bahonar University of Kerman, Kerman, Iran·
3. Department of Computer Science, Higher Education Complex of Bam, KhalijFars Highway, Bam, Kerman, Iran

*Corresponding author: vsnaeini@uk.ac.ir (V. Sattari-Naeini).

Abstract
Development of an optimal flocking control procedure is an essential problem in mobile sensor networks (MSNs). Furthermore, finding the parameters such that the sensors can reach the target in an appropriate time period is an important issue. This paper offers an optimization approach based upon the metaheuristic methods used for flocking control in MSNs to follow a target. We develop a non-differentiable optimization technique based on the gravitational search algorithm (GSA). Finding the flocking parameters using swarm behaviors is the main contribution of this paper in order to minimize the cost function. The cost function displays the average Euclidean distance of the center of mass (COM) away from the moving target. One of the benefits of using GSA is its application in multiple targets tracking with satisfactory results. The simulation results obtained that this scheme outperforms the existing ones, and demonstrate the ability of this approach in comparison with the previous methods.

Keywords: *Flocking Control, mobile Sensor Network, Target Tracking, Center of Mass, Gravitational Search Algorithms.*

1. Introduction

Wireless sensor networks (WSNs) have been greatly investigated in the past few years [1, 2, 3, 4]. The benefit of mobile sensor networks (MSNs) over the stationary ones is the environmental change adjustment [4]. Hence, MSNs can be used in various domains such as target tracking for protection of the exposed kinds of plants and underwater target observation [6, 7].

Flocks of agents are applicable to many areas including the distributed sensing, formation flying, cooperative surveillance, and point-to-point mail delivery. This phenomenal has been attracted in physics [8], mathematics [9], and biology [10]. Flocking problems have become a major thrust in the system and control theory in the recent years [11].

Cooperative control between mobile sensors is essential due to collision among them [12]. Flocking control [11] is used to resolve this issue. Flocking is a group of several mobile sensors with local interactions with an overall objective [13]. These sensors are capable of splitting, rejoining, and forming highly ordered fast convergence of COM towards the target.

Three rules have been presented by Reynolds [14]. They are considered as what follow.

Flock Centering: Each sensor attempts to remain near its neighbors (cohesion).

Collision Avoidance: The sensors keep away from collision with their neighbors (separation).

Velocity Matching: The sensors try to adjust their speed with their neighbors (alignment).

After the first flocking approach, various algorithms have been proposed for this issue. A survey on the application of flocking control has been investigated in [15]. Olfati-Saber [11] has introduced two algorithms for distributed flocking. The first one is working in free space. The second one is exhibiting this problem regarding the obstacles. In [16], flocking of robots has been investigated with a virtual leader. Two extended flocking control algorithms, one of which being flocking control with a minority of informed agent [17] and the other one being flocking of sensors with a virtual leader of varying velocity, have been proposed by Su et. al [17]. Multi-target tracking [18] is another benefit of MSN in the dynamic mode. This approach requires that some robots split from the present sensors to follow a new target. If one target disappears in MSN, the robots following that should merge with the present robots that are still following the target. Random selection (RS) and seed growing graph partition (SGGP) are the algorithms that are used for solving the problem of robot splitting/merging in multi-target tracking [19].

Improvement of the performance of target tracking regarding the obstacle using Multi-COM and Single-COM has been presented in the flocking control with single-COM and Multi-COM in [20-22]. Moreover, in order to solve the problem of designing an optimal flocking control in the obstacle space, they used genetic algorithms [23]. Some algorithms have been presented in [24] and [25], which are applicable to homogeneous MSNs. References [26, 27] follow some models for distributed flocking control. However, these works only consider the behavior of the flock without addressing target tracking.

The recent research areas have converged to the arrangement problems in stationary and MSNs [28]. A new category of the emergent motion control algorithms is anti-flocking control algorithms that dynamic coverage performances improve in MSN [29]. The AI optimization methods have been considered in many research domains. The Tabu search algorithm has been employed for optimal design of a MIMO controller [30]. GA, PSO, and ACO have been exploited to design a rotational inverted pendulum system [31]. Stability analysis and configuration control of groups of sensors have been optimized in the recent years [32]. Meanwhile, in [20], the problem of designing a flocking control approach for mobile agents to follow the moving target is advanced. Designing a network to converge to the optimal solution in an appropriate time is an open investigation problem. Natural-inspired algorithms are robust tools used in solving many optimization problems [33]. Gravitational Search Algorithm (GSA) is a recently introduced nature-inspired method whose idea is the gravity and Newton lows [34, 35]. The results of [33-42] indicate that GSA and its advanced versions are appropriated tools in

solving many optimization problems. Therefore, the strength of this algorithm encourages us to apply this method to find the optimal flocking forces.

The main contributions and novelty of this work can be summarized as what follow:

- GSA is adopted to solve the non-differentiable problem in the flocking control design to compute the coefficients of the interaction forces in the cost function to minimize the error between the moving target and the center of flocking.
- Single target moving with a circular wave trajectory is simulated to compare the performance of the proposed method with the previous ones.
- Multiple targets moving with a semi-circular and semi-sine wave trajectory are simulated to evaluate the proposed method.
- The optimal flocking control for single and multiple dynamic target trackings is presented by adding Single-COM to the parabolic trajectories.

This paper is organized as what follow. In Section 2, we introduce the Single-COM flocking control algorithm in the free space for single and multiple dynamic target trackings. In Section 3, we investigate the gravitational search algorithm. In Section 4, the problem of flocking control is formulated and the proposed method is elaborated. In Section 5, we evaluate the performance of the proposed scheme. Finally, in Section 6, we give the conclusions.

2. Flocking control in MSN
2.1. Flocking control approach in free space
A topology of flocks is shown by a graph T that includes a vertex set $v = \{1, 2, ..., m\}$ and an edge set $E \subseteq \{(x, y) : x, y \in v, x \neq y\}$. Each vertex shows one agent of flocks, while the communication link between the two agents is denoted by each edge.

$q_x, p_x \in R^n$ are the location and speed of robot x, respectively. A set of neighborhood of robot x at moment τ is defined as:

$$NB_x = \{y \in v : \| \cdot \| \leq r, v = \{1, 2, ..., m\}, x \neq y\} \quad (1)$$

where, $\| . \|$ is the Euclidean norm in R^n, and r is the neighborhood radius.

A group of moving agents (or sensors) are described with their motion relation as the following:

$$\begin{cases} \dot{q}_x = p_x \\ \dot{p}_x = u_x, x = 1, 2, ..., m \end{cases} \quad (2)$$

An $\alpha -$ lattice with the following condition is used to model the geometry of flocks [11]:

$$\| q_x - q_y \| = \gamma \quad (3)$$

In the above relation, γ is the distance between robot x and its flock-mate y. In [11], Olfati-Saber has presented a flocking control algorithm in the free space. This approach includes two control inputs as the following:

$$u_x = f_x^{\alpha} + f_x^{mt} \quad (4)$$

The first component f_i^{α} denotes a gradient-based term and a velocity consensus term as:

$$f_x^{\alpha} = \sum_{y \in NB_x^{\alpha}} \phi_\alpha (\| q_y - q_x \|_\sigma) n_{xy}$$
$$+ \sum_{y \in NB_x^{\alpha}} a_{xy}(q)(p_y - p_x) \quad (5)$$

In this algorithm, $\phi_\alpha(z)$ is the action procedure among the sensors and $\| . \|_\sigma$ of a vector is a map $R^n \Rightarrow R_+$ explained as $\| z \|_\sigma = \frac{1}{\varepsilon}[\sqrt{1 + \varepsilon \| z \|^2} - 1]$ [11]. The vector between q_x and q_y is n_{xy}. $a_{xy}(q)$ is the adjacency matrix. For more details, see [11, 20]. The second component of (4) f_x^{mt} is the distributed navigational feedback owing to the group objective.

$$f_x^{mt} = -(q_x - q_{mt}) - (p_x - p_{mt}) \quad (6)$$

where, mt-agent (q_{mt}, p_{mt}) is the dynamic target specified as follows:

$$\begin{cases} \dot{q}_{mt} = p_{mt} \\ \dot{p}_{mt} = f_{mt}(q_{mt}, p_{mt}) \end{cases} \quad (7)$$

Then the extended control protocol (4) is clearly defined as:

$$u_x = \sum_{y \in NB_x^{\alpha}} \phi_\alpha (\| q_y - q_x \|_\sigma) n_{xy} +$$
$$\sum_{y \in NB_x^{\alpha}} a_{xy}(q)(p_y - p_x) - (q_x - q_{mt}) - (p_x - p_{mt}) \quad (8)$$

In this relation, the collision avoidance and the velocity matching are contributed by the first two terms, and the end terms explain the dynamic target tracking [11].

2.2. Single-COM flocking control approach in free space

In this section, the flocking control protocol is described by adding Single-COM to the free space. COM is hard to reach the target in the Single-COM flocking control protocol (8). This makes the problem for robots to follow the target. Thus a recent limitation on the COM should be appended to this algorithm. In [20], extended flocking of robots with Single-COM of location and speed of robots are proposed in the obstacle space. Their protocol without obstacles is presented as the follows:

$$u_x = \sum_{y \in NB_x^{\alpha}} \phi_\alpha (\| q_y - q_x \|_\sigma) n_{xy} +$$
$$\sum_{y \in NB_x^{\alpha}} a_{xy}(q)(p_y - p_x) - (\bar{q} - q_{mt}) - \quad (9)$$
$$(\bar{p} - p_{mt}) - (q_x - q_{mt}) - (p_x - p_{mt})$$

The pair $(\bar{q}, \bar{p})$ is COM of locations and speeds of mobile agents, respectively, specified in (10).

$$\begin{cases} \bar{q} = \frac{1}{m} \sum_{x=1}^{m} p_x \\ \bar{p} = \frac{1}{m} \sum_{x=1}^{m} p_x \end{cases} \quad (10)$$

In relation (9), each robot should know the location and speed of other robots to compute COM $(\bar{q}, \bar{p})$. The details of the algorithm are described in [20]. Finally, based on the La and Sheng's extended algorithm without obstacle, we propose a Single-COM flocking approach with a moving target in free space as (11).

$$u_x = c_1^{\alpha} \sum_{y \in NB_x^{\alpha}} \phi_\alpha (\| q_y - q_x \|_\sigma) n_{xy} +$$
$$c_2^{\alpha} \sum_{y \in NB_x^{\alpha}} a_{xy}(q)(p_y - p_x) -$$
$$c_1^{SC}(\bar{q} - q_{mt}) - c_2^{SC}(\bar{p} - p_{mt}) - \quad (11)$$
$$c_1^{mt}(q_x - q_{mt}) - c_2^{mt}(p_x - p_{mt})$$

Here, $(c_1^{\alpha}, c_2^{\alpha})$, (c_1^{mt}, c_2^{mt}), and (c_1^{sc}, c_2^{sc}) are positive constants.

2.3. Multi-target tracking

In the multi-target tracking, each robot uses the Single-COM flocking control algorithm, which handles with one of the different targets (q_{mt_k}, p_{mt_k}) with $k = 1, 2, ..., N$ presented as (12).

$$u_x = c_1^{\alpha} \sum_{y \in NB_x^{\alpha}} \phi_{\alpha}(\| q_y - q_x \|_{\sigma}) n_{xy} +$$

$$c_2^{\alpha} \sum_{y \in NB_x^{\alpha}} a_{xy}(q)(p_y - p_x) -$$ (12)

$$c_1^{SC}(\bar{q} - q_{mt_k}) - c_2^{SC}(\bar{p} - p_{mt_k}) -$$

$$c_1^{mt}(q_x - q_{mt_k}) - c_2^{mt}(p_x - p_{mt_k})$$

The random selection (RS) algorithm operates to solve the problem of agent splitting/merging for multi-target tracking in MSN. In this algorithm, if the new target appears in the 50% of agents that are following, the present target will be chosen randomly to follow the recent target [18].

3. A Gravitational Search Algorithm (GSA)

GSA was first introduced in [33] as a novel metaheuristic search algorithm. It is basically influenced by the Newtonian laws and the notion of mass interactions [34]. In this way, the position of each mass is represented as a vector consisting of variables. As it is presented in [33], the gravitational mass of object j at the iteration t, $M_j(t)$ is computed as (13), where $fit_j(t)$ is the cost of agent j, and $worst(t)$ is the worst cost of swarms at time t.

$$M_j(t) = \frac{fit_j(t) - worst(t)}{\sum_{k=1}^{N}(fit_k(t) - worst(t))}$$ (13)

The overall force acting on the agent j at dimension m from other agents is computed by (14). Based upon the mobility rules, relation (15) shows the acceleration of the agent j in dimension m at time t. Furthermore, the next velocity of the ith agent is calculated by (16). Then the next location of the jth agent would be computed using (17).

$$F_j^m(t) = \sum_{k \in kbest\_set, k \neq j} rand_k G(t)$$

$$\frac{M_j(t).M_k(t)}{R_{jk}(t) + \varepsilon}(x_k^m(t) - x_j^m(t))$$ (14)

$$a_j^m(t) = \frac{(F_j^m(t))}{(M_j(t))} =$$

$$\sum_{k \in kbest\_set, k \neq j} rand_k G(t)$$ (15)

$$\frac{M_k(t)}{R_{jk}(t) + \varepsilon}(x_k^m(t) - x_j^m(t))$$

$$v_j^m(t+1) = rand_j \times v_j^m(t) + a_j^m(t),$$ (16)

$$x_j^m(t+1) = x_j^m(t) + v_j^m(t+1),$$ (17)

Where, $kbest\_set$ is the collection of k agents that have the best costs. G is a decreasing function

that takes the initial value G_0 and is reduced by time. $rand_k$ is a random number in the interval $[0,1]$, ϵ is a small value, and R_{jk} is the Euclidean distance between agents j and k [34, 35].

4. Proposed method

In this work, it was assumed that in the distance between the current and new positions in which the robot is moving, the computational unit of the robot is in the standby mode. Since in this duration a long distance is traversed, it has a suitable effect on power consumption. Also it is assumed that the agents are GPS-enabled. The initial location of robots is random in the space. Meanwhile, the trajectory of target is predefined.

4.1. Problem of flocking control protocol

The problem of control protocol (11) is sought the optimal results of the interaction parameters $(c_1^{\alpha}, c_2^{\alpha}), (c_1^{mt}, c_2^{mt})$, and (c_1^{sc}, c_2^{sc}) that implement the Reynolds rules for delivering the demanded flock behaviour in which the cost function (18) is minimized. Clearly, the pair $(c_1^{\alpha}, c_2^{\alpha})$ is applied to tune the forces between robot x and its flock mates (α – robot); pair (c_1^{mt}, c_2^{mt}) is applied to tune the forces between robot x and the dynamic target; and pair (c_1^{sc}, c_2^{sc}) is employed to tune the forces between the canter of flock and the target. These coefficients should be chosen as well in order to maintain the α – lattice formation, while sensors quickly converge to the target. Accordingly, the cost function is introduced as:

$$F = \frac{\sum_{x=1}^{z} \| \bar{q}_x(\tau) - q_x^{mt}(\tau) \|}{z \| \bar{q}_x(\tau = 0) - q_x^{mt}(\tau = 0) \|}$$ (18)

In the above relation, z shows the number of $\Delta \tau s$ and the simulation time is $T = z \times \Delta \tau$.

The cost function (18) presents the following terms:

- The average of Euclidean distance between COM and the dynamic target.
- The Euclidean distance of center of flock away from the moving target at the beginning time.

The cost function (18) is explicitly non-convex. Hence, in order to minimize this function, the evolutionary optimization strategy is stable since this mechanism results in a better performance in convergence percentage. GSA [33] is employed to optimize the problem of flocking control.

The term $\| \bar{q}_x(\tau = 0) - q_x^{mt}(\tau = 0) \|$ in the denominator of (18) shows the maximum distance at the beginning time, the sensors being most distant from the moving target. Moreover, the other term $\| \bar{q}_x(\tau) - q_x^{mt}(\tau) \|$ is the distance of the target away from COM at time τ. During the target tracking, this distance is decreased using the flocking control protocol (11). Decreasing the cost function depends upon how the coefficients of the interaction forces (c_1^α, c_2^α), (c_1^{mt}, c_2^{mt}), (c_1^{sc}, c_2^{sc}) are found out.

4.2. GSA-based Single-COM flocking control
In this section, GSA is adopted to solve the non-differentiable (18) in the flocking control design. The coefficients of the interaction forces in the cost function are computed via GSA. The following is a summary of the process:

Step 1. A population in the size M consisting of M possible solutions is generated randomly. Each agent is an array of the flocking parameters. Therefore, each agent X^I can be represented as:

$$X^I = [c_1^\alpha, c_2^\alpha, c_1^{mt}, c_2^{mt}, c_1^{sc}, c_2^{sc}]^I, I = 1, 2, ..., M$$

Step 2. The costs of agents are calculated by the cost function (18). All the remaining steps of the algorithm (GSA) would be conducted as described in Section 3. The best solution found by the algorithm is considered as the optimal array of the interaction parameters.

Algorithm 1 briefly shows the procedure of the proposed method.

Algorithm 1. Procedure of the proposed method
1. Identify search space
2. Generate random solutions considering X^I
3. Evaluate fitness function:
3.1. Update position of sensor x
3.2. Update velocity of sensor x
3.3. Compute distance between COM and a moving target.
3.4. Compute fitness value by (18)
4. Update $M_j(t)$ using (13)
5. Calculate total force in different directions using (14).
6. Calculate acceleration and velocity using (15) and (16).
7. Update positions using (17)
8. Repeat steps 3-7 until stopping criterion is satisfied.

5. Results and Discussion
In order to evaluate the performance of the proposed method, some experiments were conducted. We simulated a single target moving with circular wave, and the multiple targets moving with a semi-circular and semi-sine wave trajectory. The parameters were set as follow:

- GSA parameters : The search space of the coefficients of the interaction forces is considered between 0 and 10 $1 \le (c_1^v, c_2^v) \le 10$ for $v = \alpha, mt, sc$). Both the number of iterations and the

population size were set to 100. G is a linearly decreasing function starting with $G_0 = 0.125$ and ending with 0. The optimal value for G_0 is computed by the trial-and-error method.

- Parameters of flocking control in the free space: the number of sensors is 50, and the initial position of sensors is randomly distributed in the space $[0, 90] \times [0, 90]$. The parameters a and b are equal to 5 (for $\phi(z)$ [12]). For σ-norm, $\varepsilon = 0.1$; $h = 0.2$ for $\phi_\alpha(z)$. The coordinate radius is $r = 1.2\gamma = 7.5$.

- Parameters of single dynamic target: path of moving target is the circular wave path:
$q_{mt} = [210 - 100\cos(\tau), 105 + 80\sin(\tau)]^T$, where τ is $0 \le \tau \le 5.5$ and $p_{mt} = (q_{mt}(\tau) - q_{mt}(\tau - 1)) / \Delta\tau$.

- Parameters of multiple moving targets: path of thev moving target is the semi-circular wave path:
$q_{mt} = [130 - 90\cos(\tau), 250 + 30\tau + 80\sin(\tau)]^T$, where τ is $0 \le \tau \le 6$, and $p_{mt} = (q_{mt}(\tau) - q_{mt}(\tau - 1)) / \Delta\tau$.
Path of the moving target is the semi-sine wave path:
$q_{mt} = [200 + 40\tau, 50 + 50\tau + 150\sin(\tau)]^T$ where τ is $0 \le \tau \le 6$, and $p_{mt} = (q_{mt}(\tau) - q_{mt}(\tau - 1)) / \Delta\tau$.

$\Delta\tau$ is equal to 0.05 in this simulation experiment (see Figure 1).

Comparative methods: In order to indicate the superiority of the proposed method, this protocol was compared with two methods that have been proposed in the literature works. The former method is the flocking control in the free space that has been proposed by Reza Olfati-Saber [11] and the later one is the extended flocking control with Single-COM that has been proposed by Sheng and La in [19]. These methods use relations (4) and (9), respectively. The experiments are performed on single and multiple moving target trackings.

The optimal values for the interaction forces including $(c_1^\alpha, c_2^\alpha), (c_1^{mt}, c_2^{mt})$, and (c_1^{sc}, c_2^{sc}) are found using GSA regarding (11) for various sizes of robots. The results obtained are reported in table 1 by varying the number of sensors as 10, 30, 50, 70, and 90. Figure 1 shows the results of single target tracking on circular wave trajectory for the proposed method, which obtains the optimal parameters using GSA (as in Table 1); also figures 2 and 3, respectively, show the results of the flocking control algorithm without COM [11] and the extended flocking control algorithm with Single-COM [20]. Figure 4 represents the result of the multiple moving target trackings on the semi-circular and semi-sine wave trajectories using the parameters achieved by GSA for single target tracking. The results reported in table 1 are also applicable to the multiple mode. It is clearly observable that the center of flocks precisely tracks the moving targets. Figures 5 and 6, respectively, illustrate the results of the flocking control algorithm without COM [11] and the extended flocking control algorithm with Single-COM [20] in multiple moving target trackings.

In these figures, the path of target and the mean of positions of all robots are displayed in red and black, respectively. Also the initial and end positions of all robots are indicated. As it can be observed in figures 1 and 4, the targets are followed precisely and surrounded by the flocks of robots. In fact, the path of COMs coincides with the path of targets in the proposed method, while according to figures 2 and 5 that use the method proposed by Olfati-Saber [11] and figures 3 and 6 that use the Single-COM method presented by Hung La [20], the paths do not coincide and the distance between the targets and the center of flocks is high.

Figure 7(a) shows the mean progress of the cost function (18) for 50 sensors during 100 iterations by GSA. The results obtained are averaged over 10 independent runs, as the results reported in table 1. Figure 7(b) shows the distance between the center of flock and the moving target in circular wave trajectory using GSA during 100 iterations of the algorithm.

Figures 8(a) and 8(b) compare the errors between COM (center of mass) of the locations of robots and the location of a moving target (following performance) using three approaches, No-COM [11], Single-COM without iteration forces [20], and the proposed flocking protocol using the

optimal parameters of table 1 for 50 sensors. Figures 8(a) and 8(b) evaluate three methods on a single moving target and multiple dynamic targets, respectively. These figures obviously display the superiority of the proposed method in comparison with the previous ones, and clearly represent big errors between COM of locations of all agents and the location of the dynamic target for flocking control algorithm without optimal parameters shown in [11] and [20].

Figure 9(a) displays the fitness values during 100 iterations for various numbers of sensors using GSA; and figure 9(b) shows the error between COM and single moving target during target tracking using the data reported in table 1 for various numbers of sensors.

Considering the results reported in figures 1 and 4 by using the optimal flocking control leads to a better convergent speed, and errors reach zero after a few seconds. Also the parameters obtained for single target tracking as figures 4 and 7(b) have optimal results for multiple target trackings.

6. Conclusion

In this work, we investigated the optimization problem of Single-COM flocking control protocol to track a dynamic target for a mobile sensor network. The cost function was non-convex and the optimization technique based on GSA was developed. The optimal interaction forces for different numbers of sensors in the Single-COM flocking control protocol with single and multi-target tracking were proposed. Evaluation of the swarm robots-like act based dynamic target following the free space is given. The numerical results obtained validate the proposed method performance in comparison with the other approaches.

In the future, we have decided to work on the flock behavior in free and obstacle spaces. Also we would like to improve GSA with memetic as well as discussing the flocking control in 3D. In addition, the power consumption analysis is deferred to the future work.

Table 1. Optimal forces of Single-COM flocking control for different sizes found by GSA for various numbers of sensors.

Number of sensors	c_1^{α}	c_2^{α}	c_1^{mt}	c_2^{mt}	c_1^{sc}	c_2^{sc}
10	5.48098	3.73038	4.61782	4.38692	8.45326	3.0838
30	8.24948	3.7478	3.77368	5.0691	5.44878	2.11092
50	8.90246	2.63806	7.05536	4.97568	5.46172	3.4584
70	6.95232	2.17282	3.92754	8.16904	7.35568	3.13232
90	7.71056	3.28264	3.7309	5.27358	6.52208	2.34054

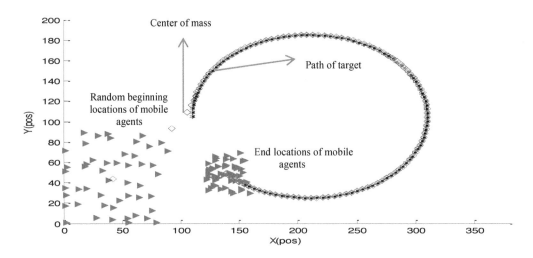

Figure 1. Beginning and ending locations of 50 mobile agents that are following a dynamic target in circular wave path with optimal parameters in table 1 by proposed flocking control algorithm using (11) and GSA.

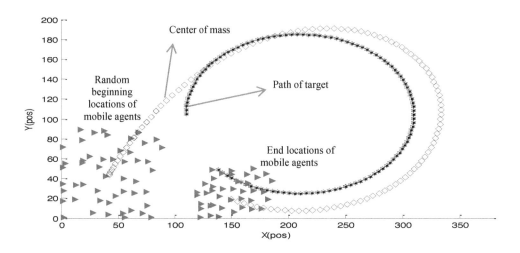

Figure 2. Beginning and ending locations of 50 mobile agents that are following a moving target in circle wave path without iteration forces using (4) [11].

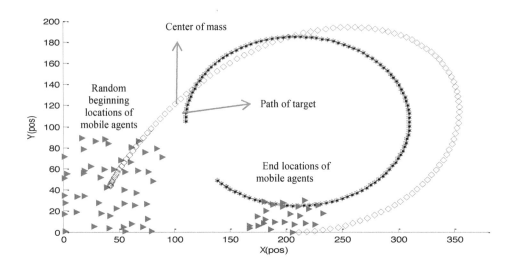

Figure 3. Beginning and ending locations of 50 mobile agents that are following a moving target in circle wave path with extended flocking control algorithm using (9) [20].

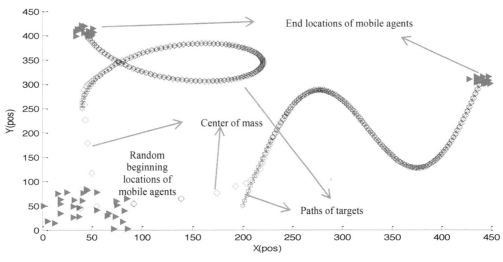

Figure 4. Beginning and ending locations of 30 mobile agents that are following two dynamic targets in semi-circular and semi-sine wave paths with optimal parameters in table 1 by proposed flocking control algorithm using (11) and GSA.

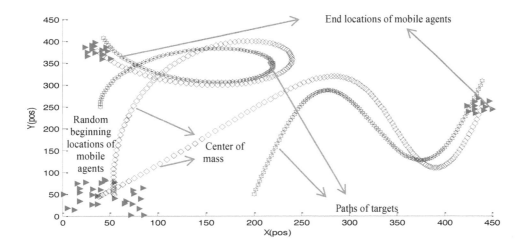

Figure 5. Beginning and ending locations of 30 mobile agents that are following two moving targets in semi-circular and semi-sine wave paths without iteration forces using (4) [11].

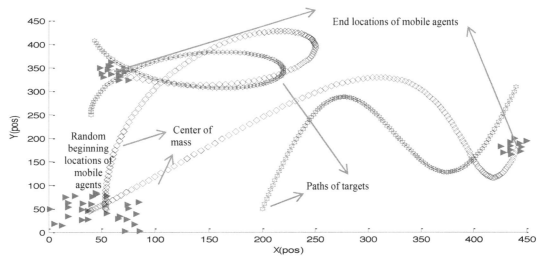

Figure 6. Beginning and ending locations of 50 mobile agents that are following two moving target in semi-circular and semi-sine wave paths with extended flocking control algorithm using (9) [20].

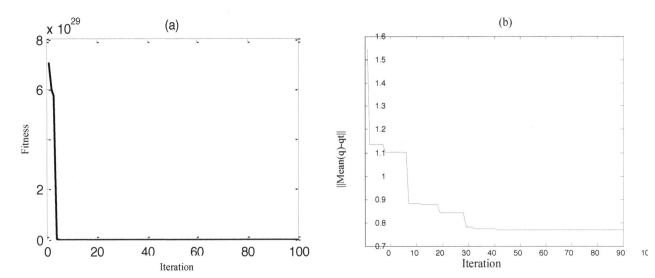

Figure 7. (a) Value of cost function during 100 iteration for 50 sensors, (b) errors between COM of locations of robots and location of target during 100 iterationa for 50 sensors.

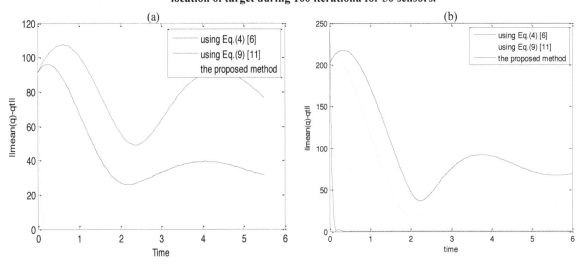

Figure 8. (a) Errors between COM of locations of robots and location of target in circular trajectory, (b) errors between COM of locations of robots and locations of two targets in semi-circular and semi-sine trajectory; all following processes for three algorithms are done on 50 sensors.

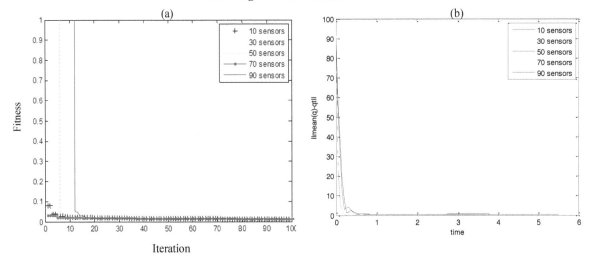

Figure 9. (a) Value of cost function for various numbers of sensors during 100 iterations, (b) errors between COM of locations of robots and location of target in circular trajectory for different numbers of sensors.

References

[1] Culler, D., Estrin, D. & Srivastava, M., (2004). Overview of Sensor Networks. IEEE Transactions on Computer, vol. 37, no. 8, pp. 41–49.

[2] Hosseinirad, S. M. & Basu, S. K., (2014). Wireless Sensor Network Design Through Genetic Algorithm. Journal of AI and Data Mining. vol. 2, no .1, pp. 85-96.

[3] Rafsanjani, M. K., Mirhoseini, M. & Nourizadeh, R. (2013). A Multi-Objective Evolutionary Algorithm For Improving Energy Consumption in Wireless Sensor Networks. Bulletin Of The Transilvania University Of Brasov, vol. 6, no. 2, pp. 107-116.

[4] Ghaffari, A., & Nobahary, S. (2015). Fault Detection Method by Using Genetic Algorithm in Clustered Wireless Sensor Networks. Journal of AI and Data Mining. vol. 3. no. 1, pp. 47-57.

[5] Kamath, S., Meisner, E. & Isler, V. (2007). Triangulation Based Multi Target Tracking with Mobile Sensor Networks. IEEE International Conference on Robotics and Automation, Roma, Italy, pp. 3283–3288, 2007.

[6] Ganguli, A., Susca, S., Martinez, S., Bullo, F. & Cortes, J. (2005). On Collective Motion in Sensor Networks: Sample Problems and Distributed Algorithms. 44th IEEE Conference on Decision and Control, and the European Control Conference, Seville, Spain, pp. 4239–4244.

[7] Biagioni, E. & Bridges, K., (2002). The Application of Remote Sensor Technology to Assist the Recovery of Rare and Endangered Species. Special issue on Distributed Sensor Networks for the International Journal of High Performance Computing Applications, vol. 16, no. 3, pp. 112-121.

[8] Vicsek, T., Czirok, A., Jacob, E. B., Cohen, I., & Schochet, O. (1995). Novel type of phase transitions in a system of self-driven particles. Phys. Rev. Lett, vol. 75, pp. 1226–1229.

[9] Mogilner, A., Edelstein-Keshet, L., Bent, L., & Spiros, A. (2003). Mutual Interactions, Potentials, and Individual Distance in a Social Aggregation, J. Math. Biol, vol. 47, pp. 353–389.

[10] Couzin, I. D., Krause, J., James, R., Ruxton, G. D., & Franks, N. R. (2002). Collective Memory and Spatial Sorting in Animal Groups, J. Theor. Biol, vol. 218, pp. 1–11.

[11] Olfati-Saber, R. (2006). Flocking for Multi-Agent Dynamic Systems: Algorithms and Theory. IEEE Transactions on Automatic Control, vol. 51, no. 3, pp. 401-420.

[12] Murray, R. M. (2007). Recent Research in Cooperative Control of Multivehicle Systems. Journal of Dynamic Systems, Measurement, and Control, vol. 129, no. 5, pp. 571-583.

[13] Jalalkamali, P. (2012). Distributed Tracking and Information-Driven Control for Mobile Sensor Networks, Ph.D. Thesis, Thayer School of Engineering Dartmouth College Hanover, New Hampshire.

[14] Reynolds, C. (1987). Flocks, Birds, and Schools: a Distributed Behavioral Model. Computer Graphics. ACM SIGGRAPH '87 Conference Proceedings, Anaheim, California, vol. 21, no. 4, pp. 25–34, 1987.

[15] Wang, Z. & Gu, D. (2006). A Survey on Application of Consensus Protocol to Flocking Control. In Proceedings of the 12th Chinese Automation and Computing Society Conference in the UK, England, pp. 1–8, 2006.

[16] Su, H., Wang, X. & Lin, Z. (2007). Flocking of Multi–Agents with a Virtual Leader Part I: With A Minority of Informed Agents. In Proceedings of the 46th IEEE Conference on Decision and Control, New Orleans, LA, USA, pp. 2937–2942, 2007.

[17] Su, H., Wang, X. & Lin, Z. (2007). Flocking of Multi–Agents with a Virtual Leader Part II: With A Virtual Leader Of Varying Velocity. 46th IEEE Conference Decision and Control, New Orleans, LA, USA, pp. 1429 – 1434, 2007.

[18] Papi, F. (2015). Multi-Sensor D-GLMB Filter for Multi-Target Tracking Using Doppler Only Measurements. Intelligence and Security Informatics Conference (EISIC). Manchester, England, pp. 83-89, 2015.

[19] La, H. M. & Sheng, W. (2009), Moving Targets Tracking and Observing in a Distributed Mobile Sensor Network. American Control Conference. MO, USA, pp. 3319-3324, 2009.

[20] La, H. M. & Sheng, W. (2009). Flocking Control of a Mobile Sensor Network to Track and Observe a Moving Target. In Proceedings of the 2009 IEEE International Conference on Robotics and Automation (ICRA 2009), Kobe, Japan, pp.3129–3134, 2009.

[21] La, H. M. & Sheng, W. (2009). Adaptive Flocking Control for Dynamic Target Tracking in Mobile Sensor Networks, In Proceedings of the 2009 IEEE International Conference on Intelligent Robots and Systems (IROS), Missouri, USA, pp. 4843–4848, 2009.

[22] La H. M. & Sheng, W. (2009). Moving Targets Tracking and Observing in a Distributed Mobile Sensor Network. In Proceedings of 2009 American Control Conference (ACC), Missouri, USA, pp. 3319–3324, 2009.

[23] La, H. M., Nguyen, T. H., Nguyen, C. H. & Nguyen, H. N. (2009). Optimal Flocking Control for a Mobile Sensor Network Based a Moving Target Tracking. In Proceedings of the 2009 IEEE International Conference on Systems, Man, and Cybernetics (SMC), San Antonio, Texas, USA, pp. 4801–4806, 2009.

[24] Tu, Z., Wang, Q., Qi, H. & Shen, Y. (2012). Flocking Based Distributed Self-Deployment Algorithms in Mobile Sensor Networks. Journal of

Parallel and Distributed Computing, vol. 72, pp. 437-449.

[25] Tu, Z., Wang, Q., Qi, H. & Shen, Y. (2012). Flocking Based Sensor Deployment in Mobile Sensor Networks. Computer Communications, vol. 35, pp. 849-869.

[26] Ngugen, T., Han, T. T., & La, H. M. (2016). Distributed Flocking Control of Mobile Robots by bounded feedback, Fifty-fourth Annual Allerton Conference, USA.

[27] Brandon, J., Wellman, Jess & B., Hoagg. (2017). A flocking algorithm with individual agent destinations and without a centralized leader, System & Control Letters, vol. 102, pp. 57-67.

[28] Chen, Z., Zhang, H. T. & Fan M. C. (2013). A Flocking Algorithm for Multi-Agents in Bounded Space. 32nd Chinese Control Conference (CCC), Xian, China, pp. 7131-7135, 2013.

[29] Ganganath, N., Cheng, C. & Tse, C. (2016). Distributed Anti-Flocking Algorithms for Dynamic Converage of Mobile Sensor Networks. IEEE Transactions on Industrial Informatics, vol. 12, no. 5, pp. 1765-1805, 2016.

[30] Hassanzadeh, I., Mobayen, S., & Kharrati, H. (2007). Design of MIMO controller for a manipulator using Tabu search algorithm, International conference on intelligent and advanced systems.

[31] Hassanzade, I., Mobayem, S. (2011). Controller design for rotary inverted pendulum system using evolutionary algorithms, Mathematical problems in engineering, vol. 2011, pp. 1-17.

[32] Ferrari, S., Foderaro, G., Zhu, P. & Wettergren, T. A. (2016). Distributed Optimal Control of Multiscale Dynamical Systems: a Tutorial. IEEE Control Systems, vol. 36, no. 2, pp.102-116.

[33] Arora, J. S. (2017). Nature-Inspired Search Methods, Introduction to Optimum Design. Academic Press, USA, pp. 739–769.

[34] Rashedi, E., Nezamabadi-pour, H. & Saryazdi, S. (2009). GSA: a Gravitational Search Algorithm.

Journal of Information Sciences, vol. 179, no. 13, pp. 2232–2248.

[35] Rashedi, E., Nezamabadi-pour, H. & Saryazdi, S. (2010). BGSA: Binary Gravitational Search Algorithm. Journal of Natural Computing, vol. 9, pp. 727–745.

[36] Rashedi, E. & Nezamabadi-pour, H. (2014). Feature Subset Selection using Improved Binary Gravitational Search Algorithm. Journal of Intelligent and Fuzzy Systems, vol. 26, no. 3, pp. 1211-1221.

[37] Chatterjee, A. & Mahanti, G. K. (2010). Comparative Performance of Gravitational Search Algorithm and Modified Particle Swarm Optimization Algorithm for Synthesis of Thinned Scanned Concentric Ring Array Antenna. Progress in Electromagnetics Research, vol. 25, pp. 331–348.

[38] Yin, M., Hu, Y., Yang, F., Li, X. & Gu, W. (2011). A Novel Hybrid K-Harmonic Means And Gravitational Search Algorithm Approach for Clustering, Expert Systems with Applications, vol. 38, no. 8, pp. 9319–9324.

[39] Li, C. & Zhou, J. (2011). Parameters Identification of Hydraulic Turbine Governing System Using Improved Gravitational Search Algorithm. Energy Conversion and Management, vol. 52, no. 1, pp. 374–381.

[40] Taghipour, M., Moradi, A. R. & Yazdani-Asrami, M. (2010). Identification of Magnetizing Inrush Current in Power Transformers Using GSA Trained ANN for Educational Purposes. In Proceeding of IEEE Conference on Open Systems (ICOS), Kuala Lumpur, Malaysia, pp. 23–27, 2010.

[41] Mirhosseini, M., Brani, F. & Nezamabadi-pour, H. (2017). QQIGSA: A Quadrivalent Quantum-Inspired GSA and its Application in Optimal Adaptive Design of Wireless Sensor Networks. Journal of Network and Computer Applications, vol. 78, pp. 231-241.

[42] Han, X. H., Chang, X. M., Quan, L., Xiong, X. Y., Li, J.X., Zhang, Zh. X. & Liu, Y. (2014). Feature Subset Selection by Gravitational Search Algorithm Optimization. Information Sciences, vol. 281, pp. 128-146.

9

A Fast and Self-Repairing Genetic Programming Designer for Logic Circuits

A. M. Mousavi [1*] and M. Khodadadi [2]

1. Department of Electrical Engineering, Lorestan University, Khoramabad, Lorestan, Iran.

2. Department of Electrical Engineering, Azad University, Arak Branch, Arak, Iran

*Corresponding author: mousavi.m@lu.ac.ir (A..Mousavi).

Abstract
Usually the important parameters in the design and implementation of combinational logic circuits are the number of gates, transistors, and levels used in the design of a circuit. In this regard, various evolutionary paradigms with different competency have recently been introduced. However, while being advantageous, evolutionary paradigms also have some limitations including a) lack of confidence in reaching the correct answer, b) long convergence time, and c) restriction on the tests performed with a higher number of input variables. In this work, we implement a genetic programming approach that given a Boolean function, outputs an equivalent circuit such that the truth table is covered, and the minimum number of gates (and to some extent, transistors and levels) are used. Furthermore, our implementation improves the aforementioned limitations by incorporating a self-repairing feature (improving limitation a); efficient use of the conceivable coding space of the problem, which virtually brings about a kind of parallelism and improves the convergence time (improving limitation b). Moreover, we apply our method to solve the Boolean functions with a higher number of inputs (improving limitation c). These issues are verified through multiple tests, and the results obtained are reported.

Keywords: *Genetic Programming, Logic Circuits, Design, Optimization.*

1. Introduction

With the emergence of new methods for the optimization problems, the research works in the design of combinatorial logic circuits have also gained a boost. This trend has paved the arena for entering evolutionary paradigms as one of the successful models for solving the optimization problems, in general, and optimization of combinational logic circuits, in particular.

In this paper, we present a method based upon genetic programming that efficiently utilizes the coding space of the logical circuits to accelerate the convergence time of the solutions. As a result, the cases we tested led to less-gate designs (with smaller number of transistors and levels) compared to the earlier works. The distinguishing facets of our approach are the utilization of a new encoding for the logical circuits and self-repairing ability so that the program will be able to recover from incomplete answers. These are utilized along

with a proper evaluation function and selection strategy. Applying these features to several test cases shows that the proposed approach is able to achieve satisfactory results in terms of the usual design criteria.

Our work and its achievements will be presented as what follow. In Section 2, we briefly review some earlier works. Section 3 begins with a brief description of genetics programming (GP) and continues with our implementation for the design of combinational logic circuits including the appropriate coding, evolutionary operators, and so on. In Section 4, the results of applying our approach to a series of previously studied circuits as well as the new ones are reported. Finally, Section 5 closes the paper with conclusions and a few suggestions for further research.

2. Related works

One of the classical methods implemented to

simplify digital functions, as taught in textbooks, is the basic Boolean manipulation techniques. These methods, which mainly consist of factoring and removing variables, could lead to a rather straightforward approach of Karnaugh Maps [15]. While the Karnaugh Maps is effective in solving problems with a few variables, problems with more variables require computer-based approaches such as Quin maccLausky [16]. With an increase in the number of design variables and constraints, the complexity of the design process increases. This fact along with a growth in the use of the computational intelligence for the optimization problems has paved the way for applying evolutionary computation paradigms to the design of electronic and logical circuits [3,4]. Earlier works in applying the evolutionary procedures to the design of logical circuits goes back to the application of genetic algorithm (GA) and genetic programming (GP) [1,5], where the emphasis was on the mere generation of circuits rather than the optimization concerns. On the other hand, others performed a comparison between the evolutionary procedures in terms of their ability in convergence. For example, [13] and [14] compare GP and GA, and show that GA may prematurely converge to non-local optima, while GP has a greater chance to find the best solutions.

In [10], a so-called Cartesian Genetic Programming (CGP) method has been proposed for the design of combinatorial logical circuits. In this work, instead of using a tree structure, which is usually used in GP, arrays of strings are used for genotypes, which is more effective in achieving optimal solutions. In a similar manner to CGP, a methodology has been proposed in [12], which is more inclined toward the implementation of Boolean functions rather than focusing on the least gates designs. In [11], GP has been employed for the design of combinatorial logical circuits considering the least number of gates, transistors, and levels. However, there are some limitations. First, the only gates used are the NAND ones. Secondly, there is no concern what so ever regarding the rate of convergence of the program. Thirdly, the results obtained are only compared with the manual designs. Finally, the evaluations reported are limited to functions with four variable inputs.In the current work, our goal was to implement the logical functions with the minimum number of gates (and to some extent, transistors and levels). At the same time, we tried to improve some

defects and shortcomings seen in similar works such as low convergence rate (number of generations to get to the answer), not reaching the desired design, high populations for achieving the desired results, and no full coverage of the truth table.

3. Implementation
3.1. Genetic programming
Genetic programming (GP) is one of the several evolutionary paradigms available for solving the optimization problems via computers. In this approach, first of all, an initial population of solutions or computer programs, each of which is a potential solution to the problem, is created. Then each of these candidate solutions is evaluated versus a so-called fitness function in order to measure its fitness. The more fit a solution is, the more chance is given for being selected in the next generation. Then through applying the cross-over and mutation operations, GP would produce a new generation of solutions from a previously elected one. These steps are repeated in GP until a convincing solution is obtained or a certain number of generations are reached.

Since how we encode the conceivable solution space would significantly affect the accuracy as well as the speed of convergence, in what follows we explain our encoding scheme.

3.2. Encoding
As mentioned in the very beginning, GP starts with a population of initial solutions that are usually generated randomly. Each of these candidate solutions is essentially a combinatorial circuit that is made up of a number of logical gates. In practice, each candidate solution circuits needs to be properly defined for the implementation of GP. This process is called encoding of the solution space. One way to do encoding is for each solution to be individually coded and entered into the GP search process. This creates a large number of independent small data chunks, where evolutionary operations such as cross-over, mutation, and evaluation of the candidate solutions would be independently applied to these small items. This approach results in a lengthy GP implementation. On the other hand, we could encode several logic circuits as a single candidate solution for the implementation of GP and aggregately apply the evolutionary operations. This approach speeds up the search cycle by introducing a kind of parallelism in the implementation. For this purpose, several

candidate solutions are gathered in a 2D array, where the number of rows determines the number of solutions and the number of columns determines the levels used in the resulting circuit. This is illustrated in figure 1 for a 5*5 array. In this figure, all the evolutionary operations are applied simultaneously to the 5 solutions. Each element of the array is itself a 1D array, where the numbers in the array indicate the type of gates used together with the inter-connections of their inputs and outputs to the other gates (1D array elements) in the main array. In this configuration, the input of each element is allowed to come only from the previous stage and the last column represents the possible outputs.

[2,0,3,0,2] [1,0,1,0,0] [2,2,4,1,5] [2,3,1,3,3] [5,1,2,2,2]

[2,0,5,0,5] [3,1,2,0,1] [2,2,3,1,5] [3,2,4,1,3] [4,3,2,0,2]

[4,0,1,0,4] [4,1,3,1,3] [5,2,5,2,0] [5,3,2,1,1] [2,3,2,3,0]

[3,0,4,0,2] [1,0,1,0,0] [3,2,4,0,2] [2,1,1,0,3] [2,4,2,4,0]

[4,0,4,0,3] [3,0,2,1,2] [1,2,5,0,2] [5,1,5,1,0] [4,1,5,4,5]

Figure 1. A typical array of 5 candidate solutions.

As it could be seen in figure 1, each element in the array is composed of five numbers with specific meanings. The first and second numbers represent the row and represent the row and column that one of the inputs of the gate should be connected, while the third and fourth numbers represent the row and column that the other input of the gate should be connected (based on two inputs gates). We interpreted the numbers 10, 20, 30, 40, … as the main input variables A, B, C, D, …. The fifth number shows the type of gate according to the equivalences: WIRE = 0, AND = 1, OR = 2, XOR = 3, NAND = 4, NOR = 5.

According to the configuration in figure 1 and depending on from which row of the last column we take the output, 5 combinatorial logic circuits are possible as the candidate solutions. For example, if we take the output from the first row of the last column, the circuit of figure 3a is obtained. In this figure, the element [5 1 2 2 2] in the first row and the fifth column is the output. This element is an OR gate whose first input comes from the output of the gate in the fifth row and the first column, while its second input comes from the output of the gate located in the second

row and the second column. The situation is better visualized in figure 2, where the inter-connections for this OR gate is drawn up to the main input variables (A, B, C, …).

When this protocol is applied to all the rows of the last column, 5 circuits in figure 3 are obtained.

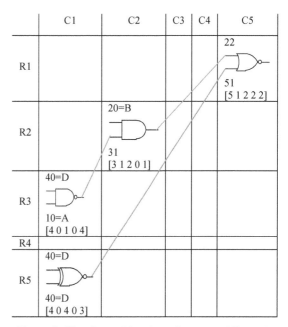

Figure 2. Circuit resulting from first row of figure 1.

3.3. Fitness function

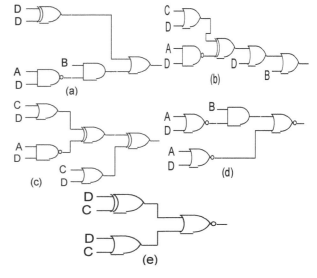

Figure 3. Equivalent circuits for array of figure 1. Last column and a) first row as output; b) second row as output; c) third row as output; d) fourth row as output; e) fifth row as output.

An important factor influencing the success of GP is an appropriate evaluation function that determines the fitness of possible solutions for their respective effectiveness in the next population. According to the common criteria of optimality for combinational logic circuits including having minimum number of gates and maximum coverage of the truth table, it is natural to consider these criteria in the definition of the evaluation function. Accordingly, the evaluation function would be a weighted sum of the number of false results (compared to the truth table) and the number of gates as in (1).

$$FF = \frac{(10 \times \frac{errors}{2^{in}}) + (\frac{gates}{31})}{11} \qquad (1)$$

In this equation, *in* is the number of inputs. E*rrors* is the number of errors of the output of the solution circuit with respect to the truth table. G*ates* is the number of gates used in the proposed circuit. The fitness function is designed so that its values are between 0 and 1. The more its value is close to zero, the more would be the fitness of the proposed solution. Nevertheless, we use the value 1-FF in our drawings such that the more close we get to the value of 1, the proposed solution would be more successful.

While the evaluation function in (1) targets solutions with the lowest number of gates, the number of columns in the array of solutions specifies the maximum number of levels of the solution. Therefore, we can use the number of columns in the array of solutions as a parameter whereby we allow it to vary between 1 and a maximum. For each value of the parameter for which the optimal solution is found such that it covers the truth table completely, we stop and the next values will not be tried. As a result, the maximum number of levels of the designs would be controllable. Note that for a specific choice for the number of columns, our approach still outputs circuits with less level than the number of columns. Thus in the evaluation tests that come in Section 4, we fix the number of columns to 5.

Therefore, with this approach and using the NAND, NOR, and XOR gates for which the number of employed transistors are compared in table 1, our implementation targets the circuits with a minimum number of gates, levels, and transistors.

3.4. Selection and evolution of generations
After the effectiveness of each chromosome in the initial population was calculated, better chromosomes of the population should be selected as the parents of the next generation. In order to maintain the diversity of the next generation,

while keeping the elite chromosomes, the roulette wheel and elitism selection approaches are being used together to select the parents for the next population. Then the usual cross-over and mutation operations would be applied to create a new generation.

Table 1. CMOS gate characteristics.

Gate type code	Gate type	Gate symbol	Area (μm)	Number of transistor
0	Wire		0	**0**
1	NOT		1728	**2**
2	AND		2880	**6**
3	OR		2880	**6**
4	NAND		2304	**4**
5	NOR		2304	**4**
6	XOR		4608	**9**
7	XNOR		5184	**9**

4. Evaluation
In this section, we illustrate our implementation of GP and evaluate its performance via Boolean functions. We also compare our results with the related works.

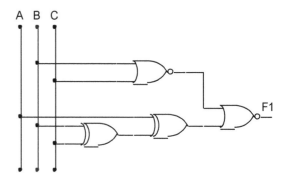

Figure 4. Circuit for F1.

4.1. Test Functions
Test 1: A function with three variables:

$F_1(A,B,C) = \sum (3,5,6)$

The optimized circuit is shown in figure 4. The convergence diagram for the circuit is shown in figure 5. The first point to note is a fast convergence process (in generation 10), as could be seen in figure 5. The second point is depicted in table 2. As it could be seen, using our approach, 4 gates and 26 transistors are used for the circuit in 3 levels.

Table 2 compares the results of other works. Note that the Human Designer 1 (HD1) uses the Karnaugh Maps plus Boolean algebra, whereas the Human Designer 2 (HD2) uses the Quine-McCluskey Procedure.

As it can be seen in this table, compared to the classic methods, the proposed method reduced the average number of gates and transistors by 44% and 35%, respectively, and also has some advantages over other approaches such as MGA [8] and NGA [6].

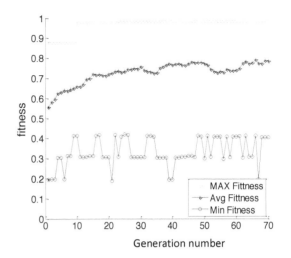

Figure 5. Convergence diagram for F_1.

Table 2. Comparison of proposed method vs. similar approaches in terms of general design parameters for function F_1.

Number of Levels	Number of transistors	Number of gates	Optimized function	Method
3	36	5	$F=C.(A\oplus B)+B.(A\oplus C)$	HD1(KM)[8]
4	35	6	$F=A'.B.C+A.(B\oplus C)$	HD2(QM)[8]
4	32	5	$F=(C+B).(B\oplus(A\oplus C))'$	NGA[6]
3	27	4	$F=(A+B).C\oplus(A.B)$	MGA[8]
3	26	4	$F=\{[(B\oplus C)\oplus A]+(B+C)'\}'$	our approach

Test 2 : A function with 4 variables

$F_2(A,B,C,D)=\sum (0,1,3,6,7,8,10,13)$.

Figure 6 shows the designed circuit using the proposed approach.

As it could be seen in figure 6, the circuit is

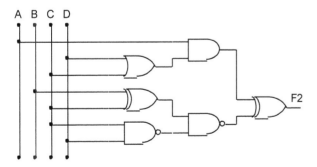

Figure 6. Circuit for F_2.

realized by 6 gates and 38 transistors in three levels. Table 3 (Human Designer 1 uses the Karnaugh Maps plus Boolean algebra to simplify the circuit, whereas Human Designer 2 uses the Sasao method [7]) also compares the results in

terms of the optimal circuit parameters. Decreasing the number of gates, transistors, and levels is evident. The convergence diagram for the circuit for function F_2 is shown in figure 7. A fast convergence process is seen in generation 37, though due to the increase in the number of inputs and function's complexity, the process is lengthier compared to F_1.

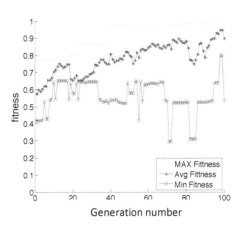

Figure 7. Convergence diagrams for function F_2.

Table 3. Comparison of proposed approach vs. other approaches in terms of general design parameters for function F$_2$.

Number of levels	Number of transistors	Number of gates	Optimized function	Method
4	56	11	F=((A′.C)⊕(B′.D′))+((C′.D′).(A⊕B′))	**HD1(KM)[8]**
5	65	12	F=C′⊕D′B′⊕CD′A′⊕C′D′B	**HD2(sasao)[8]**
5	61	10	F=(B.C′.D)⊕((B+D)⊕A⊕((C+D)+A)))′	**NGA[6]**
5	47	7	F=((B⊕(B.C))⊕((A+C+D)⊕A)′)	**MGA[8]**
3	38	6	F=((C+D).A)⊕((C.D)′.(C⊕B))′	**our approach**

Test 3: A functions with 4 variables
F$_3$(A,B,C,D)= $\sum$ (0,4,5,6,7,8,9,10,13,15).

The designed circuit for this function using the proposed approach is shown in figure 8. The circuit is implemented by 5 gates and 30 transistors in 4 levels. Table 4 shows the comparison results as well.

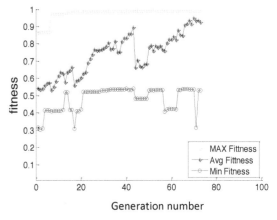

Figure 9. Convergence diagram for F$_3$.

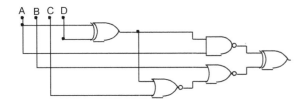

Figure 8. Circuit for F$_3$.

Table 4. Comparison of proposed method vs. similar approaches in terms of general design parameters for function F$_3$.

Number of levels	Number of transistors	Number of gates	Optimized function	Method
4	52	9	F=((A⊕B)⊕((A.D).(B+C)))+((A+C)+D)′	**HD1(KM)[8]**
5	44	10	F=A′B+A(B′D′+C′D)	**HD2(QM)[8]**
4	47	7	F=((A⊕B)⊕A.D)+(C+(A⊕D))′	**NGA[6]**
4	47	7	F=((A⊕B)⊕A.D)+(C+(A⊕D))′	**MGA[8]**
4	39	5	F=((A⊕D).C)′⊕{[(A⊕D)+C]′+B}′	**Our approach**

From table 4, one can conclude that compared to the other methods, our approach has achieved a design by an average of 25% less gates, less transistors, and thanks to less levels it produces less propagation delay. In figure 9, the convergence diagram for function F$_3$ is drawn. It reaches the solution in just 18 generations, which is faster compared to F$_2$ in spite of having more minterms. This is partially due to the type of minterms in the functions and also the inherent random factors employed in the GP process.

Test 4: A function with 5 variables

F$_4$(A,B,C,D,E)=$\sum$ (0,3,5,6,9,12,15,16,19,21,22,25,28,31)

A straightforward circuit for the implementation of this function is shown in figure 10. Also the result of applying our GP approach to this function is shown in figure 11. The pace of the convergence is also shown in figure 12. The final solution for F$_4$ is reached in generation 58, whose 5 variables and number of minterms explain this lengthier convergence compared to the previous test functions.

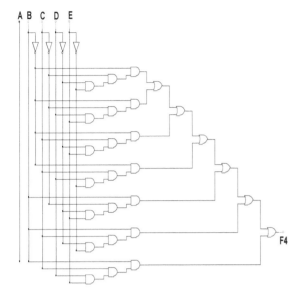

Figure 10. Circuit for F$_4$.

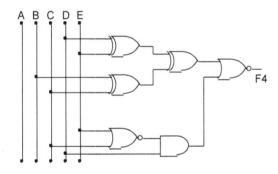

Figure 11. Designed circuit for F$_4$ using proposed approach.

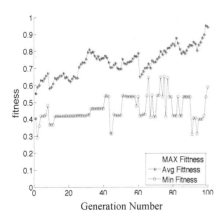

Figure 12. Convergence diagrams for F$_4$.

5. Self-Repairing

In many cases, evolutionary paradigms might get close to the optimized answers but still have unacceptable errors even with increase in the number of iterations, i.e. the resultant circuit does not fully cover the truth table. In order to overcome this problem (when the rows of the truth table are not properly covered), the following procedure is used to modify the circuit until the truth table is fully covered:

Step 1: The program outputs a circuit (F$_{GP}$) that (partially) covers the truth table (F$_{TT}$).

Step 2: A modification function F$_{CORR}$ is obtained as follows:

$$F_{CORR} = F_{GP} \oplus F_{TT} \qquad (2)$$

If F$_{CORR}$ equals zero, the output circuit fully covers the truth table, and thus there is no need for a modification circuit; else:

Step 3: F$_{CORR}$ is fed to the program as a new input as F$_{TT}$ (NEW).

$$F_{TT}(NEW) = F_{CORR} \qquad (3)$$

Then the program will design a circuit F$_{GP}$(NEW) The final output F$_{GP}$(final) is obtained using:

$$F_{GP}(final) = F_{GP} \oplus F_{GP}(NEW) \qquad (4)$$

These are shown in figure 13.

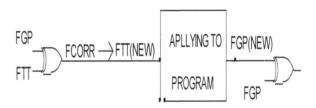

Figure 13. Block diagram for optimized circuit.

Test 5: A function with four variables.

F$_5$(A,B,C,D) = $\sum$(1,2,3,7,9,10,11)

F$_{TT}$ = [0 1 1 1 0 0 0 1 0 1 1 1 0 0 0 0]

Here, F$_5$ and F$_{TT}$ indicate the same function. The former shows the minterms and the latter shows the truth table. The circuit is shown in figure 14. Here are the outputs for this example:

F$_{TT}$	0 1 1 1 0 0 0 1 0 1 1 1 0 0 0 0
F$_{GP}$	0 1 1 1 0 0 0 0 0 1 1 1 0 0 0 0
F$_{CORR}$	0 0 0 0 0 0 0 1 0 0 0 0 0 0 0 0

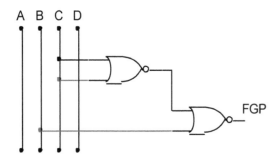

Figure 14. Circuit for F_5 with one error.

The repair process for the circuit starts with F_{CORR} as the new input F_{TT} (NEW) is fed into the optimization process. The program gives the output circuit F_{GP}(NEW) in figure 15.

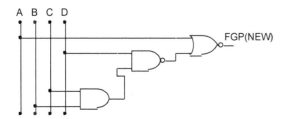

Figure 15. Repairing circuit for F_5 (F_{GP}(NEW)).

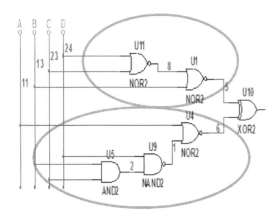

Figure 16. Final circuit for F_5.

Finally, XORing this circuit with the original circuit ($F_{GP} \oplus F_{GP}$(NEW)) gives an error-free circuit depicted in figure 16.

6. Conclusions and Suggestions

In this paper, we implemented a GP approach for optimizing combinational logic circuits. According to a number of assessments, the proposed approach shows its effectiveness with respect to the usual design criteria such as the number of gates and transistors.

Also the effective usage of the coding space of possible answers makes an inherent paralleling in the evaluation steps of the GP, which in turn speeds up the convergence process of our approach. Besides, using this strategy avoids unnecessary computation to be imposed on the program. Since the number of columns in solution arrays indicates the maximum levels of the output circuits, some flexibility comes with the implementation. For example, the program could design a wider circuit (less levels) instead of a lengthier one (more levels). Accordingly, and by using the NAND, NOR, and XOR gates, our implementation will target the designs with a minimum number of gates, transistors, and levels.

In the selection step, using a roulette wheel selection along with an elite one guarantees a sufficient dispersion in the next generation, while transfers a number of best parents to the next generation without any changes. Furthermore, a self-repairing feature produces more truthful circuits in terms of the coverage of the truth tables.

Optimization of the combinational logic circuit with feedback or memory elements could be the next step to test the applicability of our method. Also while some progresses are achieved in programs for the optimization of circuits with higher number of inputs, providing a balance between the number of inputs and an acceptable accuracy and convergence time is still a gorge for evolutionary approaches, and thus could be considered as an opportunity in the future works. In this regard, hybrid paradigms for multi-objective problems such as the one proposed in [17] could be promising.

References

[1] Holland, J. H. (1992). Adaptation in natural and artificial systems: an introductory analysis with applications to biology. A Bradford Book: MIT Press,

[2] Coello, C. A., Christiansen, A. D. & Aguirre, A., H. (2000). Towards Automated evolutionary design of combinational circuits. Computers & Electrical Engineering, vol. 27, no. 1, pp. 1–28.

[3] Kitano, H., & Hendler, J. A. (1994). Massively Parallel Artificial Intelligence. Menlo. Park, California: AAAI/MIT Press.

[4] Louis, S. J. (1993). Genetic algorithms as computational tools for design. PhD thesis, Department of Computer Science, Indiana University.

[5] Koza, J. R. (1992). Genetic Programming. Cambridge, MA: MIT Press.

[6] Coello, C. A., Christiansen A. & Aguirro, A. H. (1996). Use of Evolutionary Techniques to Automate the Design of Combinational Circuits. Department of Computer Science, Tulane University, New Orleans, USA.

[7] Sasao, T. (1993). Logic Synthesis and Optimization. Boston, London, Dordrecht: Kluwer Academic Press.

[8] Coello, C. A., Nacional, L., Avanzada, I., Aguirre, A. H. & Buckles, B. P. (2000). Evolutionary Multiobjective Design of Combinational Logic Circuits. Proc. of the Second NASA/DoD Workshop on Evolvable Hardware, Palo Alto, California, USA, July 13 – 15, pp. 161–170.

[9] Bajer, I. & Jakobović, D. (2012). Automated Design of Combinatorial Logic Circuits. Proc. of the IEEE 35th International Convention, MIPRO. Opatija, Croatia.

[10] Miller, J. F. (1999). An empirical study of the efficiency of learning Boolean functions using a Cartesian Genetic Programming approach. Proc. of the Genetic and Evolutionary Computation Conference, Orlando, Florida, USA, July 13-17, vol. 2, no. 1, pp. 1135–1142.

[11] Rajaei, A., Houshmand, M. & Rouhani, M. (2011). Optimization of Combinational Logic Circuits Using NAND Gates and Genetic Programming. Soft Computing in Industrial Applications, Springer, vol. 96, pp. 405-414.

[12] Karakatic, S., Podgorelec, V. & Hericko, M. (2013). Optimization of Combinational Logic Circuits with Genetic Programming. Electronics & Electrical Engineering, vol. 19, no. 7, pp. 86-89.

[13] Fogel, D. B. (1994). Asymptotic convergence properties of genetic algorithms and evolutionary programming analysis and experiments. Cybernetics and Systems: An International Journal, vol. 25, no. 3, pp. 389-407.

[14] Fogel, D. B. (1995). A Comparison of Evolutionary Programming and Genetic Algorithm on Selected Constrained Optimization Problems. Simulation, vol. 64, no. 6, pp. 397-404.

[15] Karnaugh, M. (1953). The Map Method for Synthesis of Combinational Logic Circuits. Transactions of the American Institute of Electrical Engineers, Part I: Communication and Electronics, vol. 72, no. 5, pp. 593-599.

[16] McCluskey, E. J. (1956). Minimization of Boolean Functions. Bell Systems Technical Journal, vol. 35, no. 6, pp. 1417-1444.

[17] Lotfi, S. & Karimi, F. (2017). A hybrid MOEA/D-TS for Solving Multi-Objective Problems. Journal of AI & Data Mining, vol.5, no. 2, pp. 183-195.

10

BQIABC: A new Quantum-Inspired Artificial Bee Colony Algorithm for Binary Optimization Problems

F. Barani[1*] and H. Nezamabadi-pour[2]

1. Department of Computer Engineering, Higher Education Complex of Bam, Bam, Iran.

2. Department of Electrical Engineering, Shahid Bahonar University of Kerman, Street, Bam, Iran

*Corresponding author: f.barani@bam.ac.ir(F. Barani).

Abstract

Artificial bee colony (ABC) algorithm is a swarm intelligence optimization algorithm inspired by the intelligent behavior of honey bees when searching for food sources. Various versions of the ABC algorithm have been widely used to solve continuous and discrete optimization problems in different fields. In this paper, a new binary version of the ABC algorithm inspired by quantum computing called binary quantum-inspired artificial bee colony algorithm (BQIABC) is proposed. BQIABC combines the main structure of ABC with the concepts and principles of quantum computing such as quantum bit, quantum superposition state, and rotation Q-gates strategy to make an algorithm with more exploration ability. Due to its higher exploration ability, the proposed algorithm can provide a robust tool to solve binary optimization problems. To evaluate the effectiveness of the proposed algorithm, several experiments are conducted on the 0/1 knapsack problem, Max-Ones, and Royal-Road functions. The results produced by BQIABC are compared with those of ten state-of-the-art binary optimization algorithms. Comparisons show that BQIABC presents better results than or similar to other algorithms. The proposed algorithm can be regarded as a promising algorithm to solve binary optimization problems.

Keywords: Artificial Bee Colony Algorithm, Quantum Computing, Rotation Q-gate, 0/1 Knapsack Problems, Benchmark Functions.

1. Introduction

The artificial bee colony (ABC) algorithm is a population-based optimization algorithm, which was developed by Karaboga in 2005 [1]. The ABC algorithm was motivated by the intelligence foraging behavior of real bees. This algorithm, due to easy implementation, low number of control parameters, and rapid convergence, has attracted the attention of many researchers to itself. In [2] and [3], the performance of the ABC algorithm has been compared with those of Genetic Algorithm (GA), Particle Swarm Algorithm (PSO), Differential Evolution (DE), Evolutionary Algorithm (EA), and Particle Swarm Inspired Evolutionary Algorithm (PS-EA) on some well-known test functions. The comparison results have indicated that ABC may be regarded as a promising algorithm to solve optimization problems.

The standard versions of evolutionary algorithms are basically used for solving continuous problems. H. Gökdağ et al. [4] have applied the PSO algorithm to detect the damaged structural elements of a Timoshenko beam. To solve the multi-pass turning optimization problems, optimization methods based on the ABC algorithm [5] and hybrid robust differential evolution (HRDE) [6] by A.R. Yildiz have been developed. Also to optimize cutting parameters in milling operations, a hybrid method based on the differential evolution algorithm and immune system has been presented [7], and a method based on the cuckoo search algorithm, reported in [8], has been introduced. I. Durgun et al. [9] and B. Yildiz et al. [10] have applied the cuckoo search algorithm and the gravitational search algorithm, respectively, to solve the problem of the optimum design of a vehicle component. Z. Izakian et al. [11] applied the particle swarm optimization algorithm for clustering time series data.

However, most optimization problems in the engineering fields are set in binary space. Different binary and discrete versions of evolutionary algorithms have been presented to solve the binary encoded problems such as the 0/1 knapsack problem, feature selection, and benchmark binary functions. H. Shi [12] has adopted the ant colony optimization, A. Lui et al. [13] have improved the simulated annealing algorithm using two kinds of solution spaces, Z. Li et al. [14] have proposed a novel binary particle swarm optimization based on the QBPSO algorithm by applying a multi-mutation strategy including single mutation operator and full mutation operator, and H. Sajedi et al. [15] have proposed a discrete gravitational search algorithm (DGSA) based on a new method for discretely updating the position of the agents for solving the 0/1 knapsack problem. S. Sunder et al. [16] have introduced a hybrid artificial bee colony algorithm called ABC-MKP, and M. Kong et al. [17] have proposed a binary ant system (BAS) based on a pheromone-laying method for solving the 0/1 multi-dimensional knapsack problem. In [18], the quantum-inspired binary gravitational search algorithm (BQGSA), and in [19], a modified GSA have been applied to solve the feature subset selection problem in data classification.

The binary artificial bee colony (BABC) algorithms can be divided into two categories, the BABC algorithm based on the continuous space and the discrete space [20]. In the first category, algorithms are based on the standard ABC algorithm and apply its formulae and operation rules to solve binary encoded problems by mapping the discrete space to the continuous space. The BinABC algorithm, proposed by Y. Marinakis et al. [21], AMABC, and NormABC, proposed by G. Pampara et al. [22] are in this category. However, it should be noted that these maps have a high complexity. The algorithms in the second category modify the food source generating formula, and replace the bit operation with the traditional vector operation. The DisABC algorithm proposed by M.H. Kashani et al. [23] is in this category.

Quantum computing (QC) is the art of applying the laws of quantum mechanics to computer science [24]. R. Feynman [25] and D. Deutsch [26] have proposed the initial idea of QC in the early 1980s. In solving computational problems, QC is stronger than classical computing. Since the

late 1990s, many studies have been done on the integration of evolutionary algorithms and quantum computing. The kind of algorithms can be classified into three categories, as follow [27]:

- Evolutionary-designed quantum algorithms, which aim to automate the combination of new quantum algorithms using EAs for quantum computers (e.g. [28, 29]).
- Quantum evolutionary algorithms (QEAs) concentrate on execution of EC algorithms in a quantum computation environment (e.g. [30-32])
- Quantum-inspired evolutionary algorithms (QIEAs) concentrate on execution of new EC algorithms using some concepts and principles of QC (e.g. [27, 33-35]).

Y. Jeong et al. [31] have proposed a quantum-inspired binary particle swarm optimization, and have applied it to solve unit commitment problems for power systems. H.B. Duan et al. [36] have combined the artificial bee colony algorithm and the quantum evolutionary algorithm quantum, introducing a hybrid method, and also N.H. Abbas et al. [37] have presented a quantum ABC inspired by quantum physics concepts to solve the continuous optimization problems. K. Han et al. [38] have introduced a quantum-inspired evolutionary algorithm for a class of combinatorial optimization, and G. Zhang has presented a comprehensive survey of the recent work in the field of quantum-inspired algorithm. To enhance the performance of ABC algorithm, G. Li et al. [39] have integrated QC into ABC and used Q-bits described on the Bloch sphere to solve continuous problems. Also X. Yuan et al. [40] have integrated ABC with QC and the chaotic local search strategy to solve the optimal power flow problem. K. Manochehri et al. [41] have presented a quantum ABC, called KQABC, by an unclear relation to produce new food sources, and have adopted it to solve 0/1 knapsack problem. Also the updating process of Q-bits in the KQABC is not clearly defined. M. Soleimanpour et al. [32] have proposed a quantum-behaved gravitational search algorithm, and H. Nezamabadi-pour [27] has presented a binary quantum-inspired GSA to solve binary encoded problems.

The admirable results achieved from combination of the evolutionary algorithms and quantum computing persuaded us to develop a new quantum-inspired version of the ABC algorithm called binary quantum-inspired artificial bee colony algorithm (BQIABC) to effectively solve combinatorial problems in binary space by applying the some concepts of quantum computing such as a quantum bit and superposition of states in the standard ABC algorithm. The use of quantum computing in ABC has enabled BQIABC to improve the exploration ability and convergence rate in obtaining optimum solutions.

The main contributions of this paper are summarized as the following:

- The artificial bee colony algorithm is combined with the quantum computing, and a binary quantum-inspired algorithm is presented to solve the binary-encoded problems.
- Binary quantum-inspired artificial bee colony algorithm (BQIABC) is proposed based on the concepts and principles of quantum computing such as a quantum bit, superposition of states, and a new rotation gate.
- In this work, a combination of ABC and QC is used to improve the convergence rate and exploration ability, and prevent trapping in local optima.
- In accordance with the ABC algorithm, a new rotation Q-gate is proposed, which determines rotation angle based on the current position and the best position so far.
- In BQIABC, a new behavior for scout bee is suggested to replace the abandoned food sources.
- A comparative study is carried out with ten other binary optimization algorithms to emphasize on the effectiveness of BQIABC algorithm.

The remainder of this paper is organized as follows. A brief review on the artificial bee colony algorithm and quantum computing that is used in this study is presented in Section 2. Section 3 presents the proposed algorithm. In Section 4, we present the experimental results and comparison with ten other algorithms on several cases of 0/1 knapsack problem, Max-Ones, and Royal-Road functions. Finally, a brief conclusion is offered in Section 5.

2. Background Knowledge
In this section, we review some background knowledge required for an easier understanding of our proposed algorithm, in brief, including artificial bee colony algorithm and quantum computing.

2.1. Artificial Bee Colony Algorithm
The artificial bee colony (ABC) algorithm [8] is a member of the class of swarm intelligence algorithms, proposed by Karaboga in 2005. The ABC algorithm is motivated by the natural behaviour of honey bees when searching for food sources. The colony of artificial bees consists of three different types of bees: employed, onlooker, and scout bees [42]. The number of employed and onlooker bees in the colony is the same, and is equal to the number of food sources around the hive. A potential solution in the optimization problem corresponds to the position of each food source, and the solution fitness is its nectar amount.

In this algorithm, the initial position of every food source is randomly generated by scout bee, and each employed bee is assigned to a food source.

$$x_{ij} = x_i^{min} + r(x_i^{max} - x_i^{min}) \tag{1}$$

where, x_i^{min} and x_i^{max} are the minimum and maximum values of the jth dimension, respectively, and r is a random number in the interval [0,1].

At each iteration t of the algorithm, the employed bee j selects a food source x_w randomly and discovers a new food source v_j around its assigned food source x_j, as follows:

$$v_{jk}(t+1) = x_{jk}(t) + \varphi_{jk}(t)(x_{jk}(t) - x_{wk}(t)) \tag{2}$$

where, $\varphi_{jk}(t)$ is a random number in the interval [-1,1] $x_{jk}(t)$ indicates the position of the jth food source in the kth dimension, and v_{jk} presents the position of the new food source j in the dimension k. The nectar amount of new food source v_j is computed. If v_j has a further nectar amount, the current food source x_j will be replaced by it.

$$x_j(t+1) = \begin{cases} v_j(t+1) & if\ fit(x_j(t)) < fit(v_j(t+1)) \\ x_j(t) & if\ fit(x_j(t)) \geq fit(v_j(t+1)) \end{cases} \tag{3}$$

There is only one scout bee in the colony. The employed bee whose food source has been abandoned becomes a scout bee and carries out a random search to find a new food source. After finishing the search process by all the employed bees, they perform a waggle dance in the hive to share the information about the nectar amount and the position of food sources with onlooker bees. Each onlooker bee chooses a food source based on a probability value associated with it, and explores a new food source around the selected food source. The probability value of food source i is calculated as follows:

$$p_i = \frac{fit_i}{\sum_{j=1}^{SN} fit_j} \qquad (4)$$

where, fit_i and SN are the fitness value of food source i and the number of food sources or the colony size, respectively. The pseudo-code of the ABC algorithm is given in figure 1.

ABC algorithm

Initialize
Repeat
    Send the employed bees onto their food sources and
      determine their nectar amounts
    Send the onlooker bees onto the food sources based on
      their probability and determine their nectar amounts
    Send the scout bees for searching new food sources
    Memorize the best food source found so far
Until (a termination condition is met)

Figure 1. Pseudo-code of ABC algorithm.

2.2. Quantum computing

The smallest unit of information in digital computers is a bit representing either 0 or 1 at a certain time, whereas Q-bit or quantum bit is the smallest unit of information in quantum computing. Each Q-bit is able to be in states "0", "1" or a combination of both states at the same time. This is known by superposition. A Q-bit is indicated as a pair of numbers (α, β), where the values for $|\alpha|^2$ and $|\beta|^2$ denote the probability of discovering the Q-bit in the states "0" and "1", respectively. The state of a Q-bit is presented as follows:

$$|\psi\rangle = \alpha|0\rangle + \beta|1\rangle \qquad (5)$$

Each Q-bit should satisfy the following normalization equation:

$$|\alpha|^2 + |\beta|^2 = 1 \qquad (6)$$

In a quantum computer, an individual q is denoted by a sequence of n Q-bits, as follows [43]:

$$q = [q_1, q_2, ..., q_n] = \begin{bmatrix} \alpha_1 & \alpha_2 & & \alpha_n \\ \beta_1 & \beta_2 & ... & \beta_n \end{bmatrix} \qquad (7)$$

In the act of observing a quantum state, it collapses to a single state. The observation process of Q-bit i is performed as follows:

$$\begin{aligned} &if \quad rand(0,1) < (\alpha_i)^2 \\ &then \qquad f_i = 0 \\ &else \qquad f_i = 1 \end{aligned}$$

Figure 2: Observation process in a quantum system.

Quantum computers apply a sequence of quantum operations to update the values for the Q-bits in each individual such that the updated Q-bits should satisfy Eq. (7). Q-gate is one of the quantum operations to update Q-bits. There are various Q-gates such as NOT gate, controlled NOT gate, rotation gate, Hadamard gate, X-gate, Y-gate, and Z-gate [24]. In most studies, the rotation Q-gate is employed more than other Q-gates. The rotation Q-gate $U(\Delta\theta_i)$ is defined as follows [38]:

$$U(\Delta\theta_i) = \begin{bmatrix} \cos(\Delta\theta_i) & -\sin(\Delta\theta_i) \\ \sin(\Delta\theta_i) & \cos(\Delta\theta_i) \end{bmatrix} \qquad (8)$$

where $\Delta\theta_i$ is the rotation angle of Q-bit i toward either 0 or 1 state. The state of Q-bit i at time t is updated as follows:

$$\begin{bmatrix} \alpha_i(t+1) \\ \beta_i(t+1) \end{bmatrix} = U(\Delta\theta_i) \begin{bmatrix} \alpha_i(t) \\ \beta_i(t) \end{bmatrix} \qquad (9)$$

3. Proposed Algorithm

The BQIABC algorithm was introduced by applying some concepts of quantum computing such as quantum bits, quantum gates, and superposition of states in the main structure of the ABC algorithm. BQIABC preserves the basic structure of the standard ABC algorithm and its main ideas, and replaces the concept of position of food sources and their updating process with new concepts. The position of each food source is defined as a Q-bit vector of length n. Each element in a food source takes a value of 0 or 1 by the probability of $|\alpha|^2$ or $|\beta|^2$. In other words, by observing a quantum state, it collapses to a single state [27]. The observation process is given by figure 2. The steps of the BQIABC algorithm are as follows:

   i.   ***Initialization***:   The   set $FB(t) = \{B_1(t), ..., B_{SN}(t)\}$ is an archive set to hold the best binary solution achieved by the onlooker and employed bees through iterations of BQIABC. At iteration $t = 0$, the set $FB(0) = \{\}$. In this step, the set $Q(t)$ of SN quantum food sources in a n-dimensional search space is randomly generated such that the normalization equation (6) is satisfied.

$$Q(t) = \{q_1(t), q_2(t), ..., q_{SN}(t)\} \qquad (10)$$

where, $q_i(t)$ is the quantum food source i that is defined as follows:

$$q_i(t) = \begin{bmatrix} \alpha_i^1(t) & \alpha_i^2(t) & & \alpha_i^n(t) \\ \beta_i^1(t) & \beta_i^2(t) & ... & \beta_i^n(t) \end{bmatrix} \qquad (11)$$

The value $\alpha_i^d \ (d = 1,...,n)$ is initially set to $\frac{1}{\sqrt{2}}$ and the value β_i^d is calculated by equation $\left|\beta_i^d\right|^2 = 1 - \left|\alpha_i^d\right|^2$.

ii. ***Observation***: the set $FW(t) = \{F_1(t), F_2(t),...,F_{SN}(t)\}$ contains the SN binary food sources (current solutions) that are made by observing on each Q-bit $q_i(t)$ in the set $Q(t)$. The binary food source i is presented as $F_i(t) = \left[f_i^1, f_i^2,...,f_i^n(t)\right]$ where $f_i^d \in \{0,1\}$. The observation process on the ith quantum food source q_i is carried out, as shown in figure 2.

iii. ***Fitness evolution***: in this step, the fitness value of each binary food source $F_i(t)$ in the set $FW(t)$ is evaluated using function *fit*.

iv. ***Updating*** $FB(t)$: in this step, N binary food sources with the highest fitness value are selected from all food sources in the set $FW(t)$ and $FB(t)$ and are replaced by the previous food sources in $FB(t)$. At $t = 0$, all binary food sources in $FW(0)$ are transferred into $FB(t)$.

v. ***Employed bees***: in this step, each employed bee i selects randomly a food source $F_w(t) \in FB(t)$ and then the rotation angle $\Delta\theta_i$ is calculated by Eq. (12). The employed bee i updates the position of quantum food source $q_i(t)$ using the rotation Q-gate in Eqs. (8, 9) and explores a new quantum food source q_i in the neighborhood of $q_i(t)$. The amount of movement towards 0 or 1 is denoted by $\Delta\theta_i$.

$$\Delta\theta_i^j = \theta(f_i^j - b_w^j) \tag{12}$$

where, f_i^j and b_w^j are the value of jth dimension of the food sources F_i and B_w, respectively, and θ denotes the magnitude of the rotation angle. To enhance the convergence of the proposed algorithm, we employed a dynamic rotation angle approach used in [43] to calculate θ.

$$\theta = \theta_{max} - (\theta_{max} - \theta_{min}) \times \frac{t}{iter_{max}} \tag{13}$$

where, t and $iter_{max}$ are the current iteration number and the maximum iteration number, respectively. Based on the above equation, the value for θ changes monotonously from θ_{max} to θ_{min}. In general, the value from 0.05π to 0.001π is considered for θ. The considered values for θ are dependent on problem [35].

Then the observation process is applied to the quantum food source q_i and is makes the binary food source F_i. If F_i has a more nectar amount, the previous food source F_i will be replaced by F_i.

$$\begin{bmatrix} \alpha_i^j(t+1) \\ \beta_i^j(t+1) \end{bmatrix} = \begin{bmatrix} \cos(\Delta\theta_i^j(t)) & -\sin(\Delta\theta_i^j(t)) \\ \sin(\Delta\theta_i^j(t)) & \cos(\Delta\theta_i^j(t)) \end{bmatrix} \begin{bmatrix} \alpha_i^j(t) \\ \beta_i^j(t) \end{bmatrix} \tag{14}$$

vi. ***Onlooker bees***: in this step, the selection probability of each food source is calculated by Eq. (4). Then the onlooker bee i chooses a food source based on the probability values associated with food sources, and explores a new food source around the selected food source similar to the employed bees.

vii. ***Scout bee***: if the number of sequential unsuccessful attempts to improve the fitness value of a food source is higher than the given value *limit*, it is considered as an abandoned food source. In this situation, the scout bee replaces the worst food source in the current iteration with the best food source in that iteration.

viii. ***Repeat***: the steps (ii)-(vii) are repeated until the stopping criterion is met.

The pseudo-code of the proposed algorithm is presented in figure 3.

4. Experimental results

In this section, vast experiments are carried out to assess the performance of our proposed algorithm in order to solve the binary encoded optimization problems. In this study, the Max-Ones, Royal-Road functions, and the 0-1 knapsack problem are considered as well-known benchmark binary problems. The BQIABC algorithm will be compared with ten binary-valued algorithms, which have been applied on the 0/1 knapsack problems, the Max-Ones, and Royal-Road functions to validate the superiority of the proposed algorithm. The experimental results are summarized in tables 2-5. In the following sections, the benchmark binary problems will be clarified in detail. It is noteworthy that all experiments have been implemented on the Matlab environment on a system with 2.40 GHz CPU and 4 GB of RAM.

BQIABC algorithm
$t = 0, FB(t) = \{\}, FW(t) = \{\}$
Initialize $Q(t)$ (Eq. 10 and 11)
Repeat
Observe $Q(t)$ and make $FW(t)$ (Fig. 2)
Calculate fitness values of $F_i(t) \in FW(t)$
Update $FB(t)$
for each employed bee i do
Generate a new quantum food source q_i in the
neighborhood of q_i using Equations (12,13,14)
Observe q_i and make F_i by (Fig. 2)
Calculate fitness value of f_i
if $fit(B_i) > fit(B_i)$ then
$q_i = q_i$
$B_i = B_i$
end if
end for
for each onlooker bee i do
Calculate the probability of food sources using Eq. 4
Select a quantum food source q_j based on probability
values
Generate a new quantum food source q_j in the
neighborhood of q_j using Equations (12,13, 14)
Observe q_j and make B_j by (Fig. 2)
Calculate fitness value of f_j
if $fit(B_j) > fit(B_j)$ then
$q_j = q_j$
$B_j = B_j$
end if
end for
Determine abandoned food source and replace it with a
new quantum food source for the scout bee
Memorize the best food source found so far
$t = t + 1$
Until (a termination condition is met)

Figure 3. Pseudo code of BQIABC algorithm.

4.1. Knapsack problem

The 0/1 knapsack problem is one of well-known binary encoded optimization problems. Given a set of N objects, where each object i having a weight w_i and a profit p_i and a knapsack with limited weight capacity C. The aim of problem is filling the knapsack with a subset of objects in such a way that the sum of weight of selected objects does not exceed the specified capacity of knapsack, whereas their profit is maximized. The 0/1 knapsack problem can be explained as follows:

$$Maximize : \sum_{i=1}^{n} p_i x_i \qquad (15)$$

Subject to the constraint:

$$\sum_{i=1}^{n} w_i x_i \leq C, x_i \in \{0,1\} \qquad (16)$$

where, x_i is 0 or 1. If x_i takes the value of "1", the object i is selected, otherwise the object is not selected for knapsack.

In the recent years, researchers have proposed several exact methods based on branch and bound, dynamic programming, and heuristic methods to deal with the knapsack problems. In this study, five test cases of the 0/1 knapsack problem with 50, 200, 400, 600, and 1000 items are employed to assess the BQIABC algorithm. All test cases are created by strongly correlated sets of data [38]. The unsorted data considered by Zhang [43] on the knapsack problems with 50, 200, and 400 items and the unsorted data has been considered by Nezamabadi-pour [27] on the knapsack problems with 600 and 1000 items. Also some of experiments reported on them are used for comparison between the proposed algorithm and other algorithms.

4.2. Binary benchmark functions

Max-ones and Royal-Road are maximization benchmark functions in binary space (see Table 1). In this study, the Max-Ones function with dimensions $n = 40, 80, 160, 320, 640$ and the Royal-Road function with dimensions $n = 40, 80, 160, 320$ were used to assess the performance of the BQIABC algorithm.

4.3. Comparative algorithms

To confirm the superiority of the proposed algorithm, it was compared with ten binary encoded heuristic algorithms. The proposed algorithm was applied on the Max-Ones, Real-Road functions, and the 0/1 knapsack problem. For comparison, we implemented KQABC [41] and used the results reported by Nezamabadi-pour [27] for the binary quantum-inspired particle swarm optimization (BQIPSO) [44], binary particle swarm optimization (BPSO) [45], modified binary particle swarm optimization (MBPSO) [46], binary gravitational search algorithm (BGSA) [47], and novel binary differential evolution NBDE [48] and the results given by Zhang [43] for the original binary quantum-inspired evolutionary algorithm (BQIEAo) [38], modified BQIEA by incorporating cross-over and mutation operators (BQIEAcm) [49], modified BQIEA by introducing new rotation Q-gate strategy (BQIEAn) [50] and conventional genetic algorithm (CGA).

Table 1. Binary benchmark functions.

Name	Function	S
Max-Ones	$f(X_i) = \sum_{d=1}^{n} X_i^d$	$\left[\{0,1\}\right]^n$
Royal-Road	$f(X_i) = \sum_{d=1}^{\frac{n}{8}} \left(\prod_{j=8(d-1)+1}^{8d} X_i^d \right)$	$\left[\{0,1\}\right]^n$

4.4. Comparative study

The comparison between binary algorithm is performed based on three criteria, the best, mean, and the worst solution found. The comparison results are reported as the mean of 30 independent runs. In BQIABC, the maximum number of iterations and the parameter value of *limit* are set to 1000 and 200, respectively. The colony size is considered to be 20.

The θ_{max} and θ_{min} value are set to 0.05π and 0.001π, respectively. Table 2 presents the comparison results of the performance of BQIABC with those of CGA, BPSO, MBPSO, NBDE, BGSA, BQIEAo, BQIEAcm, BQIEAn and BQIPSO on solving the knapsack problem with 50, 200, and 400 items.

Rows captioned by "BS", "MBS", and "WS" report the best of the best profits, mean best profits, and worst of the best profits over 30 runs.

Table 2. Comparison between BQIABC and other algorithms using the knapsack problems with 50, 200, and 400 items.

Items	Criteria	CGA	BPSO	MBPSO	NBDE	BGSA	BQIEAo	BQIEAcm	BQIEAn	BQIPSO	BQIABC
50	BS	296.45	307.05	302.23	301.98	312.16	312.17	312.13	307.25	312.22	**312.23**
	MBS	287.29	303.22	297.57	298.41	307.32	307.40	306.86	304.24	307.67	311.09
	WS	282.00	297.21	295.25	296.03	306.74	307.21	302.24	299.23	302.23	310.33
200	BS	1047.98	1107.93	1078.27	1082.35	1147.92	1178.22	1173.18	1102.08	1193.31	**1198.22**
	MBS	1027.13	1089.85	1069.09	1070.09	1120.18	1166.67	1156.22	1090.64	1184.91	1188.79
	WS	1017.15	1078.04	1058.55	1060.72	1078.29	1153.27	1143.20	1077.45	1178.23	1185.69
400	BS	2120.54	2210.46	2175.19	2181.15	2255.59	2341.36	2336.41	2211.12	2396.42	**2410.94**
	MBS	2100.85	2190.18	2156.64	2164.15	2219.28	2322.47	2315.92	2190.67	2380.10	2407.08
	WS	2086.29	2175.00	2140.68	2146.38	2191.14	2300.49	2291.25	2165.62	2366.02	2395.89

The results summarized in table 2 denote that BQIABC can present the better solutions than the other binary algorithms for all test cases. The largest difference in the performance between BQIGSA and other binary algorithms occurs in the test case with 400 items. It implies that BQIABC in more complex problems, due to its higher exploration ability, provides better results than the other binary algorithms.

Also we carried out experiments on the higher-dimensional cases of the 0/1 knapsack problem with 600 and 1000 items. The comparison results of BQIABC with BPSO, BGSA, and BQIPSO are tabulated in table 3.

From table 3, it can be observed that BQIABC finds the solutions with higher profits in comparison with the other comparative binary algorithms. As it can be seen, the distinction between the results found by BQIABC and the other comparative algorithms is very noticeable.

In [41], a basic version of quantum ABC, called KQABC, is presented to solve the 0/1 knapsack problem. Authors used a raw relation to produce and update food sources.

To confirm the superiority of BQIABC to the KQABC algorithm in solving the 0/1 knapsack problem, the KQABC algorithm was implemented based on the description provided in that paper, and the results obtained were compared with the proposed algorithm. These algorithms were implemented in the same conditions. The results obtained are tabulated in table 4.

Table 3. Comparison between BQIABC and some binary algorithms using knapsack problems with 600 and 1000 items.

Items	Criteria	BPSO	BGSA	BQIPSO	BQIABC
600	BS	3265.45	3415.23	3564.97	**3585.23**
	MBS	3242.03	3379.19	3545.32	3577.02
	WS	3219.77	3318.24	3519.56	3573.43
1000	BS	5349.12	5439.99	5866.55	**5929.91**
	MBS	5328.96	5403.17	5832.95	5911.22
	WS	5306.90	5318.24	5803.74	5887.89

Table 4. Comparison between BQIABC and KQABC.

	item / criteria	50	200	400	600	1000
KQABC	BS	279.26	1028.22	2087.63	3000.12	5229.7
	MBS	276.02	1022.94	2087.59	3100.05	5205.51
	WS	272.77	1017.74	2087.57	3100.03	5181.29
BQIABC	BS	**312.23**	**1198.22**	**2410.94**	**3585.23**	**5929.91**
	MBS	311.09	1188.79	2407.08	3577.02	5911.22
	WS	310.33	1185.69	2395.89	3573.43	5887.89

Table 4 denotes that the results found by BQIABC in comparison with KQABC have very large distinctions, and our proposed algorithm can provide better solutions for the 0/1 knapsack problem. The performance of BQIABC, BPSO, BGSA, and BQIPSO in solving two well-known binary benchmark functions with several sizes was compared in table 5. The binary functions are given in table 1. The Max-Ones function with different sizes $n = 40, 80, 160, 320, 640$ and the Royal-Road function with different sizes $n = 40, 80, 160, 320$ are considered to assess the performance of the proposed algorithm. For small size cases on solving the Max-Ones, BGSA, and BQIPSO can be found optimal solutions but by increasing the size of problem, their performance is reduced. This reduction is very sensible for BGSA. In Max-Ones with sizes of 320 and 640, there was a considerable difference between BQIABC and other comparative algorithms. The results obtained for BGSA and BQIABC are almost the same on solving the Royal-Road with size of 40 and 80. BQIABC is able to outperform BGSA, BQIPSO, and BPSO in the sizes of 160 and 320. In all sizes of Royal-Road, there was a significant distinction between BQIABC and BPSO, and between BQIGSA and BQIPSO.

Table 5. Comparison between BQIABC and some binary algorithms using Max-Ones and Royal-Road with different sizes.

Function	Criteria	BPSO [43]	BGSA [47]	BQIPSO [44]	BQIABC
Max-Ones(40)	BS	**40 (1)**	**40 (1)**	**40 (1)**	**40 (1)**
	WS	38	40	40	40
	MBS	39.251	40	40	40
Max-Ones(80)	BS	74 (2)	**80 (1)**	**80 (1)**	**80 (1)**
	WS	69	79	80	80
	MBS	71.15	79.65	80	80
Max-Ones(160)	BS	129 (2)	**160 (1)**	**160 (1)**	**160 (1)**
	WS	123	153	160	157
	MBS	125.35	157.32	160	159
Max-Ones(320)	BS	237 (4)	302 (3)	319 (2)	**320 (1)**
	WS	219	291	314	318
	MBS	227.05	308.60	316.95	319
Max-Ones(640)	BS	422 (4)	553 (3)	606 (2)	**632 (1)**
	WS	408	513	586	627
	MBS	413.60	529.85	596.15	630
Royal-Road(40)	BS	4 (2)	**5 (1)**	4 (2)	**5 (1)**
	WS	2	5	1	5
	MBS	2.95	5	2.7	5
Royal-Road(80)	BS	5 (3)	**10 (1)**	7 (2)	**10 (1)**
	WS	3	8	2	9
	MBS	3.80	9.25	3.60	9.5
Royal-Road(160)	BS	5 (4)	15 (2)	10 (3)	**16 (1)**
	WS	4	10	3	15
	MBS	4.2	11.55	6.50	15
Royal-Road(320)	BS	6 (4)	15 (3)	18 (2)	**24 (1)**
	WS	4	9	8	21
	MBS	5.00	11.19	12.00	22.5

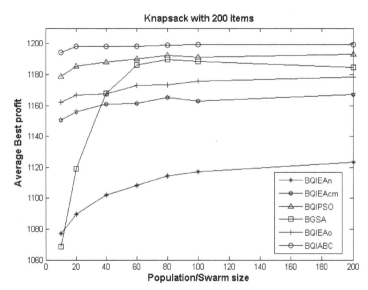

Figure 4. Effect of population size on average best profits obtained by BQIEAn, BQIEAcm, BQIEAo, BQIPSO, BGSA, and the proposed algorithm. The different swarm sizes are 10, 40, 60, 80, 100, and 200.

It can be observed in table 4 that BQIABC is able to provide better solutions in comparison with the other binary algorithms. The ability of the proposed algorithm to solve the binary encoded problems with larger sizes is mostly intuitive. In the table, rows captioned by "BS", "WS", and "MBS" report the best solution, worst solution, and mean best solutions over 30 runs, respectively. In Max-Ones and Royal-Road, the maximum number of iterations and the colony size were selected as 1000 and 20, respectively.

Figure 4 illustrates the relationship between the population size and the average best profits on the knapsack problem with 200 items. The results observed in this figure were achieved by the proposed algorithm and five binary comparative algorithms over 30 independent runs. These comparative algorithms include BQIEAn, BQIEAcm, BQIEAo, BQIPSO, and BGSA. The results for BQIPSO, BGSA and BQIEAn, BQIEAcm, BQIEAo have already been reported by H. Nezamabadi-pour [27] and G. Zhang [43], respectively. The information presented in figure 4 indicates that the increasing population size has the most influence on the optimal solutions obtained by BGSA and BQIEAn. Especially, BGSA has a significant increase from population size of 10 to 60. The BQIABC algorithm with population size of 20 could find the best solution with a profit of 1198.22. With increasing population size, the algorithms are able to find better solutions in the search space but to the contrary, the running time of algorithms will increase. In comparison with the other algorithms, BQIABC provides a better solution in all cases. In this study, the population size is considered to be 20 for the knapsack problem in all experiments.

5. Conclusions and future works

In the recent years, various versions of optimization algorithms have been widely used to solve binary problems. The artificial bee colony (ABC) is an evolutionary optimization algorithm motivated by the intelligence foraging behavior of real bees.

In this paper, we proposed a new quantum-inspired version of the ABC algorithm, called binary quantum-inspired artificial bee colony algorithm (BQIABC), to effectively solve combinatorial problems in binary space by applying some concepts of quantum computing such as a quantum bit and superposition of states in the standard ABC algorithm. BQIABC, due to its higher exploration ability, can provide a robust tool to solve binary optimization problems. BQIABC preserved the initial structure of the standard ABC algorithm. However, the concept of position of food sources and their updating process were replaced with new concepts. In this study, the 0/1 knapsack problem, Max-Ones, and Royal-Road functions were employed as binary optimization problems. To emphasize the effectiveness of BQIABC algorithm, a comparative study was done with ten other binary optimization algorithms. The comparison results illustrate that BQIABC can overcome other comparative algorithms. Also it seems that BQIABC has the ability to solve other binary optimization problems. We can consider this extension as one of the future works of this study.

References

[1] Hardy, G., Lucet, C. B. & Limnios, N. (2007). K-Terminal Network Reliability Measures with Binary

Decision Diagrams. IEEE Transactions on Reliability, vol. 56, no. 3, pp. 506-515.

[1] Karaboga, D. (2005). An idea based on honey bee swarm for numerical optimization. Technical Report-TR06, Erciyes University, Engineering Faculty, Computer Engineering Department.

[2] Karaboga, D. & Basturk, B. (2007). A powerful and efficient algorithm for numerical function optimization: artificial bee colony (ABC) algorithm. Journal of Global Optimization. vol. 39, no. 3, pp. 459-471.

[3] Karaboga, D. & Basturk, B. (2008). On the performance of artificial bee colony (ABC) algorithm, Applied Soft Computing, vol. 8, no. 1, pp. 687-697.

[4] Gökdağ, H. & Yildiz, A. R. (2012). Structural damage detection using modal parameters and particle swarm optimization, Materials Testing, vol. 54, no. 6, pp. 416-420.

[5] Yildiz, A. R. (2013). Optimization of cutting parameters in multi-pass turning using artificial bee colony-based approach, Information Sciences, vol. 220, pp. 399-407.

[6] Yildiz, A. R. (2013). Hybrid Taguchi-differential evolution algorithm for optimization of multi-pass turning operations, Applied Soft Computing, vol. 13, no. 3, pp. 1433-1439.

[7] Yildiz, A. R. (2013). A new hybrid differential evolution algorithm for the selection of optimal machining parameters in milling operations, Applied Soft Computing, vol. 13, no. 3, pp. 1561–1566.

[8] Yildiz, A. R. (2013). Cuckoo search algorithm for the selection of optimal machining parameters in milling operations, International Journal of Advanced Manufacturing Technology, vol. 64, no. 1-4, pp. 55-61.

[9] Durgun, I. & Yildiz, A.R. (2012). Structural design optimization of vehicle components using Cuckoo search algorithm, Materials Testing, vol. 54, no. 3, pp. 185-188.

[10] Yildiz, B. S., Lekesiz, H. & Yildiz, A. R. (2016). Structural design of vehicle components using gravitational search and charged system search algorithms, Materials Testing, vol. 58, no. 1, pp. 79-81.

[11] Izakian, Z. & Mesgari, M. S. (2015). Fuzzy clustering of time series data: A particle swarm optimization approach. Journal of AI and Data Mining, vol. 3, no 1, pp. 39-46.

[12] Shi, H. (2006). Solution to 0-1 knapsack problem based on improved ant colony algorithm, In proceeding of IEEE International Conference on Information Acquisition, pp. 1062-1066, 2006.

[13] Liu, A., Wang, J., Han, G., Wang, S. & Wen, J. (2006). Improved simulated annealing algorithm solving for 0-1 knapsack problem, In proceedings of IEEE the 6th international conference in intelligent systems design and application, pp. 1-6, 2006.

[14] Li, ZK. & Li, N. (2009). A novel multi-mutation binary particle swarm optimization for 0-1 knapsack problem. In proceedings of Control and Decision conference, pp. 3042-3047, 2009.

[15] Sajedi, H. & Razavi, S. F. (2016). DGSA: discrete gravitational search algorithm for solving knapsack problem, Oper Res Int J, pp. 1-29.

[16] Sundar, S., Singh, A. & Rossi, A. (2010). An artificial bee colony algorithm for the 0-1 multi-dimensional knapsack problem, Commun. Comput. Inf. Sci., vol. 94, pp. 141–151.

[17] Kong, M., Tian, P. & Kao, Y. (2008). A new ant colony optimization algorithm for the multi-dimensional knapsack problem, Comput. Oper. Res., vol. 35, no. 8, pp. 2672–2683.

[18] Han, X. H., Quan, L., Xiong, X. Y. & Wu, B. (2013). Facing the classification of binary problems with a hybrid system based on quantum- inspired binary gravitational search algorithm and K-NN method, Eng. Appl. Artif. Intell., vol. 26, pp. 580-593.

[19] Han, X. H., Chang, X. M., Quan, L., Xiong, X. Y., Li, J. X., Zhang, Zh. X. & Liu Y. (2014). Feature subset selection by gravitational search algorithm optimization, Information Sciences, vol. 281, pp. 128-146.

[20] Liu, T., Zhang, L. & Zhang, J. (2013). Study of Binary Artificial Bee Colony Algorithm Based on Particle Swarm Optimization. Journal of Computational Information Systems, vol. 9, no. 16, pp. 6459-6466.

[21] Marinakis, Y, Marinaki, M, Matsatsinis, N. (2009). A hybrid discrete artificial bee colony-GRASP algorithm for clustering. International Conference on Computers Industrial Engineering. Troyes, France, pp. 548-553 2009.

[22] Pampara, G. & Engelbrecht, A. P. (2011). Binary artificial bee colony optimization. IEEE Symposium on Swarm Intelligence, IEEE, Perth, pp. 1-8, 2011.

[23] Kashan, M. H., Nahavandi, N. & Kashan, A. H. (2012). DisABC: A new artificial bee colony algorithm for binary optimization. App. Soft Com., vol. 12, no. 1, pp. 342-352.

[24] Hey, T. (1999). Quantum computing: An introduction. Com. and Cont. Eng. Journal, vol. 10, no. 3, pp. 105-112.

[25] Feynman, R. P. (1982). Simulating physics with computers. International Journal of Theoretical Physics, vol. 21, nos. 6/7, pp. 467-488.

[26] Deutsch, D. (1985). Quantum theory, the church-Turing principle and the universal quantum computer. In Proceedings of the Royal Society of London, pp. 97-117.

[27] Nezamabadi-pour, H. (2015). A quantum-inspired gravitational search algorithm for binary encoded

optimization problems. Engineering Applications of Artificial Intelligence. vol. 40, pp. 62-75.

[28] Spector, L., Barnum, H., Bernstein, H. J. & Swamy, N., (1999). Finding a better-than-classical quantum AND/OR algorithm using genetic programming. In Proceedings of Congr. Evolutionary Computation, Piscataway, NJ, vol. 3, pp. 2239–2246, 1999.

[29] Sahin, M., Atav, U. & Tomak, M. (2005). Quantum genetic algorithm method in self-consistent electronic structure calculations of a quantum dot with many electrons. International Journal of Modern Physics, vol. 16, no. 9, pp. 1379–1393.

[30] Sun, J., Feng, B. & Xu, W. (2004). Particle swarm optimization with particles having quantum behavior. In Proceedings of congress on evolutionary computation, Portland, Oregon, USA, pp. 325–331, 2004.

[31] Sun, J., Xu, W. & Feng, B. (2004). A global search strategy of quantum-behaved particle swarm optimization. In Proceedings of IEEE Conference on Cybernetics and Intelligent Systems, pp. 111–116, 2004.

[32] Soleimanpour-moghadam M., Nezamabadi-pour, H. & Farsangi, M.M. (2012). A quantum behaved gravitational search algorithm. Intel. Info. Manag., vol. 4, no. 6, pp. 390–395.

[33] Moore, M. & Narayanan A. (1995). Quantum-Inspired Computing. Dept. Comput. Sci., Univ. Exeter. Exeter, U.K.

[34] Narayanan, A. & Moore, M. (1996). Quantum-inspired genetic algorithms. In Proceedings of IEEE Int. Conf. Evolutionary Computation, Japan, pp. 61–66, 1996.

[35] Han, K. H. & Kim, J. H. (2002). Quantum-inspired evolutionary algorithm for a class of combinatorial optimization. IEEE Trans. Evol. Comput., vol. 6, no. 6, pp. 580–593.

[36] Duan, H. B., Xu, C. F. & Xing, Z. H. (2010). A hybrid artificial bee colony optimization and quantum evolutionary algorithm for continuous optimization problems. International Journal of Neural Systems, vol. 20, no. 1, pp. 39-50.

[37] Abbas, N. H. & Aftan, H. S. (2014). Quantum artificial bee colony algorithm for numerical function optimization. International Journal of Computer Applications, vol. 93, no. 9, pp. 0975-8887.

[38] Han, K. & Kim, J. (2002). Quantum-inspired evolutionary algorithm for a class of combinatorial optimization. IEEE Trans. Evol. Comput., vol. 6, no. 6, pp. 580–593.

[39] Li, G., Sun, M. & Li, P. (2015). Quantum-inspired bee colony algorithm. Journal of Optimization, vol. 4, pp. 51-60.

[40] Yuan, X., Wang, P., Yuan, Y., Huang, Y. & Zhang, X. (2015). A new quantum inspired chaotic artificial bee colony algorithm for optimal power flow problem. Energy Conversion and Management, vol. 100, pp. 1-9.

[41] Manochehri, K. & Alizadegan, A. (2015). Designing and Comparing Classic versus Quantum Artificial Bee Colony Algorithm. Journal of mathematics and computer science, vol. 14, pp. 183-192.

[42] Karaboga D (2010). Artificial Bee Colony Algorithm, www.scholarpedia.org/article/Artificial_bee_colony_algorithm, Scholarpedia. vol. 5, no. 3.

[43] Zhang, G. (2011). Quantum-inspired evolutionary algorithms: a survey and empirical study. Journal of Heuristics, vol. 7, no. 3, pp. 303-351.

[44] Jeong Y., Park J., Jang S. & Lee K. Y. (2010). A New Quantum-Inspired Binary PSO: Application to Unit Commitment Problems for Power Systems. IEEE Transactions on Power Systems, vol. 25, no. 3, pp. 1486 – 1495.

[45] Kennedy J. & Eberhart R. C. (1997). A discrete binary version of the particle swarm algorithm. In Proceedings of IEEE Int. Conf. Systems, Man, and Cybernetics, vol. 5, pp. 4104–4108, 1997.

[46] Lee, S., Soak, S., Oh, S., Pedrycz, W. & Joen, M., (2008). Modified binary particle swarm optimization. Natural Science, vol. 18, no. 9, pp. 1161-1166.

[47] Rashedi, E., Nezamabadi-pour, H. & Saryazdi, S. (2010). BGSA: Binary Gravitational Search Algorithm, Journal of Nat Compute, vol. 9, pp. 727–745.

[48] Deng, C., Zhao, B., Yang, Y. & Deng, A. (2010). Novel binary differential evolution without scale factor. In proceedings of the third international workshop on advanced computer intelligence. Auzhou, Jiangsu, China, pp. 250-253, 2010.

[49] Li, N., Du, P. & Zhao, H. J. (2005). Independent component analysis based on improved quantum genetic algorithm: Application in hyperspectral images. In Proceedings of IGARSS, pp. 4323–4326, 2005.

[50] Zhang, G. X., Li, N., Jin, W. D. & Hu, L. Z. (2006). Novel quantum genetic algorithm and its applications. Front. Electr. Electron. Eng. China, vol. 1, no. 1, pp. 31–36.

11

Image Restoration by Variable Splitting based on Total Variant Regularizer

E. Sahragard [1], H. Farsi [1*] and S. Mohamadzadeh [2]

1. Department of Electrical & computer Engineering, University of Birjand, Birjand, Iran

2. Faculty of Technical & Engineering Ferdows, University of Birjand, Birjand, Iran.

*Corresponding author: hfarsi@birjand.ac.ir (H. Farsi).

Abstract

The aim of image restoration is to obtain a higher quality desired image from a degraded one. In this strategy, an image inpainting method fills the degraded or lost area of the image by an appropriate information. This is achieved in such a way that the image obtained is undistinguishable for a casual person who is unfamiliar with the original image. In this work, different images are degraded by two procedures; one is to blur and to add noise to the original image, and the other one is to lose a percentage of the original image pixels. Then the degraded image is restored by the proposed method and also two state-of-art methods. For image restoration, it is required to use the optimization methods. In this work, we use a linear restoration method based upon the total variation regularizer. The variable of optimization problem is split, and the new optimization problem is then solved using the Lagrangian augmented method. The experimental results obtained show that the proposed method is faster, and the restored images have a higher quality compared to the other methods.

Keywords: *Image Restoration, Image Inpainting, Deblurring, Total Variation Regularizer, Lagrangian Augmented.*

1. Introduction

Image restoration is known as one of the most important image processing techniques. It is used in various applications and areas such as medical, astronomical imaging, image and video coding, remote sensing, military, seismography, aerology, and film restoration [1]. In space exploration, the image restoration systems have been used by researchers since 1960 [2]. Providing the desired image from the degraded one is the aim of the image restoration systems. An image restoration system contains de-blurring, de-noising, and preserving fine details [3]. The information and details of the image are lost when the image is captured. The restoration not only removes the noise of images but also is widely used in blind deconvolution, image inpainting, and various image processing methods [4, 6].

Image restoration may contain several applications such as blind deconvolution, image deblurring, image inpainting, and image denoising. For each application, a special method is used for image degradation and restoration.

This paper focuses on image inpainting and deblurring. The image inpainting is a process of reconstructing the corrupted or lost parts of the image that is undistinguishable for a casual person who is unfamiliar with the original image. The image inpainting plays an important role in various image processing applications such as removal of scratches in old photographs and videos, filling in missing blocks in unreliably transmitted images, and removal of overlaid text or graphics [5]. Image demolition is caused by a non-adjusted camera, object and camera motion, reflection from uncontrollable sources, and non-ideal photographic and communication systems [5]. The most common problems involved in photography are the image blurring and noise. The blurring occurs due to a localized averaging of pixels, and significant in light limited situations and resulting in a ruined photograph. Image deblurring is the process of recovering a sharp image from a corrupted one. The blurring contains environmental blurs and motion blurs.

The reason for the environmental blurs is a light passing through the media environment with different refractive indices. The motion blurs are caused by the relative motion between a camera and a scene [7]. In this paper, we assumed that the motion blurs were distinguishable and estimable, and that the noise was Gaussian distribution with zero mean. The image restoration system includes three important parts: a) modelling the degraded image, b) formulating the image restoration problem, and c) designing an efficient and accurate method in order to solve the image restoration problem.

In the modelling part, the blurring and noise information is used to create a model of the degraded image. In many recent research works, a linear model is used to model the degraded image. Common degradations include noise, blurring, color imperfections, and geometrical distortions. The image restoration problems can be modeled using the following expressed linear degradation model:

$$y = Bx + n, \qquad (1)$$

where, B is a Point Spread Function (PSF), x is the original image, n is the noise matrix, and y represents the degraded image. Note that PSF is the degree to which an optical system blurs (spreads) a point of light. PSF is the inverse Fourier transform of Optical Transfer Function (OTF) in the frequency domain. OTF describes the Response of a linear, position-invariant system to animpulse. OTF is the Fourier transfer of the point (PSF). If PSF is specified (PSF is the same for all image pixels), Equation (1) indicates the deconvolution problem, otherwise it presents the blind deconvolution problem.

Blind Image Restoration: This technique allows the reconstruction of original images from the degraded ones even when a little or no knowledge is available about PSF. Blind Image Deconvolution (BID) is an algorithm of this type [22].

Non-Blind Restoration: This technique aids in the reconstruction of original images from the degraded ones when the process of image degradation is known, which means that the PSF information is available [22]. The image restoration problem is more accurately expressed using a non-linear regularizer. Therefore, in this work, it was tried to use this regularizer. In (1), x and y indicate the original and degraded images, respectively, and B is a linear operator that represents a blur matrix in case of blurring image or losing a number of image pixels in case of inpainting image. In order to construct the degraded image, it is required to add the linear operator of B and noise to the original

image. Depending upon the linear operator, B, which includes the blur or the lost pixels, the image restoration problem will differ. If B contains the blur, the image restoration problem changes to the deblurring, and if B indicates the lost pixels, it converts to the inpainting.

In the formulating part, the information for the degraded and original images is used to formulate the objective function and then to remove the noise and blurring from the degraded image. This function is solved using the inverse function or optimization problem. The image restoration problem that is solved by convex optimization uses unconstrained optimization, as follows:

$$\min_x \frac{1}{2}\|y - Bx\|_2^2 + \tau\phi(x), \qquad (2)$$

where, $\|.\|_p$ is p-norm, and is given by:

$$\|A\|_p = \left(\sum_{i=1}^{n}|a_i|^p\right)^{1/p} \qquad (3)$$

where, n is the number of matrix element A after reshaping.

The optimization problem contains two parts: data fidelity and smooth regularizer. In a practical research work, the regularizer is completely unable to model the characteristic of the original image. Therefore, we should compromise between the regularizer and the data fidelity. For instance, in figure 1(a), the cameraman image is degraded by the 9*9 uniform blur and additive Gaussian noise with zero mean. Figure 1(b) shows that the regularizer has a small effect, and the output noise is amplified for a very small regularizer parameter ($\tau = 0.001$). On the other hand, figure 1(C) shows that the large regularizer parameter ($\tau = 10$) provides a much smoothed image and removes the edges of image. Thus it is required that the regularizer parameter is appropriately selected such that the aforementioned problems are avoided.

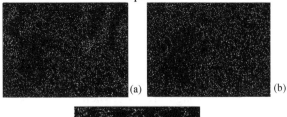

Figure 1. a) Degraded image by 9*9 uniform blur and additive Gaussian noise with zero mean b) restored image by small regularizer parameter ($\tau = 0.001$) c) restored image by large regularizer parameter ($\tau = 10$).

2. Related works

The image restoration methods are classified into three categories: 1) methods bas
ed on filtering 2) methods based on regularizer, and 3) methods based on Bayesian restoration. The image processing systems normally use a low-pass filter to model the blurring of the image. The filter-based methods contain the inverse filtering, pseudo-inverse filtering, and wiener filtering.

Equation (4) results in the restored image using (1) in the Fourier domain [2]:

$$\hat{x} = f^{-1}\left(\frac{Y(\omega_i, \omega_j)}{B(\omega_i, \omega_j)}\right)$$

$$= f^{-1}\left(X(\omega_i, \omega_j) + \frac{N(\omega_i, \omega_j)}{B(\omega_i, \omega_j)}\right) \tag{4}$$

where, f^{-1} indicates the inverse Fourier transform. $Y(\omega_i, \omega_j)$, $B(\omega_i, \omega_j)$, and $X(\omega_i, \omega_j)$ are 2D Fourier transforms of the degraded image, the blur PSF, and the original image, respectively. The simple theory and low complexity are advantages of the inverse filtering methods. However, the inverse filtering method provides an accurate restoration image when there is not additive noise in the degraded image but the degraded image normally contains an additive noise in practice. Therefore, in a noisy degraded image, the inverse filtering method provides a weak performance and unacceptable results [2].

The pseudo-inverse filtering method uses the matrix-vector form of the degraded image in which B is a non-invertible matrix. If the columns of B are lineally independent, (1) can be modified and approximated using pseudo-inverse solvation as [8]:

$$x = \left(B^T B\right)^{-1} B^T y. \tag{5}$$

The mentioned advantages of inverse filter can be enumerated for the pseudo-inverse filter. This method provides a better performance than the inverse method, although it is unable to provide acceptable results for a noisy degraded image [8].

As the name implies, the median filter is a statistics method. In this method, the median of the pixel is found, and then the pixel is replaced by median of the gray levels in their neighborhood of that pixel. The median filter is used to remove the salt and pepper noise [23].

The Wiener filter method is based upon optimization of Mean Square Error (MSE), and it provides a better performance than the inverse filter. This filter is the base of many new restoration methods because it is an optimal filter to minimize MSE. For example, the edge mapping Wiener filter has been proposed to preserve the edges and the details of images. The collaborative Wiener filter has been reported to remove image noise in a sparse 3D transform domain [9]. Although the Wiener filter is known as the most optimum method for minimization of MSE and can be efficiently solved in frequency domain, it is unable to provide a high quality for the restored image.

The regularization methods were developed to make the image restoration problem well-posed by introducing information about the original image. In this situation, there is a large number of possible solutions; additional information is required to choose the correct solution. Finally, since discontinuities cause instability in many algorithms, the solution must depend continuously upon data. The regularization methods solve this problem using the prior information about the image to calculate the estimate. It requires the selection of a regularization parameter, α, which controls the trade-off between fidelity to measurements and to the prior information.

The regularizer-based method is the second category of the image restoration methods. This method repeatedly combines additional information, and a regularizer solves the restoration problem. These methods, such as Tikhonove-Miller regularizer, are known as a framework to well-pose the restoration problem. The traditional regularizers such as L2-norm adversely affect the sharp edge restoration because the images are piecewise smoothed. Therefore, the advanced regularizers model the characteristics of the original image using non-linear penalty functions [10].

The Bayesian approach provides the means to incorporate prior knowledge in data analysis. The Bayesian analysis revolves around the posterior probability, which summarizes the degree of one's certainty concerning a given situation. The Bayes's law states that the posterior probability is proportional to the product of the likelihood and the prior probability. The likelihood encompasses the information contained in the new data. The prior expresses the degree of certainty concerning the situation before the data is taken. Although the posterior probability completely describes the state of certainty about any possible image, it is often necessary to select a single image as the 'result' or reconstruction. A typical choice is to choose an image that maximizes the posterior probability, which is called the MAP estimate. Other choices for the estimator may be more desirable, for example, the mean of the posterior density function. In situations where only a very limited data is available, the data alone may not be sufficient to specify a unique solution to the problem. The prior introduced with the Bayesian method can help to guide the result toward a preferred solution. As the MAP solution differs from the maximum likelihood (ML) solution solely because of the prior, choosing the prior is one of the most critical aspects of the Bayesian analysis.

The Bayesian restoration methods model the restoration problem using the probability theory. The Bayesian methods combine additional information of new models of the image with the prior image, and can be iteratively solved. High computational cost and being unable to provide a specific optimization framework are the disadvantages of the Bayesian methods [11].

In this work, we used the regularizer method to restore the image. There are several methods available to solve the linear inverse optimization by minimization of the objective function, which is formulated as:

$$f(x) = \min_{x} \frac{1}{2}\|y - Bx\|_2^2 + \tau\phi(x) \qquad (6)$$

where, B is a linear operator and $\phi(x)$ is a regularizer [4]. This optimization equation should find the best compromise between the candidate estimated, x, and the obtained data of $\|y - Bx\|_2^2$.

The undesired degree of equation is distinguished by the $\phi(x)$ parameter, and the relation between two parts of (6) is identified by regulating parameter (τ). The unsmooth and non-quadratic regularizers such as the Total Variant, TV, and l_p-norm are used in various image processing applications [8]. If B = I, where I is a unit vector (identity matrix), the denoising problem is confronted. If $\emptyset$ is suitable and convex, the optimization problem is strictly convex and has a unique minimizer. Therefore, the denoising function is formulated by:

$$\psi_\tau(y) = \arg\min_{x} \frac{1}{2}\|x - y\|_2^2 + \tau\phi(x) \qquad (7)$$

For example, $\psi_\tau(y) = \text{soft}(y, \tau)$ if $\phi(x) = \|x\|_1 = \sum_i |x_i|$ (the L_1 norm).

$$\text{soft}(w, \tau) = \text{sign}(w).(|w| - \tau)_+$$

where $(a)_+ = \begin{cases} 0 & \text{if } a<0 \\ a & \text{if } a>0 \end{cases}$

The soft function is shown in figure 2.

The Iterative Shrinkage Thresholding (IST) methods have been reported to efficiently and simply solve the sparsity-based restoration problems. These methods have firstly been developed as a proximal forward-backward iterative scheme in [12, 13]. In the IST method, x in the k+1 step is obtained by:

$$x^{k+1} = \psi_{\tau/\alpha}\left(x^k - \frac{1}{\alpha_k}\left(B^T\left(Bx^k - y\right)\right)\right) \qquad (8)$$

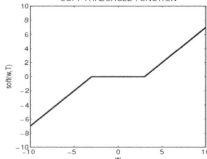

Figure 2. Soft function.

These methods are suitable and efficient when multiplication of B and B^T is dissolvable. These methods converge to minimum when $\|B\|_2^2 / 2 < a_k < +\infty$.

Another method is Two-step Iterative Shrinkage Thresholding (TwoIST), in which each current iterate incorporates to the previous two iterates. The TwoIST method is faster than the IST method. In the TwoIST algorithm, each iteration depends upon the two previous iterates rather than only on the previous one (as in IST). This algorithm may be seen as a non-linear version of the so-called two-step methods for linear problems. TwoIST was shown to be considerably faster than IST on a variety of wavelet-based image restoration problems; the speed gains can reach up to two orders of magnitude in typical benchmark problems [14].

An improved two-step variant of the IST method is called Fast IST Algorithm (FISTA). FISTA is faster than the TwoIST and IST methods. The non-smooth variation of Nesterovs optimal gradient-based algorithm is used in FISTA [15].

Sparse Reconstruction by Separable Approximation Algorithm (SpaRSA) is another fast variant of IST algorithm. This method uses a different α_k in each iteration, which is updated by α_k (where $1/\alpha_k$ is a step size) [12]. This method has been shown to outperform standard IST by selecting an aggressive step-size at each iteration. When the slowness is caused by using a small value of the regularization parameter, the continuation schemes have been found quite effective in speeding up the algorithm. The key observation is that the IST algorithm benefits significantly from warm-starting, i.e. from being initialized near a minimum of the objective function.

Neural Network Approach: The neural network is a form of multi-processor computer system with simple processing elements interconnected group of nodes [29, 30]. These interconnected components are called neurons, which send message to each other. When an element of the neural network fails, it can continue without any problem by their parallel nature [24].

Block-matching: This is employed to find blocks that contain high correlation because its accuracy is significantly impaired by the presence of noise. We utilize a block-similarity measure that performs a coarse initial denoising in local 2D transform domain. In this method, the image is divided into blocks and noise or blur is removed from each block [23].

Since the reported methods in [25, 26] are based upon non-blind de-convolution and use grayscale images, same databases, and evaluation measures, the proposed method is compared with them. The reported method in [25] is based upon the genetic algorithm, and is briefly given as follows:

Step 1: Get Blurred Image (initial image).

Step 2: Apply Fast Fourier Transform on blurred Image.

Step 3: Apply Inverse Fourier Transform, and create an initial population for applying genetic algorithm .

Step 4: Calculate the value of objective functions for the current population.

Step 5: Apply the cumulative fitness assignment criteria and selection procedure. Use genetic algorithm for selection of new population .

Step 6: Find the best individuals.

Step 7: Apply cross-over and Mutation on the new population (obtained in Step ○) in order to create a new population .

Step 8: Get the restored image using the best individuals (obtained in Step 6).

This method tries to maximize all the objectives. We proposed a fitness function criterion that is based upon individual objectives such as intensity, entropy, and edges. After evaluating fitness of all individual objectives (entropy, edge, and intensity), the combined fitness or cumulative fitness is calculated. The proposed method evaluates and maximizes all the objectives. This means that the image restoration criterion is defined as a function of entropy, edges, and intensity.

Edges can be defined as rapid changes in image intensity over a small region. In order to measure these changes, one method is to use discrete difference operators. It consists of two masks that calculate the changes in both directions, i.e. x-direction and y-direction.

We took different images with the same size. The maximum number of generation to run the program was chosen as 20; this also works as a criterion to end the evolution. Mutation has to be taken as simple mutation having probability = 0.1, arithmetic cross-over has to be taken having the cross-over probability = 0.8, selection was taken as the tournament selection, and finally, the population size had to be taken as 48.

The reported method in [26] is based upon the Wavelet transform, and is given by:

Step 1: Obtain an initial de-blurred result via the IDD-BM3D method, which will be used as the reference image for support estimation.

Step 2: Solve the resulting truncated ℓ^1-regularized problem.

In this work, we just took the anisotropic $\ell1$ norm as an example to illustrate the benefit of new regularization, though it can be also readily extended to the isotropic $\ell1$ norm.

Ones just solved a plain $\ell1$-regularized convex optimization problem, i.e. each frame coefficient was treated equally and penalized uniformly. In this case, it generates the bias, which means that the large coefficients are penalized more heavily than the smaller ones. Therefore, the customized $\ell1$-regularized model often achieves a sub-optimal performance. In practice, if the positions of the frame coefficients with large non-zero absolute values (we term the locations of large frame coefficients in magnitudes as support information) are known, we need to remove these coefficients out of the $\ell1$ norm and to use a truncated $\ell1$ norm instead in the restoration model.

The Gaussian Scale Mixture (GSM) model is developed using the simultaneous sparse coding (SSC), and its applications into image restoration are explored. It is shown that the variances of sparse coefficients (the field of scalar multipliers of Gaussians) can be jointly estimated along with the unknown sparse coefficients via the method of alternating optimization [27].

The so-called non-locally centralized sparse representation (NCSR) model is as simple as the standard sparse representation model, while our extensive experiments on various types of image restoration problems including denoising, deblurring, and super-resolution validate the generality and state-of-the-art performance of the proposed NCSR algorithm.

The patches of image x are clustered into K clusters and a PCA sub-dictionary k is learnt for each cluster. For a given patch, it is firstly checked which cluster it falls into by calculating its distances to means of the clusters, and then the PCA sub-dictionary of this cluster is selected [28].The mentioned methods are unable to converge very fast, and therefore, in this paper, we propose a new method to increase the speed and also improve the quality of the restored image.

3. Proposed method

We presented a new algorithm to solve the optimization formulation of regularized image restoration. The approach that can be used with different types of regularization is based upon the variable splitting technique. Then it solves the problem with the Lagrangian augmented optimization.

original

Blurred and noisy

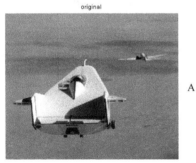

original

Blurred and noisy

Figure 3. Degraded Cameraman and Lifting-body: A) Original Image and B) degraded image with uniform blur and Gaussian noise.

3.1. Construction of degraded images for deblurring and inpainting

Assume that the aim of the proposed method is to degrade an image with a size of N*N by an m*m uniform blur, where m < N. First, a vector with the length of N is constructed so that the first m elements have the value of 1/m and the rest of the elements are zero. Next, the vector obtained is shifted to left with the size of (m-1)/2, and then it is multiplied by its transpose. Therefore, the m*m matrix is constructed, which is called the blur matrix. In order to obtain the blurred image, it requires to multiply the Fourier transform of the blurred matrix by the Fourier transform of the original image, and then to use inverse Fourier transform. The matrix obtained is Bx indicated in (1). Next, a desired noise is added to Bx, and therefore, the blurred/noisy image is constructed. In order to construct the degraded image for the inpainting case, it requires losing a number of pixels. Losing the pixels is randomly performed. In order to obtain the degraded image in (1), the random matrix is constructed such as a percentage of the original image pixels that is lost.

Note that the size of random matrix is the same as the original image. Some degraded images are shown in figures 3 and 4.

3.2. Solving problem of Lagrangian augmented optimization

In order to obtain the estimated image, x, (2) is used. The proposed method is based upon variable splitting for an optimization problem. The objective function in (2) is the sum of two functions. The main idea in the proposed method is to split the variable of x into the variable pairs of x and v such that each of them is an argument of one part in the objective function. Then the objective function is minimized under one constraint, which results in being equally the new problem with the problem in (2), given by:

$$\min_{x,v \in R^n} \frac{1}{2} \|Bx - y\|_2^2 + \tau\phi(v)$$

subject to $x = v$ (9)

The new determined optimization problem is solved by the Lagrangian augmented method. The formulation of undetermined optimization for regulated image restoration is given by:

$$f_1(x) = \frac{1}{2}\|Bx - y\|_2^2$$

$$f_2(x) = \tau\phi(x)$$ (10)

$$G = I \quad \text{i.e.} \quad v = Gx$$

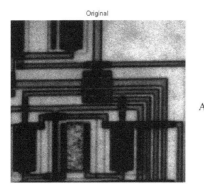

Figure 4. Degraded Cir and Peppers: A) Original Image and B) degraded image with losing 40% of pixels and Gaussian noise.

The formulation of the determined optimization using variable splitting is given by:

$$\text{objective fun} = \min_{x,v \in R^n} \frac{1}{2}\|Bx - y\|_2^2 + \tau\phi(v) \tag{11}$$

subject to $x = v$

In order to solve the determined optimization problem, it is better to use the Lagrangian augmented method, which is given by:

$$(x_{k+1}, v_{k+1}) \in \arg_{x,v} \frac{1}{2}\|Bx - y\|_2^2 + \tau\phi(v) + \frac{\mu}{2}\|x - v - d_k\|_2^2$$

$$d_{k+1} = d_k - (Gx_{k+1} - v_{k+1}) \tag{12}$$

where, μ is a positive value that is given by the user. It has been shown that the performance of the least-squares penalty is better than the Lagrangian method. In addition, the Lagrangian augmented method is converged under more principle conditions. Therefore, we propose a new method in order to solve the optimization problem, as follows:

First, k is set to zero, and $\mu > 0$, d_0, and v_0 are set to the initial values that are zero, and then it requires to solve the optimization problem given by:

$$x_{k+1} = \arg\min_x \|Bx - y\|_2^2 + \mu\|x - v_k - d_k\|_2^2 \tag{13}$$

Here, x_{k+1} is a strictly convex function, which has to be minimized. This corresponds to a linear system that is given by:

$$x_{k+1} = (B^H B + \mu I)^{-1}(B^H y + \mu(v_k + d_k)) \tag{14}$$

By obtaining x_{k+1} from the previous step, it is inserted in (15), and therefore, it requires solving the optimization problem as:

$$v_{k+1} = \arg\min_v \tau\phi(v) + \frac{\mu}{2}\|x_{k+1} - v - d_k\|_2^2 \tag{15}$$

This can be solved using (7). Then d_{k+1} is obtained by x_{k+1} and v_{k+1} in the previous step:

$$d_{k+1} = d_k - (x_{k+1} - v_{k+1}) \tag{16}$$

Next, one is added to k (k = k + 1), and the stop criterion is measured, which is given by:

$$\frac{|\text{objective fun}(k+1) - \text{objective fun}(k)|}{|\text{objective fun}(k)|} < \text{tolerance} \tag{17}$$

This criterion is equal to the changes of the objective function. If the stop criterion is satisfied, the procedure is stopped; otherwise the previous steps are repeated until the stop criterion is satisfied.

3.2.1. Variable splitting: Consider the undetermined optimization problem, which contains two terms:

$$\min_{x \in R^n} f_1(x) + f_2(g(x)), \tag{18}$$

where, the $g : R^n \to R^d$ variable splitting includes construction of a new variable as $g(x) = v$ that corresponds to a new optimization problem, given by:

$$\min_{x \in \square^n, v \in R^d} f_1(x) + f_2(v) \tag{19}$$

$$s.t : g(x) = v$$

This is equal to the optimization problem in (18). We use the variable splitting method reported in [7] to provide a fast restoration image. In [4, 10], the optimization problem in (19) is changed to (20) with consideration of the second order penalty and the periodical minimization with respect to x and v.

$$\min_{x \in R^n, v \in \square^d} f_1(x) + f_2(v) + \frac{\alpha}{2} \| g(x) - v \|_2^2 \tag{20}$$

The function of variable splitting is as the one reported by Bregman [18, 19]. This directly solves the determined optimization problem. It has been shown that when g is a linear function, i.e. $g(x) = Gx$, the Bregman's method is similar to the Lagrangian augmented method.

3.2.2. Lagrangian augmented: Consider the optimization problem with constraint as follows:

$$\min_{z \in R^n} E(z) \tag{21}$$

$$s.t \ Hz - b = 0$$

where, b = 0, $z = \begin{bmatrix} X \\ V \end{bmatrix}$ and $H = \begin{bmatrix} G & -I \end{bmatrix}$.

In this case, the Lagrangian function is given by:

$$L_A(z, \lambda, \mu) = E(z) + \lambda^T (b - Hz) + \frac{\mu}{2} \| Hz - b \|_2^2 \tag{22}$$

where, λ is a value for the Lagrangian coefficient, and $\mu > 0$ is called the penalty parameter. In this method, $L_A(z, \lambda, \mu)$ is minimized with respect to z and maintaining λ as a constant value, and then λ is updated and the minimization of $L_A(z, \lambda, \mu)$ is repeated. This procedure continues until the convergence criterion is satisfied [20].

3.2.3. Variable splitting using Lagrangian augmented method: Consider the variable splitting problem given by:

$$\min \ R(x) + \tau \phi(v) \quad s.t \quad v = Gx . \tag{23}$$

where, R(.) is the fidelity term that guarantees that x is compatible with the observed y.

In this case, the Lagrangian augmented method is given by:

$$L_\rho(x, v, \mu) = R(x) + \tau \phi(v) + \mu^T (Gx - v) + \frac{\rho}{2} \| v - Gx \|_2^2 \tag{24}$$

where, μ is the Lagrangian coefficients vector and is a constant that is selected by a user [21]. We use the Gauss–Seidel method for minimization. Therefore, the minimization problem is formulated as:

$$x_{k+1} = \arg \min_x L_\rho(x_k, v_k, \mu_k), \tag{25}$$

$$v_{k+1} = \arg \min_v L_\rho(x_{k+1}, v_k, \mu_k), \tag{26}$$

$$\mu_{k+1} = \mu_k + \rho(Gx_{k+1} - v_{k+1}) . \tag{27}$$

3.2.4. Total variation regularizer: Total variation regularizers, due to having the ability for noise cancellation and maintaining image edges, are widely used in the image restoration methods [7]. These regularizers have improved under this assumption that the image has bounded variations. If the variations of the image inside are bounded, then the sum of the absolute variations of the image inside will be limited.

Therefore, the total variation regularizers are designed to restrict the variations of the image inside. The variation is defined by:

$$\phi(x) = \sum_{w=1}^{l} \sqrt{\nabla_i(x_w)^2 + \nabla_j(x_w)^2} , \tag{28}$$

where, $\nabla_i(x_w)$ and $\nabla_j(x_w)$ are the first-order vertical and horizontal difference in the ith pixel, respectively. On the other hand, the sparsity regularizer causes the transform coefficients of the restored images to be scattered. These regularizers reduce the noise without any destructive effect on the edges.

3.2.5. Calculation of x_{k+1}: In (14), the initial vales for x_0, d_0, and v_0 are set to zero. Thus in (28), $\phi(v_0)$ that is related to the total variation regularizer can be solved and $\| Bx_0 - y \|_2^2$ can be calculated using (3). The initial objective function is then calculated using $\phi(v_0)$ and $\| Bx_0 - y \|_2^2$. In what follows, calculation of x_{k+1} is distinctly explained for the deblurring/denoising and inpainting problems.

A) Calculation of x_{k+1} for deblurring/denoising:

First, the absolute of Fourier transform of blur matrix, B, is obtained and each element is squared and added with μ:

$$(B^HB+\mu I)^{-1}, \tag{29}$$

The matrix elements obtained are then inversed. Next, the Fourier transform of $B^Hy+\mu(v_k+d_k)$ is obtained and multiplied by (20). x_{k+1} is the inverse Fourier transform of the resulting matrix.

B) Calculation of x_{k+1} for inpainting: In order to obtain the inverse of $(B^HB+\mu I)$, the Sherman-Morrison-Woodbury equation is used, which is given by:

$$\left(B^HB+\mu I\right)^{-1}=\frac{1}{\mu}\left(I-\frac{1}{\mu+1}B^HB\right), \tag{30}$$

where, B^HB is a number of zeros in the main diagonal. These zeros indicate the lost positions in the image.

Thus x_{k+1} is obtained by multiplication of $B^Hy+\mu(v_k+d_k)$ with (30).

3.2.6. Calculation of v_{k+1}: v_{k+1} can be calculated by the Moreau proximal mapping for $x_{k+1}-d_k$. This means that:

$$v_{k+1}=\psi\left(x_{k+1}-d_k\right), \tag{31}$$

where, ψ is given by equation (9). If this mapping is accurately calculated in the closed form, then it is guaranteed that the proposed method is converged.

4. Results
All experiments were executed using the MATLAB software, applied on a personal computer containing a microprocessor of Intel (R) i5CPU:2.53 GHz and 4 GB RAM. The value for μ in (13) was selected as 10% of the regularizer parameter or $\tau/10$.

The number of iterations, the processing time (CPU time), ISNR, and MSE were used as the evaluation measures. We used various images such as cameraman, Lena, moon, lifting-body, tire, coins, and peppers. For blurring, we used a uniform blur with a size of 9*9 and white normal Gaussian noise with different variances, and for inpainting, 30%, 40%, and 50% of the original pixels were lost.

4.1. Evaluation measures
In order to compare the performance of the different image restoration methods, the quantitative measures that evaluate the quality of

the restored image are very important. These measures include Improvement in SNR, ISNR, and Mean Square Error (MSE), which are calculated by [2, 9]:

$$ISNR=10\log_{10}\frac{\sum_K\left\|x-y_k\right\|^2}{\sum_K\left\|x-\hat{x}_k\right\|^2} \tag{32}$$

$$MSE=\frac{1}{M*N}\sum_K\left\|x-\hat{x}_k\right\|^2 \tag{33}$$

where, M and N are the image dimensions, x is the original image, and y_k and $\hat{x}_k$ are the observed and the estimated image in the kth iteration. In this work, in addition to these two measures, the processing time was also considered, which indicates the speed of convergence for capability of the methods.

4.2. Indexing results
4.2.1. Results obtained for deblurring
Table 1 shows the evaluation measures for the aforementioned images. The results obtained show that the proposed method improves ISNR, decreases MSE, and reduces the processing time considerably compared to the TwoIST and SpaRSA methods.

Table 1. Results of deblurring images degraded by Gaussian noise with $\sigma=0.3080$ and Uniform blur 9*9 in size.

Image	Method	Iterations	CPU time (s)	ISNR (dB)	MSE
Cameraman	TwoIST	69	16.2	7.63	94.1
	SpaRSA	123	25.7	7.86	89.2
	Proposed method	20	3.67	8.43	78.2
Lena	TwoIST	46	51.1	6.56	37.4
	SpaRSA	56	52	6.36	39.1
	Proposed method	16	13.1	7.59	29.5
Lifting-body	TwoIST	41	45.3	8.64	12.3
	SpaRSA	53	49.5	8.88	11.6
	Proposed method	24	20.3	10.4	8.14
Coins	TwoIST	61	13.8	8.87	54.4
	SpaRSA	115	23.1	8.71	56.5
	Proposed method	22	4.06	9.75	44.5
Moon	TwoIST	25	13.1	3.86	62.8
	SpaRSA	22	9.14	3.73	70.2
	Proposed method	17	6.18	3.91	67.4
Peppers	TwoIST	51	55.5	7.93	31.8
	SpaRSA	78	73.4	7.97	30.1
	Proposed method	18	14.8	8.45	27

As observed in table 1, for instance, for the Lena image, ISNR was improved by the proposed method 1.03 dB and 1.23 dB compared to the TwoIST and SpaRSA methods, respectively, and the processing time was nearly 25% of the one provided by the TwoIST and SpaRSA methods. In addition, MSE obtained by the proposed method decreased 10 units. For the Lifting-body image, the processing time required by the proposed method was less than half of the ones resulted by the other two methods and ISNR improved around 1.5 dB. In addition, MSE decreased to 3.46 and 4.16 compared to the SpaRSA and TwoIST methods, respectively.

Figure 5 shows the objective function indicated in (8) for the aforementioned images. As observed, the objective function compared to the SpaRSA and TwoIST methods is faster converged. For instance, for the cameraman image, the objective function is converged to the final value in less than 4 s, whereas 30 s is required for the other two methods at least. For the Lena image, the proposed method is converged in 3 s, whereas the SpaRSA and TwoIST methods require 30 s and 50 s, respectively, for convergence. The same results can be observed for the other images. As an example, figures 6-9 show the restored image by the proposed method. As observed, the blurred effect has been highly removed in the restored image by the proposed method.

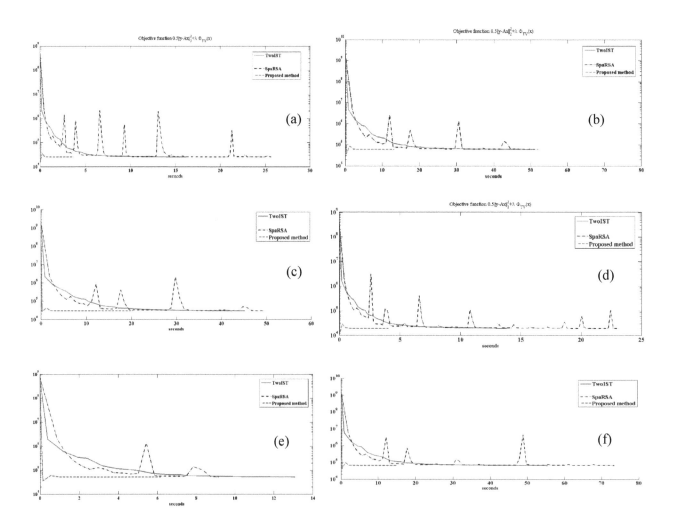

Figure 5. Output of deblurring for objective function related to equation (8) obtained by TwoIST, SpaRSA, and proposed method for images: A) Cameraman, B) Lena, C) Lifting-body, D) Coins, E) Moon, and F) Peppers.

Figure 6. Deblurring results: A) Original Image, B) degraded image, and C) restored image by proposed method.

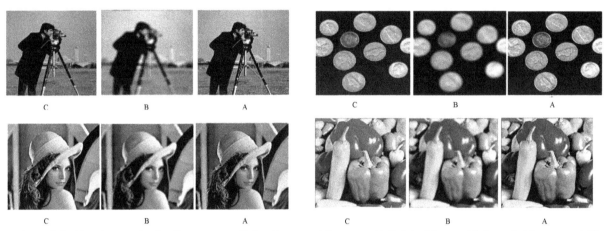

Figure 7. Deblurring results for Cameraman, Coins, Lena, and Peppers: A) Original Image, B) degraded image, and C) restored image by proposed method.

In the next experiment, the effect of different blurs with additive Gaussian noise ($\sigma = 0.3080$) was investigated. The results obtained are shown in table 2. As observed, the processing time (CPU time), ISNR, and MSE were improved compared to the other methods. It was also observed that the best results with respect to ISNR and MSE were achieved by uniform blur with a size of 9*9. In addition, the results obtained for the case of Gaussian blur with $\sigma = 1.41$ were better than the one with $\sigma = 2.83$. In the case of blur matrix in which $h_{i,j} = 1/(1+i^2+j^2)$ for i,j=-7,...7 , the results obtained provided higher ISNR and lower MSE and CPU time compared to the other cases.

In another experiment, the effect of different additive noises with uniform blur with a size of 9*9 was examined. As expected, the results obtained show that when the variance of Gaussian noise increases, ISNR decreases, MSE increases, and the quality of the restored image degrades. As an example, tables 3-7 show the results obtained for different images using different blurs and Gaussian noise with $\sigma = 0.3080$, $\sigma = 0.5$, and $\sigma = 2.0$.

In tables 5 and 7, the values for Peak Signal for the restored images by the proposed method and

other methods are shown. The PSNR values by the proposed method are higher than the results obtained by the TwoIST, SpaRSA, Genetic Algorithm, Wavelet Frame Truncated, NCSR, and SSC-GSM methods. As shown, the results obtained by the proposed method are better in terms of the Peak Signal to Noise Ratio.

In tables 5 and 6, the MSE values for the restored images by different images are shown. The MSE values by the proposed method are less than the results obtained by the TwoIST, SpaRSA, Genetic Algorithm, Wavelet Frame Truncated, NCSR, and SSC-GSM methods.

Similar results were obtained for the other images, which seem to be unnecessary to be shown.

4.2.2. Results obtained for inpainting
In the inpainting problem, the aim is the restoration of the degraded image in which a percentage of the pixels has been lost and noise has been added. In this experiment, 40% of the image pixels were lost and a normal white Gaussian noise was added to the image. For evaluation, the aforementioned images were used and the proposed method was compared to the TwoIST and FISTA methods. The results

obtained were shown in table 8. As observed, the proposed method resulted in a higher ISNR, a lower MSE, and also a shorter processing time compared to the TwoIST and FISTA methods. For instance, for the Lena image, the processing time was almost 10% of the one provided by the other two methods and improved ISNR and MSE at least 0.3 dB and 1.2, respectively. For the lifting-body image, the processing time was around 1000 s and 845 s less the ones obtained for the TwoIST and FISTA methods, respectively. Also ISNR obtained by the proposed method was 0.64 dB and 0.97 dB higher than the ones resulted by the TwoIST and FISTA methods, respectively. In this case, the proposed method provided 0.4 and 0.5 reduction in MSE

compared to the FISTA and TwoIST methods, respectively. The same results could also be concluded for other images.

Figure 10 shows the objective function resulted by inpainting for the aforementioned images. As observed, the resulting objective function by the proposed method can converge to the final value in a shorter time compared to the TwoIST and FISTA methods. For instance, in figure 10(a), which is related to the cameraman image, the objective function converges in 50 s, 200 s, and 300 s for the proposed method, TwoIST, and the FISTA method, respectively. The same results can be observed for the other images. Therefore, the objective function by the proposed method converges faster than the other two methods.

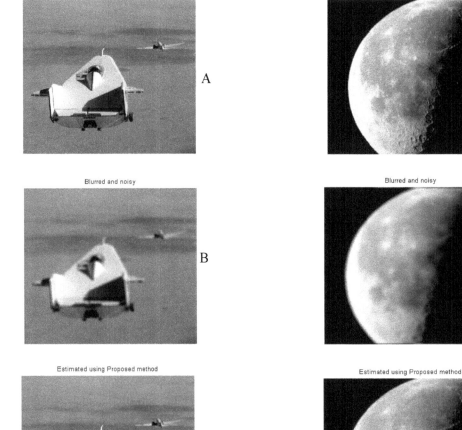

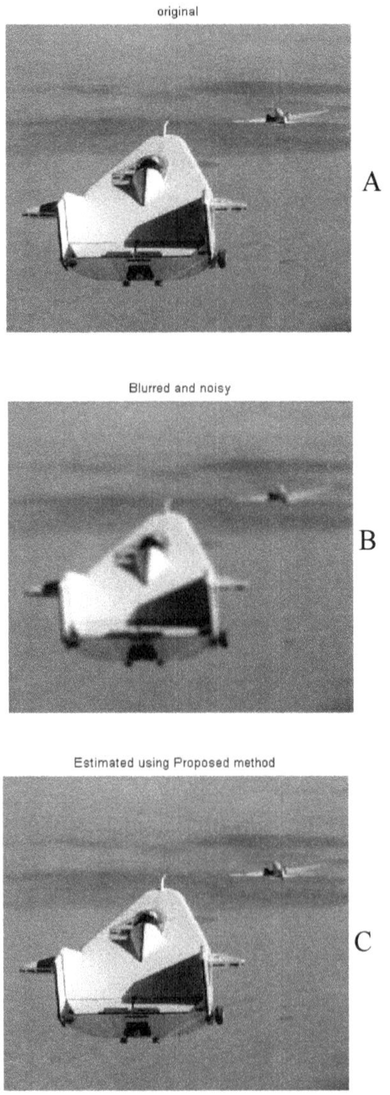

Figure 8. Deblurring results for Lifting-body: A) Original Image, B) degraded image, and C) restored image by proposed method.

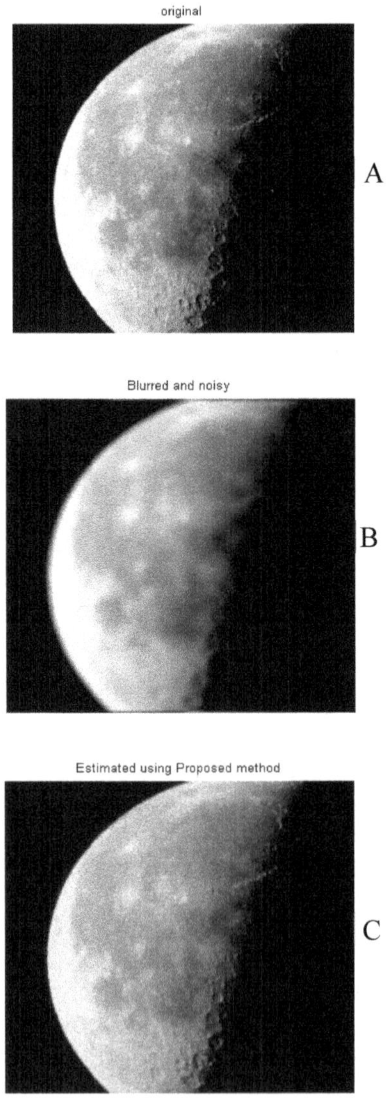

Figure 9. Deblurring results for Moon: A) Original Image, B) degraded image, and C) restored image by proposed method.

Table 2. Results of restored images degraded by Gaussian noise with σ = 0.3080 and different blurs.

Image	Method	Uniform blur with size of 9*9			Gaussian blur with σ = 1.41		
		CPU time(s)	ISNR (dB)	MSE	CPU time(s)	ISNR (dB)	MSE
Cameraman	TwoIST	62.45	5.24	94.1	26.59	3.65	113.27
	SpaRSA	64.5	5.92	89.1	22.73	3.71	107.78
	Proposed method	11.01	8.43	78.2	1.45	4.19	92.76
Lena	TwoIST	51.1	6.56	37.4	25.4	2.87	99.1
	SpaRSA	52	6.36	39.1	26.7	2.34	63.7
	Proposed method	13.1	7.59	29.5	3.9	3.42	49.8
Lifting-body	TwoIST	45.3	8.64	12.3	19.9	4.52	34.1
	SpaRSA	49.5	8.88	11.6	21.4	4.69	28.9
	Proposed method	20.3	10.4	8.14	11.9	5.73	22.7
Coins	TwoIST	13.8	8.87	54.4	16.2	4.95	67.7
	SpaRSA	23.1	8.71	56.5	29.5	4.99	65.4
	Proposed method	4.06	9.75	44.5	1.36	5.74	50.2
Moon	TwoIST	13.1	3.86	68.2	17.7	1.27	79.4
	SpaRSA	9.14	3.73	70.2	24.01	1.31	90.7
	Proposed method	6.18	3.91	67.4	1.47	2.07	70.9
Peppers	TwoIST	55.5	7.73	31.8	29.78	3.75	44.8
	SpaRSA	73.4	7.97	30.1	36.6	3.81	42.9
	Proposed method	14.8	8.45	27	4.39	4.49	37.7

Image	Method	Gaussian blur with σ = 2.83			Blur matrix $h_{ij}=1/(1+i^2+j^2)$ for i,j=-7,...7		
		CPU time(s)	ISNR (dB)	MSE	CPU time(s)	ISNR (dB)	MSE
Cameraman	TwoIST	24.21	2.57	79.7	19.25	4.64	100.6
	SpaRSA	23.18	2.69	69.8	17.45	4.61	98.2
	Proposed method	2.67	3.35	58.98	1.41	6.05	81.3
Lena	TwoIST	23.64	1.36	110	19.47	3.45	45.3
	SpaRSA	25.01	1.70	75	24.88	3.49	43.7
	Proposed method	4.12	3.29	50.45	3.25	6.21	35.4
Lifting-body	TwoIST	15.89	3.44	59.2	14.35	5.41	38.3
	SpaRSA	19.46	3.55	54.3	15.18	5.56	32.1
	Proposed method	12.10	5.41	43.9	9.42	8.35	21.6
Coins	TwoIST	14.75	3.81	79.1	13.89	4.99	60.7
	SpaRSA	23.40	3.86	63.7	22.70	5.01	62.9
	Proposed method	2.41	5.24	46.7	1.32	8.31	55.4
Moon	TwoIST	15.14	0.904	95.1	12.36	2.35	71.3
	SpaRSA	18.95	0.915	91.35	16.87	2.47	84.7
	Proposed method	2.56	1.86	79.4	1.48	4.95	61.6
Peppers	TwoIST	21.27	2.62	76	21.12	4.26	39.4
	SpaRSA	30.49	2.76	75.2	28.64	4.95	40.8
	Proposed method	5.17	4.24	60.9	3.39	7.12	30.7

Table 3. Results of restored cameraman image degraded by uniform blur with size of 9*9 and different noises.

Method	MSE				ISNR			
	Poisson noise	Gaussian noise with variance 2	Gaussian noise with variance 1	Gaussian noise with variance 0.308033	Poisson noise	Gaussian noise with variance 2	Gaussian noise with variance 1	Gaussian noise with variance 0.308033
TwoIST	$1.07'10^4$	166	148	94.1	−10.6	5.17	5.21	7.63
SpaRSA	2.86×10^3	141	138	89.1	−4.83	5.87	5.95	7.86
Wiener filter	1.11×10^4	8.93×10^3	8.93×10^3	8.93×10^3	−10.7	0.629	0.633	1.28
Inverse filter	1.06×10^9	2.5×10^6	5.5×10^5	2.4×10^5	−60.5	−35.8	−30	−14.6
Proposed method	1.99×10^3	134	132	78.2	−3.27	6.08	6.14	8.43

Table 4. Results of restored Lena image degraded by uniform blur with size of 9*9 and different noises.

Method	MSE				ISNR			
	Poisson noise	Gaussian noise with variance 2	Gaussian noise with variance 1	Gaussian noise with variance 0.308033	Poisson noise	Gaussian noise with variance 2	Gaussian noise with variance 1	Gaussian noise with variance 0.308033
TwoIST	7.14×10^3	101	100	37.4	−10.6	5.42	5.45	6.56
SpaRSA	1.79×10^3	100	99.6	39.1	−4.83	5.45	5.48	6.36
Wiener filter	9.41×10^3	3.94×10^3	3.94×10^3	3.94×10^3	−10.7	0.435	0.438	0.891
Inverse filter	4.47×10^8	1.22×10^6	7.23×10^5	4.91×10^4	−60.5	−35.4	−30.31	−15.01
Proposed method	1.27×10^3	95	80.2	29.5	−3.27	5.92	6.08	7.59

Table 5. Results of MSE and PSNR restored images degraded by Gaussian noise with σ = 2 and different blurs.

Image	Blur	TwoIST	SpaRSA	Genetic Algorithm	Wavelet Frame Truncated	NCSR	SSC-GSM	Proposed method
				PSNR				
Cameraman	9 × 9 uniform blur	25.45	25.97	27.94	27.97	28.62	28.82	28.89
	Gaussian blur: (σ =1.6)	26.27	26.35	27.48	27.78	28.33	28.39	28.53
	Motion blur: fspecial ('motion', 15, 30)	27.78	27.87	29.54	29.77	29.80	29.86	29.93
Lena	9 × 9 uniform blur	27.09	27.63	29	29.04	29.87	29.94	30.10
	Gaussian blur: (σ =1.6)	26.62	26.76	30.87	30.93	30.90	31.04	31.29
	Motion blur: fspecial ('motion', 15, 30)	28.81	28.91	31.17	31.20	31.41	31.79	32.91
				MSE				
Cameraman	9 × 9 uniform blur	185.39	164.468	104.49	103.77	89.35	85.33	83.96
	Gaussian blur: (σ = 1.6)	153.49	150.68	116.16	108.41	95.52	94.21	91.21
	Motion blur: fspecial ('motion', 15, 30)	110.17	106.19	72.30	68.56	68.09	67.15	66.08
Lena	9 × 9 uniform blur	129.74	112.22	81.86	81.1	67.00	65.93	66.84
	Gaussian blur: (σ =1.6)	141.60	137.1	53.22	52.49	52.85	51.19	48.31
	Motion blur: fspecial ('motion',15,30)	86.12	83.57	49.67	49.33	46.99	43.06	33.27

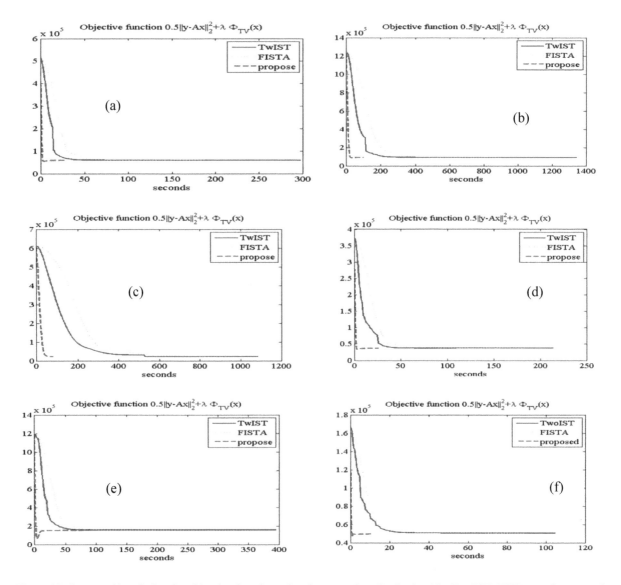

Figure 10. Output of inpainting for objective function related to equation (8) obtained by TwoIST, FISTA, and proposed methods for images: A) Cameraman, B) Lena, C) Lifting-body, D) Coins, E) Moon, F)Tire, and G) Peppers.

Table 6. Results of MSE restored images degraded by Gaussian noise with σ = 0.5 and different blurs.

image	Cameraman	Lena	Butterfly	Foreman	House	Leaves	moon	baboon	Barbara	Peppers
9 × 9 uniform blur, σ = 0.5										
TwoIST	100.71	48.32	89.94	32.89	27.73	86.51	84.74	306.96	99.10	42.18
SpaRSA	96.40	43.56	87.04	31.99	26.55	81.86	82.05	305.25	94.86	41.50
Genetic Algorithm	65.48	41.50	61.46	25.83	18.15	75.70	77.10	272.95	77.28	39.27
Wavelet Frame Truncated	64.58	42.27	59.13	22.97	18.36	75.00	76.75	275.47	76.93	40.18
NCSR	64.72	41.69	52.13	22.14	18.48	65.17	78.00	248.50	81.67	41.31
SSC-GSM	63.39	41.41	51.66	22.03	18.01	52.37	74.83	266.73	79.26	41.12
Proposed method	52.49	32.33	50.38	15.00	10.59	43.65	69.51	224.95	53.10	31.75
Gaussian blur: (σ =1.6), Gaussian noise with σ = 0.5										
TwoIST	87.92	110.05	74.99	39.09	27.87	61.96	87.52	327.40	105.70	66.85
SpaRSA	85.92	68.53	67.91	38.46	26.42	60.82	98.42	325.15	101.41	66.37
Genetic Algorithm	82.24	56.03	49.14	33.27	25.30	55.60	88.73	300.66	83.96	59.30
Wavelet Frame Truncated	81.68	53.78	50.86	26.48	23.34	54.46	92.27	293.14	85.52	58.89
NCSR	82.61	51.77	52.25	26.98	21.63	46.46	96.18	299.97	95.08	59.99
SSC-GSM	81.67	49.90	48.87	21.88	20.28	39.54	94.21	302.75	86.91	57.29
Proposed method	61.96	45.32	46.35	19.81	13.55	38.73	74.83	242.70	77.64	41.79
Motion blur: fspecial ('motion', 20, 45), σ = 0.5										
TwoIST	87.51	51.40	73.69	65.62	32.14	76.22	81.67	318.48	92.70	43.16
SpaRSA	85.92	49.78	69.87	30.34	30.34	71.96	77.28	325.15	87.72	41.22
Genetic Algorithm	76.75	39.86	53.76	22.28	21.29	59.44	71.13	263.08	75.52	44.47
Wavelet Frame Truncated	75.35	39.54	52.41	21.38	20.66	58.89	68.72	260.66	79.13	34.84
NCSR	79.63	36.99	52.73	22.70	21.09	51.53	71.13	266.73	72.29	36.23
SSC-GSM	75.52	34.28	51.53	20.61	20.00	46.57	67.46	260.06	78.40	34.84
Proposed method	52.73	30.21	30.18	11.54	11.78	25.89	62.24	227.03	51.77	24.84

Table 7. Results of PSNR restored images degraded by Gaussian noise with σ = 0. 5 and different blurs.

image	Cameraman	Lena	Butterfly	Foreman	House	Leaves	moon	baboon	Barbara	Peppers
9 × 9 uniform blur, σ = 0.5										
TwoIST	28.10	31.38	28.59	32.96	33.70	28.76	28.85	23.26	28.17	31.88
SpaRSA	28.29	31.74	28.73	33.08	33.89	29.00	28.99	23.27	28.36	31.95
Genetic Algorithm	29.97	31.95	30.25	34.01	35.54	29.34	29.26	23.77	29.25	32.19
Wavelet Frame Truncated	30.03	31.87	30.41	34.52	35.49	29.38	29.28	23.73	29.27	32.09
NCSR	30.02	31.93	30.96	34.68	35.48	29.99	29.21	23.59	29.01	31.97
SSC-GSM	30.11	31.96	30.999	34.70	35.59	30.94	29.39	23.87	29.14	31.99
Proposed method	30.93	33.05	31.11	36.37	37.88	31.73	29.71	24.61	30.88	33.11
Gaussian blur: (σ = 1.6), Gaussian noise with σ = 0.5										
TwoIST	28.69	27.71	29.38	32.21	33.68	30.21	28.71	22.98	27.89	29.88
SpaRSA	28.79	29.77	29.81	32.28	33.91	30.29	28.29	23.01	28.07	29.91
Genetic Algorithm	28.98	30.65	31.22	32.91	34.10	30.68	28.65	23.35	28.89	30.40
Wavelet Frame Truncated	29.01	30.82	31.07	33.90	34.45	30.77	28.48	23.46	28.81	30.43
NCSR	28.96	30.99	30.95	33.82	34.78	31.46	28.30	23.36	28.35	30.35
SSC-GSM	29..01	31.15	31.24	34.73	35.06	32.16	28.39	23.32	28.74	30.56
Proposed method	30.21	31.57	31.47	35.16	36.81	32.25	29.39	24.28	29.23	31.92
Motion blur: fspecial ('motion', 20, 45), σ = 0.5										
TwoIST	28.71	31.02	29.47	29.96	33.06	29.31	29.01	23.10	28.46	31.78
SpaRSA	28.79	31.16	29.68	33.31	33.31	29.56	29.25	23.01	28.70	31.98
Genetic Algorithm	29.28	32.13	30.83	34.65	34.85	30.39	29.61	23.93	29.35	32.65
Wavelet Frame Truncated	29.36	32.16	30.94	34.83	34.98	30.43	29.76	23.97	29.49	32.71
NCSR	29.12	32.45	30.91	34.57	34.89	31.01	29.61	23.82	29.54	32.54
SSC-GSM	29.35	32.78	31.01	34.99	35.12	31.45	29.84	23.99	29.78	32.71
Proposed method	30.91	33.33	33.34	37.51	37.42	34.00	30.19	24.57	30.99	34.18

As an example for inpainting, figures 11-14 show the restored image by the proposed method. As observed, the restored image is highly similar to the original one.

In the next experiment, the effect of different percentages of losing pixels with additive Gaussian noise with σ = 0.308033 and σ = 1.0

was investigated. As expected, as the percentage of losing the pixels increases, ISNR decreases, and MSE and CPU time increases. As an example, tables 9-11 show the results obtained for the Cameraman, Lena, and Lifting-body images, respectively. The same results were obtained for the other images, which seem to be unnecessary to be presented.

Figure 11. Results of inpainting: A) Original Image, B) degraded image, and C) restored image by proposed method.

Table 8. Results of inpainting images degraded by Gaussian noise with σ = 0.3080 and Losing 40% of pixels.

Image	Method	Iterations	CPU time(s)	ISNR (dB)	MSE
Cameraman	TwoIST	502	313	18.8	95.6
	SpaRSA	500	194	19	90.7
	Proposed method	73	27.5	19.2	85.7
Lena	TwoIST	502	1340	24.9	22.7
	SpaRSA	500	915	25.2	21
	Proposed method	55	100	25.5	19.8
Lifting-body	TwoIST	502	1080	7.96	30.2
	SpaRSA	500	925	7.64	30.3
	Proposed method	44	79.7	8.61	29.8
Coins	TwoIST	502	214	17.4	112
	SpaRSA	500	184	18.1	95.6
	Proposed method	78	25.9	18.3	90.9
Moon	TwoIST	502	1059	21.7	37
	SpaRSA	500	1499	21.9	35.3
	Proposed method	127	256	23.1	33.5
Tire	TwoIST	502	105	15.3	85.1
	SpaRSA	500	89	16	71.5
	Proposed method	63	11.3	16.7	61.9
Peppers	TwoIST	502	803	24.1	26.3
	SpaRSA	500	559	24.3	25.7
	Proposed method	61	72.6	24.9	22.6
Cir	TwoIST	502	294	19.3	36.8
	SpaRSA	500	204	19.4	36.2
	Proposed method	6.57	6.57	19.5	35.4

Table 9. Results of inpainting for cameraman image with different degradations.

	Method	Losing 30% of pixels			Losing 40% of pixels			Losing 50% of pixels		
		CPU time(s)	ISNR (dB)	MSE	CPU time(s)	ISNR (dB)	MSE	CPU time(s)	ISNR (dB)	MSE
Gaussian noise with variance 0.308033	TwoIST	374	66.5	19.2	313	95.6	18.8	404	144	17.9
	FISTA	274	62.7	19.5	194	90.7	19	274	135	18.2
	Proposed method	22.3	60.7	22.7	27.5	85.7	19.2	33.6	129	18.4
	Method	Losing 30% of pixels			Losing 40% of pixels			Losing 50% of pixels		
		CPU time(s)	ISNR (dB)	MSE	CPU time(s)	ISNR (dB)	MSE	CPU time(s)	ISNR (dB)	MSE
Gaussian noise with variance 1	TwoIST	315	68	19	476	101	18.5	532	143	18
	FISTA	291	64	19.3	274	93.2	18.6	288	139	18.1
	Proposed method	38.6	48.8	20.5	39.4	80.4	19.1	39.5	114	18.3

Table 10. Results of inpainting for Lena image with different degradations.

Gaussian noise with variance 0.308033	Method	Losing 30% of pixels			Losing 40% of pixels			Losing 50% of pixels		
		CPU time(s)	ISNR (dB)	MSE	CPU time(s)	ISNR (dB)	MSE	CPU time(s)	ISNR (dB)	MSE
	TwoIST	134	61.3	19.3	273	93	18.8	158	122	18.5
	FISTA	115	60.8	19.3	175	89	19	119	115	18.6
	Proposed method	10.2	59.2	19.4	10.9	85.7	19.2	11	113	18.7
Gaussian noise with variance 1	Method	Losing 30% of pixels			Losing 40% of pixels			Losing 50% of pixels		
		CPU time(s)	ISNR (dB)	MSE	CPU time(s)	ISNR (dB)	MSE	CPU time(s)	ISNR (dB)	MSE
	TwoIST	233	62.4	18.95	141	92.3	18.3	159	119	17.9
	FISTA	157	57.9	19.0	167	84.8	18.5	157	112	18.1
	Proposed method	24.1	50.1	19.2	23.4	74.8	18.9	24.9	95.4	18.6

Table 11. Results of inpainting for Lifting-body image with different degradations.

Gaussian noise with variance 0.308033	Method	Losing 30% of pixels			Losing 40% of pixels			Losing 50% of pixels		
		CPU time(s)	ISNR (dB)	MSE	CPU time(s)	ISNR (dB)	MSE	CPU time(s)	ISNR (dB)	MSE
	TwoIST	973	4.65	31.3	808	8.34	29.9	807	12	29.1
	FISTA	871	4.81	31.1	822	7.74	30.3	820	12.5	29.3
	Proposed method	38.7	4.28	34.05	46.3	7.44	30.4	57.7	11.4	29.4
Gaussian noise with variance 1	Method	Losing 30% of pixels			Losing 40% of pixels			Losing 50% of pixels		
		CPU time(s)	ISNR (dB)	MSE	CPU time(s)	ISNR (dB)	MSE	CPU time(s)	ISNR (dB)	MSE
	TwoIST	888	6.17	30	923	8.35	28.8	908	14.3	27.8
	FISTA	815	5.83	30.3	817	7.49	29	1150	12	28.2
	Proposed method	193	4.68	33.2	222	5.89	29.2	219	9.43	28.9

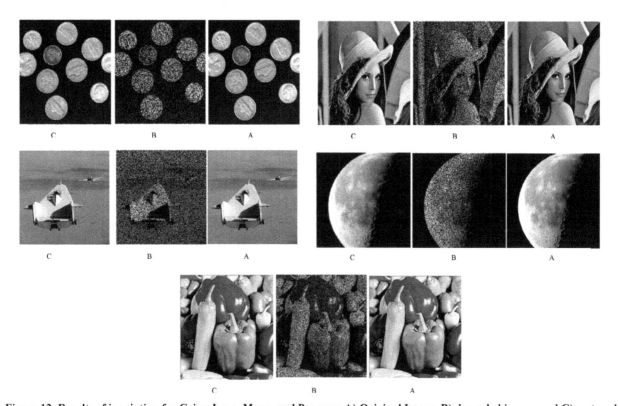

Figure 12. Results of inpainting for Coins, Lena, Moon, and Peppers: A) Original Image, B) degraded image, and C) restored image by proposed method.

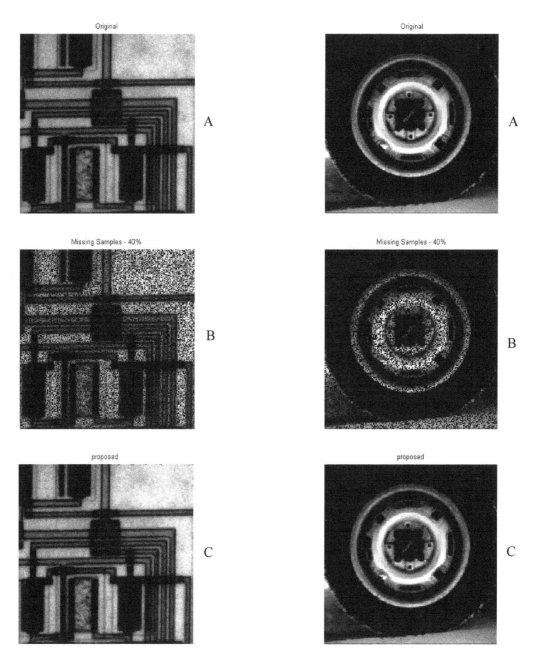

Figure 13. Results of inpainting for Cir: A) Original Image, B) degraded image, and C) restored image by proposed method.

Figure 14. Results of inpainting for Tire: A) Original Image, B) degraded image, and C) restored image by proposed method.

5. Conclusions

In this paper, a new image restoration method was proposed. It used variable splitting based upon the total variant regularizer to solve the optimization problem more rapidly. In the optimization problem, since the objective function includes two terms, one term being second-order and the other one being non-linear regularizer, the variable splitting was used. This caused the argument of each term to include an individual variable. For the new optimization problem to be equal with the initial one, the

undetermined optimization problem was converted to the determined one, and then the new problem was solved using the Lagrangian augmented method. Since image piecewise smoothed, traditional regularizers such as L2-norm affected restoration of edge sharpness and smooth the edges. Therefore, the total variant regularizer, due to maintaining the sharpness of the edges and removing the additive noise, was used. The image restoration was applied on two cases; deblurring/denoising and inpainting. In case of deblurring, different additive noises with altered blurs, and for inpainting, different types of noises with different percentage of losing the pixels were used. The performance of the proposed method was compared with the TwoIST and SpaRSA methods for deblurring/denoising, and also it was compared with the FISTA and TwoIST methods for inpainting. The evaluation measures included required time for convergence (speed), ISNR, and MSE. The experimental results showed that the proposed method provided a higher ISNR, a lower MSE, and consequently, a higher quality of the restored image with higher speed of convergence compared to the TwoIST, SpaRSA, and FISTA methods for both the deblurring/denoising and inpainting cases.

References

[1] Gonzales, R. C. & Woods, R. E. (2002). Digital Image Processing, Prentice Hall.

[2] Andrews, H. & Hunt, B. (1977). Digital Image Restoration, Prentice-Hall.

[3] Chai, A. & Shen, Z. (2007). Deconvolution: A Wavelet Frame Approach. Numerische Mathematik, pp. 529–587.

[4] Dong, B. & Feng, Cai J. & Osher, S. & Shen, Z. (2012). Image Restoration: Total Variation, Wavelet frames, and beyond. Journal of the American mathematical society, vol. 25, pp. 1033-1089.

[5] Cai, J. & Chan, R. & Shen, Z. (2008). A Framelet-Based Image Inpainting Algorithm. Applied and Computational Harmonic Analysis, vol. 24, no. 3, pp. 131–149.

[6] Babacan, S. & Katsaggelos, A. & Molina, R. (2009). Variational Bayesian Blind Deconvolution Using A Total Variation Prior. IEEE Transaction Image Processing, vol. 18, no. 1, pp. 12 -26.

[7] Wang, Y. & Yin, W. & Zhang, Y. (2007). A fast algorithm for image deblurring with total variation regularization. Rice University CAAM Technical Report TR07-10, pp. 1-19.

[8] Oliveira, J. P. (2010). Advances in total variation image restoration: blur estimation, parameter and efficient optimization. Ph.D. dissertation, Inst. Superior Técnico, Univ. ontana, Missoula, MT, USA.

[9] Tiwari, P. & Dhillon, N. & Sharma, K. (2013). Analysis of Image Restoration Techniques for Developing Better Restoration Method. vol. 3, no. 4, pp. 10-14.

[10] Leung, C. M. & Lu W. S. (1993). A multiple-parameter generalization of tikhonov-miller regularization method for image restoration. Proceedings of A silomar Conf. Signals, Systems and Computers, Pacific Grove, CA, pp. 856 -860.

[11] Babacan, S. & Katsaggelos, A. & Molina, R. (2008). Parameter estimation in TV image restoration using variational distribution approximation. IEEE Trans. Image Processing, vol. 17, no. 23, pp. 326 -339.

[12] Figueiredo, A. T. & Nowak, R. D. (2003). An Em algorithm for wavelet-based image restoration. IEEE Trans. Image Processing, vol. 12, no. 8, pp. 1 -28.

[13] Bioucas-Dias, J. & Figueiredo, M. (2008). An iterative algorithm for linear inverse problems with compound regularizers. IEEE Int. Conf. Image Processing, San Diego, CA, USA, pp. 1-4.

[14] Bioucas-Dias, J. & Figueiredo, M. (2007). A new TwoIST: two-step iterative shrinkage/thresholding algorithms for image restoration. IEEE Trans. Image Processing, vol. 16, no. 12, pp. 2992 -3004.

[15] Beck, A. & Teboulle, M. (2009). A fast iterative shrinkage-thresholding algorithm for linear inverse problems. SIAM Journal of Imaging Sciences, vol. 2, pp. 183–202.

[16] Figueiredo, M. & Nowak, R. & Wright, S. (2009). Sparse Reconstruction By Separable Approximation. IEEE Trans. Image Processing, vol. 57, pp. 2479–2493.

[17] Wang, Y. & Yang, J. & Yin, W. & Zhang, Y. (2008). A New alternating minimization algorithm for total variation image reconstruction. SIAM Journal of Imaging Sciences, vol. 1, pp. 248–272.

[18] Darbon, J. & Goldfarb, D. & Osher, S. & Yin, W. (2008). Bregman iterative algorithms for l1-minimization with applications to compressed sensing. SIAM Journal of Imaging Science, vol. 1, pp. 143–168.

[19] Goldstein, T. & Osher, S. (2009). The Split bregman algorithm for l1 regularized problems. SIAM Journal of Imaging Sciences, vol. 2, no. 2, pp. 323–343.

[20] Nocedal, J. & Wright, S. J. (2006). Numerical optimization, 2nd Edition, Springer.

[21] Boyd, N. & Chu, B. & Eckstein, J. & Parikh, E. (2011). Distributed optimization and statistical learning via the alternating direction method of multipliers. Foundations and Trends in Machine Learning, vol. 3, no. 1, pp. 1-12.

[22] Maurya, A. & Tiwari, R. (2014). A Novel Method of Image Restoration by using Different Types of Filtering Techniques. International Journal of Engineering Science and Innovative Technology (IJESIT), vol. 3, no. 4, pp. 124-129.

[23] Rani, S. & Jindal, S. & Kaur, B. (2016). A Brief Review on Image Restoration Techniques. International Journal of Computer Applications, vol. 150, no. 12, pp. 30-33.

[24] Kumar, N. & Nallamothu, R. & Sethi, A. (2013). Neural Network Based Image Deblurring. Proc. of the IEEE Conference on Neural Network Applications in Electrical Engineering, 2013.

[25] Pal Singh, D. & Khare, A. (2016). Restoration of Degraded Gray Images Using Genetic Algorithm. I.J. Image, Graphics and Signal Processing, vol. 3, pp. 28-35.

[26] He, L. & Wang, Y. & Bao, C. (2016). Wavelet Frame Truncated ℓ1-regularized Image Deblurring. Proc. of the IEEE: 8th International Conference on Wireless Communications & Signal Processing (WCSP), pp. 2472-7628.

[27] Dong, W. & Zhang, L. & Shi, G. & Li, X. (2013). Nonlocally centralized sparse representation for image restoration. IEEE Transactions on Image Processing, vol. 22, no. 4, pp. 1620–1630.

[28] Dong, W. & Shi, G. & Ma, Y. & Li, X. (2015). Image Restoration via Simultaneous Sparse Coding: Where Structured Sparsity Meets Gaussian Scale Mixture. International Journal of Computer Vision.

[29] Hosseinzadeh Samani, B., HouriJafari, H. & Zareiforoush, H. (2017). Artificial neural networks, genetic algorithm and response surface methods: The energy consumption of food and beverage industries in Iran. Journal of AI and data mining, vol. 5, no. 1, pp. 79-88.

[30] Khoshdel, V. & Akbarzadeh, A. R (2016). Application of statistical techniques and artificial neural network to estimate force from sEMG signals. Journal of AI and data mining, vol. 4, no. 2, pp. 135-141.

12

Non-linear Fractional-Order Chaotic Systems Identification with Approximated Fractional-Order Derivative based on a Hybrid Particle Swarm Optimization-Genetic Algorithm Method

M. Kosari[1*] and M. Teshnehlab[2]

1. Electrical Engineering-Control Department, K.N.Toosi University of Technology, Tehran, Iran.

2. Faculty of Electrical Engineering-Control Department, K.N.Toosi University of Technology, Tehran, Iran.

*Corresponding author: mkosari@mail.kntu.ac.ir (M. kosari).

Abstract

Although many mathematicians have searched on the fractional calculus since many years ago, its application in engineering, especially in modeling and control, does not have many antecedents. Since there is much freedom in choosing the order of differentiator and integrator in fractional calculus, it is possible to model the physical systems accurately. This paper deals with the time-domain identification fractional-order chaotic systems, where conventional derivation is replaced by a fractional one with the help of a non-integer derivation. This operator is itself approximated by an N-dimensional system composed of an integrator and a phase-lead filter. A hybrid particle swarm optimization (PSO)-genetic algorithm (GA) method is applied to estimate the parameters of the approximated non-linear fractional-order chaotic system modeled by a state-space representation. The feasibility of this approach is demonstrated through identifying the parameters of the approximated fractional-order Lorenz chaotic system. The performance of the proposed algorithm is compared with GA and standard particle swarm optimization (SPSO) in terms of parameter accuracy and cost function. In order to evaluate the identification accuracy, the time-domain output error is designed as the fitness function for parameter optimization. The simulation results show that the proposed method is more successful than the other algorithms for parameter identification of the fractional-order chaotic systems.

Keywords: *Parameter Identification, Chaotic System, Particle Swarm Optimization, Genetic Algorithm, Fractional Calculus.*

1. Introduction

In the last two decades, fractional calculus has been applied in an increasing number of fields due to the fact that the fractional-order modeling can describe the real-world physical phenomena more reasonably and accurately than the classical integer order calculus [1, 2]. It has been found that many real objects and processes in interdisciplinary fields can be described by fractional differential equations.

The diffusion of heat into a semi-infinite solid [2], voltage-current relation of a semi-infinite lossy transmission line [3], viscoelastic systems [4], dielectric polarization [5], model of love between humans [6], model of happiness [7], and model of non-local epidemics [8] are just a few examples of the fractional calculus applications.

Different methods have been proposed for the identification of fractional-order systems. Most of them consist of the generalization to fractional order systems of standard methods that are used in the identification of systems with integer order derivatives.

Although many methods have been proposed for parameter identification of integer-order chaotic systems [9-13], a little work has been done for fractional-order chaotic systems [14-16].

Time domain methods have been introduced, for example in [17, 18], where a method based on the discretization of a fractional differential equation using Grunwald-Letnikov's definition has been introduced, and the parameters have been estimated using the least-squares approach. In [19], a method based on the approximation of a fractional integrator by a rational model has been proposed. In [20], the use of methods based on fractional orthogonal bases has been introduced. In [21], identification of fractional-order systems using the modulating function method in case of noisy measurements has been proposed. Other techniques can also be found, for example in [22, 23].

In this paper, we deal with time domain identification of fractional-order non-linear systems modeled by a state-space representation. The general problem is the identification of a non-linear fractional-order system, and particularly, estimation of the fractional derivation order of fractional-order.

According to the approach proposed in [19], we intended to describe the input–output behavior of the system. Estimation of parameters of the model represents a non-linear problem that we proposed to solve using the PSO-GA method. The first problem to solve was that of numerical integration of the fractional differential system. In other words, it is necessary to propose a fractional derivation operator in order to simulate the system in a conventional way. This operator is defined using the frequency considerations derived from the approach initiated by Oustaloup [19]. The particularity of this approach is to rely on the numerical simulation of the model in order to generate the output error, and on the minimization of the resulting quadratic criterion using a PSO-GA method.

In the next section, basic definitions of fractional derivatives, integrals, and non-linear fractional-order systems are recalled. The output error method based on the PSO-GA method is applied to the identification of fractional-order non-linear chaotic system in Section III. The numerical results are presented in Section IV, followed by conclusions, summarizing the main results obtained.

2. Mathematical background
2.1. Fractional non-linear systems
Fractional-order calculus is the generalization of the classical integer order calculus. In this paper, we will consider the general incommensurate fractional-order non-linear system, represented as follows [1]:

$$_0D_t^{\alpha_i} x_i(t) = f_i(x_1(t), x_2(t), \cdots, x_n(t), t),$$
$$x_i(0) = c_i, \ i = 1, 2, \cdots, n,$$
$$y(t) = C[x_1 \quad x_2 \quad \cdots \quad x_n]^T \tag{1}$$

where, c_i is the initial conditions, α_i is the fractional orders, and $C = [0 \ \cdots \ 0 \ 1]$.

The equilibrium points of system (1) are calculated via solving the following equation:
$$f(X) = 0 \tag{2}$$
and we suppose that $E^* = (x_1^*, x_2^*, \cdots, x_n^*)$ is an equilibrium point of system (1).

2.2. Fractional derivative
There are several definitions for fractional-order derivative [2], three most commonly used ones are the Grunwald-Letnikov, Riemann-Liouville, and Caputo derivation definitions.

The Riemann-Liouville derivative definition of the order α can be described as:

$$_c^R D_t^\alpha f(t) = \frac{d^\alpha}{dt^\alpha}\left[\frac{1}{\Gamma(n-\alpha)} \int_c^t \frac{f(\tau)}{(t-\tau)^{\alpha-n+1}} d\tau\right], \tag{3}$$

where, $n-1 \le \alpha < n, n \in N$ and $\Gamma(\alpha) = \int_0^\infty x^{\alpha-1} e^{-x} dx$ is the gamma function.

The Caputo derivative definition has the following form:

$$_c^C D_t^\alpha f(t) = \frac{1}{\Gamma(n-\alpha)} \int_c^t \frac{f^{(n)}(\tau)}{(t-\tau)^{\alpha-n+1}} d\tau, \tag{4}$$

The Grunwald-Letnikov's derivation definition can be written as:

$$_c^{GL} D_t^\alpha f(t)\Big|_{t=kh} = \lim_{h \to 0} \frac{1}{h^\alpha} \sum_{j=0}^{\left\lfloor \frac{t-c}{h} \right\rfloor} \omega_j^{(\alpha)} f(kh-jh), \tag{3}$$

where, h is the sample time, $\lfloor . \rfloor$ is the flooring function, and the coefficient

$$\omega_j^{(\alpha)} = \frac{(-1)^j \Gamma(\alpha+1)}{\Gamma(j+1)\Gamma(\alpha-j+1)}, j = 0, 1, \cdots. \tag{4}$$

2.3. Fractional integration
The α th non-integer order Riemann–Liouville integral (α real positive) of a function $f(t)$ can be defined by the following relation [1]:

$$I_\alpha(f(t)) = \frac{1}{\Gamma(\alpha)} \int_0^t (t-\tau)^{\alpha-1} f(\tau) d\tau \tag{5}$$

2.4. Approximation of fractional operators
Fractional operators are usually approximated by high order rational models. As a result, a fractional model and its rational approximation have the same dynamics within a limited frequency band. The most commonly used approximation of s^α in the frequency band $[\omega_b, \omega_h]$ is the recursive distribution of zeros and poles proposed by Oustaloup [17]. Trigeassou et

al. [24] have suggested to use an integrator outside the frequency range $[\omega_b, \omega_h]$ instead of a gain:

$$I_\alpha(s) = \frac{1}{s^\alpha},$$

$$I_\alpha^*(s) = \frac{C_0}{s}\left(\frac{1+s/\omega_b}{1+s/\omega_h}\right)^{1-\alpha} \approx \frac{C_0}{s}\prod_{k=1}^{N}\frac{1+s/\omega_k'}{1+s/\omega_k} \qquad (6)$$

The block diagram of approximation of fractional integration, relation (8), can be represented as in figure 1:

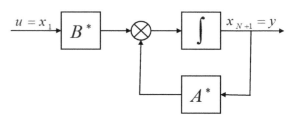

Figure 1 $I_\alpha^*(s)$ **Block diagram [19].**

The operator $I_\alpha^*(s)$ is characterized by six parameters, where ω_1' and ω_N define the frequency range, N is the number of cells (it is directly related to the quality of the desired approximation), and pulsations ω_i and ω_i' are linked by:

$$\omega_i = \lambda\omega_i', \qquad \text{with } \lambda > 1$$
$$\omega_{i+1}' = \eta\omega_i, \qquad \text{with } \eta > 1 \qquad (7)$$

The fractional order of operator is:

$$\alpha = 1 - \frac{\log(\lambda)}{\log(\lambda\eta)} \qquad (8)$$

where, λ and η are real parameters that depend on the differentiation order α. A bigger N causes a better approximation of the integrator $I_\alpha(s)$.

As $I_\alpha^*(s)$ is composed of a product of cells, we define the state-variables as the output of each cell [19], according to figure 1.

This system corresponds to the state-space representation:

$$M\dot{x} = Ax + Bu$$

or equivalently:

$$\dot{x} = A^*x + B^*u,$$
$$A^* = M^{-1}A, \quad B^* = M^{-1}B. \qquad (9)$$

where

$$M = \begin{bmatrix} 1 & 0 & \cdots & \cdots & 0 \\ -\lambda & 1 & 0 & \cdots & 0 \\ 0 & -\lambda & 1 & \ddots & \vdots \\ \vdots & \ddots & \ddots & 0 & 0 \\ 0 & \cdots & 0 & -\lambda & 1 \end{bmatrix},$$

$$A = \begin{bmatrix} 0 & 0 & \cdots & \cdots & 0 \\ \omega_1 & -\omega_1 & 0 & \cdots & 0 \\ 0 & \omega_2 & -\omega_2 & \ddots & \vdots \\ \vdots & \ddots & \ddots & \ddots & 0 \\ 0 & \cdots & 0 & \omega_N & -\omega_N \end{bmatrix},$$

$$B = \begin{bmatrix} G_n \\ 0 \\ \vdots \\ \vdots \\ 0 \end{bmatrix}, \qquad x = \begin{bmatrix} x_1 \\ x_2 \\ \vdots \\ \vdots \\ x_{N+1} \end{bmatrix}.$$

Thus fractional integrator operator corresponds to the symbolic representation given in figure 2.

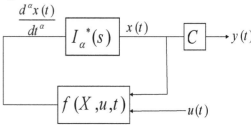

Figure 2. State-space representation of operator [19].

3. Fractional identification technique

According to figure 2, for using this approximation, the non-linear model could be approached by a state-space representation, as in figure 3:

$$\frac{d^\alpha x(t)}{dt^\alpha} \rightarrow \boxed{I_\alpha^*(s)} \xrightarrow{x(t)} \boxed{C} \rightarrow y(t)$$

$$\boxed{f(X,u,t)} \leftarrow u(t)$$

Figure 3. State-space representation of non-linear system.

Thus the approximated state space representation is:

$$\dot{X}(t) = g(X(t), u(t), t, \theta),$$
$$y(t) = CX(t) \qquad (10)$$

where, θ consists of the model parameters and operator parameters $(\omega_1', \omega_N, \text{ and } \alpha)$, $C = [0 \cdots 0 \ 1]$, and:

$$g(X(t), u(t), t, \theta) = A^*X(t)$$
$$+ B^*f(X(t), u(t), t). \qquad (11)$$

3.1. Output error method

We consider identification and parameter estimation of the non-linear model in the time domain with the help of M data pairs $\{u_k, y_k^*\}$, where y_k^* represents values of true output.

The model coefficients are conventional parameters that are easily estimated. On the other hand, the real difficulty of the problem deals with the parameter α, which corresponds to a complex reality. Thus the identification problem is non-linear, and it is justified to use an output-error technique.

Let us consider the quadratic criterion:

$$J = \frac{1}{M} \sum_{k=1}^{M} (y_k^* - \hat{y}(u, \hat{\theta}))^2 \qquad (12)$$

where, $\hat{y}_k(u, \hat{\theta})$ represents the numerical simulation of non-linear model based on estimation $\hat{\theta}$, and excited by input $u(t)$.

$\hat{y}(t)$ is non-linear in the parameters $\hat{\theta}$; thus quadratic criterion J has to be minimized iteratively by an optimization algorithm, while obtaining proper parameters, $\hat{\theta}$. In the case of linear or non-linear rational systems, the numerical simulation of the model is a very classical and simple problem. This technique [19] can be schematized by the drawing in figure 4.

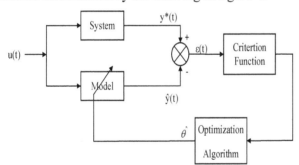

Figure 4. Output-error identification technique.

3.2. Genetic algorithm

The genetic algorithm (GA) is a kind of intelligent optimization method, proposed by Holland [25], which imitates the natural genetic phenomena of selection, cross-over and mutation operations in nature. Jong has carried out a great quantity of optimization tests with numerical functions using the Holland's theory, which proves that GA is an effective and efficient stochastic search method [26]. In the 1990s, GA was widely used in the scope of engineering such as reservoir operation optimization [27], numerical model parameter optimization [28], inverse problem research [29], vehicle routing problem [30], and routing in wireless sensor network [31].

GA starts with an initial population that contains a number of individuals, and then new individuals are produced to be better adapted to the environment with random selection, cross-over, and mutation. The best individual is eventually achieved by a number of evolution steps (generations). Every individual in a population is a feasible solution for the optimization problems, and the best individual is the optimal solution to the optimization problem. Compared with the other optimization algorithms, GA has the following advantages:

1. The optimization objective function can be either a continuous function or a discrete function [28];
2. It has the property of global search and automatic convergence to the optimal solution;
3. It is robust in dealing with complex non-linear problems;
4. The principle is simple, easy to understand, versatile, and highly maneuverable.
5. Calculation of sensitivity functions in gradient-based methods is not required.

Many improvements have been made to GA considering its wide applications including a niche technology of cross-over operation [24], a uniform mutation operation method [25], an adaptive algorithm of cross-over and mutation probability [26-27], and the hybrid particle swarm optimization (PSO) and GA method [32]. In this paper, the hybrid PSO-GA method has been used.

3.3. Particle swarm optimization

Standard particle swarm optimization (SPSO) is a kind of swarm intelligence method achieved by individual particle improvements together with cooperation and competition among the whole population [33-35]. The algorithm works by initializing a flock of birds randomly over the searching space, where every bird is called as a "particle". These "particles" fly with a certain velocity and find the global best position after some iteration. At each iteration, each particle can adjust its velocity vector based on its momentum and the influence of its best position as well as the best position of the best individual. Then the particle flies to a newly computed position. Suppose that the search space is n-dimensional, and then the position and velocity of the i th particle are represented by $x_i = [x_{i1} \ x_{i2} \ \ldots \ x_{in}]^T$ and $v_i = [v_{i1} \ v_{i2} \ \ldots \ v_{in}]^T$, respectively. The fitness of each particle can be evaluated according to the objective function of the optimization problem. The best previously visited position of the particle i is noted as its personal best position, denoted by $p_i = [p_{i1} \ p_{i2} \ \ldots \ p_{in}]^T$. The position of the best individual of the swarm is noted as the global best position $G = [g_1 \ g_2 \ \ldots \ g_n]^T$. At each step, the velocity of a particle and its new position are assigned as follow:

$$v_i(t+1) = \omega \, v_i(t) + c_1 r_1 \,(p_i\text{-}x_i)$$
$$+ \, c_2 r_2 \,(G\text{-}x_i) \qquad (13)$$

$$x_i(t+1) = x_i(t) + v_i(t+1) \qquad (14)$$

where, t is the current step number, ω is the inertia weight, c_1 and c_2 are the acceleration constants, r_1 and r_2 are two random numbers in the range $[0,1]$, $x_i(t)$ is the current position of the particle, P_i is the best one of the solutions this particle has reached, and G is the best one of the solutions all the particles have reached. The PSO algorithm performs repeated operations of the update equations above until a stopping criterion is reached. In [34], the authors have introduced a constriction factor χ into the PSO algorithm. The aim is to prevent particle explosion and to control convergence. In the PSO algorithm with a constriction factor, the velocity updating process (16) is modified to:

$$v_i(t+1) = \chi \, [v_i(t) + c_1 r_1 \,(p_i\text{-}x_i)$$
$$+ \, c_2 r_2 \,(G\text{-}x_i)] \qquad (15)$$

where, $c_1 = c_2 = 2.05$ and $\chi = 0.7298$ are the near optimal values in this PSO algorithm. With the new velocity updating (18), the PSO algorithm with a constriction factor is shown to outperform the basic PSO algorithm [34].

ω is the inertia weight that is employed to control the impact of the previous history of velocities on the current velocity. The Linear time-varying weighting function is usually utilized in the following:

$$\omega_{iter} = \frac{(iter_{max} \ \text{-} \ iter)}{iter_{max}} (\omega_{min}\text{-}\omega_{max}) + \omega_{max} \qquad (16)$$

where, ω_{iter} is the current weight, ω_{max} is the initial weight, ω_{min} is the final weight, $iter_{max}$ is the maximum iteration number, and $iter$ is the current iteration number [36, 37].

In [32], modifications have been made in PSO using GA to improve the performance and reach global maxima. The genetic operators can be used to prevent premature convergence. Using the cross-over operation, information can be exchanged between two particles that improve the likelihood of searching for the global optimum. Similarly, by applying mutation to PSO, population diversity can be managed.

Hence, a non-linear fractional identification model based on the PSO-GA method can be established through the following steps:

Step 1: Initialization: Set the counter of evolution $t=0$, randomly generate the initial positions $X(0)$ and velocities $V(0)$ and the maximum number of generation $T_m = 500$ as the termination condition.

Step 2: Individual evaluation: Calculate the fitness value of each individual in population $X(t)$.

Step 3: Obtain the new velocities $V(t+1)$ and positions $X(t+1)$ of particles using equations (17) and (18), and then update P_j and G.

Step 4: Selection operation: Apply the tournament selection operation [38] to the population.

Step 5: Cross-over operation: Apply the arithmetic cross-over operation [38] to the population.

Step 6: Mutation operation: Apply the mutation operation [38] to the population. After Steps 4, 5, and 6, new generation population will be obtained, and then update P_j and G again.

Step 7: Termination condition judgment: If $t=T_m$ as the termination conditions, the individual that has the most suitable fitness value in the processing will be selected as the optimal solution; otherwise, back to Step 2. With this, an identification model of non-linear fractional order system is established based on PSO-GA. A working flow chart of the model is shown in figure 5.

5. Simulation results

To demonstrate the effectiveness of the proposed parameter identification method for fractional-order chaotic system, simulation of the fractional-order chaotic Lorenz system is presented. All the algorithms are implemented using the MATLAB 8.1 programming language. In the simulation, the control parameters of all algorithms are set as follow: the population size $M = 20$, the initial inertia weight ω is set to χ, $c_1 = c_2 = 2.05$, the cross-over and mutation probability is equal to 0.7, and the algorithm terminates when a maximum generation number is reached; it is set to 500 generations, and the fitness function is calculated by relation (15).

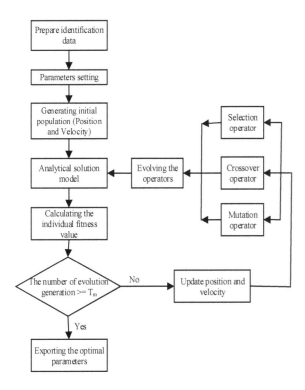

Figure 5. Flow chart for identification model parameters based on PSO-GA.

Now consider the fractional-order commensurate-order Lorenz system [39], described by:

$$_0D_t^q x(t) = \sigma(y(t) - x(t)),$$
$$_0D_t^q y(t) = x(t)(\rho - z(t)) - y(t), \qquad (17)$$
$$_0D_t^q z(t) = x(t)y(t) - \beta z(t),$$

where, σ, ρ, β, and q are unknown parameters to be identified.

In this paper, we let the true parameters of system (19) to be $(\sigma, \rho, \beta) = (10, 28, 8/3)$ and q=0.99. To obtain the standard state variables x, y, and z, we solve system (20) using the numerical algorithm derived from the G–L definition of fractional derivatives, where the initial condition $(x_0, y_0, z_0)=(0.1, 0.1, 0.1)$ and the step size $h = 0.001$. The numerical results show that it is chaotic, and its chaotic behavior is shown in figure 6. Then a frequency interval equal to 4 decades is used to approximate the fractional-order derivative with $\omega_b = 10^{-3}$ rad/s and $\omega_h = 10^1$ rad/s. Using this approximation and the same initial conditions for the step size, the numerical results for 6 cells is shown in figure 7. As it is seen, both shapes have a chaotic behavior and almost the same action. In this example, the parameters to be identified are σ, ρ, β, and q. In

the experiments, the search ranges of parameters are set as $0 \le \sigma \le 20$, $0 \le \rho \le 50$, $0 \le \beta \le 5$, $0 \le \omega_b \le 1$, $0 \le \omega_h \le 100$, and $0 \le q \le 1$.

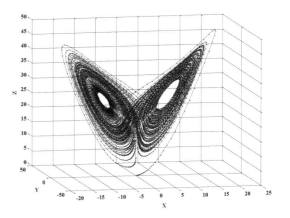

Figure 6. Chaotic behavior of fractional-order Lorenz system with G–L definition of fractional derivatives when $(\sigma, \rho, \beta) = (10, 28, 8/3)$, $q = 0.99$.

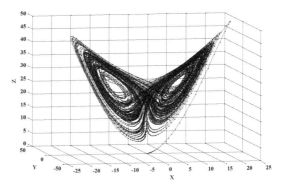

Figure 7. Chaotic behavior of fractional-order Lorenz system with approximated fractional derivatives when $(\sigma, \rho, \beta) = (10, 28, 8/3)$, $q = 0.99$, and $N = 6$.

Tables 1, 2, and 3 list the best results and standard deviations of parameters obtained by algorithms, where each algorithm runs 10 times independently.

From table 1, it can be seen that the best results obtained by GA are different from the true parameter values. According to table 2, the PSO algorithm has achieved better results than the GA method. It can be concluded that the performance of PSO is better than GA. Table 3 represents the best results using the hybrid PSO-GA method, which has derived true parameters with increase in the number of cells. Based on the results of the three tables, the hybrid GA-PSO method was found to be more effective than the other algorithms in terms of the convergence speed and preventing the premature convergence to reach the optimal state.

Table 1. Results obtained by GA method for parameter estimation of approximated fractional-order Lorenz system with 2, 3, 4, 5, and 6 cells.

Cell number (N)	σ	Std of σ	β	Std of β	ρ	Std of ρ	ω_b	Std of ω_b	ω_h	Std of ω_h	q	Std of q	Best J
0(exact)	10	-	28	-	8/3	-	0.001	-	10	-	0.99	-	-
2	8.41	3.02	27.1	4.94	2.36	0.86	0.046	0.032	10.59	6.34	0.9727	0.077	3.267
3	19.88	2.11	27.98	0.262	2.663	0.207	0.026	0.029	9.07	2.277	0.9829	0.012	0.455
4	12.9	6.42	28.07	0.273	2.63	0.555	0.025	0.032	18.11	6.151	0.9813	0.076	0.776
5	16.54	5.61	27.2	0.974	3.29	0.665	0.052	0.027	20	7.668	0.9906	0.223	3.386
6	10.98	4.26	28.03	0.844	3.109	0.572	$6.3e^{-4}$	0.003	2.67	1.391	1	0.087	1.026

Table 2. Results obtained by PSO method for parameter estimation of approximated fractional-order Lorenz system with 2, 3, 4, 5, and 6 cells.

Cell Number (N)	σ	Std of σ	β	Std of β	ρ	Std of ρ	ω_b	Std of ω_b	ω_h	Std of ω_h	q	Std of q	Best J
0(exact)	10	-	28	-	8/3	-	0.001	-	10	-	0.99	-	-
2	9.19	6.47	26.9	6.16	2.51	0.762	0.076	0.028	10.69	5.44	0.9751	0.25	1.387
3	12.93	4.91	28.004	0.035	2.663	0.005	0.002	0.002	10.08	0.013	0.989	0.0014	0.0077
4	10.009	1.87	28.000	0.329	2.6673	0.099	$9.9e^{-4}$	0.002	10.015	3.837	0.9900	0.041	0.0038
5	10.227	3.57	27.992	0.976	2.6778	0.452	$9.6e^{-4}$	0.002	9.827	3.898	0.9903	0.145	0.0347
6	6.32	3.34	27.924	1.39	2.74	0.525	0.0014	0.0005	3.88	4.466	0.9907	0.008	0.5814

Table 3. Results obtained by PSO-GA method for parameter estimation of approximated fractional-order Lorenz system with 2, 3, 4, 5 and 6 cells.

Cell number (N)	σ	Std of σ	β	Std of β	ρ	Std of ρ	ω_b	Std of ω_b	ω_h	Std of ω_h	q	Std of q	Best J
0(exact)	10	-	28	-	8/3	-	0.001	-	10	-	0.99	-	-
2	9.965	2.53	27.987	5.55	2.660	0.822	0.058	1.084	10.031	3.424	0.9819	0.1167	0.0468
3	11.324	4.16	28.001	8.384	2.6659	0.109	0.0014	0.0017	10.026	2.973	0.9896	0.0005	0.0033
4	10.000	4.12	28.000	0.050	2.6667	0.297	0.001	0.0033	10.000	8.375	0.9900	0.058	$2.8e^{-11}$
5	10.000	2.97	28.000	0.189	2.6667	0.227	0.001	0.0000	10.000	2.480	0.9900	0.0277	$2.36e^{-9}$
6	10.000	4.32	28.000	0.488	2.6667	0.520	0.001	0.0019	10.000	6.611	0.9900	0.0418	$9.7e^{-10}$

Also it could be seen that an increase in the number of cells improved the results but caused to get more complicated equations, and it was more difficult to achieve the optimum point. Hence, using 4 cells suggested better results. Figure 8 represents the objective function value (J) for algorithms with 4 cells. It shows that the hybrid GA-PSO method is better than the GA and PSO methods in terms of the convergence speed and preventing the premature convergence to reach the optimal point.

6. Conclusion

This paper proposes an identification algorithm based on the hybrid PSO-GA method in the time domain using the output error technique for the approximated non-linear fractional-order chaotic systems. The results obtained verify that this algorithm can precisely identify the coefficients and fractional-order of the Lorenz chaotic system. Taking the effective fitness function, the PSO-GA method can do the global search and solve the parameter identification issue for non-linear

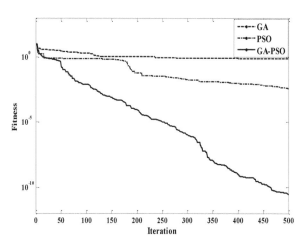

Figure 1. Objective function values J for GA, PSO, and GA-PSO methods.

to the kind of system. Effectively, with the fractional integrator operator, it is possible to consider more complex systems, and then to identify them using the proposed algorithm.

References
[1] Diethelm, K. (2010). The Analysis of Fractional Differential Equations. Springer, Berlin.

[2] Podlubny, I. (1999). Fractional Differential Equations. Academic Press, San Diego.

[3] Wang, J. (1987). Realizations of generalized Warburg impedance with RC ladder networks and transmission lines. Journal of the Electrochemical Society, vol. 134, no. 8, pp. 1915-1920.

[4] Bagley, R. L. & Calico R. A. (1991). Fractional order state equations for the control of viscoelasticallydamped structures. Journal of Guidance, Control, and Dynamics, vol. 14, no. 2, pp. 304-311.

[5] Sun, H., Abdelwahab, A. & Onaral, B. (1984). Linear approximation of transfer function with a pole of fractional power. IEEE Transactions on Automatic Control, vol. 29, no. 5, 29(5), pp. 441-444.

[6] Ahmad, W. M. & El-Khazali, R. (2007). Fractional-order dynamical models of love. Chaos, Solitons & Fractals. vol. 33, no. 4, pp. 1367-1375.

[7] Song, L., Xu, S. & Yang, J. (2010). Dynamical models of happiness with fractional order. Communications in Nonlinear Science and Numerical Simulation, vol. 15, no. 3, pp. 616-628.

[8] Ahmed, E. & Elgazzar, A. (2007). On fractional order differential equations model for nonlocal epidemics. Physica A: Statistical Mechanics and its Applications, vol. 379, no. 2, pp. 607-614.

[9] Peng, B., et al. (2009). Differential evolution algorithm-based parameter estimation for chaotic systems. Chaos, Solitons & Fractals, vol. 39, no. 5, pp. 2110-2118.

[10] Parlitz, U. (1996). Estimating model parameters from time series by autosynchronization. Physical Review Letters, vol. 76, no. 8, pp. 1232.

[11] Wu, X., Hu, H. & Zhang, B. (2004). Parameter estimation only from the symbolic sequences generated by chaos system. Chaos, Solitons & Fractals, vol. 22, no. 2, pp. 359-366.

[12] Modares, H., Alfi, A. & Fateh, M. M. (2010). Parameter identification of chaotic dynamic systems through an improved particle swarm optimization. Expert Systems with Applications, vol. 37, no. 5, pp. 3714-3720.

[13] Jiang, Y., et al. (2016). Parameter Identification of Chaotic Systems by a Novel Dual Particle Swarm Optimization. International Journal of Bifurcation and Chaos, vol. 26, no. 2, pp. 1650024.

[14] Al-Assaf, Y., El-Khazali, R. & Ahmad, W. (2004). Identification of fractional chaotic system parameters. Chaos, Solitons & Fractals, vol. 22, no. 4, pp. 897-905.

[15] Yuan, L., Yang, Q. & Zeng, C. (2013). Chaos detection and parameter identification in fractional-order chaotic systems with delay. Nonlinear Dynamics, vol. 37, no. 2, pp. 439-448.

[16] Tang, Y., et al. (2012). Parameter identification of commensurate fractional-order chaotic system via differential evolution. Physics Letters A, vol. 376, no. 4, pp. 457-464.

[17] Mathieu, B., Le Lay, L. & Oustaloup, A.. (1996). Identification of non integer order systems in the time domain. in CESA'96 IMACS Multiconference: computational engineering in systems applications.

[18] Djouambi, A., Voda, A. & Charef, A.. (2012). Recursive prediction error identification of fractional order models. Communications in Nonlinear Science and Numerical Simulation, vol. 17, no. 6, pp. 2517-2524.

[19] Poinot, T. & Trigeassou, J.-C. (2004). Identification of fractional systems using an output-error technique. Nonlinear Dynamics, vol. 38, no. 4, pp. 133-154.

[20] Aoun, M., et al. (2007). Synthesis of fractional Laguerre basis for system approximation. Automatica, vol. 43, no. 9, pp. 1640-1648.

[21] Cois, O., et al. (2001). Fractional state variable filter for system identification by fractional model. in Control Conference (ECC), 2001 European. IEEE.

[22] Dai, Y., et al. (2016). Modulating function-based identification for fractional order systems. Neurocomputing, vol. 173, no. 1, pp. 1959-1966.

[23] Moshar Movahhed, A., et al. (2017). Fractional Modeling and Analysis of Buck Converter in CCM Mode Peration. Journal of AI and Data Mining, vol. 5, no. 2, pp. 327-335.

[24] Trigeassou, J., et al. (1999). Modeling and identification of a non integer order system. in Control Conference (ECC), 1999 European. IEEE.

[25] Holland, J. H. (1975). Adaptation in natural and artificial systems: an introductory analysis with applications to biology, control, and artificial intelligence: U Michigan Press.

[26] Jong, D. & Alan, K.. (1975). Analysis of the behavior of a class of genetic adaptive systems, Engineering. College of-Technical Reports, University of Michigan.

[27] Jothiprakash, V. & Shanthi, G. (2006). Single reservoir operating policies using genetic algorithm. Water Resources Management, vol. 20, no. 6, pp. 917-929.

[28] Tang, H.-W., et al. (2010). Parameter identification for modeling river network using a genetic algorithm. Journal of Hydrodynamics, ser. B, vol. 22, no. 2, pp. 246-253.

[29] Dai, H.-c. & Wang, L.-l.. (2006). Study and application of the inverse problem on hydraulics. journal-sichuan university engineering science edition, vol. 38, no. 1, pp. 15.

[30] Shamshirband, S., et al. (2014). A solution for multi-objective commodity vehicle routing problem by NSGA-II. in Hybrid Intelligent Systems (HIS), 2014 14th International Conference on. IEEE.

[31] Kalantari, S., et al. (2011). Routing in wireless sensor network based on soft computing technique. Scientific Research and Essays, vol. 6, no. 21, pp. 432-4441.

[32] Premalatha, K. & Natarajan, A.. (2009). Hybrid PSO and GA for global maximization. Int. J. Open Problems Compt. Math, vol. 2, no. 4, pp. 597-608.

[33] Shi, Y. & Eberhart, R.. (1998). A modified particle swarm optimizer. in Evolutionary Computation Proceedings. IEEE World Congress on Computational Intelligence., The 1998 IEEE International Conference on. IEEE.

[34] Kennedy, J., et al. (2001). Swarm intelligence.: Morgan Kaufmann.

[35] Clerc, M. & Kennedy, J. (2002). The particle swarm-explosion, stability, and convergence in a multidimensional complex space. IEEE transactions on Evolutionary Computation, vol. 6, no. 1, pp. 58-73.

[36] Zheng, Y., et al. (2003). Empirical study of particle swarm optimizer with an increasing inertia weight. in Evolutionary Computation, 2003. CEC'03. The 2003 Congress on. IEEE.

[37] Zheng, Y.-L., et al. (2003). On the convergence analysis and parameter selection in particle swarm optimization. in Machine Learning and Cybernetics, 2003 International Conference on. IEEE.

[38] Larose, D.T. (2006). Data mining methods & models. 2006: John Wiley & Sons.

[39] Petras, I. (2011). Fractional-order nonlinear systems: modeling, analysis and simulation: Springer Science & Business Media.

13

Graph-based Visual Saliency Model using Background Color

Sh. Foolad[1] and A. Maleki[2*]

1. Department of Electrical & Computer Engineering, Semnan University, Semnan, Iran.

2. Faculty of Biomedical Engineering, Semnan University, Semnan, Iran.

*Corresponding author: amaleki@semnan.ac.ir (A. Maleki).

Abstract

Visual saliency is a cognitive psychology concept that makes some stimuli of a scene stand out relative to their neighbors and attract our attention. Computing visual saliency is a topic of recent interest. Here, we propose a graph-based method for saliency detection, which contains three stages: pre-processing, initial saliency detection, and final saliency detection. The initial saliency map is obtained by putting an adaptive threshold on color differences relative to the background. In final saliency detection, a graph is constructed, and the ranking technique is exploited. In the proposed method, the background is suppressed effectively, and salient regions are often selected correctly. The experimental results on the MSRA-1000 database demonstrate excellent performance and low computational complexity in comparison with the state-of-the-art methods.

Keywords: *Visual Attention, Bottom-up Model, Saliency Detection, Graph Based, Background Color.*

1. Introduction

Salient regions in a scene immediately grab one's attention. Detecting these regions in the field of vision has a computational complexity that makes it difficult even for brains [1], let alone a computer. Selecting salient regions is possible through the visual attention mechanisms. The visual attention models have many applications including target detection (e.g. finding military vehicles in a plain [2]); cutting images automatically [3]; robotic vision actions [4]; finding the tumor on a mammogram [5]; video compression [6], and image retargeting [7, 8].

From the viewpoint of information processing and attention control, there are two executive approaches. One is the bottom-up or stimulus-driven process, [9-23], which is determined exogenously by the characteristics of the stimuli themselves. Therefore, the bottom-up models select locations that have different features relative to their surroundings. Another is the top-down or goal-directed process, [32-34] which endogenously depends on the observer's intentions and demands of the task as well. Some models [24, 28] use a combination of the bottom-up and top-down features. In this work, we focused on the bottom-up saliency detection. The first attempt to understand the bottom-up attention was made by Koch and Ullman [9] (1985), whereas the first actual implementation of the corresponding saliency map was described by Niebur and Koch [10] (1996). Later works refined this model [11-14]. Itti et al. [11] proposed a bottom-up saliency detection method using center-surround differences. Their method detects the contour of the salient object instead of the whole object. Some methods search for saliency cues based on the frequency domain analysis [7, 8, 15-17]. Hou and Zhang [15] (2007) used global contrast to obtain the saliency map. In their model, edges are detected as the salient regions. Achanta et al. [16] (2009) proposed a method by maintaining the higher-frequency content of images. However, this method often recognizes some background regions as saliency. Recently, Fang et al. [7] (2012) has provided a method in the compressed domain, and calculated the saliency map by combining the feature maps (intensity, color, and texture) obtained from DCT coefficients. Also, Fang et al. [8] (2012) have presented a bottom-up method by calculating differences of a quaternion Fourier transform (QFT) between each patch and the other patches in the image. They exploited human visual sensitivity to weight these patch differences. Some other bottom-up methods define visual saliency based on the graphical framework [18- 20, 30]. Harel et al. [18] (2006) formed some activation maps using the principles of closeness and dissimilarity and combined them into a single map. These models highlight only the high-contrast edges and do not detect the interior smooth objects. Most saliency detection models use center prior [21, 27, 31], assuming that the objects near the image center are more prominent than the other regions. These models cannot detect salient regions far from the image center. Yang [20] solved the problem by estimating the center of the salient object based on the convex hull technique. However, the performance of the method depends on the accuracy of the technique for salient area extraction.

Most methods use the color, orientation, intensity, and frequency-based features for directing attention. Ma and Zhang [22] (2003) estimated saliency using a fuzzy growing method and considering only local contrasts. Hence, this method detects the object boundaries regardless of the inside of the salient regions. Achanta et al. [23] (2008) presented a bottom-up model using the color and luminance features. Borji [24] (2012) applied low-level features such as intensity, orientation and color, and high-level features such as faces, humans, and cars for saliency detection. Zhang et al. [25] (2013) proposed a saliency detection model by combining frequency, color, and location priors. Erdem [26] (2013) used the covariance of the features extracted from the image patches. Then the distances between the covariance of each patch with neighboring patches were computed for saliency estimation. Tian et al. [28] (2014) proposed a model by fusing the bottom-up (color and orientation contrast) and top-down (depth-from-focus) features.

The above-mentioned methods cannot correctly recognize the salient regions in most scenes. Determining the location of salient pixels without knowing their characteristics is difficult. In this paper, we propose a bottom-up model that consists of three stages: First, pre-processing of the input image is performed that includes segmentation into superpixels, conversion from RGB to LAB space, and calculating color mean for each LAB channel of each superpixel. Then an initial saliency map is achieved based on an adaptive threshold of the color differences relative to the background. In the end, the final saliency map is obtained by graph construction and using the ranking technique [29, 30]. In this method, the background is suppressed effectively and the salient object is highlighted more accurately in the image.

The rest of the paper is organized as follows. The proposed method is described in section 2. The experimental results on the popular large database are presented in section 3. The conclusion is discussed in section 4.

2. Proposed method

We propose a graph-based method using the background color for saliency estimation. As illustrated in figure 1, our method consists of three stages. In the first stage, we perform pre-processing on the input image. In the second stage, we detect the background and foreground regions based on the color differences in the LAB space. The color is a very important visual attribute, and the LAB space is inspired by color opponent neurons of red/green and blue/yellow in primary visual cortex (V1). Usually, the boundary regions of an image are considered as background, thus we also assume these regions as part of the background. The rest of the background and foreground regions are determined adaptively based on the color differences relative to the already assumed background regions. Accordingly, an initial saliency map is generated. In the third stage, the ranking technique [29, 30] is exploited by taking the initial salient regions as queries. Final saliency is computed based on the relevance of queries.

2.1. Pre-processing

Pre-processing is performed through three procedures. First, a given image is segmented into N superpixels using the simple linear iterative clustering (SLIC) algorithm [35]. The SLIC algorithm follows four main steps: 1) N cluster centers, $C_n = [l_n, a_n, b_n, x_n, y_n]^T$, are initialized in a regular grid space S using k-means algorithm. 2) In a $2S \times 2S$ region around each cluster center, the distance between the cluster center and each one of the pixels within the region is calculated in terms of color similarity and spatial proximity. 3) Each pixel is then associated with the nearest cluster center. Then the color average of all pixels belonging to each cluster center is computed and the color of the cluster center is updated. 4) The error is calculated between the previous and new cluster centers, and steps 2 to 4 can be repeated until the error converges. At the end of the algorithm, each cluster center, along with the associated pixels, is called a superpixel.

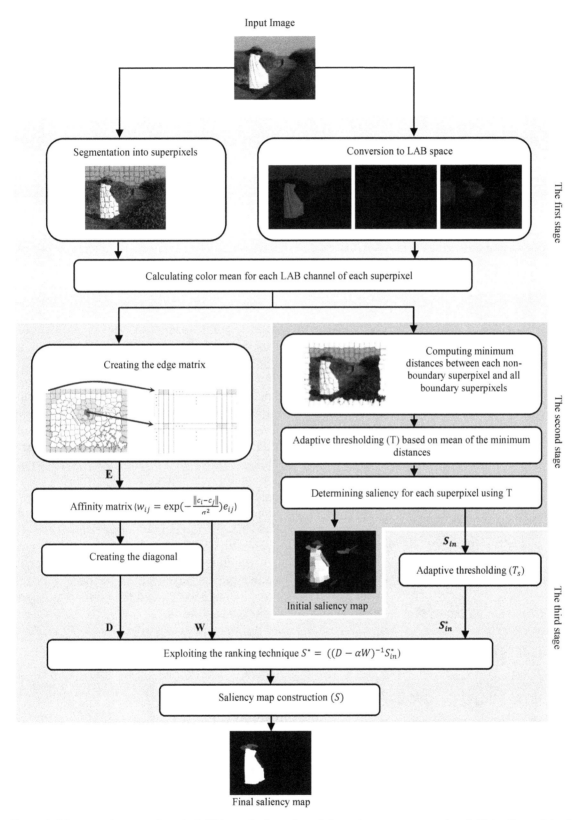

Figure 1. Diagram of proposed method. This method consists of three stages: pre-processing, initial saliency detection, and final saliency detection.

Therefore, a superpixel contains the pixels that are more uniform in terms of color and texture. Using superpixels, the structure of the salient objects is conserved, whereas the computational complexity of the image is efficiently decreased from thousands of pixels to only a few hundred superpixels. Furthermore, the superpixels maintain the image edges well and improve the quality of salient object detection. Figure 2 illustrates some images that are segmented into superpixels using the SLIC algorithm.

Figure 2. Images segmented using SLIC algorithm into about 200 superpixels.

In the second procedure of pre-processing, the given image is migrated from RGB to LAB space. Since the LAB color space is uniform and similar to human visual perception [36], it is a good choice for computing the color differences. LAB contains a luminance (L) channel and two chromatic channels: red/green (A) and blue/yellow (B). In the LAB space, the L, A, and B channels are computed through a non-linear mapping of XYZ coordinates, as follows [37]:

$$L = 116\, h\left(\frac{Y}{Y_w}\right) - 16 \tag{1}$$

$$A = 500\left[h\left(\frac{X}{X_w}\right) - h\left(\frac{Y}{Y_w}\right)\right] \tag{2}$$

$$B = 200\left[h\left(\frac{Y}{Y_w}\right) - h\left(\frac{Z}{Z_w}\right)\right] \tag{3}$$

$$h(q) = \begin{cases} \sqrt[3]{q} & q > 0.008856 \\ 7.787q + \dfrac{16}{116} & q \le 0.008856 \end{cases} \tag{4}$$

$$\begin{bmatrix} X \\ Y \\ Z \end{bmatrix} = \begin{bmatrix} 0.412453 & 0.357580 & 0.180423 \\ 0.212671 & 0.715160 & 0.072169 \\ 0.019334 & 0.119193 & 0.950227 \end{bmatrix}\begin{bmatrix} R \\ G \\ B \end{bmatrix} \tag{5}$$

where, X_w, Y_w, and Z_w are reference white points, and their values are 0.950450, 1.000000, and 1.088754, respectively.

In the third procedure of pre-processing, the color mean is computed for each LAB channel of the ith superpixel, as follows:

$$l_i^* = \frac{1}{M_i}\sum_{m=1}^{M_i} L(m) \tag{6}$$

$$a_i^* = \frac{1}{M_i}\sum_{m=1}^{M_i} A(m) \tag{7}$$

$$b_i^* = \frac{1}{M_i}\sum_{m=1}^{M_i} B(m) \tag{8}$$

where, L, A, and B are three channels in the LAB space and M_i is the number of pixels within the ith superpixel.

2.2. Initial saliency detection

Similar to our previous work [38], we detected the background and foreground superpixels by color distances. The distance between two superpixels (superpixels i and j) was computed as follows:

$$D(i.j) = c_i - c_j$$
$$= \sqrt{(l_i^* - l_j^*)^2 + (a_i^* - a_j^*)^2 + (b_i^* - b_j^*)^2} \tag{9}$$

where, $c_i = \left[l_i^*, a_i^*, b_i^* \right]$ and $c_j = \left[l_j^*, a_j^*, b_j^* \right]$ denote color means of the pixels within the superpixels i and j, respectively, and $\|.\|$ is the Euclidean distance.

The superpixels are divided into two groups: boundary and non-boundary. "Boundary superpixels" refer to the superpixels of the image boundary, and the rest are "non-boundary superpixels" (see Figure 3). Given N superpixels in the image, the R superpixels are boundary superpixels and the K superpixels are non-boundary superpixels (N = R + K). All the boundary superpixels are assumed as background, and the non-boundary superpixels have to be evaluated whether as background or foreground. To do this, the distances between each non-boundary superpixel and all boundary superpixels are computed as (9), and the minimum distance is achieved as follows:

$$MD(i) = \min_j D(i,j) \quad j = 1,2,\dots,R \tag{10}$$

where, characterizes the non-boundary superpixel and $MD(i)$ is the minimum distance between it and all boundary superpixels $(j = 1,2,\dots,R)$. If the distances between the non-boundary superpixel and all boundary superpixels are high, its minimum distance would be high as well. Therefore, it is not similar to the boundary superpixels or background, and would be considered as a foreground superpixel. The mean of minimum distance is considered as an adaptive threshold (T).

$$T = \frac{1}{K}\sum_{i=1}^{K} MD(i) \tag{11}$$

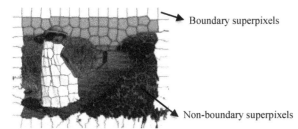

Figure 3. Boundary and non-boundary superpixels in a sample image. Yellow superpixels are boundary and others are non-boundary.

Each non-boundary superpixel whose minimum distance is bigger than T is defined as foreground. The initial saliency value for each superpixel is determined as follows:

$$S_{in}(n) = \begin{cases} MD(n) & if \ MD(n) > T \ and \\ & n \in \{K \ \ non-boundary \ \ \sup erpixels\} \\ 0 & if \ MD(n) \leq T \ and \\ & n \in \{K \ \ non-boundary \ \ \sup erpixels\} \\ 0 & if \ n \in \{R \ \ boundary \ \ \sup erpixels\} \end{cases}$$

$$(12)$$

where, $S_{in}(n)$ is the initial saliency value for superpixel n. For creating the initial saliency map, we set the initial saliency value of each superpixel for all pixels within it. For instance, the initial saliency maps of some images with their ground truths are shown in figure 4.

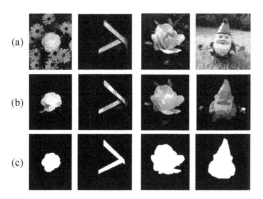

Figure 4. Examples of initial saliency maps. (a) Input images, (b) Initial saliency maps, (c) Ground truths.

Sometimes the background color is similar to the salient object color in the image. Therefore, the initial saliency map cannot recognize the salient object well, and parts of the background regions are detected as foreground incorrectly. Examples of the initial saliency maps in figure 4(b) illustrate the problem. To alleviate the problem, we used

the ranking technique based on graph construction.

2.3. Final saliency detection
We represent the image as a graph with superpixels as nodes (explained in section 2.3.1) and the initial salient nodes as queries. Then we exploit the ranking technique (described in section 2.3.2). The saliency of each node is obtained by its relevance to queries, so the final saliency map is created as the result.

2.3.1 Graph construction
We construct a connected graph G = (V, E), as shown in figure 5(a), where the nodes (V) are superpixels generated by the SLIC algorithm [35]. The edges (E) are determined by the relationship between superpixels; if two superpixels have a frontier, there is an edge between them. For example, in figure 5(a), superpixel 29 has frontiers with superpixels 21, 22, 23, 33, 32, and 28. Thus there is an edge between superpixel 29 and each of them. Each node is connected to its neighboring nodes (See the bold blue lines in figure 5(a)) and those that have frontiers with the neighboring nodes (See the blue lines in figure 5(a)). Furthermore, all the nodes on the four sides of the image are connected together (See the red line in figure 5(a)). An $N \times N$ edge matrix (E) is generated, in which $e_{ij} = 1$. If there is an edge between nodes i and j, otherwise $e_{ij} = 0$. An example of the edge matrix is illustrated in figure 5(b). According to [20, 30], the weight between the two nodes i and j is computed as follows:

$$w_{ij} = \exp\left(-\frac{D(i,j)}{\sigma^2}\right) e_{ij} = \exp\left(-\frac{c_i - c_j}{\sigma^2}\right) e_{ij} \quad (13)$$

where, $D(i,j)$ is computed as (9), e_{ij} is the element (i,j) of the edge matrix (E), and σ controls the strength of the weight. In (13), the affinity matrix (W) is created by determining distances of the nodes in the LAB color space. The weights are increased by reducing the color differences between nodes.

2.3.2 Ranking technique
To achieve the final saliency map, we exploit the ranking technique [29]. First, we apply an adaptive threshold on S_{in} in (12) and detect the initial salient nodes.

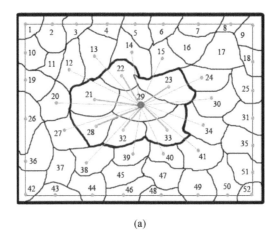

(a)

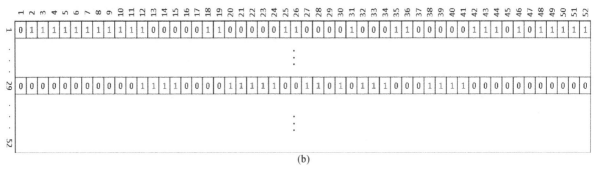

(b)

Figure 5. (a) A sample of our graph model. Blue lines indicate edges of red node (node 29), and red line shows that all boundary nodes are connected together. (b) Parts of 52 × 52 edge matrix (E) for graph (a) is shown edges of nodes 1 and 29. For each node in E, bold blue 1's indicate its edges with neighboring nodes; blue 1's refer to its edges with neighboring of them. If a node is boundary (e.g. node 1), red 1's represents its edges with boundary nodes.

$$T_s = \frac{1}{N}\sum_{n=1}^{N}S_{in}(n) \tag{14}$$

$$S_{in}^{*}(n) = \begin{cases} 1 & if\ S_{in}(n) \ge T_s \\ 0 & if\ S_{in}(n) < T_s \end{cases} \tag{15}$$

The nodes with $S_{in}^{*}=1$. are defined as initial salient nodes. We consider the initial salient nodes as queries for graph labelling.

The saliencies of the unlabelled nodes are computed based on their relevance to queries by the ranking technique:

$$S^{*} = (D - \alpha W)^{-1} S_{in}^{*} \tag{16}$$

where, W is the affinity matrix computed in (13), D denotes the diagonal matrix with $d_{ii} = \sum_{j}(w_{ij})$.

and α is the impact factor of the affinity matrix in the ranking. In (16), after computing $(D-\alpha W)^{-1}$, we set its diagonal elements to zero. This prevents the relevance of each query to itself, and weakens the contributions of other queries to the ranking [30]. Therefore, it has good effects on the results.

To generate the final saliency map (S), we set the saliency value of each node for all pixels within its corresponding superpixel, and normalize it to the range [0 1]. Figure 6 shows the impact of the graph-based ranking technique on the final saliency map.

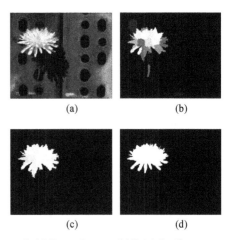

(a)   (b)

(c)   (d)

Figure 6. (a) Input image, (b) Initial saliency map, (c) Final saliency map, (d) Ground truth.

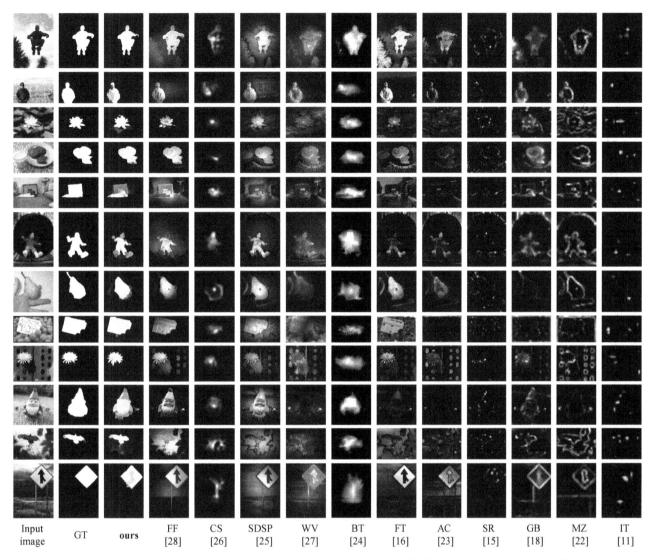

| Input image | GT | **ours** | FF [28] | CS [26] | SDSP [25] | WV [27] | BT [24] | FT [16] | AC [23] | SR [15] | GB [18] | MZ [22] | IT [11] |

Figure 7. Visual comparison of saliency maps obtained from state-of-the-art methods and our method (ours) with ground truth (GT).

3. Experimental results

We demonstrate the efficacy of the proposed method in a series of experiments, while comparing it with the state-of-the-art saliency detection models: Itti et al. [11] (IT), Ma and Zhang [22] (MZ), graph-based visual saliency [18] (GB), spectral residual approach [15] (SR), Achanta [23] (AC), frequency-tuned saliency detection [16] (FT), a model in compressed domain [7] (CD), boosting bottom-up and top-down model [24] (BT), a model based on wavelet transform [27] (WV), a saliency detection model that combines simple priors [25] (SDSP), visual saliency using region covariance [26] (CS), and a model that combines the orientation, color, and depth-from-focus features [28] (FF). In the paper, we used the original experiment results of models

FF, BT, FT, AC, SR, GB, MZ,nd IT that are available online[1], and downloaded the results of model CD from the authors' homepage[2]. Furthermore, we retrieved the saliency maps of other models including CS, SDSP, and WV from their source codes[3]. Visual comparison of the state-of-the-art methods and the proposed method with the ground truth are shown in figure 7. As shown, the proposed method is closer to ground truth than the other methods are.

3.1. Database

In our experiment, we used the popular database of MSRA-1000, a subset of the MSRA database [39], which contains 1000 images with the binary ground truths. The Ground truth was determined by the visual judgment of 9 subjects.

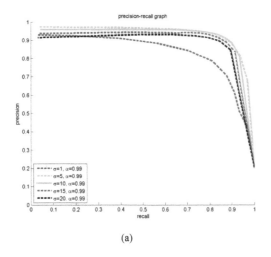 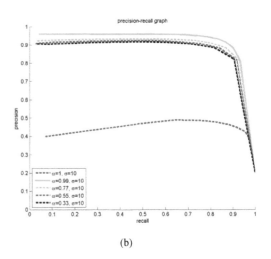

(a)   (b)

Figure 8. Comparison of precision-recall curves of proposed method on MSRA-1000 database for different values of (a) σ. parameter and (b) α parameter.

3.2. Parameters

In our experiments, we set the number of superpixels to $N = 200$. There are also two other parameters in our implementation, σ and α. These are used for controlling the edge weight in (13) and the impact of the affinity matrix in the ranking function in (16), respectively, and were empirically tuned as $\sigma = 10$ and $\alpha = 0.99$. Precision-recall curves, which determine the effects of different parameters on the MSRA-1000 database, are shown in figure 8.

3.3. Evaluation criteria

We evaluated the performance of the methods by receiver operating characteristic (ROC), precision, recall, and F-measure. In this experiment, the saliency map values in the range [0 255] are converted to binary by a fixed threshold. First, the values for the saliency map are normalized to the range [0 1]. Then given a threshold, $T_f \in [0\ 1]$, the points with saliency values higher than T_f are marked as salient and others marked as non-salient. For each image, we generate several binary saliency maps corresponding to 11 different thresholds, from 0 to 1: (0, 0.1, 0.2, ..., 1). This operation is applied to all saliency maps obtained from the database images. For each image, the binary saliency maps obtained from each saliency detection model are compared with its ground truth map. Afterward, true positive, false positive, and false negative are computed, an example of which is shown in figure 9.

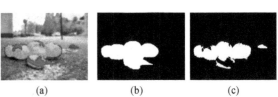

(a)   (b)   (c)

Figure 9. Classification results (a) with ground truth map (b) and a binary saliency map with a threshold equal 0.6 (c). In (a), green areas are true positives, blue areas are false positives, and red areas are false negatives.

True positive is the number of pixels that are salient in both the binary saliency map and the ground truth map. False positive is the number of pixels that are salient in binary saliency map and are non-salient in the ground truth map. False negative is the number of pixels that are salient in the ground truth map and are non-salient in the binary saliency map. The precision and recall rates for each binary saliency map are calculated as follows [28]:

$$precision = \frac{TP}{TP + FP} \qquad (17)$$

$$recall = \frac{TP}{TP + FN} \qquad (18)$$

where, TP, FP, and FN are the true positive, false positive, and false negative rates, respectively. The precision value is the ratio of correctly detected salient pixels to all salient pixels of binary saliency map, while the recall value is the ratio of correctly detected salient pixels to all salient pixels of the ground truth.

Given a ground truth map SM_G and a predicted map SM_p:

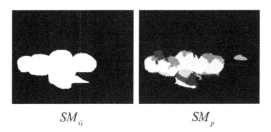

$$SM_G \qquad\qquad SM_p$$

```
Define a set of thresholds T = {T_p^i}_{i∈N}
For All thresholds in T
  Binarization of the predicted map with the threshold T_p^i.
  For All pixels in binarized maps
    If SM_G =1
      If SM_p^i =1  // SM_p^i is binarized map with threshold T_p^i
        TP++
      Else
        FN++
      End If
    Else
      If SM_p^i =1
        FP++
      End If
    End If
  End For
  Precision(T_p^i)=TP/ (TP+FP)
  Recall(T_p^i)=TP/ (TP+FN)
End For
Plot (Recall, Precision)   //for each T_p^i
```

(a) Pseudo code

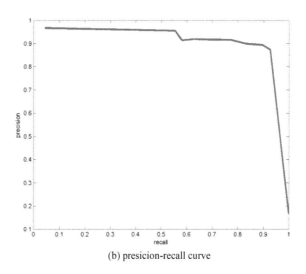

(b) presicion-recall curve

Figure 10. (a) Pseudo-code to perform a precision-recall analysis between ground truth map and predicted map. (b) the precision-recall curve for a sample predicted map.

The values for precision and recall are obtained from the binary saliency maps of all the database images, and the precision-recall curve is drawn by averaging the results for each threshold value T_f.

Pseudo-code for drawing a precision-recall curve is shown in figure 10. By the precision and recall criteria, the F-measure is obtained. Similar to [16], for each image, its gray saliency map is converted into binary by adaptive threshold (Th) that is two times the mean saliency from the saliency map.

$$Th = \frac{2}{X*Y}\sum_{x=0}^{X-1}\sum_{y=0}^{Y-1} S(x,y) \qquad (19)$$

where, X and Y are the width and height of the saliency map, respectively, and $S(x,y)$ is the saliency value of the pixel at the position (x,y).

The precision and recall are computed for each image. Then by averaging them on all the images, the F-measure is defined as:

$$F-measure = \frac{(1+\beta^2).precision.recall}{\beta^2. precision+ recall} \qquad (20)$$

where, $\beta^2=0.3$ as in [16, 25, 31] for more impact of precision than recall. The F-measure criterion for the state-of-the-art methods on MSRA-1000 database is listed in table 1.

Another way to compare experiments is to use the ROC curve that is achieved as the curve of true positive rate versus false positive rate by different thresholds over the saliency map of each image. The area under the ROC curve (AUC) [40] can be used for the quantitative assessment of the saliency detection models.

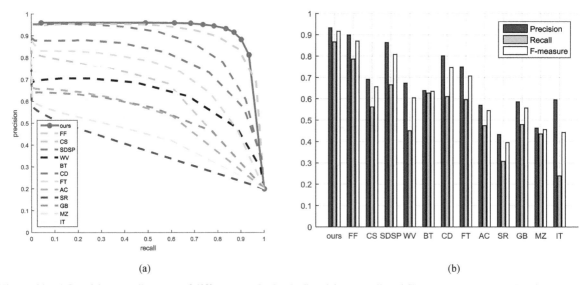

(a)   (b)

Figure 11. (a) Precision-recall curves of different methods. (b) Precision, recall and F-measure using an adaptive threshold. All results are computed on MSRA-1000 database for comparison of proposed method (ours) with state-of-the-art methods including FF [28], CS [26], SDSP [25], WV [27], BT [24], CD [7], FT [16], AC [23], SR [15], GB [18], MZ [22], IT [11].

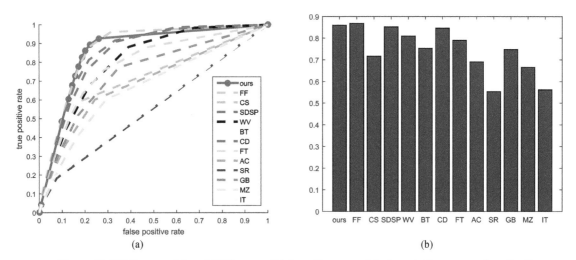

(a)   (b)

Figure 12. ROC curves (a) and AUC scores (b) for saliency models (ours is the proposed method).

Table 1. F-measure for saliency models.	
Method	F-Measure
ours	**0.9093**
FF [28]	0.8701
CS [26]	0.6564
SDSP [25]	0.8080
WV [27]	0.6040
BT [24]	0.6358
CD [7]	0.7470
FT [16]	0.7072
AC [23]	0.5444
SR [15]	0.3954
GB [18]	0.5569
MZ [22]	0.4561
IT [11]	0.4426

Table 2. Comparison of average running time.		
Method	Time (s)	Code
ours	**1.0972**	**Matlab**
CS [26]	21.223	Matlab
SDSP [25]	0.087	Matlab
WV [27]	6.777	Matlab
FT [16]	0.024	C++
AC [23]	0.127	C++
SR [15]	0.061	Matlab
GB [18]	1.563	Matlab
MZ [22]	0.07	C++
IT [11]	0.411	Matlab

We used an available code[4] to achieve the ROC curve and AUC score.

For evaluating the performance of the saliency detection models, we compare the proposed method with twelve state-of-the-art methods including IT [11], MZ [22], GB [18], SR [15], AC [23], FT [16], CD [7], BT [24], WV [27], SDSP [25], CS [26], and FF [28] on the MSRA-1000 database [39]. The precision-recall curve and F-measure metric are shown in figure 11. In addition, we use the ROC curve and AUC score for the methods that are shown in figure 12. The results obtained show that our method outperforms the state-of-the-art saliency detection methods. In addition to the saliency detection accuracy, we compared the computational cost of the proposed method with other methods. The average running time for the saliency detection methods on the MSRA-1000 database is presented in table 2 on a machine with Intel Core i5 2.53 GHz CPU and 4 GB RAM. Our method has a quite low computational complexity.

4. Conclusions

We proposed a bottom-up visual saliency detection method that detects the background and foreground regions by the color differences relative to the boundary regions of the image, based on which an initial saliency map is generated. Next, with graph construction, the ranking technique is exploited by taking the initial salient nodes as queries. The final saliency map is created by this technique. In the proposed method, the background is suppressed effectively, and the whole salient regions are highlighted uniformly. Furthermore, due to using superpixels instead of pixels, the computational complexity of the method is effectively reduced. As indicated in the experimental results on the MSRA-1000 database, the proposed method demonstrates an excellent performance against the state-of-the-arts methods. Furthermore, having a quite low run time, this method can be used for real-time applications. Since the proposed method uses the color of the boundary regions as the background features, if these features are similar to salient regions, or the image has a frame, the salient regions are not detected correctly. Our future work will focus on generating a top-down method and its combination with the proposed bottom-up method, similar to the human visual system.

References

[1] Tsotsos, J. K. (1991). Is Complexity Theory appropriate for analyzing biological systems? Behavioral and Brain Sciences, vol. 14, no. 4, pp. 770-773.

[2] Itti, L. & Koch, C. (2000). A saliency-based search mechanism for overt and covert shifts of visual attention. Vision Research. vol. 40, no. 10, pp. 1489-1506.

[3] Le Meur, O., Le Callet, P., Barba, D. & Thoreau, D. (2006). A coherent computational approach to model bottom-up visual attention, IEEE Transactions on Pattern Analysis and Machine Intelligence, vol. 28, no. 5, pp. 802-817.

[4] Siagian, C. & Itti, L. (2007). Biologically-Inspired Robotics Vision Monte-Carlo Localization in the Outdoor Environment, In Proc. IEEE International Conference on Intelligent Robots and Systems.

[5] Hong, B. W. & Brady, M. (2003). A Topographic Representation for Mammogram Segmentation, In Lecture Notes in Computer Science, pp. 730-737.

[6] Itti, L. (2004). Automatic Foveation for Video Compression Using a Neurobiological Model of Visual Attention. IEEE Transactions on Image Processing, Vol. 13, no. 10, pp. 1304-1318.

[7] Fang, Y., Chen, Z., Lin, W. & Lin, C. W. (2012). Saliency detection in the compressed domain for adaptive image retargeting, IEEE Transactions on Image Processing, vol. 21, no. 9, pp. 3888-3901.

[8] Fang, Y., Lin, W., Lee, B. S., Lau, C. T., Chen, Z., & Lin, C. W. (2012). Bottom-up saliency detection model based on human visual sensitivity and amplitude spectrum, IEEE Transactions on Multimedia, vol. 12, no. 1, pp. 187-198.

[9] Koch, C. & Ullman, S. (1985). Shifts in selective visual attention: towards the underlying neural circuitry. Human Neurobiology 4, pp. 219-227.

[10] Niebur, E. & Koch, C. (1996). Control of Selective Visual Attention: Modeling the Where Pathway. Neural Information Processing Systems, pp. 802-808.

[11] Itti, L., Koch, C. & Niebur, E. (1998). A Model of Saliency-Based Visual Attention for Rapid Scene Analysis, IEEE Transactions on Pattern Analysis and Machine Intelligence, vol. 20, no. 11, pp. 1254-1259.

[12] Itti, L. & Koch, C. (2001), Computational Modeling of Visual Attention, Nature Reviews Neuroscience, vol. 2, no. 3, pp. 194-203.

[13] Itti, L., Dhavale, N. & Pighin, F. (2004). Realistic Avatar Eye and Head Animation Using a Neurobiological Model of Visual Attention. Proc. SPIE, vol. 5200, no. 1, pp. 64-78.

[14] Lin, Y., Tang, Y., Fang, B., Shang, Z., Huang, Y., & Wang, S. (2013). A Visual-Attention Model Using Earth Mover's Distance-Based Saliency Measurement and Nonlinear Feature Combination. IEEE Transactions on pattern analysis and machine intelligence, vol. 35, no. 2, pp. 314-328.

[15] Hou, X. & Zhang, L. (2007). Saliency Detection:

A Spectral Residual Approach, Proc. IEEE Conference on Computer Vision and Pattern Recognition.

[16] Achanta, R., Hemami, S., Estrada, F. & Susstrunk, S. (2009). Frequency-tuned salient region detection. In Computer Vision and Pattern Recognition (CVPR), IEEE Conference, pp. 1597–1604.

[17] Guo, C. & Zhang, L. (2010). A Novel Multiresolution Spatiotemporal Saliency Detection Model and Its Applications in Image and Video Compression. IEEE Transaction on Image Processing, vol. 19, no. 1, pp. 185-198.

[18] Harel, J., Koch, C. & Perona, P. (2006). Graph-based visual saliency. Neural Information Processing Systems (NIPS), pp. 545–552.

[19] Avraham, T. & Lindenbaum, M. (2010). Esaliency (Extended Saliency): Meaningful Attention Using Stochastic Image Modeling. IEEE Transaction on Pattern Analysis and Machine Intelligence, vol. 32, no.4, pp. 693-708.

[20] Yang, C., Zhang, L. & Lu, H. (2013). Graph-Regularized Saliency Detection with Convex-Hull-Based Center Prior. IEEE Signal Processing Letters, vol. 20, no. 7, pp. 637-640.

[21] Goferman, S., Zelnik-Manor, L. & Tal, A. (2012). Context-aware saliency detection, IEEE Transaction on Pattern Analysis and Machine Intelligence, vol. 32, no. 10, pp. 1915-1925.

[22] Ma, Y. & Zhang, H. (2003). Contrast-based image attention analysis by using fuzzy growing. In International Multimedia Conference: Proceedings of the eleventh ACM international conference on Multimedia, vol. 2, no. 8, pp. 374-381.

[23] Achanta, R., Estrada, F., Wils, P. & Susstrunk, S. (2008). Salient region detection and segmentation. International Conference on Computer Vision Systems (ICVS), pp. 66-75.

[24] Borji, A. (2012). Boosting bottom-up and top-down visual features for saliency estimation. IEEE Conference on Computer Vision Pattern Recognition (CVPR), pp. 438-445.

[25] Zhang, L., Gu, Z. & Li, H. (2013). SDSP: A Novel Saliency Detection Method by Combining Simple Priors, in Proc. ICIP, pp. 171-175.

[26] Erdem, E. & Erdem, A. (2013). Visual saliency estimation by nonlinearly integrating features using region covariances. Journal of Vision, vol. 13, no. 4, pp. 1-20.

[27] İmamoğlu, N., Lin, W. & Fang, Y. (2013). A Saliency Detection Model Using Low-Level Features Based on Wavelet Transform. IEEE Transactions on Multimedia, vol. 15, no. 1, pp. 96-105.

[28] Tian, H., Fang, Y., Zhao, Y., Lin, W., Ni R. & Zhu, Z. (2014). Salient region detection by fusing bottom-up and top-down features extracted from a single image. IEEE Transactions on image processing, vol. 23, no. 10, pp. 4389-4398.

[29] Zhou, D., Weston, J., Gretton, A., Bousquet, O. & Scholkopf, B. (2004). Ranking on data manifolds. In NIPS.

[30] Yang, C., Zhang, L., Lu, H., Ruan, X. & Yang, M. H. (2013). Saliency Detection via Graph-based Manifold Ranking. IEEE Conference on Computer Vision and Pattern Recognition, Portland, pp. 1-8.

[31] Zhou, Q. (2014). Object-based attention: saliency detection using contrast via background prototypes, electronics letters, vol. 50, no. 14, pp. 997-999.

[32] Borji, A., Sihite, D. N. & Itti, L. (2014). What/Where to Look Next? Modeling Top-Down Visual Attention in Complex Interactive Environments. IEEE Transactions on systems man and Cybernetics systems, vol. 44, pp. 523-538.

[33] Karthikeyan, S., Jagadeesh, V. & Manjunath, B. S. (2013). Learning top-down scene context for visual attention modeling in natural images, 20th IEEE international conference on image processing (ICIP), pp. 211-215.

[34] Borji, A., Sihite, D. N. & Itti, L. (2012). Modeling the influence of action on spatial attention in visual interactive environments, IEEE international conference on robotics and automation (ICRA), pp. 444-450.

[35] Achanta, R., Shaji A, Smith, K., Lucchi, A., Fua, P. & Süsstrunk, S. (2012). SLIC superpixels compared to state-of-the-art superpixel methods, IEEE Transactions on Pattern Analysis and Machine Intelligence, vol. 34, no. 11, pp. 2274-2281.

[36] Frintrop, S. (2005). VOCUS: A visual attention system for object detection and goal directed search, Ph.D. dissertation, Rheinische Friedrich-Wilhelms-University at Bonn, Bonn, Germany.

[37] Gonzalez, R. C. & Woods, R. E. (2007). Digital Image Processing, 3rd edition, Prentice-Hall, pp. 455-456.

[38] Foolad, S. & Maleki, A. (2016). Salient Regions Detection using Background Superpixels, 24th Iranian Conference on Electrical Engineering (ICEE).

[39] Liu, T., Yuan, Z., Sun, J., Wang, J., Zheng, N. & Tang, X., and Shum, H. (2011). Learning to detect a salient object, IEEE PAMI.

[40] Borji, A. Sihite, D. & Itti, L. (2012). Quantitative analysis of human-model agreement in visual saliency modeling: A comparative study. IEEE TIP.

14

Color Reduction in Hand-drawn Persian Carpet Cartoons before Discretization using image segmentation and finding edgy regions

M. Fateh[1*] and E. Kabir[2]

1. Department of Computer Engineering, Shahrood University of Technology, Shahrood, Iran,

2. Department of Electrical and Computer Engineering, Tarbiat Modarres University, Tehran, Iran.

*Corresponding author: mansoor_fateh@shahroodut.ac.ir (M. Fateh).

Abstract

In this paper, we present a method for color reduction in Persian carpet cartoons which increases both the speed and accuracy of editing. Carpet cartoons are in two categories: machine-printed and hand-drawn. Hand-drawn cartoons are divided into two groups: before and after discretization. The purpose of this work is color reduction in hand-drawn cartoons before discretization. The proposed algorithm consists of the following steps: image segmentation, finding the color of each region, color reduction around the edges and final color reduction with C-means. The proposed method requires knowing the desired number of colors in any cartoon. In this method, the number of colors is not reduced to more than about 1.3 times of the desired number. Automatic color reduction is done in such a way that the final manual editing done to reach the desired colors is very easy.

Keywords: *Color Reduction, Hand-drawn Cartoons, Segmentation, C-means, Persian Carpet.*

1. Introduction

True color images typically contain thousands of colors, and 24 bits are assigned to each pixel. Display, storage, transmission, and processing of these images are problematic. For this reason, color quantization is commonly used as a pre-processing step for various images. Applications of color quantization in image processing include: compression [1], segmentation [2], text detection [3], color-texture analysis [4], watermarking [5], and content-based retrieval [6]. The purpose of this research work is to reduce the number of colors in a hand-drawn carpet cartoon into a preset value.

Color quantization has many techniques in RGB, HSV, HSL, and other color spaces [7, 8]. The RGB color space was used in the current work.

The process of color quantization is comprised of two steps: palette design (selection of a small set of original image colors) and pixel mapping (replacing image colors with the color palette) [9]. Color quantization methods can be classified into two groups: image-independent method that determines a fixed palette regardless of any specific image [10] and image-dependent methods

that determine an adaptive palette. The aim is to reduce the number of colors in the image with minimal distortion [9].

In another classification, quantization methods can be categorized into pre-clustering or divisive and post-clustering [1]. Pre-clustering methods are essentially based on the statistical analysis of the color distribution. They start with a single cluster that contains all colors of the image. This cluster is divided into K ones [9]. Known divisive methods include octree [11], median-cut [12], variance-based [13], center-cut [14], binary splitting [15], and rwm-cut[1] [16]. Agglomerative pre-clustering methods begin with N clusters that are the total number of colors in the image. These clusters are then joined until K clusters remain [17, 18].

Post-clustering methods first determine a basic palette and then improve it iteratively. These methods yield fetter results at the cost of increased computational time. These methods are dependent

---

[1] radius weighted mean cut

on the initial conditions; therefore, the initial palette is first constructed by a pre-clustering method and the result is improved by a post-clustering method [19]. Clustering algorithms utilized for color quantization includes C-means [20-22], min-max [23], competitive learning [24, 25], fuzzy c-means [26, 27], BIRCH [28], self-organizing map [29, 30], and divisive hierarchical clustering [31].

Some color reduction methods exploit the local properties around a pixel to find its color more precisely. Ant colony and self-growing and self-organized neural gas are examples of optimization methods utilized for this purpose [29, 32, and 33].

Patterns in a Persian carpet cartoon consist of uni-color parts or regions; therefore, segmentation-based methods are the best choices for color reduction in these cartoons. In what follows, some image segmentation methods are briefly explained.

Segmentation methods based on boundaries and edges work on the discontinuity of pixels whereas region-based methods work on similarity [34]. Also, there are hybrid methods derived from integration of the region-based and edge-based method information [35]. In this research work, a hybrid method is used.

From the perspective of user's assistance, there are three ways to set a color palette depending on the application: 1) the palette is found without knowing any default number of colors, 2) number of desired colors is set by the user, 3) the palette is provided by the user. In all three ways, several methods for color reduction and quantization have been proposed [19, 28]. In our work, the number of colors is preset by the user.

Considering that the color reduction of carpet cartoons is a new topic, in this paper, a brief description of this topic is provided in Section 2. In Section 3, the proposed method is described. In Section 4, the details of dataset are described. Then in Section 5, the experimental results are analyzed and a comparison with the results obtained by commercial software is provided. Finally, in Section 6, the conclusion is derived.

2. Principles of automatic reading of carpet cartoons

Carpet cartoons are divided into two categories: a) hand-drawn by traditional methods, and b) machine-printed by computerized methods.

Hand-drawn cartoons are divided into two categories: a) before discretization, and b) after discretization. Two samples of carpet cartoons before and after discretization are shown in

figure1. The design of a carpet cartoon after discretization is done on a graph paper.

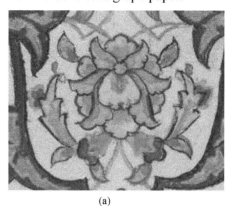

(a)

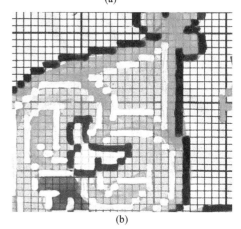

(b)

Figure 1. (a) Typical carpet cartoons before discretization; (b) Typical carpet cartoons after discretization.

The purpose and innovation of this work is the color reduction of hand-drawn carpet cartoons before discretization, which has never been done before, in order to ease the production of digital cartoons. The production of digital cartoons is of great help in establishing carpet cartoon libraries, preservation and restoration of old carpet cartoons, and automatic discretization and semi-automatic editing of cartoons.

The main concern in color reduction in conventional images is the minimization of a perceived difference between the original and quantized images. A typical conventional carpet cartoon has a palette of 10 to 15 colors. The main concern here is to have pure uni-color regions, while the fact that the quantized color of a region is close to the desired one is of less importance.

There are some commercial software products available, which assist the designer in the process of developing a carpet cartoon. However, this process is still very time- consuming and expensive. In the Iranian market, Booria [36] and Nqshsaz [37] are the most important commercial products for designing carpet cartoons. These applications reduce the number of colors to 256 perfectly. However, a further reduction in colors to tens of colors makes errors-hard to fix manually.

In the recent years, some algorithms have been proposed for color reduction in carpet cartoons [19, 38-40]. However due to the challenging problems, in particular for hand-drawn cartoons, the results are far from satisfactory. For example, color reduction with optimized C-means method [19] on part of a hand-drawn cartoon is shown in section 5 (Figure 17).

As shown in figure 2, there are two main problems to reduce color in hand-drawn carpet cartoons.

1- Varying saturation of a specific color in different parts of a hand-drawn cartoon.
2- Scanning with 256 or more colors.

The method proposed in this paper tries to solve both problems.

Figure 2. A typical hand-drawn carpet cartoon before discretization scanned by 300 dpi.

3. Proposed algorithm

The proposed algorithm consists of the following steps. 1) Image segmentation: in this step, edge detection is performed using Canny operator and edge linking is done where every closed boundary makes a separate segment. The resulting regions are of two kinds, edgy regions around the pattern edges, and plain regions including intra-pattern and background regions. 2) Finding the color of each plain region. 3) Color reduction of edgy regions with connected components labeling. 4) Final color reduction with C-means: in this step, color reduction with high accuracy is performed.

Color reduction steps in hand-drawn carpet cartoons are shown in figure 3.

In what follows, we describe the details of each color reduction step.

3.1. Image segmentation

In this step, color image is converted to grayscale, and edges are detected by canny operator (Figure 4).

In figure 4, some of the image boundaries have rupture. This rupture will cause a problem in area separation. Therefore, it is required to decrease the boundary ruptures. Then the intensity of pixels bigger than zero will be replaced by 255. Edge linking is carried out by blurring on image of edges. In continuation, the boundaries with one horizontal and vertical pixel distance will be connected till the image area separation gets done clearly and completely (Figure 5).

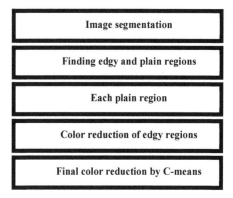

Figure 3. Proposed steps for color reduction in before-discretization carpet cartoons.

Figure 4. Edge detection by Canny operator on carpet cartoon in figure 2.

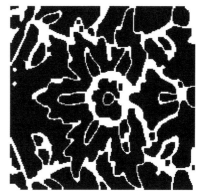

Figure 5. Blurring on edge image in figure 4.

Pattern boundaries are shown in white in figure 6. The image segmentation steps are shown in figure 7.

3.2. Finding color of each plain region

In this step, the color of each plain region is determined by the average color of its pixels for one time. If the difference between the average color and the color of any pixel is more than 10, that pixel is excluded and the average color of the remaining pixels is taken as the color of that region.

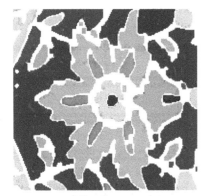

Figure 6. Final result of finding edgy regions, shown in white.

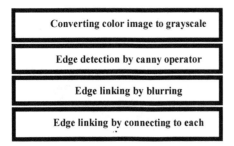

Figure 7. Steps of image segmentation.

After determining the color of each region, the number of colors in the image could be up to the number of plain regions. Using C-means algorithm, the number of palette colors is reduced to three times the number of colors preset by the user. The color distance between any region color and the palette colors is calculated. If this value is less than 15, the palette color is given to that segment; otherwise, the color does not change.

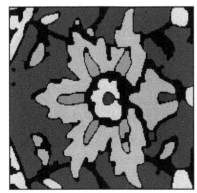

Figure 8. Finding color of each plain region in figure 2; and color reduction from 550 to 30 by C-means algorithm.

3.3. Color reduction of edgy regions

After finding the colors of plain regions, the colors of edgy regions are determined by a connected component labeling described in figure 9. In what follows, the basis of this method is described.

Image segmentation methods are divided into three groups:

- Thresholding Methods
- Boundary/Edge-based methods
- Region-based methods

The purpose of all these methods is segmentation with a high accuracy. However, it might be caused by problems in segmentation [34]:

- The segmented region might be smaller or larger than the actual one.
- The edges of the segmented region might not be connected.
- Pseudo-edges are created and real edges are missing.

In many segmentation methods based on the threshold, the threshold is determined by both general and local. The method does not have a high accuracy, because determining the exact threshold is difficult. But instead, the method has a high speed.

In edge-based methods, the number of regions is assumed to be equal to the number of closed borders. Also the gradient and laplacian algorithm is used to identify the boundary [34].

Accuracy of region-based methods is useful for segmentation. In these methods, similar regions are connected according to criteria such as color, texture and intensity. In this section, region growing and clustering are common methods. In this paper, segmentation around the edge is done by region-based methods with connected components labeling.

In this method, the Euclidian color distances of each pixel from neighboring pixels, are compared with a threshold value. If this distance is less than the threshold, the color of the neighboring pixel is replaced with the color of the central one.

A 5 by 5 window is considered and the threshold value is set by (1) where decreases as physical distance increases.

$$thershold = 15 * e^{\frac{-|x+y|}{2}} \tag{1}$$

In the above equation, x and y are the Euclidian distance of the neighboring pixel from the central one. Note that after this step, there is another one to reduce the color. Therefore, the threshold value is considered small.

Figure 10 shows a sample of color reduction for edgy regions.

3.4. Final color reduction by C-means algorithm

At the end, color reduction for the entire image is done by C-means. To ensure that the desired colors are preserved, color reduction is limited to 40-50% more than the desired number of colors, preset by the user.

The final result of color reduction is shown in figure 11. In this figure, the colors should be reduced to 16, while to keep the desired colors, the algorithm is set for 24 colors.

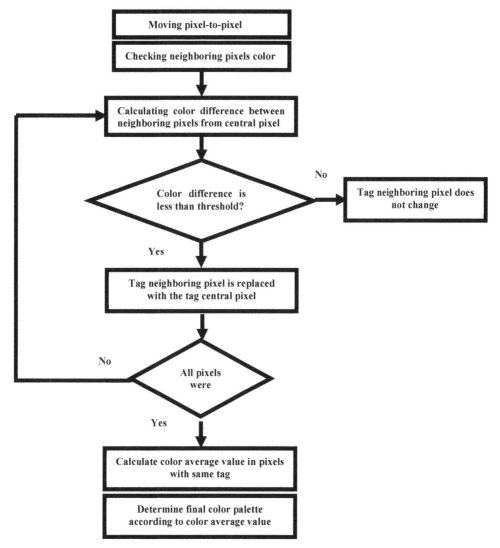

Figure 9. Flowchart for color reduction of edgy regions.

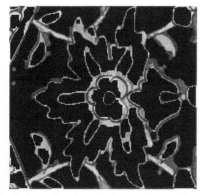

Figure 10. Color reduction of edgy regions of figure 2.

3.4. Final color reduction by C-means algorithm

At the end, color reduction for the entire image is done by C-means. To ensure that the desired colors are preserved, color reduction is limited to 40-50% more than the desired number of colors, preset by the user.

The final result of color reduction is shown in figure 11. In this figure, the colors should be reduced to 16, while to keep the desired colors, the algorithm is set for 24 colors.

Figure 11. Final reduction of colors for image of figure 2.

4. Dataset

Dataset for carpet cartoons was collected during five years from different sources [36, 37, 41]. In this work, 170 pieces of 17 carpet cartoons were used. The cartoons were from Kerman, Isfahan, Tabriz, Kashan and Qom.

- Size of each piece is between 300 by 300 and 1000 by 1000 pixels.
- The cartoons were scanned with 300 dpi.
- Color space of carpet cartoons is RGB.
- The number of colors in each piece is between 7 and 15.

90 pieces were used during the design of the method, and the remaining 80 pieces were used for the test. The ground truths for the test set were made by labeling the pixels in a semi-automatic manner, and were used to evaluate the proposed method.

As noted in Section 2, some pixels, about 5% of the total ones, are wrong in the original cartoons. In the proposed method, each region is homogeneous. Hence, the pixel color is corrected. However, if the correction does not happen, the error is not caused by the algorithm, and therefore is ignored.

5. Qualitative evaluations of results

In this Section, the results of the proposed method are examined on different carpet cartoons and compared with some conventional methods for color reduction. In our method, the final colors and number of colors are not exactly the same as the desired ones, so a quantitative evaluation is difficult. In this comparison, replacing the original colors with the similar ones is not considered as fault.

Color reduction for a sample image of the test set is shown in figure 12. The image has 522 * 524 pixels. The ground truth has 13 colors.

(a)

(b)

Figure 12. (a) A piece of a 13-color hand-drawn carpet cartoon before-discretization. (b) Resulting image produced with 18 colors.

Layer Pilot is general-purpose commercial software for color reduction of typical images. Color reduction in this software is semi-automatic [42]. In this software, the desired palette is specified by the user. The result of the color reduction by Layer Pilot is shown in figure 13. Our proposed algorithm is customized for carpet cartoons, and therefore, outperforms general-purpose software like Layer Pilot.

Part of a hand-drawn cartoon from Kerman with 15 colors is shown in figure 14.a. The colors are 5 kinds of greens, 2 gray, 2 kinds of blues, black, white, red, yellow, orange and beige. In this figure, the colors should be reduced to 15, while not to miss any desired color; the algorithm is set for 21 colors. If the colors are reduced to 15, errors resulting from merging similar colors are created. The color reduction into 15 is shown in figure 14.b. The color reduction into 21 is shown in figure 14.c.

Figure 13. Result of color reduction by Layer Pilot on figure 12.

For error analysis of figure14.b, each region is in white in figure15. In this figure, the grade color is known with the number of color. For example, dark blue and bright blue are known with blue 1 and blue 2. As seen, yellow and orange, 2 greens, white and part of beige are merged and 3 original colors are missed. Also, green 1 and white and part of gray 2, parts of green 2 and green 3 and gray 1 are merged. Gray 2 is divided into 2 colors and beige into 3 colors. In the proposed algorithm, to ensure that the desired colors are preserved, color reduction is limited to 40% more than the original number of colors.

For error analysis of figure14.c, each color is shown in figure16 by color white. As you can see, white and part of gray 2, parts of green 2 and gray 2 are merged and one color is removed. Also, gray1 and 2, green 1, 2 and 5 are divided into 2 colors and beige is divided into 3 colors. Dividing one color into 2 colors or more is not considered as error.

(a)   (b)   (c)

Figure 14. (a) A piece of a 15-color hand-drawn carpet cartoon. (b) Resulting image produced with 15 colors. (c)

Resulting image produced with 21 colors.

(1) black   (2) blue 1   (3) blue 2

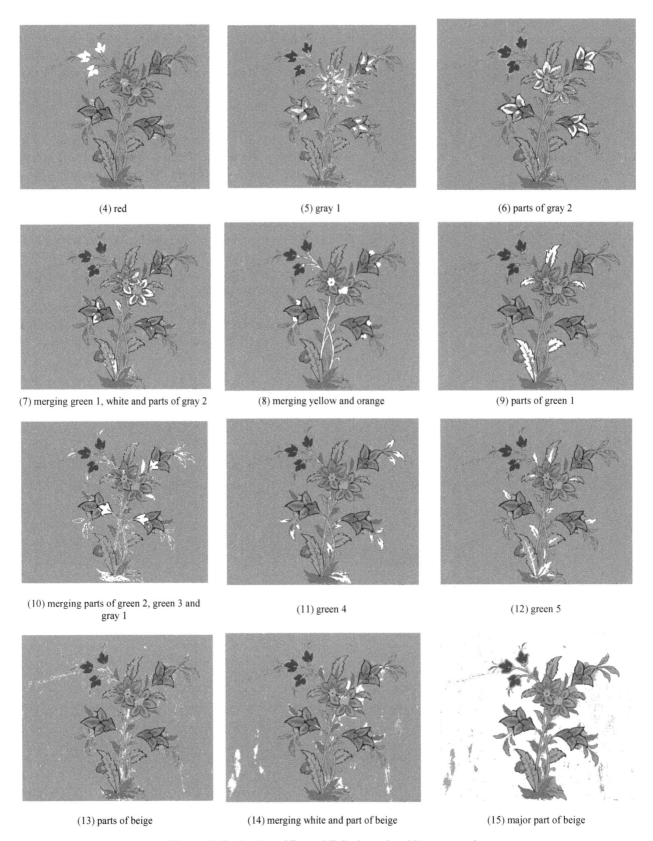

(4) red

(5) gray 1

(6) parts of gray 2

(7) merging green 1, white and parts of gray 2

(8) merging yellow and orange

(9) parts of green 1

(10) merging parts of green 2, green 3 and gray 1

(11) green 4

(12) green 5

(13) parts of beige

(14) merging white and part of beige

(15) major part of beige

Figure 15. Each color of figure 14b is shown in white, separately.

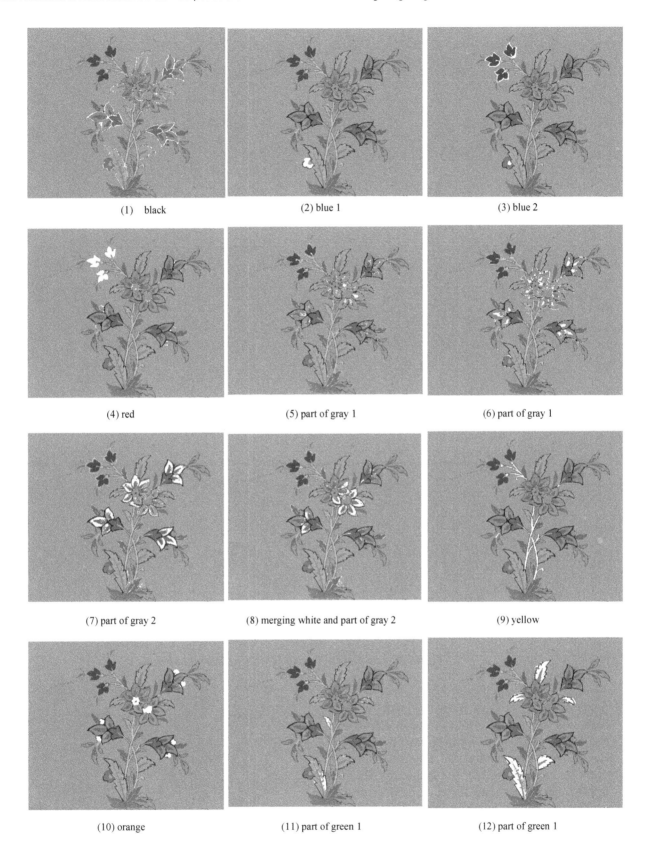

(1) black

(2) blue 1

(3) blue 2

(4) red

(5) part of gray 1

(6) part of gray 1

(7) part of gray 2

(8) merging white and part of gray 2

(9) yellow

(10) orange

(11) part of green 1

(12) part of green 1

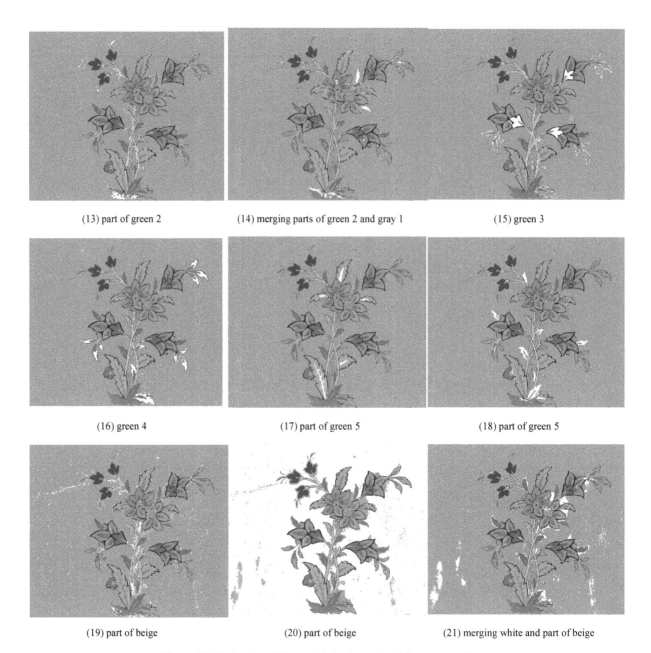

(13) part of green 2   (14) merging parts of green 2 and gray 1   (15) green 3

(16) green 4   (17) part of green 5   (18) part of green 5

(19) part of beige   (20) part of beige   (21) merging white and part of beige

Figure 16. Each color of figure 14c is shown in white, separately.

As mentioned in the previous sections, the previous methods have been designed for color reduction in machine-printed carpet cartoons and, due to the different conditions, are not efficient for hand-drawn cartoons. The methods are optimized to suit the color reduction in machine-printed carpet cartoons, and the methods are not accurate in other applications. Color reduction with the optimized C-means method [19] on part of a hand-drawn cartoon is shown in figure 17. As you can see, this result is not good for color reduction in hand-drawn cartoon.

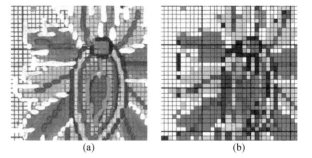

(a)   (b)

Figure 17. (a) A piece of hand-drawn carpet cartoon. (b) Image obtained by method of reference [19].

6. Conclusions

Using our proposed color reduction method, users will spend less time to convert hand-printed carpet cartoons, before discretization, into digital carpet cartoons.

Our method consists of several steps, experimentally tuned for the problem in hand. Performance of the method would have been very low if not using an appropriate technique in each step. Hence, in every part of the work, a technique is used highly appropriate for the carpet cartoons.

Steps of our method included image segmentation, finding the color of each plain region, color reduction of edgy regions with connected components labeling, and final color reduction with C-means.

In our method, the final colors and number of colors were not exactly the same as the desired colors. Since the quantitative evaluation was difficult, the qualitative evaluation of the results was selected.

References

[1] Brun, L. & Tr´emeau, A. (2002). Digital Color Imaging Handbook. CRC Press, pp. 589–638.

[2] Deng, Y. & Manjunath, B. (2001). Unsupervised Segmentation of Color-Texture Regions in Images and Video. IEEE Trans. on Pattern Analysis and Machine Intelligence, vol. 23, no. 8, pp. 800–810.

[3] Sherkat, N., Allen, T. & Wong, S. (2005). Use of Colour for Hand-Filled Form Analysis and Recognition. Pattern Analysis and Applications, vol. 8, no. 1, pp. 163–180.

[4] Sertel, O., Kong, J., Catalyurek, U. V., Lozanski, G., Saltz, J. H. & Gurcan, M. N. (2009). Histopathological Image Analysis Using Model-Based Intermediate Representations and Color Texture: Follicular Lymphoma Grading. Journal of Signal Processing Systems, vol. 55 no.1, pp. 169–183.

[5] Kuo, C.-T. & Cheng, S.-C. (2007). Fusion of Color Edge Detection and Color Quantization for Color ImageWatermarking Using Principal Axes Analysis. Pattern Recognition, vol. 40, no. 12, pp. 3691–3704.

[6] Deng, Y., Manjunath, B., Kenney, C., Moore, M. & Shin, H. (2001). An Efficient Color Representation for Image Retrieval. IEEE Trans. on Image Processing, vol. 10, no. 1, pp. 140–147.

[7] Kaur, E. N. & Kaur, E. S. (2015). Color Image Reduction using Genetic Algorithm. International Journal of Electronics Communication and Computer Engineering, vol. 6, no. 2, pp. 319-323.

[8] El-Said, S. A. (2015). Image quantization using improved artificial fish swarm algorithm. Soft Computing, vol. 19, no. 9, pp. 2667–2679.

[9] Celebi, M. E. (2011). Improving the Performance of K-Means for Color Quantization. Image and Vision Computing, vol. 29, no. 4, pp. 260–271.

[10] Mojsilovic, A. & Soljanin, E. (2001). Color Quantization and Processing by Fibonacci Lattices. IEEE Trans. On Image Processing, vol. 10, no. 11, pp. 1712–1725.

[11] Gervautz, M. & Purgathofer, W. (1988) A Simple Method for Color Quantization: Octree Quantization. New Trends in Computer Graphics, Springer-Verlag, pp. 219–231.

[12] Heckbert, P. (1982). Color Image Quantization for Frame Buffer Display. ACM SIGGRAPH Computer Graphics, vol. 16, no. 3, pp. 297–307.

[13] Wan, S., Prusinkiewicz, P. & Wong, S. (1990). Variance-Based Color Image Quantization for Frame Buffer Display. Color Research and Application, vol. 15, no. 1, pp. 52–58.

[14] Joy, G. & Xiang, Z. (1993). Center-Cut for Color Image Quantization. The Visual Computer, vol. 10, no. 1, pp. 62–66.

[15] Orchard, M. & Bouman, C. (1991). Color Quantization of Images. IEEE Trans. on Signal Processing, vol. 39, no. 12, pp. 2677–2690.

[16] Yang, C.-Y. & Lin, J.-C. (1996). RWM-Cut for Color Image Quantization. Computers and Graphics, vol. 20, no. (4), pp. 577–588.

[17] Kanjanawanishkul, K. & Uyyanonvara, B. (2005). Novel Fast Color Reduction Algorithm for Time-Constrained Appli-cations. Journal of Visual Communication and Image Representation, vol. 16, no. 3, pp. 311–332.

[18] Brun, L. & Mokhtari, M. (2000). Two High Speed Color Quantization Algorithms. in: Proc. of the 1st Int. Conf. on Color in Graphics and Image Processing, pp. 116–121.

[19] Izadipour, A. & Kabir, E.A. (2010). A method for automatic printing carpet map reading and comparing to C-means clustering. Iranian Journal of Electrical and Computer Engineering, vol. 8, no. 1, pp. 49-56.

[20] Huang, Y.-L. & Chang, R.-F. (2004). A Fast Finite-State Algorithm for Generating RGB Palettes of Color Quantized Images. Journal of Information Science and Engineering, vol. 20, no. 4, pp. 771–782.

[21] Hu, Y.-C. & Lee, M.-G. (2007) K-means Based Color Palette Design Scheme with the Use of Stable Flags. Journal of Electronic Imaging, vol. 16, no. 3, pp. 003–033.

[22] Hu, Y.-C. & Su, B.-H. (2008). Accelerated K-means Clustering Algorithm for Colour Image Quantization. Imaging Science Journal, vol. 56, no. 1, pp. 29–40.

[23] Xiang, Z. (1997) Color Image Quantization by Minimizing the Maximum Intercluster Distance. ACM Trans. On Graphics, vol. 16, no. 3, pp. 260–276.

[24] Celebi, M. E. (2009). An Effective Color Quantization Method Based on the Competitive

Learning Paradigm. in: Proc. of the 2009 Int. Conf. on Image Processing, Computer Vision, and Pattern Recognition, pp. 876–880,.

[25] Celebi, M. E. & Schaefer, G. (2010). Neural Gas Clustering for Color Reduction. in: Proc. of the 2010 Int. Conf. on Image Processing,Computer Vision, and Pattern Recognition, pp. 429–432.

[26] Izakian, Z. & Mesgari, M. S. (2015). Fuzzy clustering of time series data: A particle swarm optimization approach. Journal of AI and Data Mining, vol. 3, no. 1, pp. 39-46.

[27] Schaefer, G. & Zhou, H. (2009). Fuzzy Clustering for Colour Reduction in Images. Telecommunication Systems, vol. 40, no. 1, pp. 17–25.

[28] Bing, Z., Junyi, S. & Qinke, P. (2004). An Adjustable Algorithm for Color Quantization. Pattern Recognition Letters, vol. 25, no. 16, pp. 1787–1797.

[29] Papamarkos, N., Atsalakis, A.E. & Strouthopoulos, C.P. (2002). Adaptive color reduction. IEEE Transaction on systems, vol. 32, no. 1, pp. 44-56.

[30] Chang, C.-H., Xu, P., Xiao, R. & Srikanthan, T. (2005). New Adaptive Color Quantization Method Based on Self-Organizing Maps. IEEE Trans. on Neural Networks, vol. 16, no. 1, pp. 237–249.

[31] Celebi, M. E., Wen, Q. & Hwang, S. (2015). An effective real-time color quantization method based on divisive hierarchical clustering. Journal of Real-Time Image Processing, vol. 10, no. 2, pp. 329-344.

[32] Atsalakis, A. & Papamarkos, N. (2006). Color reduction and estimation of the number of dominant colors by using a self-growing and self-organized neural gas. Engineering Applications of Artificial Intelligence 19, pp. 769–786.

[33] Ghanbarian, A. T., Kabir, E. & Charkari, N. M. (2007). Color reduction based on ant colony. Pattern Recognition Letters, vol. 28, no. 12, pp. 1383–1390.

[34] Zuva, T., Olugbara, O. O., Ojo, S. O., Ngwira & S. M. (2011). Image Segmentation, Available Techniques, Developments and Open Issues. Journal on Image Processing and Computer Vision, vol. 2, no. 3, pp. 20-29.

[35] Wang, Y., Guo, Q. & Zhu, Y. (2007). Medical image segmentation based on deformable models and its applications. Springer, pp. 209-260.

[36] Booria CAD/CAM Systems, (2017), retrieved from http://www.booria.com/index-fa.html .

[37] Naqshsaz Software, (2017), retrieved from http://naqshsaz.persianblog.ir/ .

[38] Fateh, M., Kabir, E. & Nili Ahmadabadi, M. (2011). Color reduction for machine-printed carpet pattern by reinforcement learning. Iranian Journal of Electrical and Computer Engineering, vol. 9, no. 3, pp. 133-142.

[39] Fateh, M. & Kabir, E. (2012). Automatic reading of hand-painted carpet patterns. Iranian Journal of Computational Intelligence in Electrical Engineering, vol. 3, no. 2, pp. 15-30.

[40] Iran Carpet Company, (2014), retrieved from www.irancarpet.ir .

[41] Carpet museum of Iran, (2014), retrieved from http://carpetmuseum.ir/home.htm .

[42] Color quantization software, (2014), retrieved from http://www.colorpilot.com/layer.html .

15

Camera Pose Estimation in Unknown Environments using a Sequence of Wide-Baseline Monocular Images

S. A Hoseini and P. Kabiri[*]

Department of Computer Engineering, Iran University of Science and Technology, Tehran, Iran.

Corresponding author: peyman.kabiri@iust.ac.ir (P. Kabiri).

Abstract

In this work, a feature-based technique is proposed for the camera pose estimation in a sequence of wide-baseline images. Camera pose estimation is an important issue in many computer vision and robotics applications such as augmented reality and visual SLAM. The developed method can track captured images taken by a hand-held camera in room-sized workspaces with a maximum scene depth of 3-4 m. This system can be used in unknown environments with no additional information available from the outside world except in the first two images used for initialization. Pose estimation is performed using only natural feature points extracted and matched in successive images. In wide-baseline images, unlike consecutive frames of a video stream, displacement of the feature points in consecutive images is notable, and hence, cannot be traced easily using the patch-based methods. To handle this problem, a hybrid strategy is employed to obtain accurate feature correspondences. In this strategy, first, initial feature correspondences are found using the similarity between their descriptors, and then the outlier matchings are removed by applying the RANSAC algorithm. Further, in order to provide a set of required feature matchings, a mechanism based on the sidelong result of robust estimator is employed. The proposed method is applied on indoor real data with images in VGA quality (640 × 480 pixels), and on average, the translation error of camera pose is less than 2 cm, which indicates the effectiveness and accuracy of the developed approach.

Keywords: *Camera Pose Estimation, Feature Extraction, Feature Correspondence, Bundle Adjustment, Depth Estimation.*

1. Introduction

Camera pose estimation is one of the key issues in computer vision. In many applications, it is critical to know where the camera is located. The accurate and robust estimation of the camera position and orientation is essential for a variety of applications including 3D reconstruction, augmented reality, and visual Simultaneous Localization and Mapping (visual SLAM).

Camera tracking for a sequence of video frames is exactly the problem of camera pose estimation for each frame. For the adjacent frames of a video sequence, the camera pose has a negligible change. Moreover, the motion vector of the scene features between successive frames can be discovered using a simple patch-based similarity measure. Conversely, for wide-baseline sequences, estimation of the motion vector for feature points is not a simple task. In the computer vision literature, wide-baseline images refer to a condition where the distance between the camera center for adjacent images is noticeable or the camera orientation changes remarkably. Moreover, once the internal parameters of the camera change (i.e. zooming), the resulting images simulate the wide-baseline situation. In contrast, when the camera motion is smooth, the camera center for adjacent frames are close to each other. This leads to a negligible displacement of the points of interest in consecutive frames. This case is usually referred to as narrow-baseline. There are situations where it is more reasonable to estimate camera pose for a sequence of wide-baseline images. Reducing the computational cost, some video tracking algorithms are based upon the selected key-frames. These key-frames often form a sequence of wide-baseline frames. Also for low-quality images (like VGA), a quick movement of camera may result in a sequence of several blurred frames. Feature tracking along blurred frames is a challenging task. Hence, it is better to ignore them. The wide-baseline situation is resulted due to ignoring the successive frames. Furthermore, using a limited number of images may considerably speed up the reconstruction process.

Nevertheless, it is worth noting that the wide-baseline setting often allows a more accurate depth calculation. An increase in the depth accuracy is due to a larger, and hence, more reliable measurable disparities in the images. However, there are configurations (i.e. when the camera has rotation about its optical axis) in which the motion vector for tracked features varies significantly. In these situations, some features may introduce small disparities, while others have remarkable displacements.

For a wide-baseline case, determining the feature correspondences is a challenging task. However, with the advent of local descriptors, finding similar regions within the images taken from different viewpoints became promising. In the subsequent sections, some outstanding descriptor-based feature extractors will be introduced.

Occlusion is yet another problem for the wide-baseline case. Some features may be occluded when the camera undergoes remarkable changes in viewpoint. Occlusion usually reduces the number of matched features. It may also lead to false matchings. Generally, mitigating the undesired effects of occlusion or any problem that produces false matchings, robust estimators such as Least Median (LMed) [1] or Random Sample Consensus (RANSAC) [2] is employed. As a result, the incorrect feature correspondences are eliminated.

In this paper, the problem of camera pose estimation for a sequence of wide-baseline monocular images is addressed. The images are captured with a single camera from adjacent locations in such a way that the overlapping regions in consecutive images are adequate for obtaining the common features. On the other hand, the area of overlapping regions is not large enough to provide the feature point correspondences through correlation windows.

Camera pose estimation and 3D reconstruction are tightly coupled, i.e. to estimate the parameters of the camera motion, it is necessary to have sufficient information about the 3D structure of the scene. On the other hand, triangulating depth of newly extracted features, it is necessary to have

the camera pose from two or more views available.

1.1. Pose parameters

As depicted in figure 1, a moving camera captures images of the environment from arbitrary positions. For each view, pose of the camera is composed of two parts: the rotation matrix $R \in \mathbf{R}^{3\times3}$, which is an orthogonal matrix with $\det(R)=1$ that describes the orientation of camera, and the translation vector $t \in \mathbf{R}^3$ that indicates the distance between the origin of camera coordinate system and the world coordinate system. Accordingly, (1) is established for every 3D point in the scene [3].

$$X_c = RX_w + t \tag{1}$$

X_c, X_w are the coordinates of the 3D point with respect to the camera and world coordinate systems, respectively.

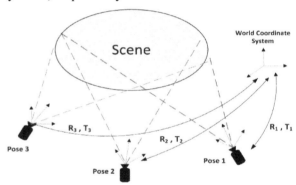

Figure 1. Multi-view camera pose estimation.

The structure of this paper is as what follows. The related works are discussed in Section 2. In Section 3, the proposed approach will be explained in details. The experimental results are presented in Section 4. Finally, the conclusions and future works are included in Section 5.

2. Relative work

Camera tracking or estimation of camera pose parameters for sequence of video frames that represents the narrow-baseline situation has been widely studied. In this research area, two main solution categories exist, i.e. Structure from Motion (SfM) and filtering. The SfM approach uses the epipolar geometry principles to solve the problem. Often to refine the estimated parameters of the camera and the depth of feature points, an additional optimization stage is required. Bundle Adjustment (BA) [4] and pose map [5] are two main strategies used for this purpose. Parallel Tracking and Mapping is a prominent work that uses BA to optimize the estimated camera Pose [6]. Some researchers have employed the pose map optimization technique to improve the accuracy of the estimated camera trajectory [7, 8]. In filtering approaches, the problem is cast in the shape of a dynamic system in which the camera pose parameters constitute the internal state of the system. Furthermore, the state transition of the system is usually a non-linear relation based on the physical nature of rigid body motion in 3D space. Meanwhile, the projection of 3D features on image plane using current rotation and translation of camera introduces the observation model of the system. Mostly, due to the non-linear nature of transition and observation model, variants of Kalman filter such as Extended Kalman Filter (EKF) and Unscented Kalman Filter (UKF) are used for pose estimation [9, 10]. Particle Filter (PF) is another solution in the context of dynamic systems, which is utilized for this purpose [11-13]. As opposed to the narrow-baseline case, the filtering techniques for wide-baseline are not easily applicable. This is due to the fact that in filtering approaches, the motion model definition is usually meaningful for small changes in the system state. However, it is not the case for the wide-baseline condition. Hence, it is more realistic to exploit SFM to handle Camera pose estimation for the wide-baseline images.

In any case, the necessary information to obtain orientation and translation of the camera is a set of point correspondences in two or more views. If these correspondences are given in 3D-3D matchings, then it is the subject of absolute orientation problem that can be solved easily using closed-form solutions proposed for this problem [14-16]. When the supplied correspondences are in the form of 3D-2D matchings, then the problem is known as Perspective n Point (PnP) in computer vision literature for which Several solutions are proposed [17, 18]. Sometimes the available information is only some 2D-2D correspondences. In such circumstances, using the notion of fundamental matrix and epipolar geometry, the camera pose parameters are estimated with ambiguity. On the other hand, multiple solutions are obtained. In order to achieve a unique solution, it is necessary to have extra information about the observed scene.

It is well-known that receiving no information about the depth of extracted scene features produces drift in camera trajectory, and increases the cumulative error, i.e. for a freely-moving camera, the captured images provide information about the geometry of the scene that can be recovered up to a scale factor using the multi-view geometry. Dealing with this problem, some

researches put markers or fiducials with known structures in the scene to control the cumulative error [19, 20]. Using multiple markers in the scene could also increase the accuracy of camera pose parameters [21].

Exploiting reference calibrated images is another technique for camera tracking in unknown environments [22, 23]. The calibrated images are those with known 3D coordinate for a sparse set of features. With reference images, the process of pose estimation reduces to data association between each new image and the reference images.

The two main contributions of this work are summarized as follow:

1) **Feature correspondences**. In order to provide a sufficient number of matched features, a combination of feature matchings based on similarity of feature descriptors and homography matrix is adopted.

2) **Propagation of depth information**. In order to enable the proposed system for estimation of the camera pose of each incoming image, a novel strategy is adopted to propagate depth information of already extracted features to subsequent images.

3. Proposed method

An overview of the proposed framework is initially presented in figure 2. In the proposed method, after the arrival of each new image, the process of camera pose estimation is performed in two stages, obtaining the matched features and estimation of camera pose parameters. To provide robust matchings, the extraction of salient and repetitive feature points is necessary. The feature extraction step will be elaborated in section 3.2. Thereafter, the extracted feature points should be matched with those of the previous image. The matchings obtained that are robust enough are used for estimation of the camera pose parameters. In Section 3.3, the issue of finding the feature point correspondences and refining them will be discussed. In the next step, camera pose for the current image is retrieved by utilizing the obtained correspondences. Since retrieving the camera pose parameters is based upon 3D-2D matchings, it is required that the depth of sufficient number of feature points among the obtained correspondences already estimated.

In the reported method, a collection of feature points with a known 3D coordinate is updated for each new image. We called this collection as fully active features. This means that with every new image, the newly extracted feature points that were matched in two recent images will be added to the previously collected feature set. Furthermore, estimating the pose parameters of the camera based on 3D-2D matchings, the feature points with known 3D coordinates are selected from this collection. It should be noted that the 3D position of fully active features is measured with respect to the world coordinate system.

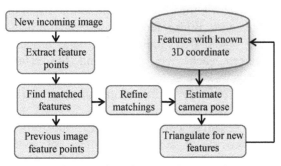

Figure 2. Overview of proposed approach.

Since the unknown parameters for camera pose estimation and depth of feature points are estimated incrementally, the associated error is accumulative. Minimizing the accumulative error, in the final step, a windowed bundle adjustment is applied to optimize the estimated pose parameters for all the input images.

In the proposed framework, there is no way to recover the depth of newly added features except using the structure of features with determined 3D position. From a set of 2D-2D matchings in two or more images, it is only possible to estimate the depth of corresponding features with a scale factor [24]. This limitation enforces the algorithm to start from a calibrated image, i.e. initially, a small amount of prior information about the scene in the form of known targets should be available. In the proposed system, a chessboard with known size is placed in front of the camera. This provides a set of feature points (corners of the chessboard cells) with known positions in the world coordinate system that allows us to estimate camera pose parameters for the first and second images. At the same time, natural features extracted and matched are triangulated using camera poses in the first and second images. Then the depth information of these features will be propagated to the subsequent images.

3.1. Wide-baseline situation

As explained earlier, in wide-baseline images, displacement of the corresponding feature points are noticeable with respect to the image size. This issue is illustrated in figure 3. The feature point displacement in two images depends upon the amount of changes in the pose parameters of the camera and the depth of the observed scene. If the

camera undergoes a significant change in position or orientation for two consecutive poses, then the associated images will be less overlapped. Hence, using the traditional patch-based similarity measures such as the sum of squared differences or normalized cross-correlation are not practical for data association. This is due to the fact that these measures are convenient for small changes in the camera view, which is not the case in the wide-baseline situation. Moreover, in cases where the distance of the camera from the scene is notable, applying a slight motion to the camera results in a noticeable displacement of the feature points. The aforementioned issues in the wide-baseline condition make the problem of feature matching a challenging task.

In addition, each feature is only visible in a small number of images. This problem causes that the necessity for triangulation of newly extracted features occurs more frequently.

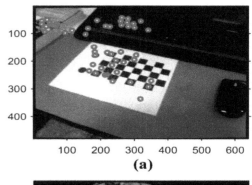

(a)

(b)

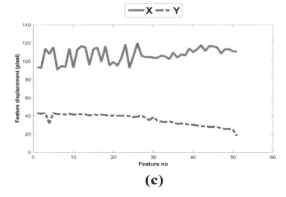

(c)

Figure 3. Wide-baseline condition (a) and (b) sparse set of feature correspondences (c) displacement of corresponding features in X and Y directions.

3.2. Feature extraction

In the proposed approach, in order to determine the relationship between images, a feature-based method is utilized. In the feature-based methods, different entities such as points, lines, region or objects can be selected as the feature. However, among them, the point features are better than the others since they are easier to detect and match. In addition, the number of detected feature points is usually more than the other types of features, and hence, it is more likely to observe them in the successive images. Many algorithms are presented to extract the feature points in images. The corners are well-known feature points. They are usually considered as the intersection of two edges. The corners may also be defined as a point where two dominant and different edge directions exist in its local neighbourhood.

Harris [25] and SUZAN [26] are famous corner detectors used in many image processing and computer vision areas such as image registration, image mosaicing, panorama stitching, and object recognition. The corners are suitable features to track in video frames since they are easily detected in successive frames and can be matched using patch-based approaches with simple similarity measures such as the sum of absolute differences or normalized cross-correlation. In contrast, for wide-baseline images, as explained earlier, image pixels undergo a remarkable displacement. Hence, it is necessary to employ features that contain descriptor. Recently, several descriptor-based feature extraction approaches have been proposed. Scale Invariant Feature Transform (SIFT) [27], Speeded-Up Robust Features (SURF) [28], and Binary Robust Invariant Scalable Keypoints (BRISK) [29] are three strong and reliable ones. They first detect the location of the feature points and then construct the associated descriptor vector from the information of image in the neighborhood of the detected location. The related descriptor vectors are invariant to scale, rotation, viewpoint, and illumination changes. This allows us to find the corresponding features using the associated descriptors by means of a simple similarity measure.

In the proposed method, the SIFT feature points were employed due to their high distinctiveness and repeatability. The generated descriptors for SIFT features are very powerful for match finding along enough overlapped images.

3.3. Feature matching and refinement

Providing accurate feature correspondences is a significant step for estimating a robust and precise camera pose parameters. As explained earlier, tracking feature points is highly susceptible to the production of incorrect matched features. Handling this problem, we require following the "detect and match" strategy to obtain the feature correspondences. In other words, initially, each incoming image SIFT features are detected, and then the presence of shared features in both the current and earlier images are matched. This task is achieved using a similarity measure between the feature descriptors. In the reported work, the cosine distance was used for this purpose, as given in (2).

$$d(D_i, D_j) = 1 - \frac{D_i^T . D_j}{\|D_i\| . \|D_j\|} \qquad (2)$$

where, $\|.\|$ denotes the L2-norm. The L2-norm of descriptor difference is also possible but it is computationally more expensive. Since the SIFT descriptors have unit norm, the similarity measure between them is calculated by a simple dot product.

The feature correspondences obtained by comparing the feature descriptors may include mismatched feature pairs, i.e. several features in the first image might be matched with a shared feature in the second image as the closest one with a minimum cosine distance. Deciding which matched feature in the second image is the correct one, the mutual consistency check is established. In order to do so, the features in the second image are paired with the features in the first one, and those that are matched in both directions are selected. This routine guarantees the mutual consistency between the matched features.

Thus the matched features may contain wrong matchings due to noise or repetitive textures. Wrong correspondences are called outliers that violate spatial consistency of image. For an accurate estimation of camera pose, these outliers should be rejected. The outlier removal is based upon the geometric constraints introduced by the motion model. RANSAC is a standard technique used for estimating the parameters of a model in the presence of outliers. The RANSAC algorithm produces the inlier correspondences as well as the parameters of the assumed model. These parameters are encoded into a 3 × 3 homography matrix (H), and for every feature correspondence $u_1 \leftrightarrow u_2$, the following equation holds:

$$\lambda u_2 = H u_1 \qquad (3)$$

u_1, u_2 are in homogeneous coordinates, and λ is the projective scaling factor. Since H is computed using the inlier correspondences, given u_1 and H, the approximate location of u_2 in the second image can be obtained. This issue will be exploited in the next section to find the paired features in specific situations.

In figure 4, feature matchings by comparison of the descriptor vectors are marked with empty red circles. The refined matchings are also illustrated with blue asterisks surrounded by a red circle. Some matchings depicted with empty red circles are not selected after refinements, even though they are visually appeared correct matchings. It is due to the fact that during the matching refinement operation, some visually correct matchings are rejected to ensure that the selected matchings are reliable.

Frame K

Frame K+1

Figure 4. Feature points marked with empty red circles are output of feature matching routine, and those marked with blue asterisks surrounded in red circles are refined matchings based on RANSAC algorithm.

3.4. Providing 3D-2D matchings

In the core of our system, the pose parameters are estimated using a set of 3D-2D feature correspondences. In the previous section, it was explained how the set of paired features were adopted. Now it is necessary to provide a collection of 3D-2D feature matchings. However, in order to be able to estimate camera pose for the current image, it is required to have at least four non-coplanar 3D-2D feature matchings.

Moreover, to achieve more accurate and reliable results, it is better to include more matchings.

Figure 5 shows the overall scheme of the adopted strategy to manage the obtained feature matchings to estimate the camera pose and to triangulate the partially active features. Let θ_k be the set of SIFT features extracted in the current image (I_k) and $\lambda_{k-1}, \gamma_{k-1}$ be the set of fully active and partially active features in the previous image (I_{k-1}). With fully active features, we mean those features whose depths are already estimated, and the partially active features are those with unknown depth but potential for matching with extracted features of the next image. From the matchings obtained in the current image, we define FA_k, PA_k as the set of ordered pairs of matchings established with fully (red arrows) and partially (green arrows) active features of I_{k-1}, respectively.

$$FA_k = \{(u_1, u_2) \mid u_1 \in \lambda_{k-1}, u_2 \in \theta_k\},$$
$$PA_k = \{(u_1, u_2) \mid u_1 \in \gamma_{k-1}, u_2 \in \theta_k\} \tag{4}$$

If the number of matchings in FA_k is greater than a pre-defined threshold, then the camera pose is computed using a method that will be explained in the next section. Immediately after that, the features belonging to γ_{k-1} are triangulated, and therefore, added to λ_k for the next stage. On the other hand, they are moved from the partially active to fully active features list.

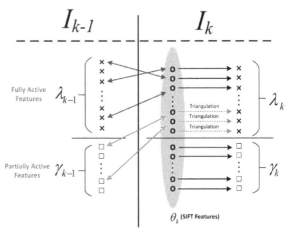

Figure 5. Overall scheme of adopted strategy followed to manage fully and partially active features.

Conversely, if the cardinality of FA_k is less than the aforementioned threshold, to recover more accurate pose parameters, we must provide more correct matchings. Doing so, the features belonging to λ_{k-1} that are not matched to any member of θ_k are moved to the new image using the homography matrix obtained from the correspondence refinement routine applied in the previous step. Some of these moved features may appear outside the image boundaries, which will be discarded. Moreover, the moved features may not accurately coincide with their true location but they can be searched within a window centred at the moved feature (blue window). Since the images are wide-baseline, searching for a precise location of matching feature within this window using simple patch-based similarity measures may lead to erroneous results.

As depicted in figure 6, u_1 is moved to u_1' using the homography matrix, while u_2 is its true correspondence. Hence, in order to obtain correct matchings, a square patch around the feature in I_{k-1} is warped using the homography matrix (red patch), and then this warped patch is searched in the foregoing window using normalized cross correlation.

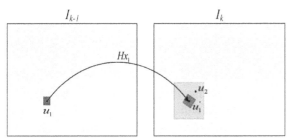

I_{k-1} I_k

Figure 6. Obtaining correspondence based on homography matrix.

3.5. Pose estimation

After determination of matched points, we proceed to estimate the camera pose parameters. As explained in the algorithm outline, the camera orientation and translation for each incoming image is estimated directly with respect to the world referential system. As illustrated in figure 7, given a set of 3D-2D feature correspondences, we aim at finding camera pose parameters embedded in the camera projection matrix. Let X_w be the world coordinate of a scene point and u be its projection on image plane; then (5) holds.

$$\lambda u = P X_w = K(R X_w + T), \text{ with}$$

$$K = \begin{bmatrix} \alpha_x & \gamma & u_0 \\ 0 & \alpha_y & v_0 \\ 0 & 0 & 1 \end{bmatrix} \quad (5)$$

where, P is the camera matrix, and R *and* T are the rotation matrix and translation vector, respectively. K is the calibration matrix that contains intrinsic parameters of the camera. α_x, α_y represent the focal length in terms of

pixels, and γ is the skew coefficient between the x, y axes and is often zero. u_0, v_0 are the principal point of the camera, which would be ideally at the centre of the image.

In this paper, in order to estimate the parameters of the camera pose in each step, the EPnP method, which has been proposed by Lepetit et al. [30] is used. EPnP is a non-iterative method with computation complexity of order O(n). As most of the solutions to the PnP problem, it tries to estimate the coordinate of reference points in the camera coordinate system. Then the orientation and translation of the camera with respect to the world coordinate is computed based on a series of 3D-3D matchings using the solutions proposed for absolute orientation problem.

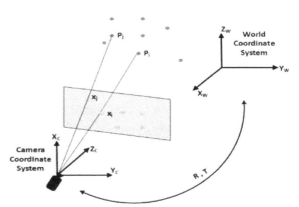

Figure 7. Camera pose estimation using 3D-2D feature points matchings.

3.6. Depth Estimation for new features

Given a feature correspondence $u_i \leftrightarrow u_{i+1}$ and camera poses encoded in camera projection matrices P_i and P_{i+1}, we are going to estimate the 3D coordinate of the associated features in the world coordinate system. According to (5), we have:

$$\lambda_i u_i = P_i X_w = \begin{pmatrix} P_{i,1}^T \\ P_{i,2}^T \\ P_{i,3}^T \end{pmatrix} X_w, \quad (6)$$

where, u_i, X_w are in homogenous coordinate, and $P_{i,1}^T, P_{i,2}^T, P_{i,3}^T$ are rows of the camera matrix P_i. Expanding (6), three equations with respect to unknown components of X_w are constructed, which are not linearly independent. Actually, two of them are independent, as given in (7).

$$\begin{cases} P_{i,3}^T x_i = P_{i,1}^T X_w \\ P_{i,3}^T y_i = P_{i,2}^T X_w \end{cases} \quad (7)$$

The same equations hold for u_{i+1}, as follow:

$$\begin{cases} P_{i+1,3}^T x_{i+1} = P_{i+1,1}^T X_w \\ P_{i+1,3}^T y_{i+1} = P_{i+1,2}^T X_w \end{cases} \qquad (8)$$

Putting together (7) and (8) and writing them in the matrix form, a linear system with four equations in the form of AX = 0 is obtained. This matrix equation can be solved using Singular Value Decomposition (SVD). It is worth noting that if a feature appears in more than two images, then the number of equations in the AX = 0 equation increase by the number of two for any added image. Considering the appearance of a feature in more than two images, the estimated depth for the corresponding point in the scene is more robust.

The above computations are applied to all new feature correspondences that are selected for inclusion in fully active features. This increases the possibility of finding enough matchings for the next incoming image.

4. Experimental results

We used a freely moving hand-held camera to capture images of a calibrated scene. The captured images were selected so that they properly represented a wide-baseline situation. Resolution of the captured images was 480×640 pixels and the algorithm works with greyscale images. It was assumed that the camera was calibrated in advance. The camera calibration was performed utilizing a flexible technique presented by zhengyou [31]. To this end, a collection of images of a chessboard with a known size taken from different viewpoints were used to estimate the intrinsic parameters of the camera. The correspondence between corners of chessboard cells and their projection on each image were then detected. Thereafter, the internal parameters of the camera were estimated by means of a closed-form solution using the correspondences obtained between the planar model and its image. The parameters obtained were then refined using a non-linear refinement based on the maximum likelihood.

A significant problem in evaluating the accuracy of the camera pose estimation methods is the lack of ground-truth data. Obtaining true pose of a moving camera w.r.t. world coordinate system is not a simple task. Using an accurate motion capture system with multiple high speed cameras is a good choice for generation of the ground-truth data. As an example of this method, Sturm et al. [32] have employed a motion capture system to construct a benchmark for the evaluation of RGB-D SLAM systems. It is also possible to generate

the translation part of the camera pose manually. Davison et al. [33] have used a hand-held camera equipped with a plump-line of known length and a hanging weight skimmed to a pre-prepared rectangular track on a cluttered desk to measure the ground-truth 3D coordinate of camera at corners of track. It is clear that measuring orientation of the camera manually is not very accurate. In order to overcome this limitation, a marker-based method was employed to generate the Ground-Truth data for camera pose. Calculation of the camera pose parameters is accompanied by correspondence of easily detectable marker points on a planar surface and their projections on image plane. In our experiments, the scene was a computer desk cluttered with various objects. A planar chessboard pattern (our marker) was stuck on it that was used for calculation of ground-truth camera pose.

At the beginning, for the first two frames, the camera pose parameters were calculated using planar chessboard markers. From the third frame onwards, estimation of camera pose parameters was carried out exploiting the natural features that were correctly matched as explained earlier.

Figure 8(a) shows the visibility of the extracted features in the input images. As it could be seen, most of the features were visible only in small numbers of images (four images in our experiment). In figure 8(b), the number of matched features before refinement after refinement and the matchings with a known depth is shown. It is obvious that the number of refined matchings is less than the number initial matchings and greater than the number of matchings with a known depth, which is an expected result.

Figure 9 illustrates the trajectory of camera in a 3D space as well as its projection on the XY plane. In spite of getting no information from the environment, the camera was tracked with sufficient precision, and its pose was estimated very close to the ground-truth data. Assume that t_{est}^k, t_{true}^k is the estimated and Ground-Truth translation part of camera pose and e_t^k is the associated error computed for I_k, as given in (9).

$$e_t^k = abs(t_{est}^k - t_{true}^k) = (e_{t,x}^k, e_{t,y}^k, e_{t,z}^k)^T \qquad (9)$$

where, $abs(.)$ denotes the absolute value function. Similarly, $r_{est}^k, r_{true}^k, e_r^k$ are defined for the rotation part of camera pose. It is worth noting that the components of rotation error were given in Euler angle representation and measured in radian.

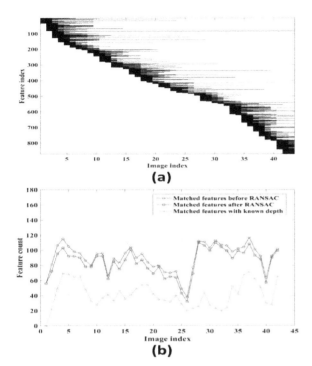

(a)

(b)

Figure 8. (a) Visibility of extracted features in images (b) Number of matched features before RANSAC after RANSAC and those matched with features whose depth is known.

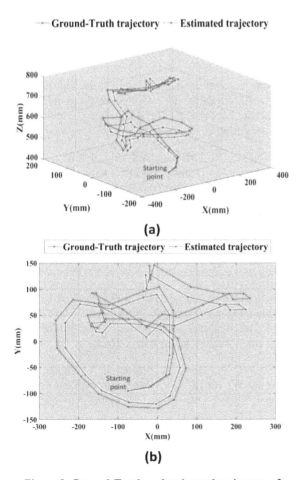

(a)

(b)

Figure 9. Ground-Truth and estimated trajectory of camera (a) in 3D and (b) projection on XY plane.

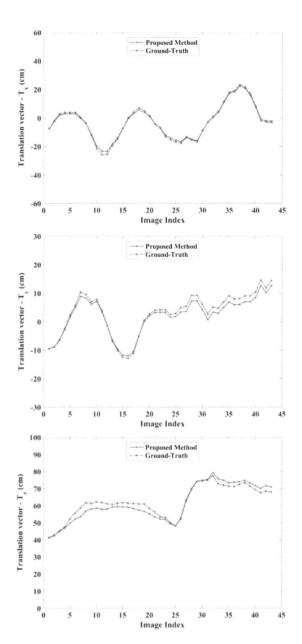

Figure 10. Estimated camera translation vector against Ground-Truth data.

Accordingly, the statistics of translation and rotation errors over all images are detailed in table 1. In figure 10, the translation components of camera pose are visualized against the computed Ground-Truth data. As it is shown, camera pose drift is negligible and the true trajectory of the camera has properly been followed.

Figure 11(a) shows the relative translation of camera center between successive images obtained from the Ground-Truth data. Figure 11(b) depicts the number of refined matchings. As illustrated in these two figures, there is a close relationship between the number of refined matchings and the translation part of camera relative pose. On the other hand, with increase in the distance of camera center in two consecutive images, the number of correct matchings was reduced.

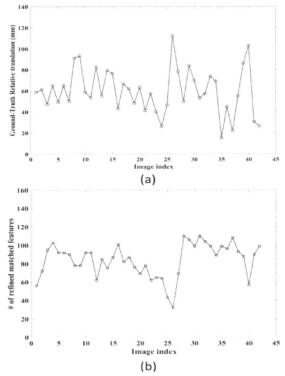

(a)

(b)

Figure 11. (a) Ground-Truth relative translation (b) Number of refined matched features between successive frames.

Table 1. Tranlation and rotation error.

	Translation error (mm)			Rotation error (radian)		
	$e_{t,x}$	$e_{t,y}$	$e_{t,z}$	$e_{r,x}$	$e_{r,y}$	$e_{r,z}$
Mean	8.41	11.89	21.46	0.17	0.26	0.08
Std	5.08	6.79	13.34	0.12	0.11	0.07
Min	0.94	0.34	0.13	0.03	0.01	0.01
Max	24.19	21.05	51.46	0.51	0.46	0.29

5. Conclusions and future works

In this work, a camera pose estimation approach was proposed for a sequence of wide-baseline images. It was considered that the camera was calibrated, and the overlapping area of the successive images was enough for acquiring a sufficient number of corresponding feature points. In the reported work, the experiments show that at least 60% of the consecutive images should be overlapped to ensure that a sufficient number of matchings are obtained.

Finding feature correspondences is the main challenge. This challenge is due to the inherent nature of wide-baseline images, in which the feature points have considerable displacement in consecutive images. In the reported work, with the exception of the first two images, no additional information about pose of the camera or position of any landmark in the scene is fed into the system. For each new image, pose of the camera was estimated according to a set of 3D-2D correspondences.

A problem that should be kept in mind is that when the number of images increases, the cumulative error for orientation and translation of camera will increase as well. If the system receives no information from the environment, then at a point in the future the error will overshoot, and as a result, the trajectory of camera undergoes an uncontrolled drift. In order to overcome this problem, it is required to either acquire some information from the scene or try to close the loop. We planned to consider the latter case in our future works. One can also investigate other feature point extractors other than SIFT and then compare the results.

References

[1] Massart, D. L., Kaufman, L., Rousseeuw, P. J. & Leroy, A. (1986). Least median of squares: a robust method for outlier and model error detection in regression and calibration. Analytica Chimica Acta, vol. 187, pp. 171-179.

[2] Fischler, M. A. & Bolles, R. C. (1981). Random sample consensus: a paradigm for model fitting with applications to image analysis and automated cartography. Communications of the ACM, vol. 24, pp. 381-395.

[3] Ma, Y., Soatto, S., Kosecka, J. & Sastry, S. S. (2003). An Invitation to 3-D Vision: From Images to Geometric Models. Berlin, Heidelberg. New York: SpringerVerlag.

[4] Triggs, B., McLauchlan, P., Hartley, R. & Fitzgibbon, A. (1999). Bundle Adjustment — A Modern Synthesis. International workshop on vision algorithms, Corfu, Greece, 1999.

[5] Kümmerle, R., Giorgio, G., Strsdat, H., Konolige, K. & Burgard, W. (2011). g2o: A General framework for Graph Optimization. IEEE international Conference on Robotics and Automation, Shanghai, China, 2011.

[6] Kelein, G. & murray, D. (2007). Parallel Tracking and Mapping for Small AR Workspaces. 6th IEEE and ACM International Symposium on Mixed and Augmented Reality, Nara, Japan, 2007.

[7] Endres, F., Hess, J., Sturm, J., Cremers, D. & Burgard, W. (2014). 3-D Mapping with an RGB-D Camera. IEEE Transactions on Robotics, vol. 29, no. 1, pp. 177-187.

[8] Engel, J., Schöps, T. & Cremers, D. (2014). LSD-SLAM: Large-Scale Direct Monocular SLAM. 13th European Conference on Computer Vision, Zurich, Switzerland, 2014.

[9] Jain, S. & Neumann, U. (2006). Real-time Camera Pose and Focal Length Estimation. 18th International Conference on Pattern Recognition(ICPR), Hong Kong, China, 2006.

[10] Maidi, M., Ababsa, F., Mallem, M. & Preda, M. (2015). Hybrid tracking system for robust fiducials registration in augmented reality. Signal, Image and Video Processing, vol. 9, no. 1, pp. 831-849.

[11] Kim, J.-S. & Hong, K.-S. (2007). A recursive camera resectioning technique for off-line video-based augmented reality. Pattern Recognition Letters, vol. 28, no. 7, pp. 842-853.

[12] Lee, S.-H. (2014). Real-time camera tracking using a particle filter combined with unscented Kalman filters. Journal of Electronic Imaging, vol. 23, no. 1, pp. 013029-013029.

[13] Herranz, F., Muthukrishnan, K. & Langendoen, K. (2011). Camera pose estimation using particle filters. International Conference on Indoor Positioning and Indoor Navigation (IPIN), Guimaraes, Portugal, 2011.

[14] Horn, B. K. P. (1987). Closed-form solution of absolute orientation using unit quaternions. Journal of the Optical Society of America A, vol. 4, pp. 629-642.

[15] Arun, K. S., Huang, T. S. & Blostein, S. D. (1987). Least-Squares Fitting of Two 3-D Point Sets. IEEE Transactions on Pattern Analysis and Machine Intelligence, vol. 9, no. 5, pp. 698-700.

[16] Horn, B. K. P., Hilden, H. M. & Negahdaripour, S. (1998). Closed-Form Solution of Absolute Orientation Using Orthonormal Matrices. Journal of Optical Socity of America, vol. 5, no. 7, pp. 1127-1135.

[17] DeMenthon, D. & Davis, L. S. (1992). Exact and approximate solutions of the perspective-three-point problem. IEEE Transactions on Pattern Analysis and Machine Intelligence, vol. 14, no. 11, pp. 1100-1105.

[18] Long, Q. & Zhongdan, L. (1999). Linear N-point camera pose determination. IEEE Transactions on Pattern Analysis and Machine Intelligence, vol. 21, no. 8, pp. 774-780.

[19] Ababsa, F.-e. & Mallem, M. (2004). Robust camera pose estimation using 2d fiducials tracking for real-time augmented reality systems. ACM SIGGRAPH international conference on Virtual Reality continuum and its applications in industry, Nanyong, Singapore, 2004.

[20] Maidi,M., Didier, J.-Y., Ababsa, F. & Mallem, M. (2010). A performance study for camera pose estimation using visual marker based tracking. Machine Vision and Applications, vol. 21, no. 3, pp. 365-376.

[21] Yoon, J.-H., Park, J.-S. & Kim, C. (2006). Increasing Camera Pose Estimation Accuracy Using Multiple Markers. Advances in Artificial Reality and Tele-Existence, Hangzhou, China, 2006.

[22] Xu, K., Chia, K. W. & Cheok, A. D. (2008). Real-time camera tracking for marker-less and unprepared augmented reality environments. Image and Vision Computing, vol. 26, no. 5, pp. 673-689.

[23] Dong, Z., Zhang, G., Jia, J. & Bao, H. (2014). Efficient keyframe-based real-time camera tracking. Computer Vision and Image Understanding, vol. 118, pp. 97-110.

[24] Hartley, R. & Zisserman, A. (2003). Multiple View Geometry in Computer Vision. 2nd ed. New York, NY, USA. Cambridge University Press.

[25] Harris, C. & Stephens, M. (1988). A combined corner and edge detector. Alvey vision conference, Manchester, UK, 1988.

[26] Smith, S. & Brady, J. M. (1997). SUSAN—A New Approach to Low Level Image Processing. International Journal of Computer Vision, vol. 23, no. 1, pp. 45-78.

[27] Lowe, D. (2004). Distinctive Image Features from Scale-Invariant Keypoints. International Journal of Computer Vision, vol. no. 2, pp. 91-110.

[28] Bay, H., Ess, A., Tuytelaars, T. & Gool, L. (2006). Speeded-Up Robust Features (SURF). Computer Vision and Image Underatanding, vol. 110. No. 3, pp. 346-359.

[29] Leutenegger, S., Chli, M. & Siegwart, R. Y. (2011). BRISK: Binary Robust invariant scalable keypoints. International Conference on Computer Vision, Barcelona, Spain, 2011.

[30] Lepetit, V., Moreno-Noguer, F. & Fua, P. (2009). EPnP: An Accurate O(n) Solution to the PnP Problem. International Journal of Computer Vision, vol. 81, no. 1, pp. 155-166.

[31] Zhengyou, Z. (2000). A flexible new technique for camera calibration. IEEE Transactions on Pattern Analysis and Machine Intelligence, vol. 22, no. 11, pp. 1330-1334.

[32] Sturm, J., Engelhard, N., Endres, F., Burgard, W. & Cremers, D. (2012). A benchmark for the evaluation of RGB-D SLAM systems. International Conference on Intelligent Robots and Systems (IROS), Vilamoura-Algarve, Portugal, 2012.

[33] Davison, A. J., Reid, I. D., Molton, N. D. & Stasse, O. (2007). MonoSLAM: Real-Time Single Camera SLAM. IEEE Transactions on Pattern Analysis and Machine Intelligence, vol. 29, no. 6, pp. 1052-1067.

16

A New Hybrid model of Multi-layer Perceptron Artificial Neural Network and Genetic Algorithms in Web Design Management Based on CMS

M. Aghazadeh and F. Soleimanian Gharehchopogh[*]

Department of Computer Engineering, Urmia Branch, Islamic Azad University, Urmia, Iran.

[*]Corresponding author: bonab.farhad@gmail.com (F. S. Gharehchopgh).

Abstract
The size and complexity of websites have grown significantly during the recent years. In line with this growth, the need to maintain most of the resources has been intensified. Content Management System (CMS) is software that has been presented in accordance with the increased demands of the users. With the advent of CMSs, factors such as domains, pre-designed module development, graphics, optimization, and alternative support have become the factors that influenced the cost of the software and web-based projects. Consecutively, these factors have challenged the previously introduced cost estimation models. This paper provides a hybrid method in order to estimate the cost of the websites designed by CMSs. The proposed method uses a combination of Genetic Algorithm (GA) and Multi-layer Perceptron (MLP). The results obtained are evaluated by comparing the number of correctly classified and incorrectly classified data, and Kappa coefficient, which represents the correlation coefficient between the sets. According to these results, the Kappa coefficient on testing dataset equals 0.82% for the proposed method, 0.06% for GA, and 0.54% for MLP Artificial Neural Network (ANN). Based upon these results, it can be said that the proposed method can be used as a considered method in order to estimate the cost of websites designed by CMSs.

Keywords: *Genetic Algorithm, Multi-Layer Perceptron Artificial Neural Network, Website Cost Estimation, Content Management System.*

1. Introduction

Some researchers have stated that the number of web pages on big websites double annually [1, 2]. However, in order to develop websites, it is required to have websites of different areas that have business-to-business relations, multi-language websites, and intranets, which integrate suppliers and business partners [3]. The number of people who increases different contents is increasing daily. These content helpers might have different writing and reception styles that demand the personal content and enhanced performance of the websites. Different media also need to manage both text and images [4, 5]. These factors make a website content management a compulsive priority.

The phrase content management of a constant source is ambiguous [6]. There are various definitions among different individuals. Some consider it as a platform that can be purchased, and the others see it as a set of approved methods or a new way to create business [7]. Since there are different definitions for content management in different areas, it has no precise and solid definition. Generally, a content management system (CMS) software is installed on a web server, and the users with different access rights can enter their own domain. According to their access rights, every user can generate, edit, and publish the content as well as information. This function is known as a management role, and it is common for almost all CMSs [8].

This paper has been organized as follows: Section 2: Related works; Section 3: Basic concepts; Section 4: Proposed method; Section 5: Evaluation criteria and data analysis; Section 6: Conclusions and future works.

2. Related works

In the recent years, many methods have been proposed for website management, their design, and production cost estimation. For example, by proposing the WEBMO model, which is a developed COCOMO II and one of the algorithmic methods, the researchers [9] have tried to estimate the effort rate for web projects. Likewise, this model calculates the cost of web projects: first by using estimators like web objects and then complexity coefficient table for object criteria, system operators, and operands calculation process along with selecting criteria complexity in the areas of e-commerce, financial and commercial applications, portals, and information services. WEBMO differs from COCOMO II by having nine instead of 7 cost drivers and variables instead of fixed capacity. This model eventually uses Pred (N) standard to evaluate the proposed model. E. Mendes et al. [10] affiliated their measurements and requirements to the number of Use Cases, total number of entities in entity-relationships, total number of pages in entity-relationship, total number of nodes in a navigation graph, number of anchors in navigation graph, and effort in person hours for designing web pages. Then by counting the number of HTML pages, the number of media files, the total number of phrases used in JavaScript code, and the cascading style sheets, the total number of internal and external links on each page, the number of media differences on each page using Case-based technique and using data extracted from 25 databases, they have tried to estimate the cost and effort of new projects. They have used the MMRE, MdMRE, and Pred (25) evaluation criteria to assess the proposed model. In another research [11], the COBRA model has been presented to estimate the cost and effort of web projects using the data from small companies. The COBRA model is a method that aims to develop understandable cost estimation of a particular company. It uses expert views and the data used in previous projects to estimate the cost and effort of new projects. Using this model, they have tested and evaluated the web objects presented by Reifer in 2000, which were completed in 12 projects, and then they proposed a model using expert views and linear regression estimation, which has been evaluated using the MMRE and Pred (25) standards. CWADEE is also another quick estimation method developed by a group of leading experts of software engineering in the University of Chile [12]. Other researchers [13] have also developed a model to estimate the cost of CMSs. They have claimed that their proposed model can be used to estimate the cost and effort of development and design based on these systems. Furthermore, they

have pointed out that the data from other content management projects has been studied. Finally, bagging predictor has been used in the linear regression model. The size of this project has been evaluated with point method by means of object modification. In order to find out different objects, their classification, and their complexity in the project, a questionnaire has been used. In order to help the project managers, a final effort has been estimated using the project size and other factors involved. For a better rate of performance of the system and the model, production characteristics, overall system characteristics, experience, and ability of the developer have been used. This model was the result of assessment and evaluation of 12 web-based projects.

In [14], a model has been proposed to estimate the cost and effort of web-based object-oriented applications. This method is a combination of the leading scholars' and researchers' theories in web projects cost estimation. This research work, which is based upon case-based reasoning, selects three similar projects from finished web-based projects, and estimates the cost and effort of the current object-oriented web-based project in accordance with the cost and effort of the finished projects. The results from the previous works have been used to assess the method.

The Naïve Bayesian algorithm has also been proposed to estimate the cost of designing content management system websites [15]. Assessments have been carried out on 99 web projects. The proposed method had a classification accuracy of 55%, and the incorrect classification accuracy was 45%. The results obtained show that the proposed method is an efficient model to estimate the cost of websites.

The hybrid of K-Nearest Neighbor (KNN) models and MLP (ANN) to estimate the cost of web project that follow CMS has been proposed [16]. Evaluation was conducted on 99 web project. The results obtained show that the accuracy precision in the hybrid model equals 0.95, and the kappa coefficient is 0.93; if compared with the MLP and KNN models, it looks much better.

The FRBFN model [17] which is a hybrid of fuzzy logic and ANN is proposed to estimate web. Evaluation was conducted on 53 web projects with 9 features. Fuzzy C-Means is used for project clustering. The results obtained show that the FRBFN model, according to the number of various clusters, has different MMRE and PRED. With increase in the number of clusters, the MMRE value decreases, and the PRED value increases.

3. Basic Concept
3.1. Effective Factors
After identifying the main requirements, a website cost is estimated based on the effective factors. The effective factors used in this paper that estimate the cost of websites are shown in figure 1.

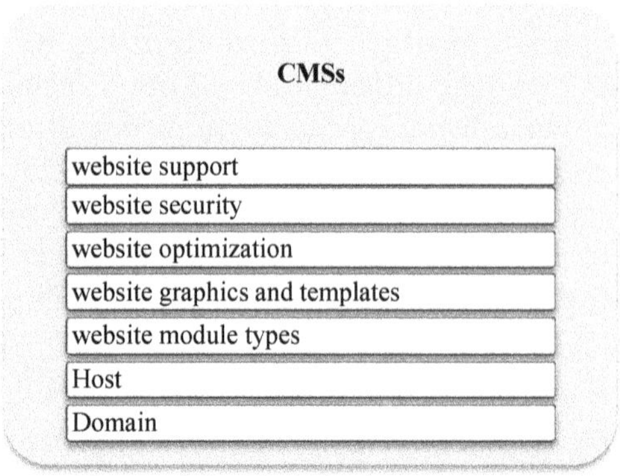

Figure 1. Factors affecting final cost of CMSs.

3.2. Genetic algorithm
Genetic algorithm (GA) is inspired by genetics and Darwin's evolutionary theory, and is based upon natural selection and survival of the fittest. GA was proposed by Holland in 1970 [18]. It is a stochastic optimization algorithm, which is suitable for complex problems with unknown search space. Like other evolutionary algorithms, GA is population-based, and has its specific parameters. The way of determining these parameters affects the performance of this algorithm. These parameters include: 1. Population 2. Fitness function 3. Chromosome representation 4. Algorithm Operators such as cross-over, mutation, and selection.

3.3. MLP (ANN)
MLP is based upon a computational unit named perceptron. A perceptron gets a vector of inputs with real values, and calculates a linear combination of the inputs. If the result is bigger than the threshold, the perceptron output is 1; otherwise, it is -1. MLP ANNs are among the most practical ANNs. These networks are capable of do a non-linear mapping with arbitrary precision by appropriately selecting the number of layers and neurons, which are mostly not large [19].

4. Proposed method
In this paper, a hybrid of GA and MLP (ANN) was used to estimate the cost of web-based software projects. In this model, the design cost of websites based on CMSs is estimated. Figure 2 shows the process of the proposed method.

In the proposed method, initially, the dataset was pre-processed, and noisy data was removed. Subsequently, the data was randomly divided into 80% training and 20% testing data. After dividing the data, the training data was used for the training phase of the proposed method. GA is used to find the most optimal parameters for MLP ANN.

After determining the testing and training datasets, MLP ANN was run. The MLP ANN used here consists of three layers:

The first layer includes the inputs that consist of 6 neurons.

The second layer acts as a hidden layer, which consists of 10 neurons, and uses the sigmoid transfer function as the activation function. Considering that the number of neurons in the hidden layer has a significant impact on the performance of the algorithm, therefore, in the proposed method based on trial and error and the iteration of the algorithm with different numbers of neurons, it can be concluded that using 10 neurons results in a better performance.

The third layer is the output layer, and has 7 neurons. In the MLP ANN, GA is used in the second layer to update the information. In each iteration, after applying the activation function, it updates the weights based on defined chromosomes using cross-over and mutation operators during consecutive iterations. In the next step, the updated weights are re-injected into the MLP ANN, and the iterations continue as long as the desired error rate has not been reached.

In the proposed method, the data whose cost has not been properly defined is used as fitness function which, in each stage, tries to reduce it.

In this paper, for evaluation of the fitness function, the accuracy criterion is used according to (1). In (1), TN represents the number of samples whose true category are negative, and the classification algorithm also correctly specifies their category as negative. TP represents the number of samples whose true category is positive, and the classification algorithm also correctly specifies their category as positive. FP represents the number of samples whose true category are positive, and the classification algorithm also correctly specifies their category as positive whose true category are positive, and the classification algorithm handles them mistakenly as negative.

$$Accuracy = \frac{(TP+TN)}{(TP+TN+FP+FN)} \tag{1}$$

After the hybrid algorithm work is completed, the results obtained from the training phase are injected to the data in the testing dataset, and the testing phase is completed as well. After the training and testing stages, the results obtained are evaluated based on the Kappa method and counting the number of right and wrong answers, and the results obtained are displayed as graphs and tables.

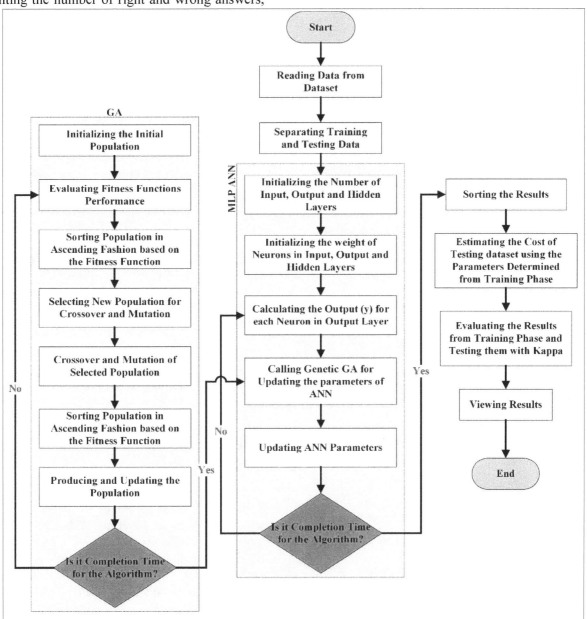

Figure 2. Process of proposed method.

5. Evaluation and results

In this paper, the Kappa coefficient and the number of correct and incorrect classifications were used to determine the accuracy of the proposed method. The dataset provided by Khaze [15] was used as the dataset. The dataset includes 99 web-based projects with 7 essential features created to specify the cost of designing the websites.

The Kappa coefficient is used to evaluate the reliability of the nominal and classifiable data. The Kappa method was proposed, for the first time, by Cohen [20]. Equation (2) is used to calculate the error coefficient.

$$kappa = \frac{\Pr(a) - \Pr(e)}{1 - \Pr(e)} \qquad (2)$$

In (2), Pr(a) is the relative observed agreement among the sets, and Pr(e) is the hypothetical probability of the agreement. The results of the evaluation of the proposed algorithm are shown in tables 1 and 2 and figures 2 and 3. Table 1 shows the values obtained to determine the Kappa coefficient for testing the dataset. Since the costs of the websites in the dataset are divided into six types, the number of sets is considered as six as well.

Table 1. Values obtained for Kappa coefficient by proposed method on testing dataset.

	Type1	Type2	Type3	Type4	Type5	Type6
Type1	2	0	0	0	0	0
Type2	0	0	0	0	0	0
Type3	0	0	2	1	0	0
Type4	0	0	2	3	0	0
Type5	0	0	0	0	2	2
Type6	0	0	0	0	0	6

Table 2 shows the values obtained for Kappa coefficient, the number of correctly and incorrectly classified data for training and testing datasets. In this table, the Kappa coefficient obtained reflects the appropriate performance of the proposed method.

Table 2. Results of evaluation of proposed method.

Materials	Training dataset	Testing dataset
Number of correctly classified data	73	15
Number of incorrectly classified data	7	4
Kappa coefficient	0.95	0.82

Figure 3 reflects the results of comparing the proposed method with GA and MLP (ANN).

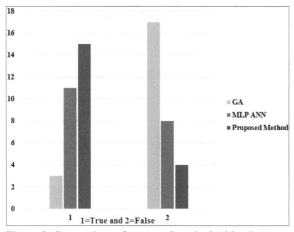

Figure 3. Comparison of proposed method with other two algorithms over testing dataset.

The comparison is based upon the number of correctly and incorrectly classified data over the testing dataset. Based on this figure, the proposed algorithm has a better performance than the other two algorithms.

Figure 4 shows the results of comparing the proposed method with GA and MLP ANN. The comparison is based upon the number of correctly and incorrectly classified data over the training dataset. Based on this figure, the proposed algorithm has a better performance than the other two algorithms.

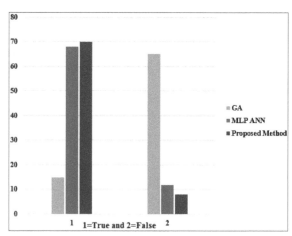

Figure 4. Comparison of proposed method with other two algorithms over training dataset.

The results of comparing the proposed method with GA and MLP ANN are shown in table 3. This table shows the number of correctly classified data, incorrectly classified data, and Kappa coefficient for the testing dataset. The Kappa coefficient for the proposed method equals 0.82%, which is an indication of an appropriate performance of proposed method.

Table 3. Results of proposed method for testing dataset.

Method	Number of correctly classified data	Number of incorrectly classified data	Kappa coefficient
GA	4	15	0.06
MLP ANN	11	8	0.54
Proposed method	15	4	0.82

Table 4 shows the results of the proposed model with 200 times of iteration of GA. Since with more iteration, diversity in GA increases, as a result, achieving an optimal solution is more probable, cross-over and mutation operators have a better chance of finding the right samples. Therefore, GA with 200 cycles of iterations in creating the optimal solution and escaping from local minimum serves best.

Table 4. Results of proposed model with 200 times GA iteration.

Materials	Training Dataset	Testing Dataset
Number of correctly classified data	76	17
Number of incorrectly classified data	4	2
Kappa coefficient	0.97	0.85

Table 5 shows the results of the proposed model with 5 layers in MLP. As shown in this table, diagnose accuracy is increased. Since MLP with increase in the number of layers can better train and test the data, and the iteration of layers reduces the error and detection of the best weight for features. If the amount of weight is to be given to a precise characteristic, then the output error reduces, and classification accuracy increases.

Table 5. Results of proposed model with 5 layers in MLP.

Materials	training dataset	Testing dataset
Number of correctly classified data	77	16
Number of incorrectly classified data	3	3
Kappa coefficient	0.97	0.86

The present paper proposes a hybrid model of GA and MLP (ANN) to achieve a higher accuracy and lower rate of error in cost estimation.

7. Conclusion and future works

With increase expansion of virtual communications, having a website is a necessity. Given the importance of cost estimation of the websites and the lack of a one hundred percent accurate method, it was tried in this work to propose a new method based on machine-learning algorithms to estimate the cost of the websites provided by content management systems. In this method, a combination of genetic algorithm and MLP ANN is used. The results obtained from the proposed method were evaluated according to the Kappa coefficient and the number of correctly and incorrectly classified data. According to the results obtained, the Kappa coefficient for the proposed method was equal to 0.82%, while it was 0.06% for genetic algorithm and 0.54 percent for MLP ANN. Based upon these results, it can be said that the proposed method has an appropriate performance in estimating the cost of websites provided by content management systems.

References

[1] Martino, S. D., Ferrucci, F., Gravino, C., & Sarro, F. (2016). Web Effort Estimation: Function Point Analysis vs. COSMIC, Information and Software Technology, vol. 72, pp. 90-109.

[2] Gharehchopogh, F. S. (2011). Neural Networks Application in Software Cost Estimation: A Case Study, 2011 International Symposium on Innovations in Intelligent Systems and Applications, pp. 69-73, IEEE, Istanbul, Turkey, 15-18 June 2011.

[3] Ghatasheh, N., Faris, H., Aljarah, I. & Iand Al-Sayyed, R. (2015). Optimizing Software Effort Estimation Models Using Firefly Algorithm. Journal of Software Engineering and Applications, vol. 8, pp.133-142.

[4] Friedlein, A. (2003). Maintaining and Evolving Successful Commercial Web Sites: Managing Change, Content, Customer Relationships, and Site Measurement, Morgan Kaufmann.

[5] Ceke, D. & Milasinovic, B. (2015). Early effort estimation in web application development, Journal of Systems and Software, vol. 103, pp. 219-237.

[6] Clark, D. (2007). Content Management and the Separation of Presentation and Content, Technical Communication Quarterly, vol. 17, no.1, pp. 35-60.

[7] Marvi, H., Esmaileyan, Z. & Harimi, A. (2013). Estimation of LPC coefficients using Evolutionary Algorithms, Journal of Artificial Intelligence & Data Mining, vol. 1, no. 2, pp.111-118.

[8]Han, Y. (2004). Digital Content Management: The Search for a Content Management System, Library Hi Tech, vol. 22, no. 4, pp. 355-365.

[9] Reifer, D. J. (2004). Web Development: Estimating Quick-To-Market Software, Software IEEE, vol. 17, no. 6, pp. 57-64.

[10] Mendes, E., Mosley, & Watson, N. I. (2002). A Comparison of Case-Based Reasoning Approaches, International Conference on World Wide Web, pp. 272-280, 2004.

[11] Ruhe, M., Jeffery, R. & Wieczorek, I. (2003). Cost Estimation for Web Applications; 25th International Conference in Software Engineering, pp. 285-294, 2003.

[12] Sergio, F., Ochoa, M., Cecilia, B. & German, P. (2003). Estimating the Development Effort of Web Projects in Chile, LA-WEB '03 Proceedings of the First Conference on Latin American Web Congress, Page 114, IEEE Computer Society Washington, DC, USA, 2003.

[13] Aggarwal, N., Prakash, N. & Sofat, S. (2010). Content Management System Effort Estimation Using Bagging Predictors, Technological Developments in Education and Automation, pp 19-24, 2010.

[14] Suharjito, R. (2012). FHS Web EE: An Effort Estimation Model for Web Application, International Conference on Advances Science and Contemporary Engineering, Procedia Engineering 50, pp. 613-622, 2012.

[15] Khaze, S. R., Ghaffari, A. & Masdari, M. (2013). Using the Naïve Bayes Algorithm for Web Design Cost Estimation with Content Management System, International Journal of Advanced Research in Computer Science and Software Engineering, vol. 3, no. 11, pp. 999-1007.

[16] Jahatloo, L. E. & Jafarian, A. (2015). A New Approach with Hybrid of Artificial Neural Network and K-Nearest Neighbor Algorithms in Cost Estimation of CMS based Web Sites Designing, Journal of Scientific Research and Development, vol. 2, no. 7, pp. 134-140.

[17] Idri, A., Zakrani, A., Elkoutbi, M. & Abran, A. (2007). Fuzzy Radial Basis Function Neural Networks

for Web Applications Cost Estimation, Innovations in Information Technologies, pp. 576-580.

[18] Holland, J. H. (1975). Adaptation in Natural and Artificial Systems, ANN Arbor: The University of Michigan Press.

[19] Samani, B. H., Jafari, H. H. & Zareiforoush, H., (2017). Artificial Neural Networks, Genetic Algorithm and Response Surface Methods: the Energy Consumption of Food and Beverage Industries in Iran, Journal of Artificial Intelligence & Data Mining, vol. 5, no.1, pp. 79-88.

[20] Cohen, J. (1960). A Coefficient of Agreement for Nominal Scales. Educational and Psychological Measurement, vol. 20, no. 1, pp. 37-46.

17

Adaptive Network- based Fuzzy Inference System-Genetic Algorithm Models for Prediction Groundwater Quality Indices: a GIS-based Analysis

A. Jalalkamali[*] and N. Jalalkamali

Department of Water Sciences & Engineering, Kerman Branch, Islamic Azad University, Kerman, Iran.

Corresponding author: ajalalkamali@yahoo.com (A.Jalalkamali).

Abstract

The prediction of groundwater quality is very important for the management of water resources and environmental activities. The present work has integrated a number of methods such as Geographic Information Systems (GIS) and Artificial Intelligence (AI) methodologies to predict the groundwater quality in Kerman plain (including HCO^3, concentrations and Electrical Conductivity (EC) of groundwater). In this research work, we investigate the abilities of the Adaptive Neuro Fuzzy Inference System (ANFIS), hybrid of ANFIS with Genetic Algorithm (GA), and Artificial Neural Network (ANN) techniques, and predict the groundwater quality. Various combinations of monthly variability, namely rainfall and groundwater levels in the wells, were used by two different neuro-fuzzy models (standard ANFIS and ANFIS-GA) and ANN. The results obtained show that the ANFIS-GA method can present a more parsimonious model with a less number of employed rules (about 300% reduction in the number of rules) compared to the ANFIS model and improves the fitness criteria and so the model efficiency at the same time (38.4% in R^2 and 44% in MAPE). This work also reveals the groundwater level fluctuations and rainfall contribution as two important factors in predicting indices of groundwater quality.

Key words: *Indices of Groundwater Quality, GIS, Genetic Algorithm, Neuro-Fuzzy, ANN.*

1. Introduction

Groundwater quality parameters are considered as serious issues in Iran, especially in areas of high-intensity agriculture and residence like Kerman plain. The impact of industrial effluents is also responsible for the deterioration of the physical, chemical, and bio-chemical parameters of groundwater[1]. Knowledge of water chemistry is important in assessing the quality of aquatic resources in order to understand its suitability for various needs. Factors controlling groundwater chemical parameters in aquifer may include water table fluctuations, factories or cities, topographic setting around the well, potential point sources near the well, and amount of rainfall. The development of optimal environmental management to prevent future groundwater contaminationobviously requires knowledge of concentrations of chemical parameters such as Na^+, Ca^{2+}, Mg^{2+}, Cl^-, HCO_3^-, and SO_4^{2-} and Electrical Conductivity (EC) of groundwater. Various numerical models are available for

predicting groundwater quality[2,3,4,5]. These models require physical descriptions concerning the porous media, suitable initial and boundary conditions for flow and transport processes, and the reactions occurring between soil and the porous matrix. Accurate quality prediction is beyond the capabilities these models provide, since the complex interaction between soil and the contaminants, the heterogeneity in physical and chemical properties of soil, and the uncertainty in estimating regional flow and transport parameters are difficult to account for in these models [2]. Although many of the models provide the required mathematical complexities to account for flow and transport processes, well-characterized soil, geology, and climatic data are not availablein regional settings especially in Iran. Therefore, alternative methods are needed to predict groundwater quality from the available information.Adaptive neuro fuzzy inference system (ANFIS) and artificial neural network

(ANN) and hybrid of them with meta-heuristic optimization methods have been used for modeling and predicting non-linear and complex environmental problems such as water and airquality and quantity with reasonable accuracy [6,7,8]; Artificial intelligence methods are non-linear modeling tools, and do not need an explicit formulation of the physical relationship of the problem. In the recent years, successful applications of soft computing techniques in water engineering have been widely published[9,10]. The objectives of the present investigation include: (1) to examine the applicability of a hybrid model (ANFIS-GA) as a tool to predict the chemical parameters of groundwater (2) to examine the impact of input parameters on groundwater quality through sensitivity analysis of the parameters used in the hybrid model.

2. Materials and methods

In this research work, the following general equation was considered for predicting the concentration of chemical parameters in water:

$$Parameter_{t+1} = F_{non}\left(X, Y, L_t, L_{t-1}, R_t, R_{t-1}\right) \qquad (1)$$

in which: X, Y: UTMX and UTMY coordination of the observed wells, respectively,R_t: monthly rainfall in the time step of t at the location of wells, R_{t-1}:monthly rainfall in the time step of$t-1$: observed rainfall values were interpolated by inverse distance weighted method in GIS environment to find rainfall values at location of wells in two mentioned time steps.L_t: level of water in the well in the time step of t, L_{t-1}: level of water in the well in the time step of $t-1$. The three different models of ANN, ANFIS, and ANFIS-GA were employed in order for the extraction of F_{non} non-linear function for each one of the chemical parameters.

Two different types of standard statistics were considered in the statistical performance evaluation.

The correlation coefficients (R^2) and mean absolute percentage error (MAPE) were used. The two performance evaluation criteria used in this work can be calculated utilizing the following equations:

$$R^2 = \left(\frac{\sum_{i=1}^{n}(H_i^o - \overline{H}_i^o)(H_i^p - \overline{H}_i^p)}{\sqrt{\left[\sum_{i=1}^{n}(H_i^o - \overline{H}_i^o)^2\right]\left[\sum_{i=1}^{n}(H_i^p - \overline{H}_i^p)^2\right]}}\right)^2 \qquad (2)$$

$$MAPE = \frac{1}{n}\sum_{i=1}^{n}\left|\frac{H_i^p - H_i^o}{H_i^o}\right| \qquad (3)$$

where,H_i^o is the observed value at the present time, H_i^p is the predicted value and n is the number of values. The best fit between calculated values would have, respectively, been $R^2=1$ and MAPE=1.

2.1. Artificial neural networks

Artificial neural networks (ANNs) are widely used for simulation of cases where deterministic models are not available or fail in fitting the data. The model is known to be generic and it can be used for a variety of problems with minor adaptations. ANN learns the data pattern using an algorithm known as "training", where many data rows [input/output] are presented to the net until it fits the data. Details about the neural network algorithm features and training process may be found in [11].

The structure of all network models that are used in this work are Multilayer Perceptron (MLP) with log-sigmoid and pure line functions as activation functions in hidden and output layers respectively. All networks are trained by Levenberg Marquardt (LM) training algorithm and the number of epochs wereset to 150.

2.2. Neuro-fuzzy structure

ANFIS is a multi-layer feed-forward network which uses neural network learning algorithms and fuzzy reasoning to map inputs into an output. Indeed, it is a fuzzy inference system (FIS) implemented in the framework of adaptive neural networks. As it can be seen in figure1, the architecture of a typical ANFIS consists of five layers. For simplicity, a typical ANFIS architecture with only two inputs leading to four rules and one output for the first order Sugeno fuzzy model is expressed [12,13].

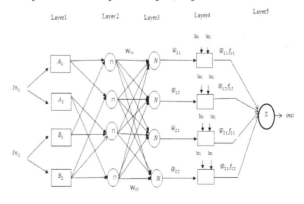

Figure 1. A typical ANFIS architecture for a two-input Sugeno model with four rules.

It is also assumed that each input has twoassociated membership functions (MFs). It is clear that this architecture can be easily generalized to our preferred dimensions. The detailed algorithm and mathematical background of the hybridlearning algorithmcan be found in Reference [14].

2.3. Proposed method

A hybrid of canonical real-coded GA, subtractive clustering and ANFIS is utilized in order to produce suitable approximate fuzzy models in terms of accuracy and parsimony.The main modeling procedure is an optimization task performed by GA, where both the accuracy and compactness of fuzzy models are subjects of optimization simultaneously. The overall optimization process by GA consists of four steps, namely, 1- Fitness assignment 2- Selection 3- Crossover 4- Mutation. Generating a fuzzy model based on subtractive clustering method is carried out in the fitness assignment part of GA. The flow chart for modeling procedure is given in figure 2. Subtractive clustering method can be used for generating a TSK fuzzymodel in whichthenumber of rules (i.e. the number of clusters) can be determined through radii parameters dedicated into dimensions. These radii are used for generating clusters. Each cluster represents a rule and regarding to the fact that clustering is carried out in multidimensional space, fuzzy sets for each rule must be obtained. The centers of MFs are obtained by projecting the center of each cluster in the corresponding dimension. The widths of MFs for each dimension are obtained on the basis ofradius $r_a$that is considered for that dimension. Therefore, each chromosome in this work encodes radii values for all dimensions (inputs and outputs) of a fuzzy model. These radii of fuzzy model are then employed by subtractive clustering for generating aTakagi-Sugeno-Kang (TSK) Fuzzy-Inference- System (FIS).

2.4. Simulation setup

After testing different sets of parameters in order to find the optimized one, the following optimized parameter set is derived.
The population size (PZ) and generation numbers (G) for GA are set to PZ = 100 and G = 50, respectively. These parameters were derived by a try and error procedure. The 1-point cross-over with the probability of 0.7 is employed. Classical mutation with probability 0.02 is used, and selection method is the roulette wheel. Number of epochs and learning rate are set to 100 and 0.2 for ANFIS.

The Gauss Membership Function (MF) is used inthe ANFIS model, and the Takagi-Sugeno-Kang (TSK) subtractive clustering method is used in all proposed models. Ranges of radii are considered to be in the interval [0.1, 2]. These values were derived from a try and error procedure.

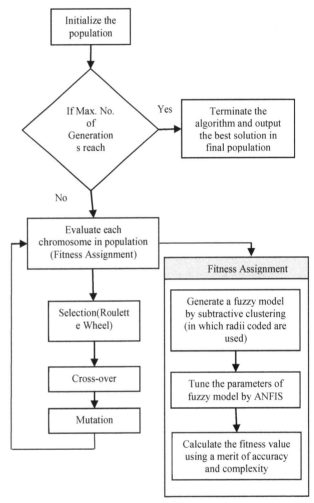

Figure 2.Steps of modeling procedure.

2.5.Spatial data analysis using spatial statistics

Geographic Information systems (GISs) are powerful computer-aided tools for varied applications ranging from sophisticated analysis and modeling of spatial data to simple inventory and management. In groundwater studies, the spatial statistics can be applied to study the distributions of non-point source contamination of groundwater on a regional scale. Spatial statistics method has also been used for various purposes such as groundwater potential, quality mapping and determination of spatial distribution of major and minor ions present in the water and has been applied in diversified applications in medical diagnosis, geology and other fields. These maps are being used as preliminary screening tools for policy and decision-making in groundwater management strategies on a regional scale[6].We used ArcGis software to carry out our spatial analysis. This software is a standard GIS analysis tool which is used in about all water resources spatial analysis around the world. We used this software for performing geo-statistics computation along with preparing maps for the observed (real) and predicted data.

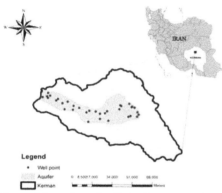

Figure 3.Location of wells in Kerman plain.

2.6. Studied area
The area studied in this research work is the aquifer of Kerman plain, which is a part of Kerman province located in the SEof Iran and in the SW of Loot desert, as shown in figure 3.

Its longitude is between 56°18″ and 57°37″ east and its latitude is between 29°30″ and 30°31″ north. This plain is a part of Iranian central plateau super watershed. The area of Kerman plain is 5420 km², 3200 km² of which is alluvium and the rest of it (2220 km²) is mountains and foothills.

In this plain, no permanent river exists. Therefore, the supply of water demands in agriculture, industry, domestic, and municipal sectors in 3200 km²highly depends on groundwater resources.Consecutive droughts and increasing the number of pumping wells the in two recent decades has been the main cause of groundwater decline that is happening at a rate of 1 to 3 m per year.

Over-exploitation of groundwater storage has caused serious problems regarding the groundwater quality indices. The depth of wells in the plain is about 57 m in average, and the mean areal precipitation is about 130 mm annually. The rainfall time series data was acquired from Kerman airport station (latitude: 30°16′ N, longitude: 56°54′E. Other data sets were collected from the Iranian Ministry of Energy (IMOE).

2.7. Data preparation
Groundwater table fluctuations is, undoubtedly, one of the most important factors in changing the concentration of chemical parameters extant in ground water. Due to the lack of quality control, data from only 27 quality-controlled wells were used for interpolation.

Further, to assess the impact of rainfall on groundwater quality, the monthly rainfall from 9 rain gage stations were estimated using theThiessen polygon method. The present study utilized groundwater information and average monthly rainfall in different lag times in order to anticipate effective qualitative factors in groundwater table using the AI methods.Table1 presents the statistical specifications of the utilized set of variables in the modeling procedure.

Table 1.Statistical parameters of data.

Variable	Mean	St.Dev	Min	Max	Skewness
water table(m)	57.04	27.22	8.92	113.88	0.22
EC(μmoh/cm)	2371	2344	240	13990	2.54
TH(mgr/lit)	533.1	405.1	100	2680	2.21
Ca(meq/lit)	4.48	3.52	0.8	25	2.16
Mg(meq/lit)	6.19	5.41	0.7	43.6	2.81
Na(meq/lit)	15.23	19.7	0.2	115	2.77
Cl(meq/lit)	14.03	18.97	0.2	120	2.84
SO$_4$(meq/lit)	7.78	8.02	0	49	2.49
HCO$_3$(meq/lit)	4.07	2.55	1	28.1	5.17

3. Result and discussion
3.1. Input Combinations
Lack of decent qualitative information in different locations of groundwater table is considered as one ofthecomplications in the wayof quality analysis of groundwater aquifer.

To this end, the present study attempted to extract the qualitative groundwater information from limited information of the aquifer such as groundwater levels, average rainfall, and local coordinates of the location. Subsequent to preparation of the information, the author attempted to predict the qualitative changes of groundwater in Kerman plain in different locations for the next month, using artificial intelligence models and the mentioned different important combinations.

Table 3. Details of ANN model architecture in test and train

chemical parameters	Input variable	No. of Hidden neurons	Train(tr) / Test(ts)	
			R^2tr/R^2ts	$MAPE_{tr}/MAPE_{ts}$
EC	4	15	0.98/0.98	0.14 / 0.13
TH	5	20	0.95/0.9	0.18 / 0.16
Mg	4	25	0.88/0.65	0.3 / 0.4
Na	4	15	0.98 /0.93	0.4 / 0.14
Ca	4	30	0.92 / 0.8	0.23 / 0.97
Cl	6	30	0.96 / 0.97	0.6 / 0.29

Table 2. Best input combinations for each chemical parameter.

	$L_{(t)}$	$L_{(t-1)}$	$R_{(t)}$	$R_{(t-1)}$
EC	×			×
TH		×	×	×
Mg	×	×		
Na	×			×
Ca		×	×	
Cl	×	×	×	×
SO₄	×	×		
HCO₃	×	×		×

The feature selection results in table 2 show that except for 'TH' and 'Ca', 'L_t' (water level in the current month) of the rest of the parameters is one of the effective factors on the anticipation of concentrations of the mentioned chemical parameters. Likewise, except for parameters of 'Mg' and 'SO₄', the effect of rainfall in either of (t) or (t-1) time steps was recognized to be among the effective factors on the prediction of concentration of parameters. The experience of technicians at Well Water Quality Assessment Lab of Kerman approves the foregone results, although, considering relatively great depth of wells (an average of 57 m) and fairly low annual rainfall (an average of 130 mm annually), the discussed effect seemed unlikely at first glance. However, although recharging of aquifer by rainfall on its surface within monthly periods seems unlikely, the discussed rainfall portrays favorable changes with quality change, in such amanner that it can be utilized for quality prediction.

3.2. AI models

Considering the limited volume of qualitative information of the aquifer in Kerman plain and the relatively large number of parameters pertaining to AI models, the development of such models is associated with a fairly significant uncertainty in calibration parameters. The modeling strategy of the present study, therefore, was based on the development of AI models maintaining the minimum possible parameters for reaching a logical and favorable fit. The three models (ANN, ANFIS, and ANFIS-GA) were employed. For the first two models to achieve acceptable functionality, we extract the number of optimal parameters including hidden layer neurons in ANN as well as the number of rules and membership functions for ANFIS through trial and error, while our model, ANFIS-GA, by employing GA, achieves the best and most accurate neuro-fuzzy model by optimization of the clustering.

3.2.1. ANN models

Table 3 shows the best ANN structures for chemical parameters along with their goodness of fitting criteria. Besides, the scatter plots of the observed values compared to the predicted values were also analyzed in selecting the most appropriate structure. To extract the mentioned table, a total number of 1620 data (5 monthlyrecorded years (2005-2010) for 27 different wells was utilized, from which 70% (1134 data) were used for training and 30% (486) for testing the models. As it will be presented later, based on fitness criteria, the models show a relatively high performances, and thus the number of data used to train and test them are enough. All the networks were Multilayer Perceptron (MLP) with the function of Log-sigmoid and Levenberg-Marquardt (LM) training algorithm.

3.2.2. ANFIS model

The following table contains the best ANFIS extracted models through trial and error and also employing GA. Gaussian membership function was used for the entire models stated in table 4. Based on this table, the ANFIS-GA model improved the performance of the model by changing the clustering radius and consequentlythe number of rules. Thus, the proposed combinational model reduced the number of parameters. The number of employed rules in the ANFIS-GA model decreased by 300%, compared to the ANFIS model, which resulted in an average increase of 38.4% for R^2 and 44% decrease for MAPE.

Table 4. Details of ANFIS and ANFIS-GA model architecture in test and train period.

Chemical parameter	Model	No. of input variable	No. of rules	No. of MF	Train		Test		Percent of improve R2	Percent of improve MAPE	Percent of decrease rules
					R^2	MAPE	R^2	MAPE			
EC	ANFIS	4	32	128	0.78	0.33	0.82	0.2			
	ANFIS-GA	4	8	32	0.99	0.1	0.99	0.1	20.7	50	300
TH	ANFIS	5	26	130	0.71	0.31	0.65	0.4			
	ANFIS-GA	5	7	35	0.95	0.15	0.91	0.14	40	65	270
Mg	ANFIS	4	17	68	0.78	0.39	0.43	0.59			
	ANFIS-GA	4	6	24	0.97	0.12	0.68	0.37	58.1	37.3	180
Na	ANFIS	4	23	92	0.77	0.8	0.85	0.25			
	ANFIS-GA	4	7	28	0.98	0.29	0.98	0.09	15.3	64	228
Ca	ANFIS	4	28	112	0.59	0.39	0.64	0.27			
	ANFIS-GA	4	4	16	0.82	0.3	0.89	0.18	39	33.3	600
Cl	ANFIS	6	21	126	0.73	0.89	0.84	0.48			
	ANFIS-GA	6	4	24	0.99	0.17	0.99	0.14	17.9	70.8	425
SO₄	ANFIS	4	27	108	0.64	0.93	0.44	0.26			
	ANFIS-GA	4	7	28	0.8	0.78	0.8	0.24	81.8	7.7	285
HCO₃	ANFIS	5	15	75	0.72	0.22	0.58	0.21			
	ANFIS-GA	5	6	30	0.94	0.13	0.78	0.16	34.5	23.8	150

Two model performance indices of R^2 and MAPE are compared in figures 4 and 5, respectively. Based on these figures, the ANFIS_GA model is preferable for all parameters over the other ones, except for the SO4 factor.

Figures 6 and 7 show the mapping of the two parameters of EC and Na, respectively as sample, and in order to compare with the prediction results and also to present some sorts of validation procedure for September 2010 in Kerman plain.

.

Figures 6 and 7 indicate the high accuracy and compactness of the ANFIS-GA model in predicting the mentioned parameters regarding the observed values. The analysis of mapping graphs of chemical parameters in the surface of the plain indicates the existence of a logical pattern of changes in the concentration. Therefore, the mentioned effect cannot be created due to local changes of concentration of chemical parameters in the location of the well caused by infiltration of pollutants from surface to the well.

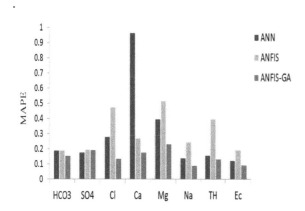

Figure 4. MAPE of chemical parameters analysis

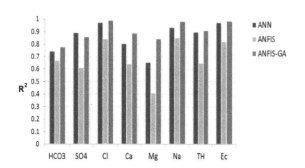

Figure 5. R^2 of chemical parameters analysis

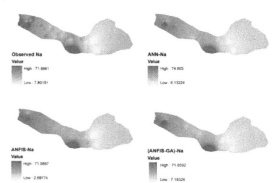

Figure 6. Observed and predicted (Na) for test period on Kerman's aquifer.

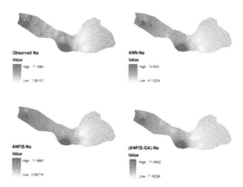

Figure 7. Observed and predicted (EC) fortest period on Kerman's aquifer.

4. Conclusions

Sensitivity analysis of different input compositions in AI models in the present work showed that the concentrations of chemical parameters were significantly affected by water level fluctuations. Furthermore, though the effect of rainfall in the under studied plain was not significant on aquifer recharge, rainfall affected the changes in the qualitative parameters of aquifer, except for Mg and SO4. Thus, it can be concluded that changes in the groundwater chemical parameters in Kerman plain depend on the level fluctuations of groundwater, location under investigation, and mean areal rainfall. The results of the studied models indicated their acceptable function in the prediction of qualitative parameters of the aquifer with a one-month lead time. Analysis of the ANFIS-GA model withobjective function showed an increase in the accuracy and compactness of this model in the testing step compared to the ANFIS model. Our proposed method aimed at providing us with an optimized composition in the structure of the ANFIS model through trade-off rise and fall between the accuracy and the number of parameters. The results maintained that a new hybrid algorithm provided both accuracy and complexity of a neuro-fuzzy model. Concerning the comparison of ANN and ANFIS models, it can be concluded that although the ANN method presented acceptable results for prediction objectives, the obtained accuracy of ANN model, being based on trial and error, cannot reach that of the ANFIS-GA hybrid model.

References

[1] Samson, M., Swaminathan, G. & Venkat Kumar, N. (2010).Assessing groundwater quality for portability using a Fuzzy logic and GIS – a case study of Tiruchirappalli city – India, Computer Modeling and New Technologies., vol.14, no.2, pp. 58–68.

[2] Jalalkamali, A., Sedghi, H. & Manshouri, M. (2011). Monthly groundwater level prediction using ANN and neuro-fuzzy models: a case study on Kerman plain, Iran, Journal of hydroinformatics, vol. 13, no. 4, pp. 867-876.

[3] Yesilnacar, M. I., Sahinkaya, E., Naz, M. & Ozkaya, B. (2008). Neural network prediction of nitrate in groundwater of Harran Plain, Turkey, Environ Geol, vol. 56, no. 1, pp. 19–25.

[4] Zhu, C., Zhou, J., Ju, Q. & Liu, D. (2008).Prediction of groundwater quality using organic grey neural network model, Bioinformatics and Biomedical Engineering.,The 2nd international conference in Shanghai, pp. 3168-3171.

[5] Seyam, M & Mogheir, Y. (2011). A new approach for groundwater, the Islamic University Journal (Series of Natural Studies and Engineering), vol. 19, no. 1, pp. 157-177.

[6] Sahoo, G. B., Ray, C, Mehnert, E. & Keefer, D. A. (2006). Application of artificial neural networks to assess pesticide contamination in shallow groundwater, Science of the Total Environment, vol. 367, no. 1, pp. 234–251.

[7] Jalalkamali, A. (2015). Using of hybrid fuzzy models to predict spatiotemporal groundwater quality parameters, Earth Science Informatics, vol. 8, no. 4, pp. 885-894.

[8] Asghari, M. & Nematzadeh, H. (2016). Predicting air pollution in Tehran: Genetic algorithm and back propagation neural network. Journal of AI & Data Mining, vol. 4, no. 1, pp. 49-54.

[9] Jalalkamali, A, Moradi, M. & Moradi, N. (2015)., Application of several artificial intelligence models and ARIMAX model for forecasting drought using the Standardized Precipitation Index, International Journal of Environmental Science and Technology, vol. 12, no. 4, pp. 1201-1210.

[10] ASCE Task Committee on Application of Artificial Neural Networks in Hydrology. (2000a). Artificial Neural Networks in Hydrology. I: Preliminary Concepts, J. of Hydrologic Engg, ASCE, vol. 5, no. 2, pp. 115-123.

[11] Anderson, D. & McNeill, G. (1992). Artificial Neural Networks Technology, Kaman Sciences Corporation, Utica, New York.

[12] Sugeno, M. (1985). Industrial applications of fuzzy control. Elsevier Science Pub.Co.

[13] Wang, Y. M. & Elhag, T. M. S. (2008). An adaptive neuro-fuzzy inference system for bridge risk assessment.Expert Systems with Applications, vol. 34, no.4, pp. 3099-3106.

[14] Jang J. S. R. (1993). ANFIS: Adaptive-network based fuzzy inference systems, IEEE Transactions on Systems Man and Cybernetics, vol. 23, no. 3, pp. 665–685.

Permissions

All chapters in this book were first published in JAIDM, by Shahrood University of Technology; hereby published with permission under the Creative Commons Attribution License or equivalent. Every chapter published in this book has been scrutinized by our experts. Their significance has been extensively debated. The topics covered herein carry significant findings which will fuel the growth of the discipline. They may even be implemented as practical applications or may be referred to as a beginning point for another development.

The contributors of this book come from diverse backgrounds, making this book a truly international effort. This book will bring forth new frontiers with its revolutionizing research information and detailed analysis of the nascent developments around the world.

We would like to thank all the contributing authors for lending their expertise to make the book truly unique. They have played a crucial role in the development of this book. Without their invaluable contributions this book wouldn't have been possible. They have made vital efforts to compile up to date information on the varied aspects of this subject to make this book a valuable addition to the collection of many professionals and students.

This book was conceptualized with the vision of imparting up-to-date information and advanced data in this field. To ensure the same, a matchless editorial board was set up. Every individual on the board went through rigorous rounds of assessment to prove their worth. After which they invested a large part of their time researching and compiling the most relevant data for our readers.

The editorial board has been involved in producing this book since its inception. They have spent rigorous hours researching and exploring the diverse topics which have resulted in the successful publishing of this book. They have passed on their knowledge of decades through this book. To expedite this challenging task, the publisher supported the team at every step. A small team of assistant editors was also appointed to further simplify the editing procedure and attain best results for the readers.

Apart from the editorial board, the designing team has also invested a significant amount of their time in understanding the subject and creating the most relevant covers. They scrutinized every image to scout for the most suitable representation of the subject and create an appropriate cover for the book.

The publishing team has been an ardent support to the editorial, designing and production team. Their endless efforts to recruit the best for this project, has resulted in the accomplishment of this book. They are a veteran in the field of academics and their pool of knowledge is as vast as their experience in printing. Their expertise and guidance has proved useful at every step. Their uncompromising quality standards have made this book an exceptional effort. Their encouragement from time to time has been an inspiration for everyone.

The publisher and the editorial board hope that this book will prove to be a valuable piece of knowledge for researchers, students, practitioners and scholars across the globe.

List of Contributors

M. Shakeri, M.-H. Dezfoulian and H. Khotanlou
Department of Computer Engineering, Bu-Ali Sina University, Hamedan, Iran

A. M. Esmaili Zaini and Gh. Barid Loghmani
Department of Applied Mathematics, Yazd University, Yazd, Iran

A. Mohammad Latif
Department of Computer Engineering, Yazd University, Yazd, Iran

H. Fattahi, A. Agah and N. Soleimanpourmoghadam
Department of Mining Engineering, Arak University of Technology, Arak, Iran

M. Mohammadpour
Young Researchers and Elite Club, Yasooj Branch, Islamic Azad University, Yasooj, Iran

M. Sina
Department of Computer Engineering, Nourabad Mamasani Branch, Islamic Azad University, Nourabad Mamasani, Iran

H. Parvin
Department of Computer Engineering, Nourabad Mamasani Branch, Islamic Azad University, Nourabad Mamasani, Iran
Young Researchers and Elite Club, Nourabad Mamasani Branch, Islamic Azad University, Nourabad Mamasani, Iran

S. M.- H. Hasheminejad and Z. Salimi
Department of Computer Engineering, Alzahra University, Tehran, Iran

F. Abdali-Mohammadi
Faculty of Engineering, Department of Computer Engineering & Information Technology, Razi University, Kermanshah, Iran

A. Poorshamam
Faculty of Basic Science, Department of Mathematic. Razi University, Kermanshah, Iran

F. Hoseini and A. Yaghoobi Notash
Department of Computer Engineering, Rasht Branch, Islamic Azad University, Rasht, Iran

A. Shahbahrami
Department of Computer Engineering, Faculty of Engineering, University of Guilan, Rasht, Iran

E. Khodayari
Department of Computer Engineering, Payamnor University of Bardsir, Bardsir, Kerman, Iran

V. Sattari-Naeini
Department of Computer Engineering, Shahid Bahonar University of Kerman, Kerman, Iran

M. Mirhosseini
Department of Computer Science, Higher Education Complex of Bam, KhalijFars Highway, Bam, Kerman, Iran

A. M. Mousavi
Department of Electrical Engineering, Lorestan University, Khoramabad, Lorestan, Iran

M. Khodadadi
Department of Electrical Engineering, Azad University, Arak Branch, Arak, Iran

F. Barani
Department of Computer Engineering, Higher Education Complex of Bam, Bam, Iran

H. Nezamabadi-pour
Department of Electrical Engineering, Shahid Bahonar University of Kerman, Street, Bam, Iran

E. Sahragard and H. Farsi
Department of Electrical & computer Engineering, University of Birjand, Birjand, Iran

S. Mohamadzadeh
Faculty of Technical & Engineering Ferdows, University of Birjand, Birjand, Iran

M. Kosari
Electrical Engineering-Control Department, K.N.Toosi University of Technology, Tehran, Iran

M. Teshnehlab
Faculty of Electrical Engineering-Control Department, K.N.Toosi University of Technology, Tehran, Iran

Sh. Foolad
Department of Electrical & Computer Engineering, Semnan University, Semnan, Iran

A. Maleki
Faculty of Biomedical Engineering, Semnan University, Semnan, Iran

M. Fateh
Department of Computer Engineering, Shahrood University of Technology, Shahrood, Iran

E. Kabir
Department of Electrical and Computer Engineering, Tarbiat Modarres University, Tehran, Iran

S. A Hoseini and P. Kabiri
Department of Computer Engineering, Iran University of Science and Technology, Tehran, Iran

M. Aghazadeh and F. Soleimanian Gharehchopogh
Department of Computer Engineering, Urmia Branch, Islamic Azad University, Urmia, Iran

A. Jalalkamali and N. Jalalkamali
Department of Water Sciences & Engineering, Kerman Branch, Islamic Azad University, Kerman, Iran

Index

Printed in the USA
CPSIA information can be obtained
at www.ICGtesting.com
JSHW051442221024
72173JS00006B/1551

9 781632 409720